# POLITICAL PROTEST AND SOCIAL CHANGE

*Also by Charles F. Andrain*

COMPARATIVE POLITICAL SYSTEMS
FOUNDATIONS OF COMPARATIVE POLITICS
POLITICAL CHANGE IN THE THIRD WORLD
POLITICAL LIFE AND SOCIAL CHANGE
POLITICS AND ECONOMIC POLICY IN WESTERN
  DEMOCRACIES
SOCIAL POLICIES IN WESTERN INDUSTRIAL SOCIETIES

*Also by David E. Apter*

AGAINST THE STATE (*with Nagayo Sawa*)
CHOICE AND THE POLITICS OF ALLOCATION
POLITICAL DEVELOPMENT AND THE NEW REALISM
  IN SUB-SAHARAN AFRICA (*edited with Carl G. Rosberg*)
THE POLITICS OF MODERNIZATION
RETHINKING DEVELOPMENT: Modernization, Dependency,
  and Postmodern Politics
REVOLUTIONARY DISCOURSE IN MAO'S REPUBLIC
  (*with Tony Saich*)

# Political Protest and Social Change

## Analyzing Politics

Charles F. Andrain
*Professor of Political Science*
*San Diego State University*

and

David E. Apter
*Henry J. Heinz II Professor of Comparative*
*Political and Social Development*
*Yale University*

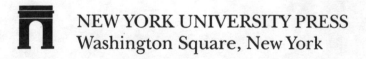 NEW YORK UNIVERSITY PRESS
Washington Square, New York

First published in the U.S.A. in 1995 by
NEW YORK UNIVERSITY PRESS
Washington Square
New York, N.Y. 10003

Library of Congress Cataloging-in-Publication Data
Andrain, Charles F.
Political protest and social change : analyzing politics / Charles
F. Andrain and David E. Apter.
p.  cm.
Includes bibliographical references and index.
ISBN 0–8147–0630–4
1. Political sociology.   2. Ideology.   3. Right and left
(Political science)   4. Protest movements.   5. Social movements–
–Political aspects.   6. Political participation.   7. Social change.
I. Apter, David Ernest, 1924–   .   II. Title.
JA76.A48   1995
320—dc20                                             94–30981
                                                        CIP

Printed in Great Britain

# Contents

# List of Tables

# Preface

At the close of the twentieth century, political protests have erupted throughout the world. The 'reds' struggle for greater socioeconomic equality. Homeless people block entry into the men's room at Los Angeles City Hall. Their red banner demands 'outhouses for people without houses.' Dressed in red satin union jackets, activists in the Justice for Janitors movement seek higher wages, greater health benefits, and more vacation time for the janitors, mainly Latina immigrants. In the People's Republic of China, 'blue' peasants revolt against 'red' tax collectors. Complaining about excessive taxes, low government prices for grain, high prices for other goods, and widespread party-state corruption, farmers throw stones at government officials and kidnap local Chinese Communist Party leaders. Pig farmers urinate on their tax collectors and confine them to the pig pen. Disillusioned with the negative consequences of rapid industrial growth, the 'greens' reject the bureaucratic state and centralized state socialism as well as corporate capitalism. They demonstrate for a decentralized state, self-governing local communities, organic gardening, a clean environment, nuclear disarmament, greater civil liberties, and expanded equality, especially for women and low-income workers. The Greenpeace ship, the *Rainbow Warrior*, sails around the world protesting nuclear-weapons testing, the slaughter of whales, the dumping of nuclear wastes, and devastation of the oceans.

Even though ecological movements have gained greater popular support in Europe and North America than in most developing nations, the greens recently have become more active in Africa and Latin America. Argentinian environmental artists paint maps filled with red water and green land masses. For them, 'red' symbolizes the blood emanating from the conflict between the northern industrialized nations and the southern part of the Americas. 'Green' represents the life that struggles to survive against deforestation activities. Amazonian Indians protest public policies destroying rain forests and the people who live there. Governments, foreign institutions (World Bank, Inter-American Development Bank), and several domestic groups – land speculators, ranchers, agribusinessmen, gold miners, oil explorers, timber-company executives – have tried to industrialize the forest areas. Opposing this deforestation drive, the Coordinating Body for Indigenous Peoples' Organizations of the Amazon stresses the need for individuals to attain harmony with nature, rather than conquer nature through technological exploitation. The Amazonian Indians perceive the earth as God's body. Hence, the land must be revered for its creative qualities, not despoiled by the reckless pursuit of rapid economic growth. Across the Atlantic Ocean, the Green Belt Movement has planted trees that prevent soil erosion and beautify the environment in over thirty African countries. Playing an important role in this movement, women plant the tree seedlings, manage the tree nurseries, and protest the construction of private skyscrapers in urban public parks.

Perceiving the political world through a multicolored kaleidoscope, this book analyzes the reciprocal impact of cultural beliefs, sociopolitical structures, and individual behaviors on protests throughout the world. It has two main foci: one empirical and the other analytical. The empirical focus examines the origins, activities, and outcomes of various protest movements that articulate economic, ethnic, nationalist, religious, feminist, ecological, and populist demands. From the analytical perspective, the book highlights three explanatory dimensions. Cultural interpretations probe the general beliefs that give meaning to people's lives. Structural analyses dissect the ways that political actors organize their activities. Behavioral explanations specify the conditions that determine political attitudes, participation, and leadership. The interaction among these three dimensions constitutes the framework for political analysis.

Part I explores cultural beliefs derived from political philosophy, ideology, religion, and nationalism. This section not only investigates ideologies – liberalism, conservatism, socialism, communism, fascism – but also interprets ideas of justice articulated by religious traditions, especially Judaism, Christianity, Islam, and Asian religions. These beliefs become especially important today, when so many protest movements base their appeal on ethnic, religious, and linguistic revivalisms.

The second part of the book studies the way that political structures at the national and international levels communicate cultural beliefs. Structural conditions facilitate and constrain the realization of cultural principles. The distribution of power within the nation- state, domestic society, and the world arena shapes the extent to which protest movements achieve their policy demands. Key theories analyzing the interactions among the state, political parties, social groups, and transnational institutions include constitutionalism, pluralism, structural realism, Marxism, Leninism, the dependency approach, and the capitalist world-economy framework.

Part III applies psychodynamic, social learning, and particularly cognitive theories to understand the behavioral relationships between political activists and the general public. We emphasize the way that tensions between cultural beliefs and structural conditions lead to protests. Attitudinal support for civil liberties shapes tactics used by protesters and influences government leaders' responses to these protests. Behavioral theories applied to political participation and leadership elucidate the motives for participation, the outcomes of popular protests, and the effectiveness of leaders in coping with movements for social change, especially revolutionary transformations. This part explains why the personalization of political power has become such a crucial feature of societies wracked by protests.

*Political Protest and Social Change* supplies an integrating focus lacking in more specialized volumes that analyze protest movements. This synthesis links theory to data. The book not only describes the major theoretical approaches but applies them to key empirical issues that deal with the interaction among political protests, public policies, and social change. It then examines the tentative answers that different theoretical perspectives give to these issues. We also evaluate the cultural, structural, and behavioral theories according to their general explanatory significance, empirical accuracy, logical coherence, parsimony, and creativity.

The theory of political opportunities offers a useful, succinct analytical framework for synthesizing explanations about political protests. This theory avoids the limitations of specific case studies, which provide too parochial descriptions, and abstract grand designs inapplicable to concrete situations. Reflecting a 'middle-range' perspective, the theory of political opportunities bridges the gap that has traditionally separated the empirical investigator from the theoretical analyst. It highlights the relationship among the cultural beliefs that shape policy priorities, the structural conditions influencing the feasibility of policy demands, and the individual behavior of government officials and protest activists.

*Political Protest and Social Change* represents one of the few books to adopt a comparative approach toward the study of protest movements. It offers a cross-national overview of current and historical political situations. Information about the United States, Canada, West Europe, East-Central Europe, China, Japan, and the developing nations broadens the scope of theoretical explanations. Even though the book explores the global issues of war, peace, and economic growth, it departs from the bipolar viewpoint that recent events have made obsolete.

Avoiding a narrow disciplinary focus, this volume synthesizes the findings of political scientists, sociologists, psychologists, and historians. The interdisciplinary orientation heightens the reader's comprehension of protests while retaining a sensitivity to the distinctive aspects of political life, especially the linkages among cultural beliefs, structures, and behavior.

Several individuals contributed to the preparation of this book. We appreciate the intellectual encouragment of Niko Pfund, editor in chief at New York University Press, and T. M. Farmiloe, publishing director of Macmillan. Others who rendered valuable assistance include Gráinne Twomey, editor, and Keith Povey, editorial services consultant. Anne L. Leu, who typed innumerable drafts of the manuscript, not only demonstrated technical expertise but also showed unflagging good will.

CHARLES F. ANDRAIN
DAVID E. APTER

# 1 Introduction: People in Protest

Political participation exploded during the twentieth century. Asserting diverse policy demands, citizens voted, joined protest movements, and supported revolutions. Today electoral participation represents the main type of political activity for most people. Even though fewer individuals engage in protests, such as demonstrations, marches, boycotts, sit-ins, and fights with police, protest behavior has recently increased. Economic movements seek greater policy benefits for their members. Unionists strike to secure higher wages, more fringe benefits (health care, pensions), and government decisions that will attain greater income equality. Peasant leagues stage land seizures. The urban poor riot against high food prices and cuts in government food subsidies. Communal movements articulate national, ethnic, and religious demands. National liberation movements strive for independence from colonial rule. Ethnic associations seek increased representation in government decisionmaking, even full autonomy or secession. Religious groups, such as the Roman Catholic base communities and Islamic revivalist organizations, struggle for a more purified political system. New civic action movements take actions against central state control. Women's associations organize against male patriarchy. Local community movements oppose the bureaucratic rule wielded by hierarchical governments. Peace movements protest military conscription, nuclear energy plants, and the arms race. The ecological movement led by the 'greens' demonstrates for disarmament, a clean environment, wilderness preservation, slow economic growth, and expanded participation by youths, women, and immigrant workers. During the twentieth century, the revolutions in the Soviet Union, China, Vietnam, Korea, Iran, and Cuba represent the most striking examples of political upheavals that led to the conquest of state power by leaders dedicated to transforming sociopolitical structures and human behavior. In 1989 elite accommodation from above and populist mobilization

1

from below produced the disintegration of Communist party domination throughout Eastern Europe.

Protest movements reflect the key aspect of political life – the relationship between the rulers and the ruled. The rulers have responsibility for making and carrying out binding policies for a society. During the late twentieth century, they face acute problems that seem intractable. These include economic poverty, state disintegration, communal violence, ethnic separatism, religious intolerance, and ecologial devastation. As pressures mount for government to resolve these problems, political leaders lack the resources to meet the expectations of conflicting groups. Popular anger grows. Protest movements organize against state authority. Public policyakers come under pressure to formulate creative solutions to the problems faced by the ruled – those individuals less actively involved in the policy process.

The relationship between the rulers and the ruled involves three analytical dimensions: cultural beliefs, structure, and behavior. Cultural beliefs stress the purposes and interpretations of rule. Structural conditions focus on the organizations through which political leaders wield power. The behavioral dimension explains how individuals interpret political messages and operate political organizations.

Using these dimensions as foci of comparative analysis, this book probes three general issues about the linkage between political protests and social change. First, why do individuals participate in protest activities, including nonviolent movements, rebellions, and revolutions? We assume that cultural beliefs, sociopolitical structures, and individual attitudes, motives, and perceptions shape the decision of some persons and groups to participate more actively than do others. What general values and policy goals guide their behavior? What structural opportunities and constraints influence their degree of participation? What personal incentives motivate individuals to overcome apathetic feelings and take political action?

Second, why do participants choose certain tactics to gain their objectives? Although formal organized opposition to ruling elites rarely emerged before the twentieth century, peasant revolts, slave rebellions, and ethnic uprisings did occur throughout history. Poor people also participated in disguised, informal political resistance. Small groups of relatives, friends, and neighbors poached, spread rumors about their overlords, and sketched millennial images that envisioned underdogs achieving political primacy.[1] When facing political domination, dissidents had to choose among different types of tactics: violent vs nonviolent, public vs covert, organized vs spontaneous, and confrontation vs the formation of alliances with other groups, parties, and government agencies. We explore the conditions that induce a protest movement to switch from nonviolent strategies – electoral campaigning, voting, petitioning, demonstrating, boycotting – to more violent tactics like property damage, physical assaults, and assassinations.

Third, what policy consequences result from the activities of protest movements? Public policies constitute an intervening variable between political protests and social change. How effectively do leaders and participants realize their policy preferences? What impact do protests wield on social change, especially on values and structural equality? How do protest movements affect the distribution of political power, such as expanded access of subordinate groups to government policy-makers?

In our analysis of these general issues, we formulate a theory of political opportunities and then apply it to protest movements.[2] Theoretically, we assume that cultural values, sociopolitical structures, and individual behaviors shape the origins, activities, and outcomes of protests. Although these dimensions are analytically distinct, they demonstrate reciprocal interactions in the empirical political world. By providing meaning to political activity and motivating people to participate in protest movements, cultural values affect their opportunities. Values both specify the desirability of certain political goals and indicate the feasibility of goal attainment. Goals and expectations of success then guide choices about the decision to participate in a protest activity.

From the structural perspective, the power of the state, political parties, domestic social groups, and foreign institutions (other nation-states, multinational corporations, the Vatican) not only hinder popular participation but also facilitate opportunities for collective political action. A highly repressive military and police may constrain demonstrations against the state, as happened at Tienanmen Square during June 1989 in Beijing. But if the state's coercive powers remain limited or fluctuate over time, protesters gain the opportunity to voice their policy demands. Under these structural conditions, the degree of state repression influences the expected outcomes that will probably result from protests. Threats of state punishment deter activism among risk-averse individuals. Yet coercion may have the opposite effect on others, indeed heighten their political activity.[3]

Playing a key role in protest movements, individuals interpret cultural values and operate sociopolitical structures. Specific leaders shape cultural beliefs into liberal, conservative, socialist, or other programs for political action. Individuals direct government institutions, political parties, domestic social groups, and transnational agencies. Along with these cultural–structural macrodimensions, such microvariables as personal attitudes, perceptions, and motives shape individual actions. Attitudes toward the protest movement, government leaders, and their public policies influence the decision to join a protest movement or refrain from participation. A person's degree and type of political activity also stem from the strength of motivations to realize social change through the political arena. The perception of opportunities – especially the expected likelihood of achieving success – leads some individuals to join a protest campaign if they view the opportunities as favorable for realizing their political objectives. In short, even if most people watch the political game from the sidelines and remain passive spectators, a few will become active players. Through protest movements, they reinterpret cultural values and try to secure changes in the dominant institutions.

## CULTURAL VALUES

Highlighting the subjective aspects of political reality, cultural interpretations probe the meaning of texts. These texts include not only verbal symbols but also rituals and ceremonies. From the cultural perspective, political life expresses a discourse of communication about power relationships. Language and rituals convey shared values that lend meaning to political experiences such as protests against government policies.

Cultural interpretations assume that generalized values account for political obedience and disobedience. To maintain their power and the political system's stability, governing officials communicate various texts – for example, ideologies, religious doctrines, nationalist myths, legal decisions – to members of society. Incumbent authorities often claim that the established system upholds moral values better than any alternative regime. They interpret the existing political and social stratification systems as natural, inevitable, and eternal. If people accept these conservative justifications of the established political system, then they will refrain from joining an opposition movement that aims to change that system.

A political system attains widespread legitimacy only if institutions transmit the dominant values and individuals understand these values, accept them, and incorporate the legitimating principles into their behavior. Political leaders need supportive institutions – ministries of information, schools, churches, mass media, political parties – to communicate the principles of legitimacy through speeches, rallies, rituals, and ceremonies. Activists within small group networks play a key role in interpreting these messages to the members. The legitimation process secures political obedience when the rulers and the ruled agree on the same interpretations of the messages that justify the established political system. Moral support for the regime may range from active loyalty to passive acceptance. Whereas some individuals enthusiastically identify with the state and its authorities, most pragmatically accept the existing regime. Perceiving no feasible alternative, they take a fatalistic, resigned attitude toward it. Pragmatic acquiescence, rather than moral commitment, explains their obedience.

Successful challenges against established authority occur only when opposition leaders transform the dominant principles of political legitimacy. Anti-regime values delegitimize the existing political system. Opponents blame the rulers and their policies for miserable social conditions. Accepting new interpretations of political reality, subordinate groups become convinced that they can transform the status quo through organized collective action.

Under the following conditions, we expect dissidents to organize political protests against the status quo. Religious values accepted by the poor articulate a 'liberation theology' designed to overcome political oppression and class exploitation. Anarchistic ideologies pervade the popular culture of the subordinates. Taking a skeptical view of political authority, anarchists seek to eliminate distinctions between rulers and ruled. Instead of

suffering under oppressive rule by state institutions and economic
elites, the people should govern themselves.

Under alternative cultural assumptions, interpretive theorists
expect greater political obedience. Dominant religious values
sanctify the established political system. The powerless believe
that the rulers govern by sacred authority and that socioeconomic
inequality is inevitable. Linked to religious values, classical
conservative ideology shapes the popular consciousness. According to conservatives, opposition to established authority brings
disorder, anarchy, and chaos. Hence, a well-ordered society needs
political hierarchy and stable authority.[4]

## STRUCTURAL CONDITIONS

Structural analysts focus on the power of governments, political
parties, domestic social groups, and transnational institutions over
the policy process. Dissecting political life, they show the ways
that these parts (membership networks) affect each other and the
whole system. The interaction between a protest movement, on
the one hand, and the nation-state, political parties, and
transnational institutions, on the other, represents a prime topic
for investigation.

Effective political action by protesters depends on favorable
structural conditions. According to resource mobilization theorists, if the structural opportunities outweigh the structural
constraints, people will participate in an opposition movement
intended to transform the political status quo. Political mobilization requires both access to resources – information, money,
weapons, organizational/communications skills – and the opportunity to use these resources. Structural opportunities reflect the
power relationships among the state, social groups, and foreign
institutions. If state repression remains limited, if social groups
attain high solidarity and autonomy from state control, and if
foreign institutions weaken the incumbent government's power
but provide resources to an opposition movement, then protesters
gain the opportunity to organize political action against the state.
In contrast, structural constraints impede participation in a
protest organization. Government repression intimidates potential
activists. Plagued by group divisions, the opposition movement

remains fragmented. Powerful state institutions monitor the actions of group dissidents. Protest movements lack the independent organizational network that can ensure compliance with the movement's norms. Foreign institutions such as other nation-states, intergovernmental agencies and transnational nongovernmental organizations provide few if any resources (weapons, expertise, finances) to the protest movement.

From these general assumptions of resource mobilization theory derive specific hypotheses that suggest the structural reasons for antistate protest activities. Expect individuals to participate in protests under the following structural opportunities. (1) State institutions wield low coercive power or alternate high repression with decreased coercion. (2) Protesters achieve extensive solidarity. They belong to homogeneous peer groups that encourage participation in protest activities. They maintain few contacts with members of different economic classes, ethnic groups, and religious organizations. (3) The protest movement retains high autonomy from tight state control. Participants become mutually dependent on each other. Personal benefits stem from cooperative interactions within the movement, which has a closed organizational network that can ensure compliance with the movement's normative obligations. (4) Foreign nation-states and international organizations provide financial support, military assistance, and specialized information to the protest movement but withdraw resources from the incumbent government. Whereas these actions of foreign institutions weaken the power of the ruling regime, they strengthen the structural opportunities of the protest movement.

Under the following structural constraints, expect lower participation in protest activities. (1) The state police, security agencies, and military apply consistently high repression over time. (2) Antiregime groups remain disunited. Most people belong to heterogeneous groups that discourage participation in protest against the state. Geographically dispersed, they come into extensive contacts with individuals from different ethnic, religious, and economic groups, particularly higher-status persons. (3) Powerful state institutions monitor the behavior of dissidents, who become dependent on the ruling elites, not the protest movement, for the satisfaction of personal goals. (4) The incumbent government receives support from foreign institutions. No foreign wars or external economic crises weaken state power. Antistate protest movements gain little foreign assistance.[5]


## MOTIVATIONS, PERCEPTIONS, AND BEHAVIORS

Behavioral theorists focus on the ways that the individual shapes the operation of political institutions. They seek to uncover the impact of cultural values and sociopolitical structures on personal actions, such as participation in a protest movement. Even if behavioral explanations never fully account for the complexities, changes, and historical contingencies that permeate political life, they do offer some insights into the mechanisms by which certain conditions produce some effect – for example, the success of protesters in realizing their policy goals. General propositions show the relationships among variables. More specific hypotheses indicate the particular conditions under which the general assumptions apply.

Cultural and structural conditions influence the subjective orientations that lead individuals to participate in political protests. Cultural values shape motives, which affect the willingness to participate or remain politically passive. Structural conditions – constraints and opportunities – influence popular expectations about the success of participatory behavior. Rational choice theory generates assumptions about the motives for participation and the perceptions of the situation that guide protesters' decisionaking. According to the rational choice formulation of George Homans, two dominant motives influence individual choices: the value attached to the goals (intended outcomes) of an action and the expected probability of successful goal attainment.[6] In choosing between alternative actions, a person selects the option that has the greater value and the greater probability of a successful outcome. If people remain strongly committed to a cause and expect that their actions will actually realize their goals, then they will participate in a protest movement. Individuals pursue both material interests and moral/spiritual values. 'Purists' participate in protest activities to assert the intrinsic worth of certain moral/spiritual/ideological principles derived from such cultural values as religion, philosophy, and nationalism. In contrast, 'pragmatists' join primarily because they perceive their protests as effective strategies for concrete benefits, such as lower taxes.

Rational choice theorists hypothesize that subjective orientations – motives, perceptions, attitudes – influence the decision to participate in protest movements. Expect lower protest activity by individuals when they hold fatalistic attitudes, remain satisfied with government policies, and blame themselves for their personal miseries. Under rarer circumstances, different motives and perceptions propel people to participate actively in a protest movement. Showing high political efficacy, protesters believe in their ability to influence the policy process. They feel highly dissatisfied because public policies have failed to attain ethical values or material benefits. These dissidents blame the incumbent government for their miserable personal situation.[7]

## CONCLUSION

Cultural, structural, and behavioral theorists make somewhat different assumptions about the relationships among cultural values, sociopolitical structures, and individual actions, motives, perceptions, and attitudes. A key issue revolves around the treatment of specific variables as independent (cause), intervening, and dependent (effect). For example, political philosophers, such as Hegel, who regard ideas as independent variables analyze the determining influence of ideologies on leaders' behavior, with political institutions the mechanism for communicating transformative values. Marx articulated a structural theory under which workers' interaction with the forces and class relations of material production generated a socialist class consciousness (normative bonds) that developed into a revolutionary motivation for systemic change. As a result of the class struggle between the proletariat and bourgeoisie, he assumed that the existing capitalist system would be transformed into another structural type – socialism. Most behavioral theorists view individual actions, perceptions, motives, and attitudes as the independent variables. Normative obligations intervene, and structural change becomes the effect. From this behavioral perspective, leaders' behavior brings about the internalization of cultural values that lead to changes in concrete structures, especially people's position vis-à-vis the ruling elite. The charismatic leader creates a new set of ideological values that produce a changed stratification system. This pattern occurs in revolutionary situations where formerly subordinate groups achieve higher wealth, status, and political power.

Why do we need theoretical perspectives to understand participation in protest movements? Theories are sets of interrelated propositions that explain general conditions, rather than particular events or actions of specific individuals. Because individual behavior and political system performance are complex, theories serve as conceptual maps for exploring the political world. By specifying certain variables as crucial, theories highlight the most significant aspects of sociopolitical life. Theoretically derived variables – cultural values, structures, behavior – represent guideposts that organize complex information into simpler categories for investigation.

Because theories posit certain regularities and direct our attention to departures from these similarities, they help explain individual behavior and systemic performance. Theoretical explanations comprise two related dimensions. General assumptions designate the basic causes, premises, and propositions that guide research. More specific hypotheses, which derive from the general assumptions, can be tested through empirical observation. They specify the scope of cultural, structural, and behavioral conditions that affect some empirical outcome, like the degree of participation in a protest movement. Using inductive strategies, analysts explore the plausibility of the hypotheses, especially the relative impact of explanatory variables.[8] We assume that a theory of political opportunities represents the best explanation for the origins, tactics, and outcomes of protest activities. More than other perspectives, it accounts for the interactions among culture, structure, and personal behavior as well as indicates the variables that most signifiantly shape political protests under diverse contexts.

# Part I
# Culture

# Introduction

Unexpected changes after the Second World War intensified cultural protests. In 1945 few people predicted that the British, French, Belgian, and Portuguese empires would be dissolved thirty years later. At the beginning of 1989 even fewer expected the abrupt crumbling of the Berlin Wall and the dismantling of the Soviet Union. One would have to rub one's eyes to imagine the ending of the bipolar world between the 'evil empire' and the 'virtuous' democracies – a development that not only framed our interpretation of the world arena but also affected domestic political life. As the bipolar world disintegrated and new multipolarities emerged, ethnic violence, local nationalisms, and religious fundamentalisms have resurfaced.

If these postwar changes highlight the need for institutional accommodation, we need to understand better the processes that will enable political institutions to overcome their vulnerability to polarized loyalties based on religious, ethnic, racial, and class affiliations. To know the conditions that facilitate the conventional politics of accommodation, we first must comprehend the conditions that lead to the unconventional politics of confrontation. How do group affiliations, economic crises, wars, natural disasters, and the spread of the mass media shape protests? In what ways do these factors hinder or expedite the accommodation of group conflicts? Whatever the cultural divisions in society, fundamentalist values, dogmatic ideologies, and the aggregation of group grievances can impede their peaceful resolution. The urge to preserve one's cultural values and even purify the society of its 'enemies' constitutes a key aspect of contemporary politics in many parts of the world. This tendency reinforces the importance of confrontation. When associated with cultural beliefs, political confrontation awakens memories. It evokes differences between people in the way they define their past and transform that past into a contemporary inheritance. Protest movements sustain their vitality not only by upholding certain values but also by opposing contradictory beliefs.

The cultural dimension of political life emphasizes how the past intersects with the present. It suggests that memory, particularly the idealization of the past, can transform freedom into grievance and grievance into freedom. Historic dreams become present realities, which often turn into nightmares when losses exceed gains and domination yields to dispossession. Cultural politics has charm. Yet it can also embody a deep yearning for solutions that endanger others. When the beliefs of protesters and their opponents become antithetical, no institutional solution, at least no democratic one, will succeed. Whether caused by ethnic polarization, racial cleavages, or religious revivalism, political crises now seem difficult to resolve. Indeed, the longing to wield power through independent nation-states reaches its peak just at a point where state authority begins to erode.

Underlying this analysis of cultural protest is the notion that contemporary societies provide infinite opportunities for people to invest interests with principle as well as transform their cherished values into interests. Why do beliefs based on religion, ethnicity, nationalism, and ideology become motivators behind political protests? Under what conditions can participants in the political struggle transform violent confrontations into nonviolent ones? How can political leaders accommodate divergent group demands, promote individual rights and their public mediation, and uphold the civil side of civil society? In our view, these issues need more probing analyses than ever before, particularly at a time when citizens have joined protest movements on an unprecedented scale.

As Part I indicates, most cultural protests involve conflicts between opposed values: moral/spiritual principles vs material interests, collectivism vs individualism, and elitism vs equality. We can best understand each type of belief – philosophy, ideology, religion, nationalism – by analyzing three issues. First, these beliefs highlight the purposes of political rule, especially the focus on moral/spiritual values and material interests. The latter refer to empirical ends (power, wealth, status), tangible benefits, and pragmatic orientations. Protest leaders and government authorities who give precedence to material interests stress efficient means, compromise, and the costs and benefits that result from behavior. In contrast, moral/spiritual values emphasize nonempirical mystical ends, symbolic goods, and ultimate expressive values. Ethical purposes, moral rules, nonnegotiable stands, and the intrinsic ends of justice, righteousness, goodness, and truth assume highest priority.[1] A second theme focuses on the relationship between collectivism and individualism. Whereas individualists regard each person as autonomous from the community, collectivists see the individual as an interdependent part of the organic society. From the collectivist viewpoint, government functions to secure the well-being of the whole community, rather than to preserve individual rights. Third, communicators of political beliefs articulate the interactions – both ideal and actual – linking the rulers with the ruled. Conceptions of freedom and equality become crucial indicators of the relationship between leaders and citizens, who often ascribe divergent priorities to elitism vs equality. In the struggle to realize their policy objectives, competing protest leaders and incumbent government officials voice different interpretations of these three value polarities. As beliefs take root in organizations, some interpretations become emphasized at the expense of others. The divergent conceptions and priorities then shape public policies and the possibilities of social change.

The meanings ascribed to philosophical treatises, ideological pamphlets, sacred scriptures, and nationalist proclamations vary according to people's historical experiences and sociopolitical positions. All political events occur in a specific historical context. As individuals learn from past experiences, they attain new understandings about the meaning of political life. These undertandings stem not only from the historical situation but also from a person's position in the contemporary social stratification system. Insiders and outsiders – functional elites and marginals – formulate divergent interpretations of similar political events. Communicators and recipients of political messages engage in a discourse that probes the meaning of ambiguous concepts. Outsiders articulate new interpretations of justice, freedom, and equality. Insiders – those with the authority to interpret political symbols – often reevaluate their traditional understandings when they encounter these new interpretations.

Three types of beliefs help us understand political life, especially the significance of protest activities. *Existential* beliefs describe, analyze, and explain conditions in the political world. They make assumptions about political reality, including the meaning of history, the nature of human beings, the relation of individual persons to the social collectivity, and the distribution of power, authority, and wealth. *Normative* beliefs refer to the goals and policy priorities upheld by political actors. Defenders of the status quo seek to justify existing conditions. Protesters usually struggle to change incumbent leaders, public policies, or structural arrangements. As key examples of normative beliefs, values and norms shape the policy process. Values denote general concepts of the desirable, such as liberty, equality, justice, and individualism. More specific norms (rules or guidelines for behavior) prescribe the rights and obligations of particular roles. For example, legal rights of due process constitute relevant norms for attaining the general value of liberty. Justice is partly realized through legal guarantees against self-incrimination and forced confessions. *Imaginative* beliefs include utopian visions portraying a future perfect society. Perceiving a contradiction between existing conditions and a regenerated society, visionary protesters imagine a radical transformation toward a political system where altruism, material abundance, harmony, and justice prevail.[2]

Through expressive symbols, abstract values and more specific norms assume concrete significance. Expressive symbols comprise several types – words, pictures, people, physical objects, and rituals. Slogans, myths, songs, and anthems illustrate verbal symbols. Pictorial symbols include flags, posters, and murals. Charismatic leaders embody national or ideological values. Physical objects such as monuments and crosses symbolize shared meanings. All these expressive symbols assume crucial significance when displayed during rituals – for example, parades, demonstrations, mourning processions, festivals, and ceremonies such as saluting a flag, taking an oath, or staging a protest at a mass rally. By communicating shared meanings, these rituals inculcate a collective identity, promote group solidarity, and either legitimize officials' right to rule or else challenge the legitimacy of incumbent authorities.[3]

Cultural values, norms, and expressive symbols shape both sociopolitical structures and individual behaviors. Traditions, religious commandments, ideological prescriptions, and constitutional laws prescribe cultural norms. These rules specify the rights and obligations of sociopolitical structures, not only government agencies but also social groups, movements, and political parties that seek greater access to the policy process. Normative expectations specify the scope of political authority, policy jurisdictions, and responsibilities of policymaking organizations. If the normative rights and obligations are incorporated into structural operations, the political system functions in an institutionalized way. Individuals comply with the dominant norms because they voluntarily accept these normative guidelines as binding on them or because they fear the structural sanctions levied against them for noncompliance with the normative obligations. Few disruptive protests against political authority occur. Aggrieved individuals seek solutions to their problems through private agencies and through established political parties, representative legislatures, bureaucracies, and courts. When an incongruence occurs between cultural norms and structural performance, role ambiguity, role conflict, and fragmentation plague the political system. Political structures function according to informal customs that diverge from the formal rules upheld by the established regime. Conflicts may emerge between individual achievement and more collectivist, ascriptive bases for making political decisions – for example, the possession of inherited personal qualities such as age, gender, kin ties, and ethnic affiliation. Equality before the law conflicts with special privileges for political elites. Moral–spiritual values – civic virtue, religious standards of righteousness, ideological purity – clash with informal decision rules that dispense concrete payoffs to the individual officeholder, friends, and relatives. Under these cultural conditions of deinstitutionalization, the policy process often becomes deadlocked. Corruption runs rampant. As protest movements gain strength, pressures arise for a renewed political system.

Political beliefs guide and justify individual behavior. They shape personal values, intentions, goals, and preferences for collective action. By influencing expectations about the possible consequences of alternative decisions, causal attributions determine personal motives. Individuals are more likely to feel motivated to participate in a political action when they perceive that structural opportunities outweigh the structural constraints and that their participation will lead to goal attainment. Just as normative obligations affect the operation of political structures, so cultural norms prescribe how individuals should behave in specific role situations. Beliefs about individualism vs collectivism (concern for others), material wellbeing vs moral-spiritual values, freedom vs equality, and evaluation of 'public goods' vs 'private goods' both constrain and facilitate the decision to join a protest activity or support the incumbent regime.[4]

Analysts who probe cultural interpretations, political protests, and social change raise several issues. First, what are the origins of political beliefs? How did the historical context – both the structural conditions and the dominant values in a particular era – influence the content of political ideas? In what ways did the writings of other theorists affect a philosopher's interpretations of political life? Second, what cultural, structural, and behavioral variables influence the interpretation of political beliefs by members of different audiences? What was the original meaning of cultural texts to their authors? How are such texts as sacred scriptures, constitutions, and ideologies reinterpreted to meet current conditions? In the conflict between divergent ideologies, why do some interpretations emerge triumphant over others? What is the explanatory importance of the structural historical context, the contemporary social networks and power realities, people's cultural heritage, and the personal experiences of individuals exposed to the dominant media? Third, what is the impact of political beliefs on political institutions and behavior? How are ideas institutionalized and internalized? How do the processes of institutionalization and internalizaion affect social change? In what ways do programmatic beliefs shape public policies?

To answer these questions, analysts have used two different approaches: political culture and discourse theory. Advocates of a political culture approach take a behavioral perspective toward explaining cultural interpretations. Through sample surveys, questionnaires, and interviews, investigators explore individuals' subjective orientations – their knowledge, cognitive beliefs, feelings, evaluations – revealed in verbal behavior. Taking the role of a detached observer, the social scientist tries to uncover the necessary and sufficient conditions that explain these orientations. Crucial explanatory variables include childhood socialization, adult learning, reactions to economic conditions, perceptions of government performance, and particularly exposure to messages from the mass media, political parties, workplace, educational institutions, neighborhood, and family. Faced with stimuli from these diverse socializing agencies, each individual formulates distinctive political beliefs – for example, political trust, alienation, efficacy, and fatalism. These orientations give some clues about predispositions to join protest movements or to support the incumbent authorities. Adherents of the political culture approach usually employ a short-run time perspective. Few longitudinal studies of the same individuals take place.

Although some analysts such as Lucian Pye and Harry Eckstein rely on qualitative interviews to gather information, most political culture theorists – for example, Gabriel Almond, Sidney Verba, Ronald Inglehart, Robert Putnam, Seymour Martin Lipset, Philip Converse – use quantitative methods. Their data derive from sample surveys and semantic differential scales. Multiple regression, factor analysis, path analysis, and content analyses represent precise techniques for explaining the origins and impacts of political attitudes, perceptions, and motivations. Through these quantitative measurements, analysts ascribe meaning to the respondents' answers to survey questions.[5]

In contrast, discourse theorists – for example, Clifford Geertz, Victor Turner, Robert Bellah, Mikhail Bakhtin, Roland Barthes, Ferdinand de Saussure, Pierre Bourdieu, Jürgen Habermas – prefer a qualitative hermeneutic approach that focuses on narrative understandings of texts and their meanings. Every cultural interpretation occurs in a historical context, which shapes the meaning attributed to verbal discourses, events, experiences, and situations. Individuals interpret political communications according to a specific context that comprises the historical background, contemporary power networks, peer group pressures, and dominant cultural symbols. Linguistic communications – philosophical treatises, ideological pamphlets, political speeches, religious scriptures, nationalist communiqués, radio reports, television broadcasts, newspaper articles – express shared meanings about power relationships. They label political situations as good or evil, just or unjust. Defenders of a hierarchical order justify rule by 'top dogs' and 'insiders.' Antiregime protests voice the interests of the 'underdogs' and 'outsiders' who remain on the margins of political life. Hence, the struggles over meaning become struggles for power. Elites want to maintain their power to interpret and reinterpret cultural symbols. Dissidents try to legitimate new interpretaions of old beliefs. Whether articulated by an incumbent government official or a protest leader, the cultural meanings in language shape political actors' goals and their decisions.

Through the interpretation of texts, discourse theorists seek to clarify meanings and to apply historical experiences to current conditions. According to Greek mythology, Hermes communicated the messages of the gods to individuals. Yet because these messages were ambiguous, Hermes had to explicate their hidden meanings and connect them to ethical values. Similarly, conemporary analysts who adopt the hermeneutic approach try to comprehend the meaning of political messages. They assume that political life expresses several possible meanings, not just one. To interpret these esoteric meanings, we need to comprehend the actor's intentions, situation, and language. Because language provides meaning to ambiguous political events and values, the interpretive theorist who seeks to decode latent meanings empathizes with the author of a philosophical text, an ideological writing, a court decision, and a religious scripture. By identifying with the author's contextual situation, the interpreter comes to understand the relevance of past experiences to present needs, the meaning of past events to future prospects, the relationship between personal life and political decisionmaking, and the impact of particular events on the whole context.

Rather than drawing a sharp distinction between their own values and others' beliefs, discourse theorists identify with the people they study. The observer's personal commitments, moral pain, intellectual puzzles, and ethical predicaments sensitize her relationships with other participants in the wider political community. Through imaginative insight into individuals' minds, discourse theorists learn the languages, myths, and metaphors by which political actors organize their worldviews. Hence, the meaning of ambiguous political situations becomes clarified.[6]

The discourse theorist's interpretation of texts proceeds in a qualitative way; analysis takes a narrative form. The researcher emerges as a story-teller who relies on her creative imagination, intuition, hunches, and playfulness for understanding why the poor rebel against their oppressors or why the state can effectively quell disobedience, even when the political situation provokes mass frustrations. As Andrew M. Greeley indicates: 'Our work begins with old, twice-told stories, passes through a process of formalization, and then becomes the raw material for new stories to be stored in the trash cans for the Muse on her next romp.'[7] From this narrative perspective, events unfold in a historical sequence. Past events constrain present activities and shape future outcomes. Knowledge about political meanings and their impact on social change relates to a precise historical context.

Instead of remaining atomized respondents to a sample survey, individuals participate in a 'discourse of community' that can change the status quo. Conceptual schema help them understand the political situation and may give them the motivation to change not only their cognitions but sociopolitical structures as well. Discourse theorists view cultural interpretations as providing meaning at a time of widespread conceptual confusion. Rapid social changes stemming from growing societal complexity, urbanization, economic growth, depression, war, and plagues lead to ambiguity about the meaning of personal existence. New cosmologies arise to explain these rapid, unanticipated changes. Structural conflicts produce contradictory values. For example, socialist ideology protests capitalist industrialization. Nationalist movements campaign against colonial domination. Fundamentalist religious beliefs reject secular humanism. These political movements campaigning for social change erect a free 'mobilization space' where they can articulate a 'semiotic space.' Reformist movements seek incremental change, prefer to negotiate interests, and rely on pragmatic tactics that secure concrete benefits. In contrast, more radical movements attempt to transform the status quo, assert the purity of ultimate ends, and reject the politics of accommodation. For these radical leaders, the vision of a transformed political system conveys profound role reversals: The last shall be first. The formerly excluded will become included as active players in political decisionmaking. The marginals will join the inner circle. Political beliefs embodied in rituals serve as 'episodic discourses' that clarify meanings of political life and outline strategies for political action to secure social change.[8]

Political beliefs shape the policy process because they ascribe meaning to political actions and highlight certain policy priorities on leaders' political agenda. First, beliefs diagnose policy problems; that is, they specify those issues that leaders regard as most important for policy resolution. For example, what role, if any, should the government play in coping with such issues as high unemployment, low economic growth, poverty, ethnocentrism, ecological devastation, domestic violence, and wars in other nations? What people or impersonal forces have caused that social problem? Second, cultural beliefs designate possible solutions to a pressing issue. To what extent should policy officials rely on government institutions or on agencies such as business firms, unions, churches, families, and voluntary associations? If government officials assume main responsibility for handling a problem, should they give preference to monetary, fiscal, or regulatory policies? Third, leaders, whether government authorities or protesters, use cultural beliefs to mobilize support behind their programs. Interpretations of political reality specify the most appropriate tactics, persuasive messages, and enthusiastic target audiences. Government officials use beliefs to justify their decisions and to gain acceptance for their policies. Protesters articulate beliefs that challenge the incumbent powerolders for enacting unjust policies. Movement leaders who link general concepts to the specific needs of individuals achieve the greatest support. Under this condition, they communicate slogans, stories, myths, and folktales that resonate with the audience's personal experiences. Hence, aggrieved individuals feel motivated to participate in the protest activity that calls for basic policy changes.[9]

Part I relies on the political culture approach and especially discourse theory to clarify the evolutionary impact of political beliefs on protest movements. Chapter 2 analyzes the historical development of philosophical and ideological principles, with a focus on their contemporary effect. Chapter 3 interprets the way that religious values shape policy priorities and ascribe meaning to the political situation in times of rapid social change. Chapter 4 on nationalism explicates the values that have historically influenced concepts of national identity. All three belief systems – ideology, religion, nationalism – not only prescribe value priorities but also sketch causal attributions that either enhance or constrain the opportunity for individuals to participate in protest movements.

# 2 Political Philosophies, Ideologies, and the Quest for Meaning

The concept of 'ideology' originated during the late eighteenth century as a protest against religious superstition and monarchical authority. At the time of the French Revolution, Destutt de Tracy (1754–1836) attacked the divine right of the king to rule and challenged orthodox religious traditions associated with the Roman Catholic Church. Committed to Enlightenment principles, the philosopher de Tracy viewed ideology as a 'science of ideas' based on the objective knowledge gained from the physical senses, not from abstract metaphysics or principles of religious faith and sacred political authority. Through reason, logic, education, and empirical investigation, social scientists could not only understand political reality but also control and change the social environment. According to de Tracy, intellectuals must play a critical role in forging sociopolitical change. Because government authorities often distort reality, conceal information, and communicate falsehoods, social scientists had the responsibility to unmask these distortions and illusions. When Napoleon Bonaparte gained power at the start of the nineteenth century and later faced political defeats, he denounced Destutt de Tracy and his philosophical group as *idéologues* who spread false doctrines that undermined state authority.

In the mid-nineteenth century, Karl Marx perceived ideology as an agent of change and an instrument for maintaining the status quo. For him, intellectuals upheld a critical function when they illuminated capitalist realities, unmasked illusions, and articulated a 'socialist consciousness' that would help obtain a new economic system. From another perspective, Marx contrasted scientific socialism with unscientific ideologies based on false consciousness. In this view, ideology constitutes both a rationalization for actions taken on nonideological grounds – the struggle for capital accumulation, political power, and status –

23

and a subjective blinder that distorts an accurate understanding of the sociopolitical situation.[1]

Political analysts today interpret ideology in more detached terms. For them, it represents a systematic set of principles linking perceptions of the world to explicit moral values. An ideology not only interprets the meaning of events but also posits the need to change or maintain the existing situaion. By merging the empirical with the evaluative dimensions, ideology stirs individuals to take political actions that will realize a program for upholding or reconstructing society.[2]

Philosophical and ideological principles guide political activities. They specify the scope of political authority, highlight policy priorities, and motivate leaders to view some policy options as more desirable and feasible than others. As John Maynard Keynes indicated during the Great Depression of the 1930s:

> The ideas of economists and political philosophers, both when they are right and when they are wrong, are more powerful than is commonly understood. Indeed the world is ruled by little else. . . . The power of vested interests is vastly exaggerated compared with the gradual encroachment of ideas. . . . It is ideas, not vested interests, which are dangerous for good or evil.[3]

When political leaders deliberate policy options, ideological and philosophical ideas prescribe certain organizational procedures that guide the debate and shape the selection of an adopted policy. After a policy has been implemented, political beliefs evaluate the implementation process and the policy outcomes in terms of such general standards as efficiency, utility, equality, liberty, and justice. By justifying the policies and their outcomes, incumbent government officials try to gain moral acceptance for their rule. Dissident ideologues who do not hold government power often challenge established authority, protest existing policies, and offer proposals for change.

How do political beliefs generate social change? The degree of change depends on the content of beliefs, their institutionalization, and the internalization of values. If an ideology or philosophy regards change as desirable and feasible, leaders who hold these dynamic beliefs will more likely realize social change. Revolutionary, reformist, conservative, and reactionary belief systems sketch divergent goals. Revolutionaries express the greatest commitment to a fundamental transformation of the existing society. They support increased economic and cultural equality, expanded opportunities for group mobility, the exchange of group positions (young people supplanting the aged, peasants overthrowing landlords), and a change in the value bases of ranking people – for example, from inherited personal qualities to ideological or economic achievement. In contrast, reformists favor more evolutionary, individualistic changes. They want to narrow the gap between rich and poor, enlarge individual opportunities for upward mobility, reward people for their personal achievements, and promote greater representation of diverse individuals in government decisionmaking. Conservatives voice the need for only limited modifications in the social stratification system. Although individuals enjoy spiritual equality before God, on earth those with certain ascriptive qualities – men, ethnic elites, members of a royal lineage – should continue to rule. Reactionaries want to restore the power of displaced political elites, whether these comprise male patriarchs, ecclesiastical officials, landlords, or monarchists. For them, a more rigid, elitist social stratification system becomes necessary to purify the social system of all the contaminating influences of permissive 'modernization.'

Political beliefs actually shape social change only when they become institutionalized and internalized. Various institutions communicate messages about the feasibility and desirability of change. Political institutions include government agencies, political parties, ideological institutes, and public schools; they help translate public policies into action. Important social groups comprise ethnic associations, ecclesiastical institutions, and such economic organizations as business enterprises, labor unions, and peasant leagues. Social movements often transmit new political values. International institutions like the Arab League, Roman Catholic Church, the International Monetary Fund, the World Bank, multinational corporations, the Voice of America, the British Broadcasting Corporation, and Radio Moscow propagate political messages beyond the nation-state to areas all over the world. Particularly when an institution has extensive resources, maintains a complex stable organization to process these resources, and gains legitimacy for its values and procedures, it can more easily translate its change-oriented beliefs into political action. Institutions facilitate the internalization of values among individuals. People accept beliefs as morally valid if a powerful institution communicates messages that seem comprehensible and relevant to their lives. Internalization becomes more likely when the expected gains for accepting the belief outweigh the expected losses, either material or moral. Individuals who become highly dependent on small groups or larger-scale organizations that can monitor members' compliance with dominant values usually show a strong commitment to institutional beliefs about the need for social change.[4]

As we examine different philosophical and ideological orientations toward social change, the Enlightenment represents the dividing line between traditional ideas and contemporary beliefs. Beginning in the sixteenth-century European Renaissance, the Enlightenment vision reached its apogée during the Age of Reason in the latter part of eighteenth-century France, Britain, and Prussia. Enlightenment philosophers upheld the values of modernity, rationality, secularity, and individualism. Power and wealth took precedence over civic virtue and spiritual goodness as dominant purposes of rule. This outlook challenged the medieval Catholic synthesis formulated by St Thomas Aquinas.

## THE MEDIEVAL CATHOLIC SYNTHESIS

St Thomas Aquinas (1224–1274), the foremost medieval theologian of the Roman Catholic Church, sketched an exalted vision of the political order that partly derived from Aristotelian ideas. Making frequent references to 'the Philosopher' Aristotle, Aquinas assumed that political rulers should not only promote peace and order but also strive for the common good, happiness (just rule), and virtuous living. For him, the main purpose of politics revolved around the pursuit of civic virtue, which took precedence over efforts to secure material goods for the people. Even if the government could never fulfill the highest human purposes – eternal salvation, the enjoyment of God, and eternal good, which only the Church can provide – the state should coordinate diverse community activities and guide individuals toward the temporal common good.

According to Aquinas, the community well-being assumes priority over the pursuit of individual interests. Along with Aristotle, Aquinas assumed that no individual can live in isolation from other human beings, mainly because each person needs society to secure all the requirements for the good life. Whereas Aristotle believed that the individual was by nature a political being who could find no identity outside the *political* order, Aquinas placed greater emphasis on the moral-spiritual benefits that people gained from *social* institutions, including the family, civic associations, and especially the Church. Synthesizing Greek Athenian principles with New Testament concepts, he based his interpretation of the Church on the organic community – the *corpus mysticum* – portrayed by St Paul in First Corinthians 12:12–13, 27. For Aquinas, the Church functions as the mystical body of Christ, who becomes the Logos – the cosmic figure merging the biblical Word of God with the Athenian divine Reason.[5] The sacrament of the Eucharist brings unity to the participants. Just as blood gives life to the human body, so the blood of Christ partaken in the Eucharist provides life (shared values) to the Church. The interdependence of bodily organs resembles the functional interdependence of members within the religious community. Whereas the human body seeks a harmonious functioning of its parts, order constitutes a primary ecclesiastical objective. Just as the brain directs the human body, so Christ heads the Church, with the Pope serving as the vicar of Christ on earth. The human body forms a hierarchy, with the head at the top and feet at the bottom. Similarly, the Church needs hierarchical arrangements, with the Pope at the head and the laity at the bottom.

Like Aristotle, Aquinas formulated a hierarchical relationship between the political rulers and their subjects, with reason, law, and virtue restraining the actions of political leaders. Aquinas viewed the tyrant as the worst leader, for he pursues his private interests, rules arbitrarily, rejects legal restraints, and harms the community. Because the tyrant commits sedition by violating order, justice, and the common good, Aquinas upheld the right to disobey a tyrant, even to overthrow him. In contrast, Aquinas regarded monarchy as the best form of government. The ideal king represents God on earth. He embodies reason, practices virtue, pursues the common good, and makes decisions restrained by law. Like Aristotle, Aquinas stressed the need for government by laws, not by the arbitrary will of the rulers. The king's laws should consist of propositions rationally deduced from the principles of justice that God imparts to human beings. The will of the sovereign has the force of law only when regulated by reason. Since few kings display perfect civic virtue, Aquinas preferred a mixed government that would secure temperance, balance, and countervailing restraints among different ruling groups. Based on Aristotle's formulations, this mixed government would enable the monarch to rule, assisted by a virtuous aristocracy. The people would share in government power by electing the king and aristocrats. By allowing people a participatory role in political decisionmaking, the rulers would dissuade their subjects from rebelling. Hence, unity, order, and equilibrium would result.[6]

## THE ENLIGHTENMENT AND MODERNITY

The Enlightenment, which began in sixteenth-century Renaissance Europe and reached its apogée during the last half of the eighteenth century, emerged as a protest against the medieval Catholic synthesis. Enlightenment theorists sketched an interpretation of modernity based on secularization, individualism, and active participation in politics to transform society. Moral/spiritual/intellectual values became separated from material interests. Secularization prevailed. Rather than promoting civic virtue and religious values, goverent functioned primarily to realize material interests: physical security, economic prosperity, and concrete benefits to individuals. Among both rulers and ruled, power, wealth, and status began to take precedence over spiritual priorities. Political leaders concentrated on gaining and maintaining power. Citizens sought material happiness through public policies.

Enlightenment philosophers asserted a more individualist orientation than did St Thomas Aquinas. Rather than perceiving the political system as an organism, they viewed it as a machine composed of individual parts. Unlike the organs of the human body, the parts of a machine can be removed and replaced without destruction of the whole. Similarly, in society, the individual scarcely depends on the political community for his or her identity. Instead, each person holds an autonomous status. Through reason, the individual can improve personal conditions, understand the world, and change the sociopolitical environment. Whereas Aristotle and Aquinas had viewed reason as an ultimate virtue, Enlightenment theorists regarded reason as a technical means to master nature. Reason gives individuals the freedom to reject dogma, think for themselves, criticize unjust public policies, and reform society. As Immanuel Kant wrote in 1784: 'Enlightenment is man's emergence from his self-incurred immaturity. Immaturity is the inability to use one's own understanding without the guidance of another. . . . The motto of enlightenment is therefore: *Sapere aude!* Have courage to use your *own* understanding!'[7] During the Age of Reason, Baron d'Holbach took a similar view about the need for the individual to emancipate the self from the dominance of medieval tradition, intellectual dogma, religious superstition, and political authority:

> The *enlightened man* is man in his maturity, in his perfection, who is capable of pursuing his own happiness; because he has learned to examine, to think for himself, and not to take that for truth upon the authority of others, which experience has taught him examination will frequently prove erroneous.[8]

Under the Enlightenment, the political distance between the rulers and the ruled narrowed. Aquinas had sketched a hierarchical relation between political leaders and their followers. Advised by philosophers and theologians who knew the transcendent good, virtuous rulers had the responsiility to govern their subjects with wisdom and knowledge. By contrast, Enlightenment theorists who formulated assumptions about a social contract held that individuals no longer remained passive subjects but became active citizens who gained the right to protest existing authority and even to overthrow political regimes.

These Enlightenment principles shaped the attitudes toward change expressed by classical liberals, democratic socialists, and Marxist communists. Despite their disagreements about the purposes of political rule and the role of the state vis-à-vis society, they all believed in science, material progress, and the application of reason to change society. For them, progress meant movement from simplicity to complexity, from small-scale maneuvers to large-scale operations, and from physical nature's mastery over human beings to individuals' conquest of nature. Although liberals, socialists, and communists assumed the dominance of society over the state, the state actually played a crucial role promoting social change. For all three ideologies, political development revolved around the management of a complex society, adaptability to changing situations, and either evolutionary reform or a fundamental transformation of society.[9]

## Classical Liberalism

Classical liberals accepted the Enlightenment beliefs about individualism, rational self-interest, secularization, and government based on a social contract. During seventeenth-century England, liberalism emerged at the same time as capitalism. Liberal merchants, manufacturers, financiers, and intellectuals articulated ideas that diverged from medieval Catholic theology supporting the monarchy, the mercantilist state, feudal status distinctions, and the established church. Politically, liberals demanded a more representative government based on parliamentary rule. Impersonal law, not a monarch, should undergird political authority. Economically, liberals favored greater freedom for the private entrepreneur. Individuals should have the opportunity to pursue their self-interests – wealth and social status – free from tight state controls. Classical liberals supported the expression of sacred and secular values in different realms. The separation of church from state maximized individual freedom. Religious toleration enabled the individual to pursue salvation free from orthodox controls. In short, classical liberals stressed the primacy of individual freedom over the hierarchical, collectivist order linked to medieval Catholicism. Government functioned mainly to regulate the individual pursuit of power, wealth, and status. Citizens gained greater participation in political decisionmaking.[10]

Even though Thomas Hobbes scarcely advocated limited government or equality between rulers and the ruled, his philosophical beliefs shaped the orientations of later liberals, such as John Locke, Adam Smith, and Jeremy Bentham. Like these liberals, Hobbes took a mechanistic, individualist view of society. Rejecting the organic analogies of Aristotle and Aquinas, Hobbes perceived the political system not as a natural organism sanctioned by God but as an artificial machine established by individuals. Motivated by self-interest, desire, reason, and prudence, individuals agreed to leave the state of nature and establish a political regime. The state of nature featured violent conflict, physical insecurity, self-destruction (the war of 'every man against every man'), and anarchy. Ambiguous rules and divergent interpretations of political concepts caused disorder. In contrast, in the political system where a sovereign power rules, individuals experience greater peace, interpersonal cooperation, security, self-preservation, conceptual clarity, and order. In a competitive world of war, scarce resources, and conflicts among self-interested individuals, government guarantees security, personal survival, and productive lives.

Building his arguments on the covenant tradition of the Bible and on the logical reasoning associated with geometry, Hobbes specified a contractual relationship uniting the rulers with the ruled. Through the calculating use of reason, individuals established a covenant that authorized the sovereign – either one man or an assembly – to act for them, to define the general interest, and to prescribe their rights and duties. Preferring an absolutist monarchical ruler, Hobbes prescribed multiple duties for the sovereign. The 'Leviathan,' a 'mortal god' with terrifying power that remained beyond human control (Job 41:1–34), formulates laws, interprets these rules, and enforces them. Multiple, divergent interpretations of scripture endanger political order; priests and prophets challenge temporal rule. By fusing religious with political authority, the sovereign must interpret both secular laws and sacred commandments derived from the Bible. As a 'Sovereign Definer,' the ruler backs up his interpretations with coercive force. Obedience stems from both fear of temporal death as well as fear of eternal damnation. Enforcing clearly defined rules binding on the whole society, the state applies sanctions against self-interested individuals who violate the rules of the political game. Peace, cooperation, and the attainent of mutual benefits result. In the ideal commonwealth sketched by Hobbes, the people act as subjects, as rule observers. Obedience to the sovereign rests on fear of disobedience. The educational system teaches individuals the duties of citizenship, respect for the rules, the need to restrain self-interests, and the importance of showing awe before the sovereign. Justice denotes equal treatment by the sovereign, that is, political equality before the sovereign's laws. If the sovereign no longer guarantees citizens their survival, personal security, and life necessities, then they have the right to withdraw their loyalty.[11]

Although John Locke placed individual interests at the center of his political theory, he departed from Hobbes in formulating a more constitutionalist version of the social contract. Unlike

Hobbes, Locke supported a close linkage among political freedom, capitalism, and religious toleration. Motivated by self-interests – the desire to maintain life, expand liberty, and preserve property, – individuals strive for economic benefits, greater conveniences, and higher productivity. According to Locke's agrarian capitalist orientation, individuals behave as rational producers who satisfy human needs, master the world, and conquer physical nature. He praised the hard-working individual who improved the land through drainage, crop rotation, and the use of more productive farm machinery. Favoring private ownership of landed property, Locke held that private enclosures of commonly-held land were necessary to increase the productive use of land. Trade in surplus food enhanced societal prosperity and thereby benefited everyone.

Because property rights – defined broadly as life, liberty, and estate – were insecure in the state of nature, Locke assumed that people established a social contract authorizing a limited, consensual government. For him, the ideal relationship between rulers and ruled rested on a mixed constitution that avoided monarchical absolutism and populism. He preferred a political system blending constitutional monarchy, the dominance of the landed aristocracy in the House of Lords, and elections to the House of Commons. Such institutional mechanisms as majority rule, legal restraints on government authority, a balance of power between a representative legislature and the executive, and impartial justice administered by independent courts maintained representative, limited government. This complex system of constitutional government reflected the emerging complex capitalist economy based on trade, competitive markets, widespread property rights, and manufacturing.

Locke believed that government functions mainly to defend individual liberty, protect private property, mediate conflicts, and maintain life. Government should promote religious toleration. Since all individuals have moral autonomy in their private lives, they, not a state church, must assume responsibility for their own salvation. Government officials also need to protect individuals in their pursuit of private wealth, so that the virtues of industry, sobriety, and thrift will bring economic rewards. When nearly all citizens possess private property, their stake in society helps maintain political order. Political rulers must employ coercive power against those who violate individuals' rights to life, liberty, and estate. Yet if the government rules arbitrarily and threatens private property rights, then the majority of property owners have the right to revolt against despotism and establish a new political system, as did the American colonists during the late eighteenth century.[12]

The Scottish liberal Adam Smith protested the mercantilist state and upheld the capitalist economy emerging in Britain during the late eighteenth century. Like Locke, Smith was a methodological individualist. He saw individuals as the key unit of society. Motivated by their self-interests – the pursuit of wealth and especially social status, – they deserved to be treated with dignity. Taking a secular, utilitarian view of government responsibilities, Smith wanted the government to maintain religious toleration. Instead of promoting religious orthodoxy, it should perform useful activities that furthered the efficient accumulation of wealth. These functions included the protection of private property, defense against foreign attack, the administration of justice, education, and the construction of public works (roads, bridges, harbors, canals) that facilitate commerce and a competitive market. For him, justice involved freedom from oppression, particularly from both the avaricious rich and the envious poor who threaten the security of private property. Even though these responsibilities could justify a wide scope for government power, Smith wanted the political regime to allow the competitive market extensive independence from state control. Opposed to state mercantilism and private monopolies, he favored international trade, unrestricted domestic commerce, and consumers' freedom of choice. His conception of the links between rulers and the ruled upheld the impersonal rule of law, not governance by arbitrary officials. Even though Smith supported 'natural liberty,' he rejected economic and political equality. True, he sought to avoid the extremes of opulent wealth and poverty; workers should receive high wages to buy goods. Yet, for him, capitalism represented a hierarchical system. Laborers remained subordinate to the capitalists. Inequalities of wealth provided incentives for individuals to improve their conditions. In the political system, Smith also favored political hierarchy; an enlightened elite of landowners, parliamentarians, and intellectuals like himself should make the crucial public policies. This elite would deter merchants from gaining special government favors for themselves and from establishing monopolies that interfered with a free market.[13]

Utilitarian theorists, particularly Jeremy Bentham, stressed the methodological individualism associated with the modern public choice approach. He perceived society as the aggregate of individuals: 'The interest of the community [is] the sum of the interests of the several members who compose it.'[14] The ruled primarily pursue their self-interests – pleasure, wealth, and status. Government has the main obligation to defend these interests, secure private property, and promote happiness. Unlike Aristotle, who equated happiness with conformity to public virtue ('perfect goodness'), Bentham defined social happiness as the greatest pleasure of the greatest number. He evaluated the relationship between government officials and the people according to a utility criterion or a pleasure/pain calculus. For him, utility meant the subjective preferences of individuals – the perceptions of their own rewards, benefits, advantages, satisfactions, goodness, and happiness. If government supplied personal benefits (pleasures) at minimal costs (pains), then it maximized social utility. No government official could possibly know each individual's utility or source of satisfaction. Hence, government must exercise a limited scope of power; it should enable individuals to enjoy pleasure and achieve security from pain. Yet many individuals remain unaware of their own interests; they deceive themselves. All societies face interest conflicts based on jealousy, rivalry, and hatred. For these reasons, legislation and education constitute key government obligations. Legislators must enact laws that punish evil actions that harm others and more importantly reward good actions that benefit the community, even if individuals perceive no self-interest from performing them. Good legislation implies enlightenment in both instrumental and moral virtues. Enlightened educators teach prudence: rational calculation of interests, information about rewards and punishments, self-control, and the internalization of utilitarian principles. Education also promotes moral character, especially benevolence, so that individuals gain happiness by helping others and feel unhappy when others suffer injustice. During his later years, Bentham supported a republican form of government. From his perspective, an elected legislature of rational individuals would formulate policies ensuring the community interest. Enlightened, educated voters would support the market system, parliament, impersonal laws based on reason, and the separation of church from state. According to

Bentham, these institutional arrangements produce social happiness and restrain rulers' power over the populace.[15]

Although the utilitarian John Stuart Mill accepted many of Bentham's views, Mill placed greater emphasis on the need for government to uplift the moral character of the community. Both agreed that government policies should be evaluated by their consequences in promoting the greatest happiness of individuals. Mill, however, rejected self-interested individualism and expressed ambivalence toward political equality. For him, government functioned not just to provide individual benefits but more importantly to ensure that individual interests coincide with the good of the whole community. Educational and other sociopolitical institutions must teach wisdom, intelligence, and a noble character. Not all satisfactions or pleasures reflect equal moral value: 'It is better to be a human being dissatisfied than a pig satisfied; better to be Socrates dissatisfied than a fool satisfied.'[16] Government's major obligation centered on developing individuals' potentialities, especially their moral virtues and intelligence.

Mill took an ambivalent view toward political equality. On the one hand, his egalitarian sentiments supported every person's right to equal treatment under the law. He favored an expanded suffrage to include women. Public policies should help eradicate poverty, diminish the income gap separating rich from poor, and expand equal economic opportunities. Mill protested domination by the capitalist elite. From his standpoint, capitalism brought excessive inequalities, egotism, class conflict, and inefficient monopolies. It also stunted individual development. Government officials must regulate trade, wages, and working hours, as well as protect the elderly, children, and workers from deleterious, unhealthful conditions. Whereas Mill opposed government ownership as too monopolistic and inefficient, he supported cooperative enterprises that would enable workers to own capital, elect managers, and share profits. On the other hand, Mill feared the tyranny of the majority and wanted an educated elite to govern. He upheld civil liberty as the primary value; it expanded choices, diversity of views, and individual/minority rights. Mill assumed that a meritocracy of intellectuals, politicians, and administrators – persons with superior virtue, talent, and intelligence – would best preserve political liberty, increase aggregate happiness, and improve people's moral and intellectual qualities. According to him, educated individuals with superior knowledge, skills, and wisdom should have the greatest voting rights. He favored excluding from the franchise those who paid no taxes, collected poor relief, had undergone bankruptcy, and remained illiterate. Unlike the educated elite, these poorer individuals lacked the ability to think independently, to transcend their narrow class interests, and to promote the common good.[17]

The same tensions that faced John Stuart Mill also confront modern liberals. Although they all take an individualist orientation, they disagree about the scope of government power and about the relative priority accorded freedom and equality. Whereas libertarians prefer a minimal state and assert the primacy of freedom over equality, egalitarian liberals want government to implement extensive social service programs. For them, public policymakers should give the highest priority to freedom but must also work for more equal politico-economic conditions.

Libertarian philosophers, public choice theorists, and neoclassical economists affirm the virtues of the free market economy, a flexible price system, and limited government. As methodological individualists, they assume that society is a collection of self-interested individuals. Motivated to benefit themselves, people prefer to maximize the utility of themselves and their families more than the well-being of the nation, the poor, or the sick. Each individual can best judge his or her own utility. No government official has the information about the benefits that bring the greatest satisfaction to each person in society. Hence, government should perform only limited functions: preserve private property, secure law and order, enforce contracts, and protect individuals against force, fraud, and theft. Because government bureaucracies wield power inefficiently and usually fail to achieve their intended goals, libertarians want the competitive market to undertake most activities. They believe that most government policies – in-kind benefits, progressive income taxes, price controls, wage controls, rent controls, regulation of transportation – are both inefficient and inequitable. Marginal costs usually exceed marginal benefits; hence, inefficiency results. Wealthier individuals gain more benefits from these programs than do the poor – a situation that creates inequities. Because of these inefficiencies and inequities, libertarians, public choice theorists, and neoclassical economists favor a government with limited control over citizens. Just as in the market consumers exert their sovereignty, so in the political system individuals must retain the power to maximize their choices free from state interference.

Public choice theorists reject both political and economic equality. For example, William H. Riker defends classical liberalism – what he calls 'eighteenth-century Whiggery' – against modern populism, which asserts that people's preferences should become public policy and that freedom rests on the translation of popular wishes into the law. For Riker, citizens must play a restricted role in political decisionmaking. They vote legislators into office. Faced with a choice of competing party candidates, they have the right to dismiss elected officials from office. The main political particiants should be legislators, who form coalitions, negotiate compromises, trade votes, and make marginal policy adjustments. Similarly, James Buchanan and Gordon Tullock perceive voters as too ignorant and uninformed to participate actively in the policy process.

Besides rejecting political equality, libertarians remain skeptical of public policies that redistribute wealth to poorer citizens. Opposed to the 'feudalist' bureaucratic welfare state, social democracy, state socialism, and Keynesian government policies that stimulate aggregate demand, Friedrich Hayek denounces all institutions and policies intended to realize greater economic equality: trade unions, central government planning agencies, public housing, and in-kind transfers for health care, education, and food. Private capital investment takes precedence over government programs to expand consumer expenditures. Viewing individual liberty as a natural right, libertarian philosopher Robert Nozick wants to maximize individuals' free choice to spend money and use their property as they see fit. He regards equal economic rewards and even equal opportunities as neither desirable nor feasible. The only just redistribution of wealth occurs through voluntary transfers, not coercive government policies.[18]

Although egalitarian liberals affirm the need for individual freedom, they diverge from the libertarians in supporting a more activist government that will implement programs to attain social justice. According to John Rawls, justice involves the implementation of both freedom and equality. For him, freedom takes the highest priority. It means pluralism, diversity, tolerance, consensual power, and constitutional democracy. All these conditions restrain government's power over individuals. A social contract or agreement on the rules of the political game secures cooperation and freedom. Government officials must impartially apply these rules to all persons, regardless of status. By agreeing on rules for settling conflicts, people learn how to cooperate. Through discussion, dialogue, and the process of reaching agreements, political participants reconcile their conflicting concepts of freedom, equality, and justice. Government must guarantee each person an equal right to basic liberties – the freedoms to express ideas, organize associations, vote, run for office, and enjoy legal protection. Regardless of their status, all persons should have an equal opportunity to gain public office. Everyone must enjoy the same fair opportunities to realize goals. If there occurs an unequal distribution of primary goods – free thought, free movement, free choice of occupations, right to hold public office, income, wealth, self-respect – then government policies should maximize the benefits of the least advantaged individuals. Consensus on such moral virtues as fairness, civility, tolerance, and reasonableness restrains the individual pursuit of material interests.

Rejecting the materialistic individualism stressed by public choice theorists, Philip Selznick seeks to reconcile supposedly contradictory principles: individualism vs communitarianism, material interests vs moral virtues, and freedom vs equality. According to his interpretation of 'communitarian liberalism,' individuals can enjoy full autonomy to realize their potentialities only in a community that values citizenship, civic virtue, and shared public goods (social integration, education, public safety) over the pursuit of material self-interests. For him, an inclusive moral equality and policies that facilitate equal opportunities take priority over equality of shared poverty. Committed to Enlightenment values, Selznick rejects centralized bureaucratic authority, ideological monism, dogmatism, arbitrary conventions, and the imposition of doctrines on passive subjects. Instead, his concept of freedom upholds decentralized constitutional authority, multiple loyalties, tolerance of ambiguity, skepticism, and extensive civic participation. Engaged in dialogue about public issues, citizens become active players in the policy process.

Similarly, Bruce Ackerman views political decisionaking as a liberal dialogue where individuals justify their diverse policy positions, reconcile conflicts, and achieve mutually beneficial exchanges. Under this ideal system of rational conversation, individuals attain both liberty and equality. No group exploits or dominates others. All individuals enjoy equal respect and an opportunity to participate in the liberal dialogue. Public policies guarantee that every person experiences material equality at the start of adult life. Along with Ronald Dworkin, Ackerman assumes that greater equality of resources enhances active citizenship and participation in political life. Opposed to both laissez-faire and state socialism, Ackerman advocates a mixed market economy as the foundation of political dialogue. According to this egalitarian viewpoint, government programs for education, health care, housing, and employment expand individual equality of opportunities and also create more egalitarian socioeconomic outcomes. Through these public policies, government institutions, private firms, and voluntary associations cooperate to realize a freer, more equal society.[19]

At the close of the twentieth century, liberalism has become the dominant ideology throughout the world. According to Francis Fukuyama, 'There is a fundamental process at work that dictates a common evolutionary pattern for *all* human societies – in short, something like a Universal History of mankind in the direction of liberal democracy.'[20] Although acknowledging that all political systems have not yet institutionalized liberal democratic principles, Fukuyama assumes that liberal democratic ideals have emerged triumphant in the world culture. Not only in North America, Britain, and Europe but also in the less developed nations, political leaders assert their belief in liberty, equality, individual worth, competitive elections, the rule of law, and universal suffrage. Public policies reflect the priority placed on free trade, international competitiveness, state deregulation, privatizaion, and certain 'neoliberal' austerity programs preferred by public choice theorists: wage restraints, reduced social service expenditures, decreased state subsidies and state employment, and tight control of the money supply.[21] Economic liberalism based on markets and private property thus takes ideological precedence over state socialism or Scandinavian social democracy.

## Democratic Socialism

Protesting the public choice interpretation of liberal democracy, modern democratic socialists uphold the need for a more egalitarian, cooperative society than operates under capitalism. In most West European nations, social democratic and labor parties win the highest or second highest proportion of votes in national elections to the parliament. Allied with trade unions and cooperatives, these socialist parties communicate their beliefs to the public. Particularly in Britain and Sweden, R. H. Tawney, Andrew Gamble, Ian Gough, Pat Devine, David Miller, Hjalmar Branting, Ernst Wigforss, and Tage Erlander have articulated the principal tenets of demoratic socialism: constitutional government, civil liberties, political equality, and a modified market system that extends politico-economic rights to employees and consumers. Whereas liberal democrats stress competitive individualism, democratic socialists perceive individuals as more altruistic and cooperative. The individual finds meaning in the community, not in the atomized conditions prevailing under capitalism. Viewing society as a fellowship, democratic socialists assume that people will realize their highest potentialities only in a socialist society governed by democratic procedures. Under liberal capitalism, the state concentrates on materialistic ends. It promotes capital accumulation and compensates for market imperfections. Public policies encompass means-tests, private implementation of government programs, and cash transfers. In contrast, democratic socialists want government policies to realize both moral values and material interests. Government must advance the equal respect and dignity of all individuals, regardless of social status. Its policies should provide universal benefits, particularly through in-kind programs for public housing, public health care, and public education. In their conception of the relationship between the rulers and ruled, liberal democrats perceive a conflict between freedom and equality. For them, individual freedom takes precedence over equality of conditions. Democratic socialists, however, see no tension that separates freedom from equality. Although rejecting absolute equality of economic resources, they believe that freedom can thrive only in a society where the present gap between rich and poor has considerably narrowed. Public policies must equalize opportunities, guarantee a minimum income for all, and ensure that each person gains equal respect. These egalitarian programs will liberate the oppressed, empower the powerless, enrich the poor, assimilate the marginalized, and extend equal dignity to those of low status.

Like the modern classical liberals, contemporary democratic socialists disagree about the proper scope of government power and the need to rely on the market. Market-oriented socialists assume that the competitive market has certain virtues: decentralized decisionmaking, efficiency, and freedom of consumer goods, like cars, furniture, clothes, restaurants, and resorts. Hence, socialists should reject the extension of state-owned firms and instead support autonomous, worker-owned cooperatives that compete with private firms. Small-scale private businesses that meet consumer needs should also be supported.

Socialists who place less faith in the 'free market' articulate plans for democratic socialism that blend market mechanisms with public planning at the central and local level. Large-scale state-owned enterprises control electricity, railroads, oil, and foreign trade. Central government agencies plan the economy for the whole society. They regulate markets, control profits, direct economic investment, coordinate innovation and research, and equalize employment opportunities. The central state also meets social service needs. Through high, progressive taxes on income and wealth, governent redistributes resources to the poor. Public expenditures for food, clothing, public housing, health care, education, and employment ensure that all individuals attain minimum standards of well-being. Central government policies curtail high concentrations of wealth and political power, thereby strengthening individual rights. Along with these centralized policies, decentralized initiatives at both the public and private levels promote participatory democracy, active citizenship, and political equality. Cooperatives, consumer unions, self-managed firms, tenants' associations, and local organizations of parents, teachers, and students formulate new policy initiatives, administer social services, and adapt national plans to local conditions. For example, under proposals for self-managed firms, their governing boards would include diverse representatives: workers, customers, suppliers, community officials, ecologists, local citizens, and even employees of competing firms. These members would formulate general decisions about production, investment, allocation of resources, and tasks of the labor force. Managers would then implement these decisions. Smaller-scale private enterprises meet the changing demands of consumers for goods and services. Through these programs, democratic socialists expect that a transformed egalitarian politico-economic system will realize democratic planning of investment and resource allocation, extensive employee involvement in the workplace, and widespread popular participation in self-governing communities. Responding to popular preferences, a socialist democracy will secure substantive changes, not just procedural modifications. Policymakers will become more accountable to the general citizenry than under liberal democratic capitalism. As a result of expanded popular participation, individuals will learn collective decisionmaking skills, develop their potentialities, gain equal opportunities for self-realization, and realize their basic rights to well-being, dignity, and freedom.[22]

During the era from 1950 through the early 1990s, market-oriented socialists wielded far greater policy influence than their more visionary comrades who stressed expanded political and economic equality. Socialist-dominated governments in West Germany, Belgium, the Netherlands, France, Spain, Portugal, Greece, Australia, and New Zealand enacted neoliberal austerity policies. Budgetary restraint, monetary stability, and expanded business profits took priority over government efforts to lower joblessness, enlarge social service benefits, and equalize incomes. Whereas democratic socialist ideology stressed workers' management, full employment, egalitarian redistribution measures, and state control of private enterprises, neoliberal policies sought to make the capitalist economies more competitive and efficient. Reliance on market mechanisms superseded government planning. Government promoted capital accumulation through encouraging foreign and domestic private investment. State officials granted the managers of state enterprises extensive autonomy, so that they would have incentives to compete efficiently on the world market and earn a profit. Austerity programs reduced workers' real wages, curtailed employment in state industries, decreased taxes on the wealthy, and raised fees for gasoline, electricity, and public transportation.

Why did egalitarian democratic socialists face difficulties realizing their ideological programs and transforming capitalism into socialism? As we have seen, democratic socialists advocated modern Enlightenment values: reason, universal equality, solidarity, optimism about future progress, and the belief in universal principles for constructing a just society. After the 'golden age' of economic prosperity that ended around 1975, postmodern values became more popular. Unlike Enlightenment principles, postmodernism expressed greater doubts about instrumental rationality, equality, solidarity, progress, and universally applicable laws of policy science. Instead, postmodern theorists emphasized nonrational myths, particularistic differences, atomization, and a pessimistic view of the future as chaotic and uncontrollable. The decline of the manufacturing sector and the growth of the service sector also impeded opportunities for social democratic parties and blue-collar industrial unions to realize their policy preferences. Workers found fewer jobs in manufacturing, state enterprises, and public corporations. Occupational differentiation fragmented working-class solidarity. Dominated by multinational corporations, the world capitalist economy impeded the power of national governments to implement social democrats' egalitarian programs. The collapse of East European state socialist economies meant a declining faith in public planning. The liberal commitment to market mechanisms and privatization grew stronger. Government officials no longer gave the highest priority to full employment and egalitarian income redistribution. Even social-democratic leaders enacted policies designed to promote market efficiency, expand international competition, and curtail inflation.[23]

## Communism

Marx, Engels, and Lenin organized protests against the evolutionary reformism of social democracy. They perceived revolution, not evolution, as the most effective way to secure equality, freedom, and well-being. Rather than reform society through the political application of reason, enlightened individualism, and education, the communists sought to transform the sociopolitical system – that is, end the class basis of rule, liberate the ruled from their oppressors, and institute greater socioeconomic equality. Material ends – higher economic productivity and a more equal distribution of economic rewards – became infused with moral/spiritual/ideological value. Instead of functioning as an isolated atom, the individual should become part of a collective cause realizing a new sociopolitical order. Contrasting actual and ideal political systems, the communists equated feudalism and capitalism with the domination of the rulers over the ruled. In the ideal communist system, the centralized bureaucratic state, corporate capitalism, and the hierarchical Church would no longer dominate their subjects. All people would live in full freedom and equality.

Marx's interpretations reflected basic Enlightenment notions. He assumed that reason leads to liberation from oppression. Rather than depend on revelation and religious authority, philosophers through theory and empirical investigation can understand and transform the world. Like the Enlightenment thinkers, Marx believed in progress. As societies move from one stage to higher stages – for example, through slavery, feudalism, capitalism, socialism, and communism – progress occurs. As the productive forces become more developed, individuals can master the physical environment and expand their choices. Marx concurred with the Enlightenment assumption that science has both a voluntaristic and deterministic strain. Marx's interpretation of 'scientific socialism' sketched the 'natural laws' of capitalist development; these laws stressed the dialectical processes by which capitalist production generated the class antagonisms that inevitably led to socialist transformation. Yet Marx also remained optimistic about the power of human beings to realize fundamental change. Taking a quasi-voluntarist position, he wrote: 'Men make their own history, but not of their own free will; not under circumstances they themselves have chosen but under the given and inherited circumstances with which they are directly confronted.'[24]

Sketching the political relationships between rulers and ruled, Marx contrasted capitalist society with the advanced phase of communism. Under capitalism the propertied classes rule the proletariat. They shape state policies, influence government bureaucrats, and secure an ideological domination over society, so that official definitions of the general interest become synonymous with the capitalist class interest. During the transition period between capitalism and communist society, the state operates as the 'revolutionary dictatorship of the proletariat,' which Marx interpreted as the exercise of political power by the working class. The industrial proletariat, which has become a majority of the people, uses coercive force to achieve the communist revolution: the abolition of class distinctions, the collective ownership of capital, and the liberation of the productive forces. In the advanced phase of communism, the state as an agent of class rule will cease operating because antagonistic class interests no longer prevail. Workers will gain liberation from bureaucratic state oppression and class rule. Society regains its freedom from the state. Under the 'associated mode of production,' a planned economy controls collective production and distribution; workers function as free, social, and associated individuals. The market, monetary exchanges, commodity production, private ownership of capital, and the division of labor disappear. Only in this advanced communist society will political equality emerge. The workers will all participate as equals in the decisionmaking process. Participatory democracy based on rational consensus will serve as the structural mechanism for making public policies affecting the whole society. Public officials will remain accountable to the workers who elected them.[25]

Adopting many Marxist ideas to the Russian context, Lenin, the founder of the Soviet state, articulated a more elitist concept of political rule than had Marx. Lenin perceived that only through the organization of anticapitalist protests by a vanguard party would Russia ever realize full communism. Even though Marx placed little emphasis on individual autonomy, interest diversity, and pluralism, he did favor workers' political parties and unions that maintained independence from both the capitalists and socialist intellectuals; these parties and unions would lead the struggle toward an eventual communist society. For him, the 'dictatorship of the proletariat' meant workers' control of the state. Lenin made this concept the cornerstone of the new Soviet regime. Under Lenin's interpretation, the proletarian dictatorship hardly denoted rule by the proletarian majority. Instead, it meant coercive force wielded by the Communist Party and by the Cheka (the All-Russian Extraordinary Commission for Combating Counter-Revolution, Sabotage, and Speculation) – a security police agency that Lenin established two months after the Bolshevik seizure of government power. During the transition stage between the overthrow of capitalism and the advent of socialism, Lenin saw the need for the Communist Party and the state to employ ruthless coercion to suppress the former exploiters and to destroy all symptoms of disintegration, such as crime, corruption, profiteering, and anarchy, that accompanied the breakdown of the *ancien régime*. According to Lenin, the Communist Party must play a vanguard role in the construction of socialism. In his view, most people are apathetic, inert, dormant, convention-ridden, and guided by habit; they readily accept the need for subordination and control. Even workers, especially unskilled and untrained ones, are constrained by trade-union consciousness. Motivated by their passions, appetites, and self-interests, they compromise their principles, pursue short-term personal gains, and collaborate with 'petty bourgeois' reformers. Faced with an opportunistic proletariat, Lenin wanted a vanguard party elite of professional revolutionaries, intellectuals, and enlightened workers to forge socialist class consciousness among the masses. Through political organization, popular education, and general leadership, the Party has the responsibility to arouse the masses from their political slumber, enlighten them, and guide them through socialist construction. As the vanguard of the proletariat, the Communist Party must remain committed to reason, the purity of Marxist principles, long-term planning, sacrifice for the collective good, and proletarian solidarity. Public policies infuse material objectives – rapid industrializaion, central economic planning, redistribution of wealth to the poor – with socialist ideological value. Purges of corrupt 'anti-Party' cadres maintain the vanguard's ideological purity.[26]

Lenin posited a dominant role for the state until the establishment of 'full communism.' Whereas Marx had referred to a 'first phase' and a 'more advanced phase of communist society,' Lenin equated the first phase with socialism and linked the higher stage to full communism. Because classes still prevail in the socialist stage, a powerful central government must smash the bourgeoisie and construct socialism, which Lenin associated with industrialization, large-scale collective production, advanced technology, and 'electrification of the entire economy.' Political elitism, as embodied in a powerful state and a vanguard Communist Party, takes precedence over political equality. Individualism becomes subordinate to the collective interests of the Communist Party, the Soviet state, and the proletarian class. The party-state promotes both moral and material welfare. Communist Party leaders see themselves as political educators teaching new socialist values and creating new Soviet citizens. Along with the party, the state spearheads rapid industrialization, spurs socialist construction, coordinates economic production, plans comprehensive social service programs, and tries to equalize economic opportunities for citizens, especially poor farmers and factory workers. Through these policies, Lenin assumed that the proletariat and peasantry would live under more equal conditions than during the czarist regime. Only with the emergence of full communism will people achieve complete equality and genuine political freedom. Because no antagonistic classes will remain, the state as an agency of class repression will vanish. For Lenin, however, socialism and especially full communism lay in the distant future. During the transition period to these stages, a centralized state and vanguard party must govern the society.[27]

Although Leninist principles wielded the greatest influence over the communist movement during the twentieth century, today these vanguardist, elitist beliefs have come under challenge from pluralist communists in West Europe, East-Central Europe, and Latin America. The Italian Communist Party renamed itself the Democratic Party of the Left. Its leaders support a multiclass state, alliances with other parties, the electoral road to socialism, and expanded mass participation by factory workers, small farmers, and small-scale businesspeople. In Eastern Europe competitive elections, autonomous unions, decentralized government, a stronger policymaking role for parliament, and a separation of power between the party and the state have become more widespread than under Communist Party rule. Latin American Marxists reject Lenin's emphasis on ideological monism, armed struggle, the proletarian dictatorship, and a single vanguard party led by a revolutionary leader. Instead, most support ideological pluralism, autonomous social groups, consensual alliance formation, a shared or collective vanguard that leads the class struggle, and a popular front of all exploited groups: workers, peasants, students, revolutionary Christians, neighborhood groups, radical feminists, ecologists, humanists, Indians, and even 'progressive' sectors of the military.[28]

In contrast with the pluralist communists, the anarcho-communists have voiced a more radical perspective toward social change. Attracting limited support in such places as France, Italy, and Spain between the two world wars, the anarchists staged protests against the state bureaucracy, monopolistic capitalism, and the Roman Catholic Church. Viewing parliamentary rule, political parties, and elections as too reformist, the anarcho-syndicalists attempted to transform society from capitalism into socialism through mobilization from below. Workers' councils, popular assemblies, neighborhood associations, unions, and producers' cooperatives enabled workers to take direct action. The anarcho-syndicalist Georges Sorel advocated the destruction, not the reform, of the state. For him, direct action – the general strike – represented the most efficient tactic for establishing a revolutionary syndicalist society governed by trade unions. Syndicalists had to propagate a set of myths that motivated the masses for action. These myths were nonrational, emotional images that justified the meaning of suffering, proclaimed the certainty of victory, served as a guide to violent action, and reinforced military solidarity. Even though Sorel defended the Bolshevik overthrow of the Russian oligarchy, his opposition to bourgeois 'cowardice,' gradual reformism, and the parliamentary politics of dialogue also resembled fascists' beliefs, particuarly their commitment to irrational, emotional, violent political activity.[29]

## REACTION AGAINST THE ENLIGHTENMENT

Not only Sorel but also conservatives, fundamentalists, and particularly fascists protest key tenets of the Enlightenment philosophy. Despite crucial differences about the purposes of rule, especially the importance of religious values in political life, the three groups reject the Enlightenment stress on reason as a means to understand and change the world. For them, emotional, mystical beliefs take precedence over skeptical scientific inquiry. Action based on nonrational sentiments becomes more important than intellectual reflection. Opposed to the pluralist diversity of modernization, they seek to restore the organic values of the premodern era. Secular and sacred values are fused, not differentiated. The collective whole – an Islamic community, a Christian *corpus mysticum*, the Aryan race, the German *Volk*, the Italian nation – assumes primacy over the individual parts. The purposes of goverment rule stress the purification of the community from contaminating influences – communists, secular humanists, Jews, subversives – so that the health of the organic community is restored. The relationship between rulers and ruled rests on a hierarchical, patriarchal foundation. Men dominate the political community. Women remain subservient to the heads of the family and the national fatherand.

Despite these similarities, crucial differences separate the fascists from conservatives and fundamentalists. Whereas fascists break with religious orthodoxy, conservatives and fundamentalists emphasize religious values in sociopolitical life. They also voice a more pluralist interpretation than did either Hitler or Mussolini, the dominant fascist leaders between the two world wars.

## Conservatism

Contemporary conservative ideologies reject the Enlightenment principles associated with classical liberalism, socialism, and especially communism. Tradition, mysticism, sacred values, collective responsibilities, and political elitism take priority over reason, secular skepticism, individual rights, and mass participation in political life. The philosophies of St Augustine, St Thomas Aquinas, and Edmund Burke have influenced conservative theorists today. Like Christian theologian St Augustine (354–430), they perceive individuals as dominated by original sin, self-love, an evil will, and irrational passions. Hence, any hope of future progress based on human reason seems doomed. Because self-imposed restraints cannot check individuals' tendencies toward self-indulgence, powerful collective institutions such as the state, the established church, and the family must restrain the evil tendencies of human nature. The major purposes of governent revolve around the regulation of moral behavior: promoting civic virtue, planning for the common good, and educating individuals for responsibility to the community. Law and education assume crucial importance as the conveyors of moral/spiritual values. Conservative public policies stress prayer in schools and training in moral character as the overriding objective of public education. They seek laws that prohibit abortion, ban pornography, and restrict homosexual rights.

Opposed to both the socialists' stress on income equality and the liberals' commitment to secular individualism, pluralist conservatives support government policies that promote religion, family life, and group diversity. Often allied with religious institutions, conservative parties, especially the Christian Democrats on the European continent, favor government subsidies to private church schools. Since the Second World War the conservatives have also upheld the need for communal institutions – the government, church, family – to help individuals. From the early

1950s through the mid-1970s, English tories such as R. A. Butler and Harold Macmillan advocated a welfare state that promotes class harmony, political order, incremental reform, and social planning. Adopting a paternalistic outlook, these tories assumed that political elites have the obligation to assist less fortunate members of the national family. On the European continent, Christian Democrats in West Germany, Austria, Belgium, the Netherands, and Luxembourg have asserted similar paternalistic values. They stress the importance of governent social services, especially old-age pensions and child allowances, that strengthen the family. Pledged to maintain a diverse society, conservatives favor different social insurance programs for different occupations. Although conservatives want government to regulate private economic firms, they reject powerful state efforts to secure more equal economic rewards through progressive taxes or egalitarian expenditures. Rather than maximizing income equality, government institutions should allocate child benefits to parents, pensions to the elderly, and health care to the sick.

For classical conservatives, collectivist values take precedence over the individual pursuit of self-interest. Particularly in Europe and Latin America, conservatives share St Thomas Aquinas' view of society, the political system, and the established Church as hierarchical organisms. Because society is a complex, differentiated organism, only slow, evolutionary growth must occur. Activist attempts to secure rapid, fundamental changes would upset the societal equilibrium and create disorder. Instead, government officials must maintain the organic harmony of society, where functional relationships bind all individual members together in a tight sense of community.

Both monistic and pluralist conservatives advocate an elitist relationship between rulers and ruled. The political system functions as a human organism. Just as the head dominates the body, so the elite must govern the body politic. If the feet were to become equal with the head, society would disintegrate. Attempts to attain political equality between the rulers and the ruled would lead to anarchy. Hence, conservatives see the need for a powerful state and strong leadership to preserve order, authority, and tradition. *Monistic* organizations such as the Societies for the Defense of Tradition, Family, and Property want a powerful state and established church to uphold patriarchal authority. For them, the proper linkage between rulers and ruled rests on an

Augustinian foundation. The state wields coercive power; subjects dutifully obey. In contrast, the *pluralists* now dominant in conservative and Christian Democratic parties throughout West Europe and Latin America favor shared power restrained by law. Even though the British philosopher Edmund Burke (1729–1797) remained skeptical of the mass public's competence to make wise judgments about complex policy issues and restricted the citizen's political role to voting for parliamentarians, he rejected arbitrary government ruled by corrupt, cruel leaders. From his conservative perspective, a parliamentary elite of professional experts should make decisions based on the eternal law of justice. Similarly, according to conservative pluralists influenced by St Thomas Aquinas, a government limited by legal restraints counteracts the leveling, conformist, egalitarian tendencies of contemporary mass society. Law provides political order. It specifies the obligations that the individual owes the community. Yet the law also protects the individual from the twin dangers of a standardizing bureaucratic state and the conformist pressures of the majority. Guided by the law, legislators thus have the duty to pursue the good of the whole community, not the particularistic interests of isolated individuals or the mass majority. From the pluralist conservative perspective, various social groups – voluntary associations, local communities, regional organizations – bring needed diversity to society. Within the political system, local governments, autonomous courts, and quasigovernmental organizations check central state authority, thereby ensuring that social change will occur in an evolutionary way.[30]

## Fundamentalism

Throughout the world a growing protest against the Enlightenment paradigm comes from the fundamentalists. Like conservatives, they reject secularization and the modernist faith in reason, scientific skepticism, and material progress. Yet fundamentalists downgrade the conservative emphasis on pluralism, diversity, and evolutionary change. For them, ideological monism, exclusivism, simplicity, and apocalyptic change emerge triumphant over belief in pluralism, inclusivism, complexity, and gradual social change. The term 'fundamentalism' originated in the United States during the era immediately before the First World War, when Protestant evangelicals published twelve paperbound books entitled *The Fundamentals: A Testimony to the Truth.* These fundamentals rejected theological and sociopolitical modernism: historical biblical criticism, the social gospel, evolution, secular humanism, liberalism, socialism, and communism. Instead, the fundamentalists affirmed traditional tenets of the Christian faith, such as the literal inerrancy of the Bible, the trinitarian God, the deity of Christ, the virgin birth, his bodily resurrection, and his second coming. Today the term 'fundamentalist' applies to revivalist groups throughout the world – not only US evangelicals but also Protestant Pentecostalists in Latin America, the Muslim Brotherhood in Egypt and Jordan, the Algerian Islamic Salvation Front, the Iranian Shia theocrats, and the Israeli Shas, Torah Flag, and Agudat Yisrael. They draw support from individuals who have suffered the negative consequences of modernization. These include former rural residents who move into the cities, achieve some formal education, but reject the secularized lifestyle of urban life, with its corruption, permissiveness, tolerance, and pursuit of pleasure. To these individuals, modernization has brought disequilibrium, not harmony or progress.

According to fundamentalist protesters, society must revive the purity of its sacred roots. They recognize no sharp distinction between public and private affairs, between sacred and secular concerns, or between normative and empirical reality. Sacred values and material secular interests should be fused, not separated. State laws, policies, and institutions must rest on a religious foundation. For the fundamentalists, the major purposes of government revolve around the regulation of private and public morality. Schools and courts must restore moral values to the community. Along with other government institutions, they must cleanse the community of modern vices: premarital sex, pornography, abortion, homosexuality, drug addiction, gambling, and alcoholism. Public schools must conduct orthodox prayers and teach traditional religious values. Courts should enforce religious law based on a literal interpretation of sacred scripture, which contains only one unchanging meaning for all times. Rather than stress the rights of individual self-expression, fundamentalists assert the paramount importance of collective institutions, including the family, the nation, and the religious community. They want public policies to restore the health of these communal institutions. The fundamentalist interpretation of the interaction between rulers and ruled supports neither civil liberties nor political equality. Political freedom implies the rights of deviant groups to spread decadent, impure ideas. Upholding a patriarchal *ethos*, fundamentalists want women to remain subordinate to their husbands and fathers. Women perform traditionally subservient roles in raising the children and preserving family values. Men interpret the sacred scriptures, govern state institutions, and dominate public policymaking.[31]

## Fascism

Although fascists share the fundamentalist commitment to a patriarchal order, reject diversity, and perceive the world divided between the pure and the impure, fascists reject the fundamentalists' priority on sacred religious traditions. Instead, they uphold the collective interests of the race and nation, not the church or spiritual community. Powerful secular leaders such as like Adolf Hitler and Benito Mussolini embodied the national will.

Fascists, who attained their greatest political power between the two world wars, sought dramatic changes in the sociopolitical order as well as a reversion to a preexisting society, such as the Roman Empire or the medieval teutonic empires. Benito Mussolini, the fascist leader who ruled Italy from 1922 through 1943, stressed the need for fascists to borrow freely from all ideologies, whether revolutionary or reactionary: 'We do not believe in dogmatic programs. . . . We permit ourselves the luxury of being aristocratic and democratic, conservative and progressive, reactionary and revolutionary, legalists and illegalists, according to the circumstances of the moment, the place and the environent.'[32] Whatever ideology fascists reinterpreted for the immediate political situation, they rejected the Enlightenment principles of reason, individualism, representative government, and the separation of sacred values from secular issues.

As Mussolini indicated, fascists accepted and rejected aspects of conservatism, classical liberalism, and communism. From conservatism, they borrowed notions about the dominance of personal leadership, the subordination of women, and the organic state and society, with its stress on functional interdependence and harmony. Yet fascists opposed the conservative support for a powerful established church that controlled education, the courts, and citizens' moral behavior. Like classical liberals, fascist ideologues supported private ownership of capital, economic efficiency, and the unequal distribution of income. Yet fascists rejected such liberal political principles as minority rights, individual self-expression, parliamentary democracy, and constitutional restraints on the state. Unlike liberal capitalists, the fascists denounced free world trade but favored extensive state regulation of private economic firms.

Although Mussolini was originally a Socialist party leader from 1908 to 1914 and Adolf Hitler led the National Socialist German Workers' (Nazi) Party, both strongly rejected democratic-socialist ideas, especially the support for autonomous trade unions, civil liberties, political decentralization, and egalitarian public policies that redistributed income to the poor. Under German Nazi and Italian Fascist rule, economic policies hardly reduced income inequalities. In Italy fascist decisions benefited large landowners and large industrilists. Similarly, German elites – civil servants and business executives in the iron, steel, and chemical industries – retained their privileges under the rearmament policies that militarized the German state by the end of the 1930s.

Fascism showed a closer resemblance to the Leninist interpretation of communism than to democratic socialism. Like Lenin, fascists stressed the supremacy of the collective over the individual, the need to organize the single political party like an army, and rule through the exercise of a strong will. Yet in other respects, fascism departed from Leninist principles, especially the ideological stress on class conflict, an eventual classless society, and workers' ownership of capital. Lenin advocated party domination of the state, collective leadership, an atheistic society, and a society based on the working class. In contrast, fascists assigned greater decisionmaking powers to the state vis-à-vis the party. They emphasized personal leadership, rejected atheism, and identified collectivism with the nation or the race, not with an economic class.

The relationship between rulers and ruled rested on a hierarchical, elitist, patriarchal, monistic foundation. One male leader, one strong organic state, and one party governed a homogeneous people. Nazi posters with Hitler's photograph proclaimed: 'One people, one Germany, one *Führer*!' The Italian word *fasces* refers to the Roman symbol of power – a bundle of rods bound together by thongs, with an axe head at one end. For Mussolini, this symbol implied that a single will had to govern fascist Italy. No class conflicts provoked by socialists or communists should disturb the unity of state and society. Both Hitler and Mussolini asserted that the best men should rule free of mass pressures from below. Leaders exercise authority. Followers obey. Because individuals are born unequal, neither political nor socioeconomic equality is possible. Inferiors must defer to their superiors. Equal duties to the nation-state and its leader form the basis of national solidarity. Some of Hitler's Nazi followers viewed him as the Redeemer of the Reich, who saved the German nation from Jews, Marxists, and foreign powers. A few fascists perceived Mussolini as a national deity restoring the ancient glories of imperial Rome.[33] According to both Hitler and Mussolini, the main political tasks revolved around defending the fatherland, liberating the nation from its enemies, and restoring national glory.

Although Mussolini and Hitler died at the end of the Second World War, fascist beliefs still influence protests against the values of liberal pluralism, tolerance, universalism, and egalitarian reform. In the United States, fascism remains alive among prisoners and youth gangs, with their commitment to violence, patriarchal dominance, emotionalism, and protection of one's 'turf.' The White Aryan Resistance and the Fourth Reich Skinheads use violence against Jews, Asians, African-Americans, immigrants, and homosexuals. Throughout Western Europe fascist political parties – the German *Republikaner*, the Austrian Freedom Party, the Belgian *Vlaams Blok*, the French *Front National*, the British National Party – attract some popular support, mainly from men who feel threatened by economic modernization, especially free trade, multinational corporations, labor mobility across nations, transnational market integration (European Union), and the declining power of the nation-state over economic decisionmaking. Like Hitler and Mussolini, contemporary fascist leaders stress collective values: nationalism, ethnocentrism, and the need to purify the national community of 'contaminating' influences – Jews, communists, socialists, other leftwingers, and particularly non-European immigrants from Africa, the Middle East, and Asia. Hostile to political freedom and equality, fascists advocate personal leadership, male dominance, a strong police, and a powerful military. Rejecting the liberal 'permissive' society, they want state institutions to enforce discipline through such punitive policies as capital punishment, corporal punishment, and long prison sentences for crimes committed by immigrants. Moralistic values infuse material interests. Contemporary fascists favor private property, income inequality, and economic policies (low taxes, high tariffs) that benefit small entrepreneurs – groups that have suffered under large-scale modern capitalism and the influence of multinational corporations. Glorifying the national fatherand, fascists seek a healthy organic state, a nation purified of 'parasitic' foreigners and 'dissolute' liberals, socialists, and communists.[34] With the decline of Communist Party regimes during the late 1980s, protest movements voicing these fascist beliefs regained strength in East-Central Europe.

## CONCLUSION

What impact do ideological protests wield on social change? As we have seen, this impact depends on the content of the ideological beliefs, their institutionalisation, and the extent to which individuals have accepted these values. Conservatives support gradual, evolutionary change that does not upset society's organic harmony. For them, an established church serves as the key institution for transmitting its basic messages. So long as individuals remain within the ecclesiastical network and never expose themelves to divergent beliefs, then the church hierarchy will impart the basic tenets of the church to the parishioners. Contemporary fundamentalists operate within powerful small-group settings, usually a nonbureaucratic church or mosque. To the extent that members actively participate within this all-encompassing church network, they will probably accept the political and religious teachings of the clergy about social change. Classical liberals favor reformist changes, such as expanded, more egalitarian opportunities for individuals to gain upward mobility. In the contemporary Western world, private business firms, the mass media, and research centers articulate the values of liberal capitalism. Particularly in the United States, the principles linked to 'Lockean liberalism' have gained widespread support; here, business groups and commercial farms have wielded extensive political influence. In contrast, in Scandinavia, especially Sweden, democratic socialism functions as the dominant belief system. The Social Democratic Party, powerful labor unions, and cooperatives communicate egalitarian views. Compared with American and British citizens, Swedes hence seem more ready to accept the egalitarian policies linked to an activist social service state. Throughout Eastern Europe, the Communist Party and its auxiliaries – unions, peasant associations, professional organizations, youth groups – interpreted the principles of Marxism–Leninism. Even though the official ideology advocated a transformaion of the existing sociopolitical system, in practice East European communists abandoned the mass struggle for fundamental change. Instead, they tried to maintain their power and to secure modifications of basic instituions, such as greater adaptability to modern technology. Efforts to reshape popular attitudes proved unsuccessful. Different religious, ethnic, and regional values retained a more powerful hold over the individual than did 'socialist consciousness.'

The attempt of Hitler and Mussolini to transform personal beliefs also failed. Through single parties and mass rallies, these two leaders sought to institutionalize their fascist ideologies. So long as Hitler appeared responsible for greater prosperity and national glory, some Germans supported him, if not all his specific Nazi views. Yet when defeat in the Second World War appeared inevitable, acceptance of the Aryan myths rapidly waned. Compared with Hitler, Mussolini never gained the institutional power needed to socialize the population. The Catholic Church, the monarchy, the army, the state civil service, large-scale industrialists, and landowners continued to retain some influence free from Fascist Party control. Hence, Mussolini's eclectic fascist principles never became widely internalized.[35]

Although nearly all modern ideologues assert the dominance of society over the bureaucratic state, in practice they uphold a powerful state to propagate their ideological messages. Committed to the free competitive market, classical liberals advocate limited government restrained by constitutional guarantees and pluralist autonomous social groups. Yet liberals envision comprehensive activities for the state in preserving market mechanisms. It needs to promote efficiency, rectify market failures, limit negative externalities (pollution, unhealthy food), protect property rights, construct an economic infrastructure, socialize the work force, and defend capitalist interests through the use of military and diplomatic power in the world arena. Democratic socialists want to decentralize the policymaking process to local cooperatives and popular movements. But these fragmented institutions lack the power to realize egalitarian objectives, especially against the resistance of large-scale domestic private business enterprises, multinational corporations, and foreign nation-states that shape the contemporary world capitalist economy. Although both Marx and Lenin rejected the oppressive state associated with class rule, under the Soviet regime Lenin organized a powerful state that would defeat the counter-revolutionaries, construct socialism, and defend the USSR against foreign attack. Pluralist conservatives favor strong intermediary institutions that come between the individual and the state; yet they also believe that the state must defend order and traditional values. Fundamentalists assert the primacy of the spiritual community vis-à-vis corrupt impure governments. Nevertheless, their reliance on the state to regulate private and public moral behavior gives government institutions extensive power to control society. Hitler claimed that his Nazi policies reinforced the primacy of the German *Volk* over the discredited government institutions operated by the Weimar Republic officials. In practice, however, the Nazi state wielded greater coercive control over the populace than did any previous German state.[36]

Despite this ideological support for a strong state to propagate basic beliefs, government power to reshape society actually remains limited. Even where revolutionary ideologies dominate, government agencies can more easily coerce individuals and secure behavioral compliance than they can transform human attitudes or engineer fundamental transformations in the socio-political situation. As democratic socialist R. H. Tawney recognized, the Kingdom of God cannot be attained through political action. According to him, political leaders and citizens must concentrate on realizing a freer, more egalitarian society, not paradise on earth.[37]

# 3  Religion and Political Vision

Albert Hirschman recounts the story of the Polish rabbi who impressed a Kraków congregation with his psychic powers. One sabbath while saying prayers in the Remuh synagogue, he suddenly exclaimed: 'The rabbi of Warsaw has just died.' Since Warsaw is located over 150 miles to the north of Kraków, the people in the synagogue marveled at the clairvoyance of their rabbi. Yet doubts began to emerge when some Jews from Kraków visited Warsaw two weeks later and saw that the rabbi there was still alive – indeed, healthy enough to preside at the Sabbath services. On returning to Kraków, these Jews told their colleagues about their rabbi's mistaken judgment. Although some of his detractors snickered, other faithful supporters rushed to his defense. 'Oh yes,' they retorted, 'he may have been wrong about a few specific details. But what great vision our rabbi has.'[1]

For political protesters who seek either to realize a new sociopolitical order in the future or to restore a paradise lost, religious visions inspire people to change the world. Religious images draw a sharp contrast between the present evil world and a reconstructed society committed to the highest spiritual ideals. For example, Psalm 146 warned the Jews against trusting political leaders whose ambitious plans perished with them at death. Instead, the Psalmist urged the people to trust in the God of Jacob – the Lord who 'executes justice for the oppressed, gives food to the hungry, sets the prisoners free, protects strangers in Israel, uplifts the downtrodden, helps widows and orphans, but ruins the plans of the wicked.'

Influenced by the Messianic traditions of Judaism, the first-century Christians depicted visions that gave meaning to their lives, motivated them to endure suffering, and promised the ultimate triumph of righteousness. The *Revelation to John* protested Roman oppression and the tendency for upwardly mobile Christians to accommodate themselves to the Roman political order by serving in the army, civil service, or imperial palace at

59

the close of the first century CE. John portrayed Rome as Leviathan, the great beast from the sea, and viewed the imperial cultic priesthood that coordinated worship of the emperor as Behemoth, the great beast from the land. Serving the two beasts and their master the dragon Satan, the 'great harlot' Rome embodied the prostitution of spiritual purity expressed in Christian love.[2] In contrast with Rome, John's Utopian order envisioned a new Jerusalem that united heaven with a transformed earth:

> I saw a new heaven and a new earth, for the first heaven and the first earth had vanished, and there was no longer any sea. I saw the Holy City, new Jerusalem, coming down out of heaven from God, made ready like a bride adorned for her husband. I heard a loud voice proclaiming from the throne: 'Now God has his dwelling with mankind! He will dwell among them and they shall be his people, and God himself will be with them. He will wipe every tear from their eyes. There shall be an end to death and to mourning, crying, and pain, for the old order has passed away!' . . . Jerusalem, the Holy City, . . . shone with the glory of God. It had the radiance of some priceless jewel, like a jasper, clear as crystal (Revelation 21:1–4, 10–11).

In this new Jerusalem, God enlightens people, who live under purity, love, peace, and abundance. Later secular revolutionaries used the metaphor of the new Jerusalem to transform the mundane, profane world according to a transcendental vision of ethical perfection.

What are the political implications of religious beliefs? For several reasons, religious values have historically played a vital part in political protests. First, they represent a form of 'cultural power' or 'symbolic capital' that articulate ultimate purposes, transcendental meanings, and ethical ideals. Members of religious communities share ultimate ends that transcend the empirical world. Sacred symbols offer meaning behind ambiguous historical events, provide a purpose for living, explain the reasons for suffering, and specify guidelines for moral behavior. Not only the religious vocabulary but political discourse communicates interpretations of the public good: justice, virtue, equality, freedom, and equity.[3]

Second, religious values justify and criticize the exercise of political power. Before the nineteenth century, few political systems drew a sharp distinction between sacred values and secular beliefs. Kings claimed to rule by divine grace. Clergy consecrated the kings, thereby legitimating their rule. Monarchs, emperors, and czars often viewed themselves as the representatives of God on earth. Their policies supposedly reflected divine commandments. During the late twentieth century, kings no longer rule most societies. The more 'secular' values of statehood and nationalism comprise the dominant political beliefs. Yet political leaders still justify their right to rule on the basis of sacred values. In some revolutionary societies, such as North Korea, industrialization and the socialist transformation of the economy assume ultimate significance, with Marxist–Leninist ideology and nationalism representing a new form of secular political religion.[4] Even in democratic countries that have preserved the autonomy of the church from state control, elected officials still appeal for support in terms of moral-spiritual values like justice, personal rectitude, public virtue, and pursuit of the common well-being.

Besides legitimating the exercise of political power, religious figures often use sacred spiritual values to protest the operation of the political system, the behavior of its leaders, and dominant public policies. Challenges against political oppression, economic exploitation, and status degradation reverberate through the political discourse. The World Council of Churches implements programs that combat racism and uphold economic justice. Composed mainly of Catholics and evangelical Protestants, 'pro-life' groups reject abortion policies, equating abortion with murder. Catholic advocates of 'liberation theology' oppose conservative governments. Staging protests against both communist and anticommunist Asian regimes, Buddhist monks charge that government policies violate the highest spiritual values of Buddhism.

Third, religious institutions strive to translate general ethical values into specific government policies. Few clergy draw a sharp distinction between personal and public morality. Affirming guidelines for moral behavior, they try to influence education, legal, health, and family policies, especially decisions affecting marriage, divorce, birth control, abortion, pornography, and homosexuals' rights. Clergy also work to implement policies that will secure greater ethnic equality, income equality, justice for the oppressed, and world peace. Particularly in nations where the government subsidizes religious institutions, church officials often seek lower taxes on ecclesiastical property as well as higher expenditures for their hospitals and educational institutions.[5]

Fourth, religious values shape attitudes toward sociopolitical change and the opportunities for realizing a transformed society. As we saw in the last chapter, the content of cultural beliefs, the power of institutions that interpret them, and their internalization in personal behavior affect the achievement of social change. Dynamic religious beliefs voiced by reformists and revolutionaries stimulate an activist orientation toward the world. Viewing the world as empirically real, they stress the tension between empirical realities and spiritual ideals – between 'what is' and 'what ought to be.' These ideals motivate people to change the status quo. Rather than fatalistically resigning themselves to the existential situation, individuals postulate sociopolitical change as both desirable and feasible. Militant radicals struggle to transform existing regimes. For them, poverty and injustice derive from structural causes, not from personal sins. As political activists, these militants seek to liberate the oppressed, empower the powerless, and attain economic equality. These secular programs assume sacred significance. Egalitarian relationships take priority over deference to hierarchical elites. The prospects for a transformed society increase when no strong clerical organization blocks change or particularly when religious institutions facilitate specific changes. Under the latter condition, a powerful religious institution maintains high solidarity; individuals become dependent on it to attain their goals. The institution has the control capacities to ensure compliance with its normative obligations. Hence, individuals feel pressured to internalize religious beliefs that highlight the need for change as both desirable and feasible. With numerous resources, a complex organization, and legitimacy, powerful religious institutions led by 'liberation theologians' can pressure government officials to promote sociopolitical change.

More generally, however, conservative and reactionary clergy dominate ecclesiastical institutions that impede the realization of rapid, comprehensive social changes. Conservatives usually stress personal salvation, not the liberation of the whole society through political action. Differentiating material interests from moral–spiritual values, they assume that religious institutions should concentrate on saving the individual. Poverty stems from personal failures; the churches and private charities, rather than the government, should take main responsibility for helping the poor. Dedicated to maintaining the politico-economic status quo, these conservatives urge deference to religious hierarchs and government officials. Unlike conservatives, reactionary fundamentalists reject the existential order; they want to restore an ideal past society. Perceiving the world divided between the pure and the defiled, they defer to their own patriarchal church leaders who guide the 'elect' toward personal salvation in a communal context. Yet fundamentalists may defy political authority, especially if they label government officials as 'pagans' or 'infidels.' Fusing secular and sacred principles, fundamentalists assume that the religious values of abstinence, discipline, self-control, and frugality are more likely to produce material success than are public policies enacted by a 'profane' government.[6] From the fundamentalists' perspective, only by capturing control of state power do they hope to restore the traditional religious values associated with paradise lost.

In sum, we assume that a dialectical tension between secularization and sacralization explains the continuing importance of religious values in modern political life. As Durkheim pointed out, the structural differentiation linked to modernization produces atomization, fragmented identities, impersonality, and bureaucratization. Individuals gain greater autonomy from community controls. Tolerance for 'deviant' lifestyles grows along with the pluralism of worldviews. People become citizens of a nation-state that provides individual social services; neither the family nor the church assumes this responsibility as they did in the past. Secular rationalization implies a dynamic society that engineers rapid growth and material progress. Through reason, technology, and the experimental sciences, individuals can understand and control not only the material world but also the social environment. Opposed to the Enlightenment beliefs of individual autonomy, rationalization, and modernization, protests that arise against secularization assert the priority of sacred values. Sacralization movements reject the mundane world of instrumental technical rationality and the profane world of pluralistic tolerance. They uphold expressive transcendental values, mystical ultimate ends, totalistic collective identities, warm personal ties, and communal spontaneity. During the twentieth century, protesters have invoked these religious values when they resisted colonial rule, ethnic group domination, cultural oppression, and secular modernization. If they gain state power and implement their orthodox religious values in public policies, then secular protests emerge to challenge the sacralization of politics.[7]

Throughout the world during all historical periods, religious values have formed an integral part of society's political culture. Both theorists and theologians articulate the meaning of ethical ideals, spiritual principles, and divine laws for contemporary political conditions. As interpreters of political hermeneutics, they move up and down Jacob's stairway that connects heaven with earth. The following sections analyze the changing interpretations of diverse sacred beliefs, including three Asian religions – Confucianism, Hinduism, Buddhism – Judaism, Christianity, and Islam. We explore two key questions. How do religious values influence public policies? What is the power of churches to secure social change?

## ASIAN ENLIGHTENMENT

As the ancient religion of China, Confucianism upheld the values of enlightenment that shaped the emperors' public policies. Confucianists made no differentiation between the 'sacred' and the 'secular' realms. The mandarins – scholar–gentry literati – performed both ritual and decisionmaking activities. The emperor was regarded as the son of heaven; the mandarins coordinated reverence for the emperor and the ancestral spirits. In the policy arena, the Confucian literati implemented the government decisions formulated by the emperor and his advisors. Rather than focusing on a transcendental salvation beyond one's earthy existence, Confucian priorities stressed the humanistic principles that should govern everyday life. Civic virtue, filial piety, respect for superiors, reverence for the ancestors, and rule by knowledge assumed highest importance. Rectitude and enlightenment represented the primary political virtues. Government responsibilities included education in moral virtues – right conduct, propriety, self-discipline, familial piety. Political rulers had to act as the moral exemplars for society. Traditional Chinese government meant rule by virtuous men, not impersonal law. The hierarchical relationships that bound the ruled to the rulers dissuaded mass peasant protests against the ruling elites. Just as in the family the superiors (fathers) ruled subordinates, so in the political system men governed women and the old dominated the young. The educated mandarins who demonstrated their mastery of the Confucian classics and passed the written examinations ruled over the less-well-educated peasants.

Collectivist principles, not individualism, underlay Confucian beliefs. Identifying individualism with selfishness, anarchy, license, and lack of self-control, the mandarin upheld the need for duty to others, primarily the extended family (kin, clan) and the wider Chinese community. According to the Confucian ethic, the individual's fate depended on society's well-being. Individual achievement came to those who obeyed father and emperor, the symbols of Chinese collectivism, rather than to those gratifying their personal desires.

Although Confucian beliefs justified social stability, order, respect for tradition, and obedience to the established rulers, they also checked the political power of the emperor. If he did not govern in a virtuous way, he supposedly had lost the mandate of heaven. Under this condition, people had the right to rebel against an immoral government. Confucian principles not only legitimated the emperor's right to rule but also supplied the mandarins with the ethical justifications to restrain the emperor's power.[8]

Confronted by the worldwide influence of European technological values during the twentieth century, Confucian principles began to lose their vitality; Asian scholars sought new ideological perspectives, whether Marxism–Leninism or capitalism, that would replace Confucianism as the dominant belief system. Particularly in mainland China, Vietnam, and North Korea after the Second World War, Marxism–Leninism reinterpreted traditional Confucian values to modern conditions. Communist Party ideologues functioned as the new mandarins who governed the populace. Their focus on the importance of political education, governance by moral example, and deference to hierarchical authority figures resembled the mandarin tradition of enlightenment. Like Confucianism, the new political religion articulated by Chinese, Vietnamese, and North Korean communists blended secular interests with sacred values. It united the policymaking and ritual dimensions of political life. 'Secular' political ends – winning wars, educating the populace, industrializing the economy, creating a healthy citizenry – became endowed with 'sacred' significance. As in the traditional Confucian society, collectivism – loyalty to the nation and to smaller groups – took precedence over individual freedom and self-interest. Even though maintaining some continuity with Confucian traditions, the Communist party leaders also proclaimed the revolutionary aspects of Marxist–Leninist ideology. Whereas Confucian principles had emphasized harmony, stability, political apathy, and fatalism, Asian Marxist–Leninists sought fundamental transformations of their societies. Upholding a comprehensive role for the Communist Party, they asserted the need for conflict, change, active political participation, and mastery over fate.

In the non-communist areas of East Asia, especially Taiwan, Singapore, and South Korea, political leaders have reinterpreted Confucian beliefs to promote rapid economic growth. Rather than a powerful Communist Party, other structures, such as a strong bureaucratic-authoritarian state and private business corporations, communicated the new reinterpretations to the people. Taking a pragmatic attitude toward Confucianism, leaders of these institutions emphasized the importance of family solidarity, community obligations, consensual decisionmaking, educational achievement (literacy, technical skills), hard work, and frugality – all worldly orientations. Austerity values promoted family savings that financed domestic capital investment. Collectivist values, which affirmed loyalty to the nation, family, and kin, motivated individuals to cooperate for the cause of higher national growth rates. By encouraging obedience to superiors, Confucian capitalism asserted the need for labor discipline. No established Confucian church blocked development policies implemented by government officials, foreign investors, and domestic private entrepreneurs. Even if Confucian beliefs did not directly promote rapid economic growth, they helped facilitate the structural–behavioral conditions that brought extensive socioeconomic changes to East Asia.[9]

Unlike Confucianism, the beliefs of Hinduism, the dominant religion of India, have justified a more static sociopolitical order. Before the twentieth century, mass protests rarely emerged to challenge the traditional framework. Whereas the Confucian mandarins regarded the existing world as real, Hindus perceive empirical life as illusion – maya. The spiritual essence of human life revolves around the eternal cycle of birth, death, and rebirth.

Individuals seek to attain a higher caste status in the next life, not a transformation of the existing sociopolitical system. Collectivism, not individualism, regulates social interactions. According to Hinduism, personal identity stems from ascribed caste status, not from individual achievements. Members of each caste must maintain their ritual purity. Higher-status 'pure' castes avoid contaminating contacts with lower-status 'impure' caste members. Based on particularistic normative obligations, the caste system specifies different occupations, marriage arrangements, and laws for each caste. *Dharma* (rules of social interaction) depend on an individual's social status, stage of life, and inherited personal qualities. These rules deter upward mobility.

Before the British government established territorial control over India during the nineteenth century, the upper castes – notably the Brahmin priests – functioned as the enlightened rulers of a hierarchical system. No strong central state maintained social order. Hindu *dharma* urged obedience to the rulers, not to an institutionalized government. Although the kings wielded arbitrary power, their power remained unstable. The government enacted low taxes, maintained few defense capabilities, and provided few social services. Brahmin priests, not the kings, ensured order within each caste and village. Hence, political instability – the rapid turnover of rulers – coincided with social stability based on *dharma* law and the caste system.

Not until the twentieth century, with the struggle for independence from British colonial rule, did serious challenges to the caste system emerge. The top leaders of the Indian National Congress Party, which led the territory to political independence, denounced caste practices. The Indian constitution abolished untouchability and forbade discrimination based on caste status. Public policies enabled the ex-untouchables or 'scheduled castes' to secure greater access to higher education, political representation, and government employment. The disorganized, disunified structure of Hinduism allowed more egalitarian beliefs such as Pandit Nehru's secular nationalism, Christianity, and Marxism to gain a foothold in certain regions of India, particularly the cities. Hindu tolerance – the perception that all faiths seek the same truth – also encourages some openness to modern ideas. Nevertheless, the cultural values stressing the need for Hindus to retain continuity with past customs block fundamental social change. Lower castes in the villages confront considerable discrimination and violence. Rural women enjoy few egalitarian rights. Stigmas of spiritual pollution and economic deprivation still prevail. Without powerful political or religious institutions to forge a basic transformation of society, change occurs at a gradual pace.

During the 1990s several Hindu revivalist groups mobilized protests against some reformist changes enacted by the secular, pluralist Indian government. The Rashtriya Swayamsevak Sangh (RSS), the Bharatiya Janata Party (BJP), and the Vishwa Hindu Parishad (VHP – World Hindu Party) asserted sacred, communal, and elitist principles aimed against British common law, Christians, Muslims, and Buddhists. Led by urban upper-caste youths who were educated but unemployed, these revivalist organizations rejected the government's egaliarian treatment toward the lower castes and Muslims. The 'backward classes' and tribal peoples have gained quotas or 'reservations' in federal government employment and access to higher education, thereby facilitating upward mobility for a few lower-caste Indians. Muslims won representation within the Congress Party and the right to have their own Islamic family law. With ties to the Middle East, some Indian Muslim entrepreneurs attained upward mobility, wealth, and a share of political power. Several lower-caste individuals turned toward Islam, Christianity, and Buddhism as ways to attain greater social equality. The former marginals – untouchables and Muslims – no longer show such deference as before, particularly in the cities. These evolutionary changes in social status alienate higher-caste Hindus, who fear downward mobility. Hence, they want to revive a monolithic Hindu nation based on the cult of Lord Ram, a mythical god-king who ruled by elitist *dharma* law. Hindus now comprise 80 percent of the Indian population. These communalists seek a homogeneous Hindu nation where diverse groups no longer share equal rights and a common citizenship.[10]

Compared with both Confucianism and Hinduism, Buddhism has placed greater stress on equality and opportunities for personal salvation from present conditions. Whereas low-status people, especially peasants and women, identify Confucianism with hierarchy, harmony, and the sanctity of the present order, they find the Buddhist principles of universalism and equality more appealing. Except in Sri Lanka, most Buddhists reject the caste system. Stressing individualism, Buddhist values rarely justify rigid caste or class divisions. Secular law, not Buddhist religious law, regulates social interactions in most Southeast Asian countries today.

Despite this egalitarian, individualist ethos, Buddhist monks have rarely played an active political role in transforming the social order and securing a more equal relationship between government rulers and the ruled. For Buddha, the enlightened one, the highest priority centered on the realization of nirvana – the quality of absolute blessedness in which the individual gains release from the cycle of reincarnation. People reach this spiritual stage by transcending the suffering that pervades the material world. Rather than societal transformation, contemplation of spiritual reality and renunciation of material possessions become the primary objectives. Historically in places like Burma, Thailand, Laos, and Tibet, Buddhist monks advised kings, legitimated their rule, and provided education. Except under atypical circumstances, such as Tibet where the senior *lamas* (monks) ruled a theocracy from 1642 to 1959, Buddhist clergy rarely exercised dominant political power. During the twentieth century, they generally played an opposition role. For example, in the 1930s they rallied against the British colonialists in Burma. Recently some young urban monks protested Burmese military domination. Tibetan Buddhists have rebelled against Chinese Communist Party oppression. Vietnamese Buddhist clergy mounted demonstraions against the Catholic President Ngo Dinh Diem, who ruled South Vietnam from 1954 through 1963. Buddhists also opposed the state socialist policies introduced by the Vietnamese Communist Party after 1975. Despite these oppositional activities, Buddhists have lacked the powerful, unified church structures and the motivation to organize fundamental social change. No powerful Buddhist political parties have emerged to struggle for fundamental societal changes.[11]

## JUSTICE AND JUDAISM

In contrast with the ancient Asian religions, the beliefs of Judaism show a greater receptivity to sociopolitical change. Prophets such as Elijah, Isaiah, Jeremiah, Ezekiel, Hosea, Amos, Micah, and Haggai perceived a close connection between politics and ethics.

As messengers of God, they sketched a vision of the ideal society. For them, no sharp distinction separated public and private ethics, the community and the individual, religion and politics, the temple and the state, beliefs and actions, and material interests and moral–spiritual values. Instead, the prophets fused all these apparent antitheses. Perceiving the empirical world as real, not illusory, they sought to cleanse the political community of moral impurities, so that both society and human behavior would become transformed. From the prophetic perspective, the articulation of the gap between ethical values – justice, righteousness, mercy, generosity – and the actual practices of both the political rulers and the people constituted the main impetus behind change. According to the prophets, only by placing the highest priority on spiritual holiness will the Jewish people realize material abundance ('milk and honey') in the promised land. Prophetic messages envisioned a transformed society committed to the highest ethical and spiritual principles. For example, Jeremiah foresaw a time when everyone will internalize the wisdom, knowledge, teachings, and law of God:

> The days are coming, says the Lord, when I shall establish a new covenant with the people of Israel and Judah. . . . I shall set my law within them, writing it on their hearts. I shall be their God, and they will be my people. No longer need they teach one another, neighbor or brother, to know the Lord. All of them, high and low alike, will know me, says the Lord (Jeremiah 31:31, 33–34).

For the Hebrew prophets, justice, mercy, and humility before God represent the prime political virtues. The prophet Micah asked: 'What does the Lord require of you but to act justly, to love kindness, and to walk humbly with your God?' (Micah 6:8). Mercy meant compassion, forgiveness, and steadfast love. Humility implied loyal service to God. Justice or righteousness involved obedience to God's moral law. The Jewish people believed in a binding commitment or covenant between them and their one god Yahweh. In the covenant with Abraham, God promised them the land of Israel. The covenant with King David proclaimed that the future kings after David would govern the Israeli nation. According to the covenant declared to Moses on Mount Sinai, Yahweh obligated the people to articulate their sacred beliefs to the world, obey God's will, and demonstrate this obedience in their law, ethical behavior, and daily living. The Jews had the free will to accept or reject this covenant. Even though the Hebrew Bible tried to reconcile the virtues of justice and mercy, a tension between these two qualities of God still remains. On the one hand, God acts justly; he rewards the obedient and punishes those who transgress the divine legal commandments. On the other hand, Yahweh shows mercy and forgives those who repent of their sins – that is, change their behavior so that spiritual values assume highest priority.

The Jewish prophets drew a sharp contrast between the ideal and actual relationship that linked the rulers with the ruled. Priests, prophets, and kings made the key political decisions. Descendants from the tribe of Levi, the priests performed sacrifices, presided over religious ceremonies, and upheld the Mosaic law. Prophets – messengers called by God – anointed the king, advised him, legitimated his decisions, but also challenged his actions. Prophets played a superior role to kings, who governed the Jewish people for only a brief period. After King Solomon died in 922 BCE, the monarchy split into two kingdoms. Israel, the northern kingdom, survived two hundred years; prophets like Elijah and Elisha challenged the power of the charismatic kings who ruled Israel. The southern kingdom of Judah maintained its integrity until 587 BCE. Hereditary monarchs descended from King David governed Judah, the site of the temple in Jerusalem, where the priests fulfilled more important responsibilities and the prophets held less authority than in Israel. In both kingdoms, however, the prophets attacked idolatry – the worship of false gods – and injustice toward low-status people. For example, Psalm 72 reflects this prophetic message:

> Teach the king to judge with your righteousness, O God.
> Share with him your own justice,
>> so that he will rule over your people with justice and govern
>> the oppressed with righteousness.
> May the land enjoy prosperity; may it experience righteousness.
> May the king judge the poor fairly; may he help the needy and
>> defeat their oppressors (Psalm 72:1–4).

As defenders of the oppressed, prophets rebuked the kings for failing to keep the covenant with God, to love mercy, and to practice justice. Despite this vision of a consensual relationship between rulers and ruled, brutal monarchs usually dominated Jewish society. Faced with a coercive political sitution, the prophets felt a divine calling to declare God's will to society, to specify the moral basis of the political community, to denounce coercive rule, and to proclaim the hope for redemption, which meant both spiritual and political transformation.

For the Jews, communal spiritual values took precedence over the pursuit of self-interests. Primordial and spiritual values fused to instill a shared national identity. The Jews spoke one language, Hebrew. Membership in primordial groups – twelve tribes, clans, villages, and families – reinforced their cohesion. Participation in a common ethnic history and wars with alien powers further cemented the solidarity of the Jews, who believed that they lived in a sacred land where Yahweh also dwelled. Their main religious ceremony, the Passover feast, celebrated the flight of the whole Hebrew community from their Egyptian oppressors. Belief in one god, the Mosaic law, the divine commandments, and the prophetic teachings represented the spiritual values that strengthened communal ties. Particularly after the destruction of the two kingdoms – Israel in the north and Judah in the south – the Jews looked for a messiah to restore their political independence and establish a recontructed society based on spiritual redemption. Originally, the concept of a messiah referred to the whole Israeli people, a 'kingdom of priests and a holy nation' (Exodus 19:6). Later emerged the idea of a vanguard group that would provide an example to others. Finally, the notion of messiah became personalized in a priest, prophet, rabbi, or king. For example, a king like the model King David – God's Anointed (*meshiah Elohim*) – would redeem Israel and thereby uphold the Davidic covenant, which ensured Jews' political independence under David's descendant. Yet whether the Jews perceived the messiah as the community faithful, the vanguard elect, or a single person, they all agreed that the messiah would transform the whole society, not just isolated individuals.[12]

After the Roman destruction of Jerusalem in 70 CE, Jews went into exile until the establishment of the Israeli state in 1948. Inspired by Theodor Herzl during the late nineteenth century, the Zionist movement emerged in Europe to proclaim the need for an independent state for Jews. Perceiving Zionism as a Messianic vanguard movement of the oppressed Jewish people, Herzl synthesized liberal, socialist, and nationalist principles. Liberalism implied equal rights for Jews and Arabs. Socialism involved common ownership of land in the kibbutz and a powerful role for trade unions in politicoeconomic decisionmaking. Nationalism meant that the Jewish nation would regain state sovereignty. Although the Declaration of Independence refers to Israel as a 'Jewish state,' it operates as a secular political system, not as a theocracy. Two secular parties – the Labor-Yachad Alignment and the Likud – dominate political life. Only a minority of Israeli citizens – probably under a third – perceive themselves as Orthodox Jews. Nevertheless, the small religious parties play a key role in the formation of coalition governments. Rabbinical courts interpret Orthodox law, which regulates marriage, divorce, and inheritance. These religious courts also adjudicate policy issues related to abortion, dietary laws, the basis of Jewish identity, and the use of public transportation and the mass media on the Sabbath.

Even though the European Zionist settlers who founded the Israeli state took a secular view of nationalism, recently a more Orthodox, biblical concept of messianism has emerged as a protest against secular Zionism. Rather than a homogeneous society, contemporary Israel is split by ethnic and religious cleavages. Among Jews, around 55 percent are Sephardim descended from those who came to Israel from Arab countries in Asia and Africa. The remaining 45 percent include Ashkenazim – descendants of European and North American Jews. Within the pre-1967 Israeli borders, Jews represent slightly over 80 percent of the population; however, the proportion of Jews in areas including the occupied territories constitutes only 60 percent. Jews are split between Orthodox believers and more secular individuals who rarely observe Orthodox religious laws or customs. Faced with internal diversity, growing consumerism, and threats of invasion by Arab states, the Gush Emunim (Bloc of the Faithful) messianic movement emerged in 1974 to articulate an Orthodox, biblical, militaristic nationalism. Comprising mainly young Orthodox settlers who graduated from state religious schools, the Gush Emunim members invoke biblical analogies to justify Jewish settlement in the occupied territories – areas they regard as ancient Judea and Samaria. For them, the land of 'Eretz Yisrael' assumes mystical, sacred value as a gift from God. Settlement of this holy land reaffirms the redemptive covenant between God and Abraham. Wars with Arab states prepare the way for the coming of the Messiah. Their concept of messianic nationalism takes an apocalyptic view. The old political order has ended. A new order will soon emerge. During the transition period, which Gush Emunim activists view as the 'Era of Redemption,' Jews must reject compromises with Israeli secularists, liberals, socialists, Europeans, Americans, and particularly Palestinians and Arabs. Instead, the Israeli state needs to restore the military power wielded by King David's monarchy. Military weapons convey spiritual value in the holy war against Israel's enemies. Not only Talmudic scholars but also soldiers and vigilante settlers must mobilize to redeem Israel according to the sacred Zionist vision. Militants envision that Torah law, not rules inherited from the Ottoman Empire and British colonialism, will govern the reconstituted political system, which they label the 'Torahcratic republic.'[13]

## VIRTUE AND THE CHRISTIAN COMMONWEALTH

The Christian movement that emerged from Judaism during the first century CE portrayed a sharp tension between the spiritual and political orders. The followers of Jesus believed that he was the Messiah. 'Christ' is the Greek term for messiah, the 'Anointed One.' To his disciples in Jerusalem, Jesus was a charismatic figure who arose to overcome Roman occupation forces and restore the kingdom to Israel. Jesus, the Greek translation of the Hebrew name Joshua, means 'Yahweh is salvation.' Just as Joshua had led the Jews to the promised land, so Jesus would lead his followers out of Roman oppression into the Kingdom of God. Yet Jesus came not as a warrior like King David but as a nonviolent martyr. Viewed like Isaac as the 'beloved son' of God and as the paschal lamb, Jesus sacrificed his own life so that others would gain eternal life. His kingdom represented the spiritual reign of God, not a political kingdom with an army, military conquests, specific territory, and civil servants. He brought the sword of right-eousness, rather than a physical weapon. His twelve disciples corresponded to the twelve tribes of Israel. They and his other followers expected him to come again in final victory. Meanwhile, they had the responsibility to organize a new community – a vanguard fellowship that would prepare the way for the realization of the Kingdom of God on earth.

Asserting the priority of moral-spiritual values over material interests, Jesus contrasted Roman imperial domination with the Kingdom of God. Under the rule of Herod the Great (40–4 BCE) and the three sons who succeeded him, the government showed primary loyalty to Rome, not to the Jews. Herod built luxurious palaces, levied high taxes, exploited tenant farmers, and expropriated land that went to his absentee landlord friends. Cruelty, repression, and corruption prevailed. The Roman military ruled by coercive power, monopolized wealth in the few, and elevated their own status above the lowly. In the Kingdom of God, however, spiritual values would take precedence. As Jesus told his disciples: 'Do not be anxious, saying, "What shall we eat?" or "What shall we drink?" or "What shall we wear?" For the Gentiles seek all these things, and your heavenly Father knows that you need them all. But seek first his kingdom and his righteousness, and all these things shall be yours as well' (Matthew 6:31–33).

The values that Jesus proclaimed represented a nonviolent protest against the Roman imperialists, the Herodian ruling dynasty, and their collaborators in the priestly aristocracy. His vision of the Kingdom of God embodied antithetical values from those that legitimated the established stratification system. Denouncing Herod Antipas, who ruled Galilee from 4 BCE to 39 CE, as a 'fox' – a sly but dangerous tetrarch – Jesus urged his followers to serve others, not dominate them: 'You know that, among the Gentiles, rulers lord it over their subjects, and the great make their authority felt. It shall not be so with you. Among you, whoever wants to be great must be your servant, and whoever wants to be first must be the slave of all – just as the Son of Man did not come to be served but to serve and to give his life as a ransom for many' (Matthew 20:25–28). Hence, service based on *agape* (divine sacrificial love), not coercive power, would pervade interpersonal relations in the Kingdom of God. Economic sharing would replace the pursuit of individual wealth and exploitation of the poor by the rich. Humility before God would transcend the strivings for higher social status on earth. Proclaiming the inclusive nature of God's love, Jesus directed his message at the 'lost sheep,' the outcasts of society: women, children, beggars, lepers, the poor, the disabled, prostitutes, tax collectors, and others regarded as sinners by the religious and political establishment. Jesus' concept of equality between men and women, children and adults, rich and poor rejected the elitist exclusivism practiced by the rulers of his time. As a rabbi, prophet, and healer, Jesus included the marginals in his spiritual kingdom.

Naturally, this 'good news' about the Kingdom of God scarcely evoked a positive response from the Roman authorities. Their imperial system was based on the Emperor Caesar, who recognized no other kings. The Roman rulers commanded the people to worship the emperor as a god. State cults with political priests coordinated loyalty to Rome and the emperor. When Jesus proclaimed the Kingdom of God, he threatened Roman rulers and wealthy priestly aristocrats in Jerusalem who administered Jewish law and collaborated with Roman officials. The cleansing of the temple challenged the power of corrupt priests who managed currency exchanges, regulated temple commerce, and exploited the poor, especially destitute widows. Rather than urging Jews to pay taxes to the Roman emperor, Jesus gave an ambivalent reply: 'Pay Caesar what belongs to Caesar and God what belongs to God' (Mark 12:17). To the Jewish nationalists seeking freedom from Roman domination, this ambiguous response implied that only God, not Caesar, deserved any loyalty or tribute. Because of Jesus' activities in Jerusalem before Passover and his widespread popular support, the Roman leaders, along with their allies the chief temple priests, sentenced him to death. According to Jewish law, people found guilty of religious crimes such as blasphemy died by stoning. The Romans, however, sentenced Jesus to death by crucifixion – a capital punishment administered only to those judged guilty of the political crimes of treason, sedition, rebellion, and insurrection. Around 30 CE at the start of the Passover season, the Roman military executed Jesus for the crime of claiming to be 'king of the Jews.' For the later followers of Jesus, the cross represented not a sign of Roman humiliation but a symbol of spiritual victory that overcame or 'crossed out' oppression.[14]

From the crucifixion of Jesus in 30 until the destruction of Jerusalem by the Romans forty years later, the followers of Jesus constituted a movement or sect within Judaism. This movement perceived Jesus as the messiah; his teachings unified the messianic community. Redemptive sacrifice, altruism, empathy for the outcasts, and *agape* (divine love that transcends self-interest) served as shared spiritual values binding members together. They pledged to pursue the ethical principles voiced by the prophet

Micah and reiterated by Jesus: mercy (steadfast love), justice (righteousness – a right relationship with God), and humility (a humble fellowship with God). Two key rituals embodied these sacred values. In the ceremony of the Eucharist, the followers of Jesus gave thanks for his coming and looked forward to his return and to the establishment of the Kingdom of God on a transformed earth. This meal corresponded to the Passover feast, at which the Jewish people commemorated their past deliverance from their Egyptian oppressors and expressed the hope for an ideal future order. Christian baptism resembled two Hebrew rituals – immersion and circumcision – that symbolized initiation into the Jewish community. The Pharisees and Essenes viewed immersion as a ritual of purification. Male circumcision symbolized the need for obedience to Yahweh, loyalty to the covenant with God, and identification with the Jewish community. The early Christians who followed Paul's teachings renounced the need to practice circumcision. For them, baptism represented the key purification ritual that signaled a spiritual rebirth, a commitment to obey God, and repentance of their sins – a behavioral change.[15]

Twenty years after the crucifixion, the apostle Paul emerged as the authoritative interpreter of the Christian faith. Some Gentiles who heard Paul perceived him as Hermes, who communicated the divine message of God to mortals (Acts 14:12). Although a Pharisee, Paul knew Greek, held Roman citizenship, and saw his role as a mediator between the Gentiles and Jews – a Jewish envoy who proclaimed the gospel ('good news') to the Gentiles. According to Paul's mystical vision, Jesus Christ mediated between heaven and earth. The Heavenly Man made in the image of God became incarnated in the Messiah on earth. As the second Adam, he brought eternal life and salvation not only to the Jews but to the whole world. By supplying solidarity to the early Christians, the heavenly Christ became more important than the historial person Jesus, whom Paul had never met. From Paul's perspective, spiritual love and faith unified the Christian community. God's divine grace (charisma) was mediated through Christ, who embodied sacrificial love. Through the baptismal ritual of purification, Christians experienced the death of the old person, a spiritual rebirth, and union with Christ. The Eucharist celebrated Christ's presence and expressed hope for his early return. Paul, who saw Christians as a messianic body formed around Christ, portrayed the community in organic terms:

You were baptized into union with Christ, and now you are clothed, so to speak, with the life of Christ himself. So there is no difference between Jews and Gentiles, between slaves and free men, between men and women. You are all one in union with Christ Jesus. If you belong to Christ, then you are the descendants of Abraham and will receive what God has promised (Galatians 3:27–29).

From this organic community Paul saw emerging a new spiritual person who has empathy for other people, not merely a concern for the self (Philippians 2:4).

Paul drew a sharp distinction between members of the spiritual community and people who remained outside. Insiders expressed a spiritual transformation, mental renewal, and ethical regeneration. Their lives manifested spiritual values: eternal life, light, and love. In contrast, those outside the organic community remained under the spell of the material world: death, darkness, and sin.

Unlike the original Jesus movement in Jerusalem, Paul took a more acquiescent stance toward the political order. Whereas the early Jewish Christians had strongly opposed Roman oppression, Paul abandoned the injunction to resist Roman rule. He postulated the existence of two separate societies: the secular and the spiritual. Christians inhabited the spiritual domain, which assumes some political qualities like 'commonwealth' and 'citizenship.' According to Paul's letter to the Philippians (3:20), 'Our commonwealth is in heaven.' In this heavenly commonwealth, Christian citizens lived according to spiritual virtues, not according to earthly appetites and desires. In his letter to the Ephesians (2:19), he wrote: 'You Gentiles are not foreigners or strangers any longer; you are now fellow citizens with God's people and members of the family of God.' Thus Christians lived in a divine community outside the Roman political order. To this heavenly commonwealth, they owed their main allegiance. From it, they derived their common identity that transcended the pursuit of self-interest. Yet Paul, unlike some Jewish Christians around Jerusalem, did not urge disobedience to Roman secular authority. People must respect their political rulers, pay taxes, and refrain from overthrowing the state by violence:

Every person must submit to the authorities in power, for all authority comes from God, and the existing authorities are instituted by him. It follows that anyone who rebels against authority is resisting a divine institution, and those who resist have themselves to thank for the punishment they will receive. Governments hold no terrors for the law-abiding but only for the criminal. You wish to have no fear of the authorities? Then continue to do right and you will have their approval, for they are God's agents working for your good. But if you are doing wrong, then you will have cause to fear them. . . . They are God's agents of punishment bringing retribution on the offender. For this reason you must obey the authorities – not just because of God's punishment but also as a matter of conscience. That is also why you pay taxes, because the authorities are working for God when they fulfill their duties. Pay, then, what you owe them; pay them your personal and property taxes. Show respect and honor for them all (Romans 13:1–7).

Despite this appeal for submission to political authority, Paul never assumed that loyalty to the state took precedence over loyalty to God. Worship of the state meant idolatry. From Paul's viewpoint, Jesus, not Caesar, was Lord. The sacred realm of the heavenly commonwealth reflected divine love and spontaneity, which contrasted with the coercive power and bureaucratic organization in the secular political order. Communal ties naturally emerged from the sacred realm. A tension developed between it and the secular state. Taking an eschatological view of history, Paul expected an imminent end of the evil world order. His apocalyptic visions revealed the mysteries of historical development to his followers. Paul assumed that Jesus Christ would soon return, abolish all government powers, and establish the Kingdom of God on earth – a theocracy ruled by God the Father and Jesus the Messiah (1 Corinthians 15:20–25).[16]

This conflict between two different orders – the secular and the sacred, the coercive and consensual, the state and society – has underlain political life in European societies since the emergence of Christianity. After the Romans destroyed Jerusalem in 70 CE, the Christian movement moved its center to Rome. Christian ties to Judaism weakened. Gentiles gave the strongest support to the Christian gospel. As the first century drew to a close, many Christians abandoned their hope for the immediate return of Christ and the abolition of the Roman political regime. Some

Roman officials began accepting the Christian faith. The Christian bishop in Rome (the pope) gradually consolidated his power over other bishops. The Roman Catholic Church, which began as a spontaneous community, developed into a more bureaucratic organization that could impede or facilitate social change. In 324 Constantine consolidated his rule over the disintegrating Roman Empire and became the first Christian emperor. Whereas in the past most Roman political rulers had persecuted the Christian movement, now they declared their intention to protect Christians and even help maintain Church unity. Catholic clergy, along with secular government rulers, emerged as the ruling establishment. The Church gained state support and subsidies, including tax exemptions, land, funds for construction, and participation in state bureaucratic offices. Whereas the early Jesus movement had stressed personal holiness, decentralization, and egalitarianism, the institutionalized Roman Catholic Church provided salvation through the priestly administration of the sacraments, operated a more hierarchical, centralized, bureaucratic organization, and combined elitist rule with an inclusive, universal membership.[17]

Shortly after the death of Constantine, the Christian theologian St Augustine (354–430), a bishop at Hippo, sketched a vision of two distinct societies – the heavenly city and the earthly city. This idea originated with St Paul, who had contrasted the secular with the heavenly commonwealth. When Paul was writing his letters to the newly-established Christian churches, Rome persecuted the followers of Jesus. When, however, St Augustine wrote *The City of God*, Christian clergy had established close links with the secular Roman rulers. Hence, St Augustine had to formulate a new interpretation of the relationship between the sacred and secular orders. The Psalmist (87:2–3) had described Jerusalem as the 'city of God.' For Augustine, the city of God became a Christian utopia free of all the evils St Paul associated with actual political life – conflict, disunity, struggle, instability, corruption, oppression, and destitution. According to Augustine, the earthly and heavenly cities constituted two invisible cities – that is, two models of society. Drawing a sharp contrast between the two, he perceived that only in the Heavenly City could people find an authentic sense of community. Whereas the earthly city loves the self, the Heavenly City loves God. From this distinction stem the different characteristics of the two cities. In the earthly city, self-love leads to conflict, coercion, 'the lust for domination,' rule by powerful leaders, and a scarcity of goods. In the Heavenly City, however, the love of God produces unity, consensus, interpersonal service, rule by God, and abundance. The earthly city contains both good and evil people. Only good people – those committed to the sacrificial love (*agape*) exemplified by Jesus Christ – inhabit the Heavenly City. There, 'both those put in authority and those subject to them serve one another in love, the rulers by their counsel, and subjects by obedience.'[18] Only in the Heavenly City can people find true fellowship, justice, community, unity, and eternal peace.

The sharp contrast that Augustine drew between the two cities asserted the superiority of spiritual values over material interests based on political power, wealth, and status. From his perspective, the political order could never satisfy people's highest spiritual needs because imperial states like Egypt and Rome ruled through coercive power. No earthly state could ever attain true justice – conceived by Augustine as the rule of God over individuals, reason over the passions, and the soul over the body. Instead, true justice will emerge only in a community ruled by Christ. Nevertheless, Augustine did see some positive purposes served by the political regime. Although only the City of God provided eternal peace, the state could maintain order, harmony, and peace on earth. By bringing unbelievers into the Roman Catholic Church, the state could help the Church – an imperfect embodiment of the Heavenly City – achieve the salvation of individual souls.[19]

Today within the Roman Catholic Church, conservatives, reformists, and radicals articulate beliefs influenced by Jesus, Paul, Augustine, and Thomas Aquinas. Resisting the attempts of tenant farmers to organize a peasant league in northeast Brazil, a monistic conservative landlord echoed the words of St Paul: 'Everything has been ordained by God. He knows what He is doing. If He gives land to me and not to you, to reject this is to rebel against God. . . . You have to accept poverty on earth in order to gain eternal life in heaven.'[20] Pope John Paul II affirms a more pluralist conservative vision based on his interpretations of Augustine and Thomas Aquinas. Particularly within the Church, the laity must submit to the patriarchal authority of the ecclesiastical hierarchs, rather than support liberation theology. Viewing the Church as a hierarchical institution, he insists that priests, nuns, and laity obey the Pope, cardinals, and bishops. Obedience to Church authority takes priority over civil liberties for Catholics doubting traditional Catholic teachings. The Church must not only reform the social structures that maintain oppression, misery, and material deprivation but give precedence to the alleviation of spiritual poverty – the alienation from God that causes social injustice. Instead of striving for fundamental sociopolitical change, the Church should concentrate on its sacramental, pastoral role that stresses liberation from sin and personal piety, so that individuals can enjoy the divine gift of eternal happiness. In the political system, the pope wants government run by virtuous leaders. It should provide order, ensure church autonomy, aid the poor, and guarantee workers their economic and human rights, including the right to stage nonviolent strikes for improved working conditions and for programs that enhance the common good. Committed to a corporate model, Pope John Paul II views government as an organic political body that needs unity, collective harmony, and class solidarity. He urges Catholics to avoid both the individualistic license of capitalist materialism and the collectivism of state socialism. From his perspective, centrally planned economies impose excessive state control, negate pluralism, and place an exaggerated emphasis on historical materialism. Although capitalist societies uphold private property and decentralization, the pope criticizes them for promoting excessive economic inequalities and pursuing profit as the supreme good. When the market becomes the way to satisfy all human needs, then society reaps political disorder, social injustice, and contempt for human dignity. According to the pope's conservative standpoint, government and Church attempts to secure evolutionary change must maintain political order and society's organic harmony.[21]

In Western Europe and Latin America Christian Democratic parties have sketched a reformist vision of society. In such countries as Germany, Italy, the Netherlands, Belgium, Austria, Costa Rica, El Salvador, Venezuela, and Chile, Christian Democrats assume a policy stance between market liberals and social democrats. Supporting the social service state, they favor expanded opportunities for all individuals to gain upward mobility. Comprehensive health-care policies, generous pensions, child benefits, and day-care programs represent valuable ways to strengthen the family. Committed to pluralism, many Christian

Democrats prefer that the Church implement such public policies as education, health care, and income-maintenance. The relationship between the rulers and the ruled rests on a legalistic foundation. All groups should retain the structural autonomy to voice civil liberties against undesirable public policies such as abortion and divorce. Justice implies equal treatment under the law.[22]

Latin American advocates of liberation theology voice more radical demands for sociopolitical change than either conservative Catholics or reformist Christian Democrats. For liberation theologians such as José Miranda, Rubem Alves, Gustavo Gutiérrez, and Leonardo Boff, Marxism represents a mode of critical analysis to challenge capitalism and economic dependency in Latin America. Just as St Thomas Aquinas adapted Aristotelian principles to medieval Europe, so liberation theologians apply Marxist analysis to understand the Latin American sociopolitical situation. Rejecting atheism, philosophical dogmatism, dialectical materialism, and Stalinism, they uphold humanism, civil liberties, skepticism, and personal dignity. Assuming that capitalist social structures produce economic exploitation, political oppression, and status degradation, they want government and Church to liberate the outcasts and show a 'preferential option for the poor.' Rather than remaining atomized or withdrawn from political involvement, individuals must join communal movements that secure greater equality, feed the hungry, and transform the world. Liberation theologians link the general principles of the Bible to the concrete needs of oppressed people. The meaning of political experience derives from biblical texts. Fusing moral/spiritual values with material concerns, they strive to realize the Kingdom of God on earth. For them, faith becomes manifest in Christian love, 'orthopraxis,' and active service behind the cause of bringing justice to the poor.

Priests and nuns active in *comunidades eclesiales de base* (Christian communities at the base) teach a liberation theology and help their parishioners free themselves from political and economic oppression. In neighborhoods and villages, the CEBs organize poor people, especially small farmers, shopkeepers, vendors, artisans, and bus drivers. Around fifteen to twenty families gather to read the Bible, discuss its relevance for contemporary conditions, celebrate the sacraments, and work for such community improvements as increased literacy, more health-care centers, better housing, and greater protection for human rights. These activities reflect a commitment to an egalitarian relationship between rulers and ruled. Equality denotes a decentralized participatory democracy where women, poor people, and the marginals enjoy equal respect. Freedom implies liberation from both individual and collective sins: class exploitation, political oppression, social injustice. Opposed to individual fatalism, the CEBs uphold personal political efficacy, individual responsibility, self-improvement, self-esteem, and the possibility of securing social change through widespread community participation. Individual effectiveness combines with a collectivist orientation. Viewing the Roman Catholic Church as the 'People of God,' CEB members develop an awareness of their solidary power to transform the status quo. For them, sharing, reconciliation, and mutual understanding take priority over class conflict. The major purposes of government revolve around both the enhancement of all people's moral dignity and the reconstruction of society, especially through policies that secure greater income redistribution and political freedom.

During the 1970s radical Catholics in Nicaragua united with the Sandinistas to overthrow the coercive Somoza dynasty. On the island of Solentiname, Father Ernesto Cardenal linked the gospel stories to farmers and fishermen fighting for deliverance from Somoza's tyranny. Just as Jesus struggled to liberate the oppressed from the rule of Herod Antipas, so the Sandinista revolutionaries reenacted the story of Christ's redemptive sacrifice when they gave up their lives for ultimate victory over Somoza in 1979. Some Solentiname artists even painted a picture of Jesus rising from the tomb and bearing a resemblance to the Sandinista founding leader Carlos Fonseca. Besides struggling against state oppression and class exploitation, the radical Nicaraguan Catholics placed a high value on equality – not just more equal access to material benefits like education, health care, land, and jobs but also the spiritual equality that stems from Christian love, sacrifice, human dignity, and service to the people. In short, the Nicaraguan advocates of liberation theology supported a transformed church actively engaged in sociopolitical change. For these radical Catholics, a more equal relationship between rulers and ruled on earth assumed equal importance with spiritual salvation in the heavenly world.[23]

Besides the radical Catholics, the Protestant evangelicals represent another populist movement organizing the poor throughout Latin America. Although articulating divergent theological positions, both movements advocate spontaneity, social equality, individual change, personal efficacy, and a biblical view of justice. Moral/spiritual values fuse with material interests. Not only CEB members but Protestant Pentecostalists seek liberation from personal sin and expanded economic opportunities for upward mobility. Active participation in communal church services strengthens the individual's personal relationship with God. Despite these similarities, Catholic radicals and Protestant fundamentalists take divergent stands toward the relationship between rulers and ruled. Whereas some liberation theologians view Marxism as a method for analyzing the impact of capitalism in Latin America, evangelicals reject any Marxist influence. Appealing to the urban poor who recently migrated to the cities from the rural areas, the Pentecostalists passively accept political authority, including military rule. Even though they concur that an authoritarian military regime violates human rights, they remain highly pessimistic about their effectiveness in reforming an unjust, corrupt political system. Rather than ally with radical Catholic or Marxist groups struggling to overthrow conservative despots and transform society, evangelical churches stress individual solutions for social problems. Personal liberation from sin takes priority over the reconstruction of society. Church activities revolve around the need to internalize such values as self-control, moral purity, temperance, sexual restraint, discipline, hard work, political order, and the sacred meaning that the Bible offers a profane world. All these evangelical values appeal to the urban poor, who feel that neither the government nor the Roman Catholic Church meets their personal needs.[24]

## ISLAMIC LAW AND JUSTICE

Like the Protestant evangelicals in Latin America, the Muslim revivalists throughout the Middle East, Asia, and Africa articulate a spiritual vision that rejects the pluralist values of liberal modernization. During the last century, the United States, Britain, France, and other European powers tried to modernize the Third World. They differentiated sacred from secular values.

Economic growth heightened income inequalities between urban and rural areas and within the cities. Rapid social upheavals sprung from urbanization, incipient industrialization, secular education, and the spread of the mass media. All these changes brought political, economic, and cultural dependence on the capitalist core societies in North America and Western Europe.

The domestic power situation also explains the growth of Islamic revivalism during the last two decades. Governments and ruling parties repressed most opposition groups. Only the mosques retained the communications networks to challenge public policies that failed to respond to popular needs. As economic stagnation worsened, Islamic associations increasingly provided education, health care, family assistance, housing, legal aid, credit, insurance, and jobs to the urban poor. Government agencies and other private institutions, however, benefited mainly wealthier city residents. For the Islamic revivalists, domestic secularization tied to Western influences also meant cultural decadence and alienation from indigenous values. Islamic ethical principles and laws appeared a more spiritual foundation for public policies than did norms based on secular ideologies.

As a protest against the dysfunctional aspects of modernization, Islamic revivalist movements have gained growing support among urban residents who emigrated to the city from the rural areas. They comprise the followers of such movements as the Muslim Brotherhood in Egypt and Jordan, the Tunisian Renaissance Party, the Algerian Islamic Salvation Front, the Lebanese Hezbollah (Party of God), and the Palestinian Hamas. Young educated urban professionals – scientists, engineers, physicians, teachers, clergy, lawyers – lead these movements. Their religious and political beliefs reflect a protest against Westernization. The primary purposes of political rule combine moral–spiritual values with material interests. Although seeking government assistance for science, engineering, and technology, Muslim revivalists reject Western materialism, individualism, conspicuous consumpion, and secularism. For them, the spiritual domain encompasses secular pursuits. Rather than differentiated from secular, mundane activities, the sacred Islamic law (the Shariah) shapes all aspects of life. Justice derives from the Koran and the sayings of the prophet Mohammed. Collectivism takes priority over individualism. Individuals can find meaning, purpose, and moral guidelines for daily behavior only in a communal context – the *umma* (Islamic community). The Islamic revivalists seek a relationship between rulers and ruled that secures liberation from Western political, economic, and cultural influences. They reject political leaders who have aligned with Western nation-states, benefited from multinational investments, and supported 'permissive' Western lifestyles such as alcohol consumption, women's rights, and abortion.[25]

However important the recent Islamic revival, Muslim clergy since the Second World War have rarely developed the motivation or the autonomous power to lead movements for fundamental sociopolitical change. The *ulama* – teachers of the Islamic law – usually uphold the need for Muslims to retain their traditional values, especially obedience to Koranic legal injunctions, fasting during Ramadan, and Islamic, not Westernized, education. According to them, Islamic law should shape the educational curriculum, content of the mass media, court decisions, and such aspects of family life as marriage, inheritance, and divorce. Even though the Koran upholds the spiritual equality between men and women, the *ulama* have accorded women only limited legal rights. Compared with men, women inherit less property, experience greater impediments to gaining a divorce, and must remain more secluded from active participation in political life. For all Muslims, whether male or female, submission to the Islamic community – the *umma* – takes precedence over individual freedom. According to traditional interpretations of the *ulama*, 'excessive' individual liberty associated with pluralist modernization leads to anarchy, disorder, chaos, and self-indulgence. When uneducated by Islamic religious scholars, people give vent to their insatiable passions. Hence, social institutions such as the family, state, and especially the Muslim courts must implement the Islamic law, restrain individual passions, and enjoin individuals to subordinate their desires to the dictates of the *umma*. Particularly among Sunni, the *ulama* have rarely challenged oppressive relations between the rulers and ruled. Islam means 'submission to Allah,' the sovereign lawgiver and judge, the sole source of law and authority. Lacking access to powerful ecclesiastical institutions, the *ulama* usually remain subordinate to government officials and concentrate on upholding the sacred Islamic law.

Despite their agreement on most spiritual beliefs and religious customs, the two dominant sects within Islam – Sunni and Shia –

take a divergent attitude toward political authority. Over 85 percent of Muslims belong to the Sunni group. More politically quiescent than the Shiites, the Sunni *ulama* retain less political autonomy from the state. 'Sunni' means people who follow the customary practices of Mohammed and the *umma* community. Perceiving Islamic law as unchangeable, the Sunni clerics recognize no need for charismatic spiritual leaders who interpret the Koranic law to changing conditions. With a weak clerical institution, a fatalistic view of political reality, and a traditional view of law, the Sunni clergy have usually taken a conservative view of sociopolitical change.

In contrast, the Shia *ulama*, particularly in Iran and Lebanon, have spearheaded the movement for societal transformation. The Shiites dominate Iran as a theocracy, comprise over one half the Iraqi population, and attract numerous followers in Lebanon and Bahrein. According to Fouad Ajami, the Iranian leader Ayatollah Khomeini tried to rally groups excluded from Arab wealth and political power:

> The pied piper of the Muslim oppressed exposed in a harsh and glaring way the great weakness, the forbidden secret, of Arab nationalism: that it was Sunni domination dressed in secular garb. . . . The Shia underclass and its clerical tribunes came with trumpets and scripture to offer what mainstream society everywhere has always dreaded: redemption and deliverance. And they came to settle an account that was in many ways as old as Islam itself. It was the rebels against those who had acquired earthly political kingdom, the children of the millennium against the settled classes.[26]

Compared with the Sunnis, the Shiites take a more dynamic view of law, maintain a more powerful clerical institution, and can mount a stronger opposition to government rule. With less fatalistic attitudes and stronger feelings of political efficacy, the Shia have shown greater readiness to mobilize for political action and to sacrifice for the spiritual cause. 'Shia' means partisans of Ali, the son-in-law of the Prophet Mohammed. According to the Shiites, all spiritual leaders should descend from Ali and Hussein, Ali's son whom Sunni rulers killed during the late seventh century. As a result of their minority status within Islam and the martyred death of their founder, the Shiites developed an oppositional stance toward political rulers. Spiritual leaders –

*imams* – emerged who performed both political and religious functions. They and the *ulama* not only interpreted the Islamic law to meet changing conditions but also challenged political authority as impure.

Since Shia Islam became the Iranian state religion in 1502, the clerics (mullahs or *ulama*) maintained partial independence from government control; hence, they had the power to mobilize their followers against government rulers. Skilled at rhetoric, the mullahs could articulate popular grievances to the Shiites, who comprise over 90 percent of the population. Religious taxes and charitable contributions from the bazaar merchants financed the mosques. During the late 1970s the urban mullahs had the financial resources to lead the anti-Shah revolution and to establish an organizational network that directed the revolution against the monarch. They established a theocratic political system in 1979. The Ayatollah Khomeini, the charismatic spiritual leader who spearheaded this revolution, perceived the Shia clerics as the enlightened vanguard of the Islamic revolution to create a new purified society. From his viewpoint, because they knew Islamic law and practiced justice, they could best fulfill the requirements for political leadership. They had the duty to awaken, enlighten, and guide the masses, as well as to make key public policies. In sum, when excluded from government power, the Shia attacked political tyranny. After gaining government control in Iran, however, they repressed their opponents, labeling them as 'unbelievers' who deviate from the mullahs' reinterpretations of Islamic law.

Despite the traditional support for a fusion of secular with sacred values, the mullahs have implemented profound sociopolitical changes within Iran. Wielding greater political power than ever before in Iranian history, they dominate key government agencies, particularly judicial, education, and propaganda institutions. Implemented by government theocrats, Shariah law extends to all aspects of human life. Propagating Islamic beliefs and legal norms, the schools try to create a 'new Islamic person.' The Islamic revolutionary government has symbolically upgraded the status of the urban poor but has restricted women's rights, particularly their right to gain a divorce, participate in the policy process, and hold professional jobs outside teaching and nursing. A republican form of government, not a monarchy, rules Iran. The parliament now plays a greater role in government decisionmaking than during the Shah's regime. Bureaucratic authority, including reliance on written laws, has expanded. The government now employs a high percentage of the labor force and wields an extensive scope of power.

Even though Ayatollah Khomeini struggled to win support for his Islamic revolution throughout the Muslim world, he mainly appealed to the Shiites within Iran. Sunnis in Iraq and other states failed to rally behind the ayatollah's call for redemptive sacrifice and promise of eventual revolutionary victory. Even in Iraq, most Shiites backed their Sunni-dominated government in the war with Iran. Thus religious nationalism emerged triumphant over political movements that try to unite religious followers across several nations.[27]

## CONCLUSION

This chapter has explored two related issues: the power of churches to influence public policies and the impact of religious values on sociopolitical change. First, the policy influence of religious institutions depends on their structural interactions with government agencies. Under a theocratic regime or in states where priests hold dominant public offices, the clerics' interpretations of religious beliefs determine public policies. Tibet (1642–1959), inner Oman (1913–1955), and the Islamic Republic of Iran represent the most notable examples. If government leaders suppress church autonomy and establish a secular political religion that venerates the nation, religious leaders lack the power or opportunity to shape public policies. Rather than participate in politics, churches concentrate on prayer, faith, and theology. In pluralist societies where the secular and sacred realms retain some autonomy, religious and government institutions experience a creative tension. Church leaders and laity wield some power to press their claims on policymakers. Even if religious values usually legitimize existing policies, interpretations of sacred beliefs also challenge public policymakers to reform unjust conditions.[28]

Second, the power of churches to secure sociopolitical change depends on their organizational networks and on the policy preferences of religious leaders. Whatever the differences within each religious faith, Judaism, Christianity, and Shia Islam have generally shown the greatest support for changes in human behavior and societal structures. Jews, Christians, and Muslims view the empirical world as real. From their perspective, history reflects a linear path toward eventual redemption. Evolutionists perceive a gradual unfolding of the Kingdom of God on earth. More revolutionary apocalypticists foresee a cataclysmic destruction of the present evil order and the institution of a new redeemed society. Both assume that God actively intervenes in history to help people achieve personal and societal transformation. The tension between spiritual ideals and empirical realities has motivated the struggle to secure greater justice. Jews, Shia Muslims, and especially Roman Catholics operate complex institutions. Particularly since the Vatican Council II (1962–1965), Roman Catholics have shown increased opposition to authoritarian regimes in Eastern Europe, Latin America, South Korea, and the Philippines. Compared with the Sunni clergy, the Shia hold more abstract, eschatological beliefs and administer more powerful religious institutions. These cultural values and structural resources have inspired them to lead movements that protest conservative Sunni domination.

In contrast, Hindus and Buddhists take a more conservative view that regards the empirical world as unreal and illusory. For them, history occurs in a cyclical, not a linear, pattern. Civilizations rise, fall, and rise again. Religious challenges against corrupt government officials proclaim the need to restore traditional virtues, not make fundamental changes in sociopolitical structures. Lacking powerful, complex, nationwide ecclesiastical institutions, neither Hindu nor Buddhist leaders have the structural resources to transform society. Committed to cultural conservatism, their religious beliefs express little willingness to restructure the sociopolitical order according to a Utopian vision.

Faced with the conservative orientations of Confucianism, revolutionary leaders in China, Vietnam, and North Korea after the Second World War perceived the need to create a new secular political religion. Descendants of Confucian literati, the Communist Party cadres formulated a utopian vision of a restructured sociopolitical order. Mass political movements organized popular participation to overthrow the autocratic state and institute a fundamentally new regime. Like the Gush Emunim and the

Iranian Shia revolutionaries, the Asian communist intellectuals polarized the world between the pure and the defiled, thereby using sacred or ideological values to justify violence against the *ancien régime*. Nationalist symbols blended with Marxist–Leninist eschatological principles. The mission to redeem the nation from foreign impurities became associated with the ideological struggle to transform society from capitalism into communism.[29] Of these two causes, nationalism emerged triumphant by the 1990s, when the revolutionary commitment to state socialism waned.

# 4  Nationalism and Political Identity

During the early fifteenth century, the French people felt no strong national identity. Feudal lords dominated several regions. Allied with the feudal fiefdom Burgundy, the English controlled most areas of present-day France. Roman Catholic Church authority extended over a more universal community. The French King Charles, who remained subordinate to both the feudal lords and the Church, governed only a few provinces within the central and southern areas of France. In 1429 if English troops had captured the city of Orleans, they would have controlled the whole French territory. Faced with this disintegrating political situation, Charles VII proved unable to mobilize the French forces against England.

Unexpectedly, a seventeen-year-old woman, Joan of Arc (1412–1431), appeared on the scene to create a stronger identification with the French nation. In his play *Saint Joan*, George Bernard Shaw imagined her telling a French squire and military captain:

> We are all subject to the King of Heaven; and He gave us our countries and our languages, and meant us to keep them. If it were not so it would be murder to kill an Englishman in battle; and you, squire, would be in great danger of hell fire. You must not think about your duty to your feudal lord, but about your duty to God . . . . I will teach them [the French soldiers] all to fight that the will of God may be done in France . . . . There will be but one king there: not the feudal English king, but God's French one.[1]

As a creature of the Middle Ages, Joan linked French identity to religious values; from her perspective, King Charles VII embodied the sacred French nation. She also linked national identity to language. Since the French and English spoke distinctive languages, they should live in separate political communities. Spurred on by a sense of shared identity linked to language, territory, sacred beliefs, and the king who symbolized

93

these sacred, primordial values, Joan successfully rallied the
French soldiers against the English abortive attempts to seize
Orleans. At Rheims Cathedral, she later had Charles VII
crowned king of all France, thereby helping to save her nation
from English conquest.

Since the emergence of modern nationalist movements during
the fifteenth century, the nation has assumed mystical value.
Whereas Europeans' primary identity used to derive from their
membership in a feudal fiefdom or in the universalist Roman
Catholic Church, the national community became the object of
faith and emotional appeal. Like the Church, it was regarded as
eternal and transcendental – a community that demanded
ultimate allegiance.

Through political discourse, national identities, such as
religious attachments, are constantly created and recreated,
interpreted and reinterpreted. In nations like France, the
monarch first embodied national values. National identification
later spread to the whole people at the time of the French
Revolution. Changing national identities reflected the interaction
between rulers and ruled. Initially, nationalist myths perceived
the king as the head of the body politic, the father of his people,
and the imitator of Christ who wielded divine authority. At the
feet of the body politic, the ruled were passive subjects – children
with limited authority. When, however, national identity shifted
to the whole people, the ruled became more active citizens. No
longer viewed as children, the people acted as adults who
overthrew despotic monarchs like Louis XVI and established a
new nation-state with a stronger national identity. In France, the
revolutionary Jacobins during the 1790s perceived the nation as
the Supreme Being and worshipped the goddess Liberty. The
nation, not the king, created all valuable things. At least in
theory, the distance narrowed between rulers and ruled.
According to the notion of popular sovereignty, the people rose
to the head of the body politic. They had to fight and die as
martyrs for the national cause.[2] As Liah Greenfeld points out,
revolutionary French nationalism reflected a spiritual faith:

France the nation bore an unmistakable resemblance to France
the king's state and France the Church. . . . It was not just a
nation, it was the Great Nation, *la Grande Nation*, the most
national of nations, which carried to perfection the virtues

required by the new cult. . . . *La Grande Nation* was the reincarnation of *le roi très chrétien*. Like he of old, the eldest son of the Church, the defender of Christianity, who spread its message with fire and sword, she carried and spread the gospel of Nationality – liberty and equality – with fire and sword. The crusading nation succeeded the crusading king.[3]

As the French case illustrates, nationalist movements arose as a protest against oppression by feudal lords, ecclesiastical hierarchs, and colonial occupiers. Resenting their inferior status, nationalists proclaimed the need for dignity, respect, and equality. They articulated a common identity based on shared values. People with a common cultural heritage felt attached to a territory larger than a feudal estate or city but smaller than an empire, a universal religious community, or all humanity. Nationalist values unified a people but divided one nation's inhabitants from those in other nations.

Historically, national identity has stemmed from three basic values: primordial, sacred, and civil. Primordial values designate those first-order attachments based on common origins. People related to others through family ties and more inclusive ethnic affinities perceive a solidarity that derives from their shared history and contemporary lifestyles. Similarly, those who speak the same language, live in the same geographic region, and show a reverence for the land perceive themselves belonging to the same nation.

Sacred values, which include religious and ideological beliefs, constitute another communal source of national identity. As dynastic empires collapsed and religious institutions became more pluralistic, nationalism assumed sacred significance. Until the nineteenth century, one's political identity rested on a commitment to 'ultimate ends' that transcend empirical reality. Traditional societies fused sacred with secular values. Regarded by his subjects as divine, the dynastic ruler performed religious rituals, which helped to preserve social solidarity. Laws regulating human behavior reflected a spiritual foundation. In contrast, in modern political systems people differentiate secular and sacred values. Civil law becomes separated from religious norms. National identity derives from a commitment to secular beliefs, particularly those linked to empirically observable results like economic growth, expanded educational opportunities, and improved physical health. Despite the growing secularity of modern political life, sacred values have scarcely disappeared. Instead, they have reappeared in a nationalism based on spiritual or ideological values – for example, Shia Islam in Iran and 'socialist patriotism' as interpreted by President Kim Il Sung in North Korea. Portrayed as a holy organic community, the nation assumes spiritual significance. As in traditional societies where the political system was merged with the church, national solidarity arises from membership in a community of 'true believers' who share a common faith.

Although communal values based on primordial and sacred ties convey powerful emotional attachments, we assume that socio-political actors formulate these identities and that they undergo continual revision. Like ethnicity and religion, nationalism expresses a discourse of meaning, shared identity, and solidarity. Through political rituals, leaders articulate new interpretations of national identity. Ideological mobilizers, ethnic entrepreneurs, party heads, media figures, and government officials recreate symbolic meanings to gain support for their policy priorities. As sociopolitical conditions change, old communal identities gain new interpretations. For example, primordial identities linked to ethnicity arise in opposition to a hegemonic elite that denies equal status to a subordinate ethnic group; thus *Négritude* challenged Eurocentrism. Nationalisms that focus on spiritual values often reflect a protest against secular modernization, cultural alienation, and government suppression of opposition religious movements.

National leaders who uphold civil values play the most significant role in democratic societies that respect political freedom. Civility highlights the need for tolerance, mutual respect, empathy, and political dialogue among individuals with conflicting interests. Civil values maintain a shared attachment to the political role of a citizen and to general political institutions that fairly treat diverse groups. National identity upholds 'unity in diversity.' Individuals share multiple loyalties. Rather than pledging allegiance to a monolithic, homogeneous nation, citizens have ties to many groups. Yet they attain unity because of their common regard for just political institutions and for impartial legal procedures. National solidarity derives from civility – values stressing dispersed power, the rule of law, and a concern for the general well-being that transcends the interests of particular ethnic, linguistic, religious, and economic groups. In a pluralist society, each group agrees to reconcile differences, accommodate positions, and gain mutual concessions. Through this process of compromise, national unity results. Under a civil society, the rule of law guides public policymaking and assumes sacred value. Laws not only restrain the ruled but also dissuade the rulers, especially the police, military, and bureaucrats, from making arbitrary, brutal decisions. Several political parties compete for office to representative legislatures. Independent courts protect the civil liberties of assembly, association, and petition. Widespread participation in political decisionmaking promotes individual dignity, self-esteem, and citizenship. Individuals perceive themselves members of an inclusive political community that shares a concern for the common good. A public mass educational system teaches the meaning of civil values, particularly citizens' legal rights and duties. During the post-Second World War era, national identity based on civil values has prevailed in North America, West Europe, and such Third World states as Costa Rica – areas where pluralism and classical liberalism have thrived.[4]

This analysis of national identity raises three crucial questions. First, what historical events and philosophical ideas influenced the emergence of nationalist movements? How did domination by aristocratic elites, Roman Catholic Church hierarchy, and colonial rulers provoke a nationalist response? Second, why did certain types of nationalism become dominant in particular areas? Important types include hegemonic, organic, and pluralist nationalism. Hegemonic nationalism asserts the dominance of one ethnic group over the rest. Organic nationalism demands that all people commit themselves to a set of monistic sacred or ideological values; the nation represents an organic community in which monolithic collective values supersede the pursuit of individual interests. Pluralist nationalism thrives in societies where social groups retain extensive autonomy and citizens abide by civil values. Third, what impact does nationalism wield on public policies and social change? We assume that this impact stems from the institutionalization and internalization of nationalist values. Participation in common institutions like the state, public schools, courts, churches, and the mass media strengthens national identity. These institutions communicate nationalist values, stimulate national awareness, and allocate common goods to people living in the same territory. When representatives of the indigenous population gain control over governent, they secure the power to make public policies that affect employment opportunities, educational curriculum, court decisions, and language. By shaping values and access to material benefits, these government leaders reinforce people's national identity.[5]

## NATIONALISM AND PRIMORDIAL VALUES

Even though most contemporary nations comprise several different ethnic groups, national identities still rest on primordial values linked to the family and ethnic group. The word 'nation' derives from the Latin term *nasci* – to be born. Primordially, nationalism implies that members of a nation share a common ancestry or heritage. As John Schaar has indicated: 'A nation is a birth, hence a group of persons made kindred by common origin. Nations are also continually reborn, through the death of old customs and institutions and the generation of new ones. A nation has a unique birth and is also a continuous rebirth.'[6] Rituals such as singing the national anthem and pledging allegiance to the flag stimulate a re-creation of national solidarity. Familial sentiments become fixed on the nation. Patriotism means loyalty to the fatherland or mother country; the Greek term *patris* refers to fatherland. Russians refer to their nation as 'Mother Russia.' US residents view the American nation as 'home sweet home.' Leaders of the Vietnamese Communist Party urge their comrades to defend the socialist homeland. In traditional societies such as pre-twentieth-century Japan, people perceived the nation as an extended family and the emperor as father of the country. During the present era, leaders who spearheaded the movement for national independence from colonial rule became known as fathers of their country.

A major reason for the continuing importance of ethnic groups in political life stems from their close ties with nationalist values. The term *ethnicity* derives from the Greek word *ethnos*, meaning a people or nation that shares common ancestors. In contrast with Japan, Korea, and such European nations as Iceland, Norway, Portugal, and Poland, most countries in Asia and Africa contain several different ethnic groups. Attachments to a single ethnic group and its political institutions often conflict with identifications toward the polyethnic nation. Hence, the nationalist leaders who led the Asian and African territories to political independence after the Second World War stressed the anticolonial struggle against European domination as the basis for national identity. Composed mainly of professionals such as intellectuals, teachers, authors, journalists, lawyers, and priests, these nationalist leaders also highlighted the distinctive cultural contributions of non-European ethnic groups. Yet because of this ethnic diversity, national identification remains weaker than in Japan or most West European nations.

The strength of nationalist identification depends on people's ethnic homogeneity, their mobilization around a 'core culture,' and the power of the nation-state. Ethnically-homogeneous individuals who share similar primordial values view other people as members of the same national family. Leaders in core areas (centers of communications, traffic, and economic exchanges) reinforce national awareness. A powerful nation-state – a centralized, differentiated set of administrative institutions that control a territory and monopolize the right to make binding, authoritative rules over that territory–further strengthens national identity. Japan illustrates a society with high ethnic homogeneity, mobilization around a core area (Tokyo), and a historically powerful state. Nigeria represents one of the many African countries with considerable ethnic diversity, several core areas, a weak central government, and hence limited identification with the polyethnic Nigerian nation. The Hausa-Fulani, Yoruba, and Igbo ethnic groups comprise around two thirds of the Nigerian population; the remaining third includes two hundred other ethnic peoples. Numerous core areas – Lagos, Ibadan, Calabar, Kano – compete for popular allegiance. At the time of national independence in 1960, the three regional governments, not the federal government, wielded decisive policymaking power. Even today, because of the large size and ethnic heterogeneity of Nigeria, regional governments retain considerable policy influence. Confronted with an ethnically pluralist society, most Nigerian leaders have tried to use the nation-state as a structural means to create stronger attachments to the Nigerian nation.[7]

Hegemonic nationalists reject the ethnic diversity found in societies such as Nigeria. Under hegemonic nationalism, collectivism assumes primacy over individual rights. Nationalist leaders insist that all individuals and all subordinate ethnic groups submit to the values of the dominant ethnic group. According to this view, the nation and its leaders embody one popular will and a monolithic general interest. The relationship between rulers and ruled assumes a hierarchical form. Political elites perceive that the nation fulfills both moral–spiritual and material interests. Distinctive cultural beliefs associated with the dominant ethnic group assume mystical value. Linguistic policy tries to instill these values in school children. Members of the ruling ethnic group use their power over public policymaking to gain concrete payoffs: contracts, licenses, subsidies, jobs, educational opportunities, and health facilities. Government officials employ coercion against subordinate ethnic groups seeking similar material benefits from public policies.

Nazi Germany represents the most striking case of hegemonic nationalism during the past sixty years. In Nazi Germany only the Aryan race could hold membership in the German nation. Non-Aryan peoples, especially the Jews, faced repression and ultimately extermination. All Germans had to pledge their loyalty to *der Führer* Hitler, who alone articulated the national will of the German fatherland. Hitler fancied himself the redeemer of the Reich, who brought salvation to the German *Volk*. As Nazi Germany became more militarily aggressive during the late 1930s, the mystical feudal cult of blood and soil exhorted German youths to sacrifice their lives for national glory. The Bloodflag symbolized the sacrifices that Germans had to endure against the nation's enemies.[8] With the defeat of the Third Reich in 1945, hegemonic nationalism declined but scarcely disappeared.

During the post-Second World War era, hegemonic nationalists have contended for dominance in many African societies. For example, in the Republic of South Africa attempts by one ethnic group to wield hegemonic control over an ethnically diverse population has led to extensive political violence. South Africa contains four major ethnic groups: black Africans (75 percent, including Zulu, Xhosa, Sotho, Tswana), whites (15 percent, including 10 percent Afrikaners and 5 percent English), coloureds (7 percent), and Asians (3 percent). Cooperative relationships between two former antagonists – the African National Congress (ANC) and the National Party – have stimulated both whites and blacks to rally behind organizations that uphold racial homogeneity. Whereas the National Party used to win majority electoral support from the white population, control the state, and subjugate Africans, by the early 1990s its power had waned. Seeking a multiracial, decentralized government, it began to share decisionmaking authority with the ANC. Several white racist neofascist organizations protested this development. The Afrikaner Resistance Movement, the Afrikaner People's Guard, the Afrikaner Volksfront, and the Boer Republican Army strove to realize a racially pure *volkstaat* based on blood (armed struggle) and soil (reverence for the Boer land settled by Afrikaners). Calvinist principles of predestination justified hatred toward the 'impure' nonwhite races. For these hegemonic nationalists, the Afrikaners represented the predestined elect – the chosen people – whereas black Africans appeared as the descendants of Ham, whose son Canaan was cursed by Noah as 'lowest of slaves' to his brothers (Genesis 9:25). Besides black Africans, other 'enemies' included the English, coloureds, liberals, socialists, and communists. Although most Africans supported the African National Congress, which favored a nonracial, regionalized, democratic state, a few blacks organized hegemonic nationalist movements. Opposed to the ANC, the Inkatha Freedom Party rallied rural residents and urban migrants among the Zulu to support an independent Zulu kingdom. Articulating a more revolutionary socialist message, the Pan-Africanist Congress and the Azanian African People's Organization demanded a wholly African state free of any white English or Afrikaner representation. All these calls for ethnic purification caused extensive political violence in South Africa, not only between blacks and whites but within the two large racial groups as well. Economic marginalization, cultural alienation, police support for racist organizations, and the gap separating educated urban residents from poorer rural dwellers exacerbated hegemonic nationalism in both racial communities.[9]

After the collapse of Communist Party rule in East-Central Europe during the late 1980s, hegemonic nationalists gained greater power. Before the First World War several empires had dominated that region: the Ottoman, Czarist Russian, and Austro-Hungarian. Between the two world wars, Nazi Germany established its hegemony. When the Second World War ended, the Soviet Union replaced Nazi Germany as the dominant ruling power. All these historical experiences of imperial rule shaped contemporary nationalist identities. Economic collapse and state disintegration stimulated intellectuals, professionals, and white-collar employees – those with bureaucratic and communications skills – to campaign for one dominant ethnic group controlling the state. Slovak leaders won independence from Czechs. Bulgarians limit the rights of Turks. Hungarians in Romania, Serbia, and Slovakia face discrimination. The Estonian majority (61 percent) denies Russians (30 percent) citizenship rights. Everywhere Jews and Gypsies come under attack.

The hegemonic nationalism emerging in the East European post-communist era upholds collectivist, spiritual, and elitist values that downgrade civil ties. Collectivism as manifested in the purity of the ethnic community and the demands for ethnic homogeneity takes precedence over individual rights. The relationship between the rulers and ruled reflects a monistic interaction that pits citizens against noncitizens, who lack political rights because of their ascriptive (inherited) qualities. The pluralist accommodation of diverse interests becomes subordinate to elitist polarization. Strong emotional attachments to the nation as a sacred entity transcend the more rational stress on compromising economic demands and securing concrete benefits that will bring mutual concessions to an ethnically diverse community.

Particuarly in former Yugoslavia, ethnic, religious, and economic conflicts reinforced each other to provoke civil war and national disintegration. During the late 1980s over 85 percent of Yugoslavs identified with their republic – for example, Serbia, Croatia, Bosnia, – rather than with the Yugoslav nation. Younger urban residents who participated in the League of Communists expressed the strongest national identification, especially if they belonged to ethnically-mixed families. Yet as the power of the League of Communists declined at the federal level and each republic gained greater authority over economic and political decisionmaking, civil ties to the Yugoslav nation waned. Ethnic nationalism grew stronger. In 1991 the wealthier Catholic republics of Slovenia and Croatia formed independent states. Influenced by its Orthodox traditions, the poorer Serbs fought for a greater Serbia. In the impoverished southern region of ex-Yugoslavia, Muslim Bosnians (around 40 percent of that republic's population) waged a losing battle against the more powerful Serbs and Croats. Hegemonic nationalism thus led to the disintegration of the Yugoslav state as rival ethnic-religious groups used violence in their struggle for dominance.[10]

## THE RELIGIOUS BASIS OF NATIONALISM

As the history of East-Central Europe and most other areas indicates, national identity usually stems from a close linkage between sacred and primordial values. For example, the contemporary Jewish citizens of Israel regard themselves as an ethnic group. They have all descended from a common ancestor Abraham, experienced a historical struggle against various Gentile oppressors, and speak the same language Hebrew. Yet their distinctive sacred values – the belief in one transcendent God and in the covenant between God and the Jewish people – also give Israelis their sense of national identity. Confucian principles supplied solidarity to the Han Chinese and the Chinese nation. Shintoism strengthened the national solidarity of the Japanese. During the late 1800s the Russian novelist Fyodor Dostoyevsky perceived a tight linkage between the Russian Orthodox faith and the Russian national identity. In the novel *The Possessed*, Shatov articulated the holy mission of Mother Russia:

> God's personality is a synthesis of the entire nation from the beginning of its existence to its end. . . . If a great nation does not believe that it alone to the exclusion of any other possesses the sole truth, if it does not believe that it alone is destined to and can regenerate and save the rest of the world through the truth it holds, it immediately ceases to be a great nation and becomes merely an ethnographical designation. . . . Now, the only God-bearing nation is the Russian nation. . . . I believe in Russia and in the Russian Orthodox Church. I believe in the body of Christ. I believe that His new coming will take place in Russia.[11]

In the United States, John Jay, the first chief justice of the Supreme Court, asserted that English Christians comprised the core of the early American nation. Today some Buddhist monks want to base the Sri Lankan national identity on Buddhism and the Sinhalese ethnic group. Viewing the Sinhalese as a 'lion race' purified by Aryan blood, they exclude the Hindu Tamils (18

percent of the population) from membership in the Sri Lankan
nation.

When a people live under foreign oppression, a religious
organization articulating spiritual and political values often
spearheads the nationalist movement. Between the two world
wars, British colonialists and white settlers dominated East and
Central African territories. Because the colonial power forbade
overt political activity by Africans, separatist churches and
prophetic movements expressed the African demand for national
independence. Buddhist monks led the drive for Ceylon's (Sri
Lanka's) liberation from British colonialism. With a base in India,
the Dalai Lama and his Buddhist followers guide the nonviolent
struggle against Chinese oppression of the Tibetan people. In Iran
the Shah, allied with Britain and the United States, autocratically
ruled the nation. Suppressed by the Shah's military and secret
police, Iranians rallied around a coalition led by Muslim *mullahs*,
who demanded an Islamic republic and a termination of
American–British domination over military affairs and economic
investment. In Poland the Roman Catholic Church has
historically articulated nationalist demands. Threatened by
Germany and Austria on the west and by Russia on the east,
the Polish nation-state disappeared between 1795 and 1918.
During this time, the Roman Catholic Church in Poland kept
alive the spirit of Polish nationalism. Today the Polish Church not
only proclaims the universal spiritual values of the Catholic faith
but also the need for Poland to remain free from Russian
domination.[12]

Particularly in Europe and North America, nationalist leaders
articulated spiritual principles based on ancient Judaism and
early Christian theology; these sacred values strengthened
identification with the national cause. Echoing the ideas of the
Hebrew prophets, nationalist intellectuals evoked the concept of a
chosen people – a 'holy nation' destined to fulfill divine
obligations. According to the nationalist assumptions, God
actively intervened in the nation's history; a messiah would
emerge to deliver the people from persecution by outside powers.
Like the ancient Hebrews, contemporary nationalists looked for a
collective salvation. In his letters to the early Christian churches,
Paul perceived a new spiritual person emerging from an organic
community. He drew a sharp distinction between the 'redeemed'
members of the spiritual community and the 'lost' people who

remained outside. These motifs – the reborn person, the organic community, and the polarization between insiders and outsiders – reappeared in nationalist movements that emerged in Europe during the fifteenth century. St Augustine's conception of the sacred and secular orders also influenced later European nationalists. For them, the nation assumed the same sacred qualities that Augustine had attributed to the heavenly city. Through the nation, the person found redemption. Just as religion used to claim the individual's highest loyalty, the national cause represented the ultimate commitment. Like the religious prophets, nationalists urged an end to the pursuit of self-interest. The national good became the prime value that reinforced solidarity. Nationalists also contrasted the nation with the imperial state. When dominated by a foreign power, citizens faced coercion and military force. As members of the national community, they live in fellowship, love, brotherhood, sisterhood, and equality. To attain these communal values, the nationalists struggled to liberate the nation from its foreign oppressors.[13]

The political power of Augustine's visible city – the Roman Catholic Church – declined in western Europe when the Renaissance and the Protestant Reformation stimulated the growing nationalist spirit. From the fourteenth through the sixteenth centuries, nationalism began to replace universal religion as the main value unifying people. The Renaissance urged a return to Greco-Roman ideas, such as secular humanism. It encouraged the development of a dynastic state, in which the centralizing monarch embodied the nation. Later, the dynastic state transformed into the nation-state – a specialized administrative structure separate from the Roman Catholic Church. The nation belonged to all the people, not just the monarch and his aristocratic family. Renaissance writers like Niccolò Machiavelli launched an attack against the Roman Catholic Church and the Holy Roman Empire. Promoting a new science of statecraft, Machiavelli saw power and interest as the main components of a political system. Political life revolved around conflicts over scarce resources. Rulers concentrated on securing, maintaining, and expanding political power. The ruled showed insatiable desires for power, wealth, property, and status – all scarce resources. Amid this individualist world of limited goods but unlimited ambitions, political leaders needed a collective cause that would dampen interest conflicts. Unlike medieval Catholic theologians, Machiavelli hardly viewed perceived moral regeneration or the pursuit of spiritual virtues as a primary political end. According to him, Christianity affirmed passive values: humility, self-denial, and martyrdom. Instead, Machiavelli wanted a new politicized religion based on Roman martial virtues that would encourage citizens to defend the national fatherland. National salvation became the major collective cause that would curb mass desires, instill discipline, and promote self-sacrifice behind the mission of liberating such emerging nations as Italy from her 'barbarous domination' by foreign oppressors.[14]

Like the Renaissance, the Protestant Reformation led by Martin Luther and John Calvin contributed to the rise of nationalism. Luther perceived the church as an invisible assembly of the faithful, not as a visible ecclesiastical institution with power to check the state. Leading the revolt against the Roman Catholic Church, he removed all intermediaries between rulers and ruled. Just as the individual stands in a direct relationship to God, no intervening forces like an ecclesiastical institution should come between people and their nation-state. Luther allied with nationalistic German nobles and princes striving for political independence from the Church in Rome. By translating the Bible from Latin into German and by urging everyone to read the Bible, Luther facilitated the national language becoming a primary source of common identity. Luther also wrote religious hymns in German. From this innovation, nationalist anthems developed and reinforced national solidarity. The Reformation movement outside Germany promoted the growth of new religious sects. Protestant leaders felt that each person, not just the church, could interpret the Bible, now translated into national languages. Most often, these new sects became national denominations in Scandinavia, Britain, Scotland, and the United States.

As a mass movement, nationalism began with the English Puritans during the first half of the seventeenth century. They revived the main tenets of Hebrew nationalism. Rather than obeying king and bishops, the Puritans proclaimed that only the Bible represented the valid source of political authority. Perceiving the English nation as the new Israel, they saw themselves as a chosen people destined by God to spread a new national gospel. Like the residents of ancient Israel and Judah, the Puritans upheld the importance of covenants and law. They formulated a written constitution or covenant for England. The written law became invested with sacred value.

Although the Puritans executed King Charles I in 1648, their rule over England lasted only a short period. The Puritan zeal based on ideological uniformity, individual purity, impersonal law, and the absolute sovereignty of God declined. The monarchy was restored when Charles II ascended the throne in 1660. Nevertheless, the monarchists failed to restore the pre-Puritan *ancien régime*. Although the king ruled, the need for him to secure parliament's cooperation restrained his power. The written constitution was abolished; yet legal rights became more firmly established than before the Puritan Revolution. English nationalism thus rested on more pluralist foundations.[15]

Even if the Puritans lost power in England, they achieved greater success in the American colonies. At the start of the 1600s, not all Puritans had the patience to await the revolution in England. Many sailed to Massachusetts, where they established a government modeled after Hebrew principles. Puritans looked on America as the 'promised land,' the new Israel. The settlers represented the chosen people. The old European world symbolized Egypt. If the Hebrews felt united by a covenant with God, the New England pioneers had their Mayflower compact. Under this covenant, Puritan ministers served as impersonal agents of the Bible, the word of God. He alone wielded full sovereignty. Although refraining from holding government office, ministers did determine the eligibility of church members, who had the sole right to vote for elected officials – governors, deputies, magistrates – and to participate in town meetings, which discussed both political and religious issues. Along with ministers, magistrates had the obligation to abide by the laws of Scripture. If a political ruler, like a tyrannical monarch, violated these holy laws, the people could overthrow him, as the English Puritans had beheaded King Charles I in 1648.

During the 1770s the Puritan ministers in New England spearheaded the revolution against the British colonial system. Asserting the absolute sovereignty of God, Puritans wanted the Bible, not the king or colonial government, to function as the source of political authority. Charging that colonial rule was illegitimate, the Puritan clergy claimed that King George III had violated the laws of Scripture and the covenant between the rulers and the ruled. Hence, the people had the right to overthrow the imperial system and establish national independence. For the Puritans, British political oppression brought moral decadence; colonial rulers resembled the dragon and two beasts depicted in Revelation 13. National liberty represented a sacred cause to attain personal holiness.

The civil religion that emerged after the end of the Revolutionary War included not just the Bible Commonwealth of Massachusetts Bay Colony but the whole American nation. Puritanism became Americanism. At the end of the eighteenth century, many Americans perceived the American nation as a regenerated community of righteousness, the new Israel gaining independence from the Egyptian house of bondage (decadent Europe). George Washington acted as a second Moses, the divine agent who guided the exodus from British imperial rule toward the promised land. The 1787 US Constitution that regulated interactions between the government and citizens resembled the Hebrew covenant linking God to the Jewish people. Whereas the Articles of Confederation represented a polytheistic system giving extensive sovereignty to the separate states, the Constitution that established a stronger government embodied political monotheism. Early Americans saw the United States as a political model for the world. Its representatives had the duty to proclaim the gospel of liberty and law to other nations.[16]

Compared with the early American nationalists, the French revolutionaries, especially the Jacobins, implemented a more fanatical cult of the nation. Under the *ancien régime* of King Louis XVI, hierarchy and patriarchal authority characterized the interactions between rulers and ruled. Just as the father dominated his children, so the king governed his subjects. Although the masses remained fatalistic and politically inert, intermediary groups like professional associations, corporations, and regional communities intervened between the people and the monarch. Asserting collective rights, these associations bargained over material interests with central government officials. Tradition and custom also checked the power of the state. Even if elitist, the political system reflected some pluralist features. The French revolutionaries engineered a fundamental ideological transformation in the national political culture. Moral zeal and secular religion mobilized the population. As Alexis de Tocqueville commented, 'The ideal the French Revolution set before it was not merely a change in the French social system but nothing short of a regeneration of the whole human race. It created an atmosphere of missionary fervor and, indeed, assumed all the aspects of a religious revival.'[17] Proclaiming the Enlightenment virtues of universal human rights and the rights of citizens, French revolutionaries fused nationalism with universalism. Ideological monism triumphed over cultural pluralism. The sovereignty of the people replaced the sovereignty of the monarch. Mass participation in politics grew as citizens became exposed to a national education, national propaganda, and national military conscription. Political equality took priority over elitist privilege. Landed aristocrats, Catholic bishops, royal dynasties, and provincial associations no longer governed the nation. Instead, French revolutionaries wanted the citizenry to rule. Ideological will based on reason, not tradition or custom, shaped political action. Consumed by moral zeal, Jacobins like Robespierre polarized the nation between patriots and counterrevolutionaries. A powerful state emerged to embody the popular will.

Dominant in the French revolutionary governments from 1793 to 1794, members of the Jacobin club instituted a political religion that invested the nation and state with sacred value. The Jacobins included mainly merchants, shopkeepers, artisans, journalists, publishers, teachers, lawyers, and doctors – groups that dominated later twentieth-century nationalist movements. They ordered some Catholic churches closed and converted into temples of reason. Nationalistic ceremonies resembled religious rituals. At the feast of the Supreme Being, the French showed their adoration for the goddess Liberty. The official scripture became the revolutionary Declaration of the Rights of Man. Jacobins gave political sermons, sang national anthems, such as the Marseillaise, took an oath of loyalty to the French republic, and pledged to have no 'other altars than those of the Fatherland.' In all these nationalistic ceremonies, the Jacobins worshiped *la patrie*, the nation or fatherland. Whereas during medieval times the Latin word *patria* had meant either the City of God or particular localities, *la patrie* referred to the whole nation. Before the revolution children had received a Roman Catholic education. Now they went to public schools, where nationalist propaganda replaced church indoctrination. Teachers propagated the national doctrines of patriotism and citizenship. People used to live and die for the Catholic faith. Now Jacobins urged them to die for the national cause. 'Mort pour la Patrie' – Death for the fatherland – became the rallying cry that mobilized the populace behind wars against domestic and foreign enemies. All these French Revolutionary themes – national equality, patriotism, populist militarism, moral zeal, public education dedicated to the propagation of national virtues–influenced the nationalist movements arising in nineteenth-century Europe and Latin America as well as twentieth-century Asia and Africa.[18]

Even though Marxist–Leninist leaders proclaim the universalist values of proletarian internationalism, the revolutions that they directed in Russia, China, North Korea, Vietnam, and Cuba strengthened nationalist sentiments. These revolutionaries established a more encompassing political religion than the Jacobins had ever achieved during their brief control over the French government. Under communist rule, the party, nation, and leader gained sacred value. Although Lenin criticized party members who made an analogy between the Communist Party and the church, his support for party primacy and the vanguard role of the Bolsheviks in the new Soviet state produced a comprehensive political religion after Lenin died in early 1924. The Communist Party assumed functions performed by the Russian Orthodox Church under the czars. The party was viewed as a charismatic organization striving to redeem Russian society from economic backwardness and capitalist oppression. Marxist–Leninist ideology represented the cornerstone of new sacred beliefs. The struggle to construct a socialist society and eventually realize full communism paralleled the early Christian efforts to accelerate the attainment of the Kingdom of God on earth. Lenin's stress on organization resembled St Paul's organizing activities. Educating the populace, the party spread both nationalist and socialist values. Lenin envisioned the public schools as propagators of political education. They would create a new Soviet man and woman who would industrialize the country, build socialism, and achieve full communism. Schools also had a responsibility to teach national pride, Soviet patriotism, and the national values expressed in the Russian language and literature.

Particularly under Stalin's rule, Soviet leaders, like the Russian Orthodox clergy, faced a tension between nationalism and universalism. During the late 1890s, Stalin had studied at an Orthodox theological seminary. There, Orthodox priests taught the sacred beliefs that Holy Mother Russia was the center of

Christendom, Moscow was the Third Rome, and the Russian state and church had the mission to redeem the world. Both Marxism and the Christian faith have communicated a set of universalist principles. Marx wanted the workers of the world to unite against capitalist exploitation. Despite this universalist ethos, Stalin affirmed nationalist values. Opposed to the concept of polycentrism, under which many centers of communism retain their national autonomy, he perceived Moscow as the center of world communism. For him, the Communist Party of the Soviet Union had the duty to redeem the world from economic backwardness and to liberate oppressed peoples from capitalist exploitation.

Until the disintegration of the USSR in 1991, Soviet leaders used political saints, secular rituals, and holy traditions to strengthen national solidarity. Whereas during the 1930s and 1940s the veneration of Stalin resembled a religious cult, Lenin became the moral exemplar after Stalin died in 1953. Rituals associated with the membership in the Young Communist League (Komsomol) promoted conformity to collective causes: patriotism, hard work, and socialist competition. Pilgrimages to war memorials and labor monuments provided a public opportunity for adolescents to express national pride, respect for the armed forces, and dedication to hard work. On work Saturdays, Komsomol youths built bridges, constructed houses, or harvested a crop. Through all these rituals, supposedly secular activities became sanctified. Teachers and textbooks also exhorted students to defend the Revolution and the Soviet nation, as did the Soviet army during the Second World War – called in the USSR the Great Patriotic War. By encouraging participation in holy traditions, Soviet leaders tried to reinforce citizens' attachments to the nation.[19]

In other Marxist–Leninist states, the Communist Party relied on political religion to promote national identity. During the Chinese Cultural Revolution (1966–1976), followers of Chairman Mao Zedong opened study meetings with a hymn, such as 'Song of the Helmsman.' They viewed Mao as the Great Helmsman guiding China to national glory and socialism. Chinese teachers and textbooks focused on Mao as the model of exemplary behavior. He became the model of austerity, sacrifice, and ideological awareness – the political educator who enlightened the masses in the Long March and later in the caves of Yenan.

Teachers exhorted youths to emulate Mao by advancing the revolutionary class struggle and sacrificing for the Chinese Motherland. Spiritual rectification and moral redemption took precedence over the pursuit of individual material interests. The transformation of agriculture and the industrialization of the Chinese nation assumed spiritual significance.[20]

In the Democratic People's Republic of Korea (North Korea), the ruling Korean Workers' Party (KWP) perceived President Kim Il Sung as the embodiment of primordial and sacred values. He appeared as the 'Father of the Nation,' 'Redeemer of the Nation,' 'Great Sun,' 'Ever-Shining Sun,' and 'Sun of the People.' In Korean 'Il Sung' means 'becoming the sun.' Hence, Kim Il Sung represented the source of political enlightenment, the nation's sun who brought paradise on earth. Kim's portrait, monuments, and statues intruded everywhere. Nearly all citizens wore a button with his picture. KWP activists urged teachers to propagate the values of President Kim Il Sung: socialist patriotism, love for the socialist fatherland, national defense, and collectivism as manifested in the dominance of the group, party, and nation. As a presidential monarch, Kim Il Sung functioned like the father of his people, using the 'Mother' Party to guide his children. Primary-school pupils showed their loyalty to President Kim – the Exemplar, 'Great Leader,' 'General-issimo,' and 'Father–Chieftain.' According to DPRK policy-makers, 'thought decides everything.' Through emulating the thoughts of Kim Il Sung and exercising the will to master the environment, Party activists were expected to construct a powerful socialist nation. In this voluntarist policy process, Kim Il Sung acted as a Hobbesian 'Sovereign Definer.' As supreme leader, he defined the meanings of political concepts and enforced his definitions of the public good. For him, beliefs determine political reality; hence, language – the mode for communicating ideas – became crucial. Linguistic purges tried to eliminate conceptual confusion, deter dissent, promote political order, and create a closed, sanitized society. By deleting Japanese, Chinese, English, and 'bourgeois' terms from the Korean vocabulary and by modernizing the language so that all people can understand it, political elites used linguistic reform as a way to strengthen Korean nationalism and reinforce the cult of Kim Il Sung, who supposedly saved the Korean language from foreign contamination.[21]

Cuban leaders also used political saints, secular rituals, and holy traditions to advance nationalism and the socialist revolution. In Cuba, however, dead martyrs, rather than living rulers, served as political saints rallying the people behind civic virtue: idealism, sacrifice, and altruism. After Fidel Castro led the overthrow of the Batista regime during the late 1950s, he exhorted Cubans to venerate the martyrs Camilo Cienfuegos, Che Guevara, and Haydee Tamara Bunke Sider (Tania) as saints who had sacrificed their lives for the revolutionary cause. Holy days, which included July 26 (commemoration of the storming of the Moncada garrison), May 1 (celebration of workers' international solidarity), and July 10 (Day of the Martyrs of the Revolution), promoted national unity. Secular rituals tried to enhance support for revolutionary socialist values and the nation-state. The most important rituals included testimonials of solidarity, registration of children's births by the parents' Committee for the Defense of the Revolution, and funeral processions that honor the Revolution's martyrs. At mass rallies in Havana, Fidel Castro concluded each speech with this slogan: 'Patria o Muerte. Venceremos' ('Fatherland or Death. We shall overcome'). Like the French revolutionaries two hundred years ago, he exhorted the people to sacrifice their lives for national salvation.[22]

As these examples of revolutionary symbolism suggest, states that institutionalize political religion uphold organic nationalism. Fusing secular with sacred values, this monistic interpretation of nationalism denies social groups any authority to intervene between the individual and the nation-state. Ruling ideologues view the political system as one organic community in which the collective will supersedes individual interests. Nationalism becomes a sacred cause. Patriots – the apostles of the new sacred order – must sacrifice themselves for national redemption. In a healthy organism, the parts work in harmony with the whole. In the political system, dissension represents illness. To restore the nation's health, its leaders must exorcise from the body politic the polluted ideas that spread disease. Just as the brain guides the human organism, so in society the political elite – the head – should dominate everybody else. A vanguard relationship thus structures interactions between rulers and ruled. Charismatic leaders, ideologues, and technocrats guide the people. The charismatic leader – the one who demonstrates the gift of grace – seeks the moral-spiritual redemption of society. Ideologues propagate the values of reborn men and women. Technocrats make the key public policies about methods to secure greater economic abundance, which becomes endowed with sacred significance.[23]

## PLURALIST NATIONALISM AND CIVIL VALUES

Unlike organic nationalism, pluralist nationalism upholds the primacy of civil values, constitutional liberalism, and unity in diversity. The sacred and secular realms retain autonomy. According to liberal nationalists, political life cannot provide spiritual salvation. People should seek salvation in the church, temple, or mosque and look toward private organizations and government institutions to satisfy material needs, such as employment opportunities, education, and health care. Although the nation-state primarily functions to fulfill individual interests, spiritual values also become important in political life because the law assumes sacred value. Under pluralist nationalism, the rule of law guides public policymaking. The law regulates group conflicts; hence, dissatisfied groups refrain from relying on violent tactics to resolve a problem. Legal procedures limit the coercive actions of powerful organizations, both private corporations and government institutions like the military, police, and bureaucracy. Constitutional government narrows the gap that separates rulers from the ruled. Competitive parties, independent voluntary associations, and legal procedures help make the government accountable to the governed, so that political institutions represent the needs of diverse groups. Rather than the national community overwhelming the individual, autonomous groups and representative government seek to realize individual human rights. Political activists uphold the civil values of tolerance, diversity, mutual loyalties, and widespread citizen participation in political discourse. Entrepreneurial leaders, legislators, and judges dominate political decisionmaking. In the market economies where pluralist nationalism thrives, political entrepreneurs supply policy benefits in exchange for popular support. Legislators pass laws that ratify the victories secured by group coalitions. Court judges clarify, systematize, and institutionalize the rules that regulate the group struggle. Pluralist nationalism hence secures a balance between conflict and consensus. Although divided by conflicting interests, people attain unity by their commitment to civil values.[24]

Most Third World nations lack the structural and cultural conditions that reinforce a widespread commitment to pluralist nationalism. For example, since India attained political independence in 1947, the secular brand of pluralist nationalism advocated by the first prime minister Jawaharlal Nehru has waned; organic nationalism based on Hindu sacred values has grown stronger. British classical liberalism, democratic socialism, and Brahmin tolerance all influenced Nehru's civil nationalism. For him, the secular values of material prosperity, industrialization, science, and rationality transcended primordial and religious cleavages. Individual human rights took precedence over the assertion of particularistic communal ties. The relationship between rulers and ruled rested on a heterogeneous, pluralist foundation: liberal democracy, federalism, civil law, tolerance, and a synthesis of diverse cultural values. During the decades after political independence, the power of urban, secular British-educated leaders declined. The governing Congress Party lost its ideological and organizational cohesion. Corruption and patron–client ties shaped its activities. Traditional rural leaders gained increasing authority in the states. Politicians in regional and local elections appealed for ethnic, caste, and religious support. Muslims and Sikhs were more unified and better organized than Hindus, who comprise over 80 percent of the nation's people. Muslims gained special legal rights over family planning, marriage, divorce, and education. The prosperous Sikhs secured high representation in the civil service. Resenting these concrete benefits obtained by the two minority religious groups, Hindu communal organizations like the Rashtriya Swayamsevak Sangh (National Volunteer Corps), the Vishwa Hindu Parishad (World Hindu Party), and the Bharatiya Janata Party (BJP) articulate a communalist interpretation of organic nationalism that revives Hindu status, religious identity, and economic wellbeing. Opposed to the civil values of secular progress, religious tolerance, equal rights for individuals, and the accommodation of diverse interests, the Hindu revivalists seek a political system that gives priority to mystical values, communal obligations, and majority rule by Hindus, not minority rights for Muslims or Sikhs. According to these communalists, the interaction between government officials and citizens must rest on a monistic, homogeneous relationship, rather than on the pluralist ties upheld by Pandit Nehru. Working through several groups – schools, training institutes, health clinics, credit unions, cooperatives, temples, missionary agencies – they mobilize the Hindu masses, especially in northern India, to assert their distinctive religious communal identity. Because of the weak welfare state, fragmented labor movement, and impotent national political parties, the central government provides few social services to the poor. In response to this need, the Hindu revivalist groups win popular support by supplying such concrete benefits as education, health care, pensions, and loans.[25] Ideological monism combines with economic pluralism, at least within the Hindu community.

Since the end of the Second World War, the greatest support for pluralist nationalism has emerged in North America and Western Europe. Public policymakers highlight the importance of civil values. Perceiving that citizens hold diverse, not identical, interests, leaders encourage various social groups to unify behind common political ends: freedom, justice, fair treatment, equal opportunities. The accommodation of interests supersedes assimilation policies that try to impose identical values on all individuals, whatever their ethnic or religious heritage. Citizens retain their separate group ties while striving for a national identity in representative political institutions.

Despite the persistence of religious and particularly ethnic discrimination, pluralist nationalism in North America and Western Europe today rests on a more institutionalized foundation than before the Second World War. In the United States, ethnic prejudice has waned. Particularly after the Second World War American nationalism became more inclusive of diverse ethnic-linguistic groups. Reacting against the Nazi doctrines of Aryan supremacy and the Japanese racial hegemony in southeast Asia during the Second World War, US policymakers in the postwar era passed laws that extended national membership to non-Europeans. The 1952 McCarran-Walter act abrogated the provisions of the 1790 naturalization legislation granting naturalized citizenship only to white people. In 1965 the Immigration Act eliminated previous policies biased toward European settlers; under this act, Asians and Latin Americans gained greater opportunities to emigrate to the United States. Today nearly half the US citizens believe that immigrants should maintain their own distinct cultures, rather than assimilate into a melting pot. For the pluralist nationalists who uphold these civil values, the United States represents a smorgasbord, not a pot where everyone melts into a homogeneous white majority. Praising the cultural diversity of American nationalism, pluralist Ronald Takaki indicates:

> Like the crew of the *Pequod* in Herman Melville's epic story, Americans represent the races and cultures of the world. On deck, Captain Ahab and his officers were all white men. Below deck, there were European Americans like Ishmael, Africans like Daggoo, Pacific Islanders like Queequeg, American Indians like Tashtego, and Asians like Fedallah. . . . As Americans, we originally came from many different shores, and our diversity has been at the center of the making of America. . . . As we hear America singing, we find ourselves invited to bring our rich cultural diversity on deck.[26]

For many citizens who originally emigrated from Latin America and Asia, America represents a land of freedom and opportunity, a country where individuals can gain an education and protest government policies without fear of government persecution.

In Canada as well, pluralist nationalism has gained greater support since the 1960s. Most Canadians view tolerance as their primary national virtue. Compared with Americans, they more strongly uphold the right to racial intermarriage. Most citizens support civil liberties, especially legal guarantees for unpopular groups to speak freely, hold rallies, and avoid wiretaps by the security service. The federal government implements a relatively inclusive immigration policy. Whereas before 1967 80 percent of immigrants came from European countries, from 1981 through 1991 three fourths came from Latin America, the Caribbean, Africa, and especially Asia. Most eligible immigrants have become Canadian citizens. Today Canada represents a poly-ethnic nation of diverse ethnic groups, including French, English, Germans, Irish, West Indians, East Indians, Chinese, and indigenous peoples. Ethnic, linguistic, and religious groups have gained widespread political rights. During the last three decades, citizens of Quebec province, where 80 percent of Francophone Canadians live, secured extensive autonomy to regulate language policy, education, and economic development. Influenced by the Quebec movement toward greater autonomy from the federal government, the ten Canadian provinces now wield greater political influence vis-à-vis the central government than do the fifty American states. Yet as the provinces assert their political, economic, and cultural autonomy, the power of the federal government in Ottawa wanes. The national identity becomes more fragmented. Few national institutions have the power to integrate the diverse Canadian society. Provincial governments control education and many public corporations. Regional parties demand greater provincial independence from the federal government. Popular ties to the region remain strong, especially in Quebec where over half the citizens during the early 1990s favored political independence for their province along with economic union with the rest of Canada. Hence, extensive social pluralism and institutionalization of ethnic–linguistic autonomy have led to a fractured national identity. Growing popular doubts about the wisdom of policies supporting multiculturalism and immigration have recently emerged.[27]

During the 1990s the European Union (EU) faced conflicting pressures toward pluralist and hegemonic nationalism. On the one hand, several developments strengthened civil values among West Europeans. Social pluralism, democratic institutions, and the market economy promoted tighter integration within the EU. EU institutions, especially the Commission and Parliament, increased their decisionmaking authority. Greater inter-European trade, travel, and the expansion of higher educational opportunities, along with a pan-European mass media, promoted a European consciousness. Well-educated youths who work as professionals, support civil liberties, and seek greater citizen participation in political life perceived themselves as both citizens of their own particular nation and as European citizens. In particular, university-educated young people who regard themelves as 'leftwingers' and who identify with leftwing parties (the Greens and small socialist parties such as the Dutch Pacifist Socialist Party) upheld ethnic tolerance and the rights of immigrant workers from North Africa, the Middle East, and Asia. These pluralist Europeans supported European Commission activities, wanted to accelerate European unification, and perceived substantial benefits from participation in the EU. For them, the defense of individual freedom and human rights took priority over the defense of the nation. Tolerant Europeans not only adopted a universalistic value perspective but assumed that the expected benefits of promoting immigrants' opportunities outweigh expected costs. On the other hand, the decline of nation-state power, increased strength of the EU, greater market penetration by the multinational corporations, and rise in immigration from East Europe, Africa, the Middle East, and Asia have all stimulated protests against pluralist nationalism, civil values, and ethnic tolerance. Particularly in Germany, Austria, France, and Italy – centers of Axis power during the Second World War – neofascist organizations uphold collectivist values, reject European integration, and want to purify the national community of non-European immigrants, Jews, Gypsies, and leftwingers. For these hegemonic nationalists, ethnic diversity challenges such value priorities as primordial ties, political authoritarianism, and the economic wellbeing of the indigenous European population. Their national identity revolves around a monolithic, homogeneous community. Increased pressures from these neofascist parties and public hostility to rising immigration have led governing parties to enact more restrictive legislation against immigrants.[28] Despite this ethnic hostility, pluralist nationalism appears stronger in Western Europe than in Eastern Europe, where hegemonic nationalism attracts greater popular support.

## CONCLUSION

This examination of nationalist political culture has analyzed three general issues. First, what historical events shaped the emergence of nationalist movements? As we have seen, nationalism arose as a reaction against several forms of domination. From the fourteenth through the seventeenth centuries in Europe, the Renaissance and Protestant Reformation movements struggled against political domination by the Roman Catholic Church and the Holy Roman Empire. During the late eighteenth and early nineteenth centuries, nationalist leaders in the Americas guided colonial territories toward political independence from British, French, and Spanish colonial rule. After the Second World War Asian, Middle Eastern, and African territories gained liberation from European colonialism. Nearly all these nationalist movements attempted to escape control not only from foreign domination but also from aristocratic control by landlords, traditional chiefs, and maharajahs. Struggles for national independence usually pitted these aristocrats against middle-class professionals like intellectuals, teachers, students, doctors, lawyers, journalists, and clergy who articulated nationalist values.

Second, why do hegemonic, organic, and pluralist nationalism become dominant in particular areas? Hegemonic nationalism emerges where a politically–powerful ethnic group feels threatened by either foreign states or by rival domestic groups. Dominant ethnic leaders assert their cultural hegemony over all challengers. Organic nationalism has flourished in societies where clerical officials help govern a relatively powerful state as bureaucrats and political educators. Examples include territories historically influenced by Roman Catholicism (Latin America), Christian Orthodoxy (Russia), Confucianism (China, Vietnam, Korea), and Shia Islam (Iran). Pluralist nationalism shapes policies in countries with a competitive market economy, dispersed political power, and free world trade. Under these conditions, civil values regulate not only market exchanges but political conflicts among competing interest groups.

Third, how does nationalism influence public policies and social change? This impact derives from institutionalization of nationalist values. The state plays a key role in the institutionalization process. Through its control over churches, schools, courts, and the media, it promotes rituals, dispenses resources, and thereby stimulates greater national solidarity. Nationalist rituals define national identity, designate criteria for membership in the nation, legitimate the operation of national political institutions, express conflict with alien 'out-groups,' and uphold certain procedures for settling disputes among 'in-groups.' By enacting public policies that grant jobs, contracts, licenses, and subsidies to their supporters, politicians can strengthen national solidarity.

Yet specific economic policies depend more on structural conditions than on nationalist values, particularly in the under-developed areas. Nationalism basically means that the indigenous people control the state and articulate an authentic culture uncontaminated by foreign influences. Although nationalism upholds Africa for the Africans, it remains silent about the precise programs for government responsibilities. For example, political elites used African socialism as an ideological tactic for strengthening national solidarity in communally plural societies. Even though this nationalist ideology attacked colonial exploitation, rejected South African racial oppression, and urged a return to African communal values, it hardly guided economic policies about the roles of the state, private traders, private farmers, and foreign investors. Whatever their economic ideology, nearly all contemporary African territories have maintained an expansive state sector. The central government controls investment, operates numerous state enterprises, and employs a high number of personnel as a proportion of the nonagricultural labor force. Recent government policies encourage greater privatization and competition within the economy. Civil servants often become executives within subsidiaries of the multinational corporations. Rather than influenced by specific nationalist beliefs, all these policies stemmed from structural conditions, especially the changing power positions of African state elites, private merchants, and foreign business executives.[29]

The impact of nationalism on domestic social change depends on the ideological values of nationalist leaders and the power of the organizations that they control. Organic nationalists advocate conservative, reactionary, or revolutionary changes. Most organic nationalists prefer to maintain the existing social order. In Iran, however, the Islamic revolution restored the mullahs to greater social status, wealth, and political power than they had ever held under the *ancien régime*. The communist revolutions in Russia, China, Vietnam, North Korea, and Cuba engineered transformations in sociopolitical relationships. Greater social equality, stronger political institutions, and a more fervent national identity emerged. Hegemonic nationalism asserts conservative values; it seeks to retain the cultural domination of one ethnic group. Pluralist nationalists advocate reformist changes. They want expanded equal opportunities for all groups, more representative political institutions, legal restraints on rulers' power, and a mixed economy where government and private businesses share responsibilities.[30]

# Part II
# Structure

# Introduction

Whereas cultural values shape the purposes of protest movements, sociopolitical structures influence the feasibility of goal attainment. A protest movement that has access to numerous resources (wealth, weapons, information, authority, organizational-communications skills) and effectively uses these resources to overcome opposition, coordinate isolated individuals, and mobilize apathetic groups will achieve the greatest policy successes. Political accomplishments also depend on other structural variables, including the degree of coercive power wielded by the state, the ability of protest leaders to form coalitions with other groups, the opposition mounted by influential elites against the protest movement, and the power of transnational institutions to hinder or facilitate the movement's activities. From this perspective, structural conditions not only expand opportunities for successful political action but also constrain the power of protest leaders to realize their objectives.[1]

In the most general sense, 'structure' refers to a pattern of social relationships among the parts, either concrete membership groups or more analytical dimensions. We can empirically observe and physically separate concrete structures – membership networks like the nation-state, domestic social groups, political parties, and foreign institutions. From the activities of these concrete organizations, social scientists infer more analytical structures or patterned interactions among the parts. As elaborated by Marion Levy, Jr, analytical structures of society include role differentiation, solidarity, economic allocation, and political allocation.[2] In the political system, power constitutes the major structural variable. Analytical dimensions of power comprise centralization, coerciveness, coordination, autonomy from other structures, and scope (range of activities performed). We can assess the power of such concrete structures as the nation-state, social groups, and foreign institutions in terms of these analytical aspects. For instance, a 'strong' state exerts centralized power, monopolizes coercive force, achieves high coordination among government agencies, maintains autonomy from social groups and foreign institutions, and carries out a wide range of activities. If protest movements demonstrate these five structural characeristics, they too can wield effective power to overcome resistance, unify the disorganized, and mobilize support behind their policy goals.[3]

Sociopolitical structures wield a reciprocal impact on cultural values and individual behavior. Political leaders need concrete structures – mass media, parties, social movements, small groups, government agencies – to communicate their values and norms. Values specify general purposes of political action. Norms indicate the rules of the political game, that is, the rights and obligations of concrete structures involved in the policy process. These normative rules explicate the scope of political authority, policy jurisdictions, and responsibilities of decisionmaking organizations. If governing institutions incorporate the normative rules into their operations, the political system operates in an integrated, institutionalized way. Making demands on representative government agencies, protest movements use nonviolent tactics. When, however, a conflict arises between cultural norms and structural performance, role ambiguity, role conflict, and corruption result. Political structures function according to informal customs that diverge from the formal rules proclaimed by incumbent government elites. For example, formal equality before the law conflicts with informal customs that grant certain high-status families or ethnic groups unequal access to political power and the wealth that accrues from control over government office. Under this cultural condition of deinstitutionalization, corruption runs rampant. The ruling political system loses its legitimacy. Protest leaders who promise a more purified government often organize popular resistance against the ruling elites and rely on violent tactics to gain political power. Protest activists rally behind guerrilla bands, popular militias, and rebel armies as structural means for achieving government control.

Structural conditions also affect the prospects for individual disobedience toward established governments. Structural crises often stem from wars, foreign invasions, military defeats, depressions, skyrocketing inflation, growing income inequalities, and natural disasters, such as floods, droughts, and earthquakes. All these structural shocks upset the equilibrium between demands on government and supplies (resources) to satisfy these demands. Demands on government increase, but resources decline. Government officials cannot implement public policies that cope with this incongruence between supply and demand.

The consensual coalition that used to support the incumbent government dissolves. Government agencies, especially the army, police, and security forces, rely on greater coercion to maintain the political system. At least in the short run, high coercion consistently applied over time may intimidate protesters, who regard overt resistance as too costly. Yet over the long-range period, repression can unintentionally undermine the rulers' authority and strengthen opponents. By intensifying moral anger against incumbent officials, punitive government actions often rally dissident protesters to defy the regime. When the government loses administrative control over society, the risks of incurring punishment decline. As government coercion decreases from a high to a medium level, protesters retain their anger against an unjust political system but feel more politically efficacious about challenging the established authorities. Hence, the structural crises lessen the constraints that used to deter protesters from resisting the government's mandates. Protest movements experience greater opportunity to gain control over government offices and implement their policy preferences.[4]

When structural analysts dissect political life, they concentrate on three general issues. First, which concrete structures make the crucial decisions over society? Which agencies dominate the public policy process? Possibilities include formal government institutions, capitalist enterprises, trade unions, political parties, and transnational organizations such as foreign nation-states or multinational corporations. This issue of 'who rules' highlights the interactions between the rulers and ruled, especially the restraints that citizens can place on government officials to make them more accountable.

Second, in what ways do political institutions achieve order in both the domestic and international arenas? If by 'order' we mean the nonviolent management of conflict, the relationships among the state, domestic social groups, and foreign institutions can lead to varying degrees of order. Political institutions can generate order in several ways. By employing extensive coercion against political protesters, fear of disobedience can limit conflict from below. Besides this Hobbesian strategy, government officials often rely on more consensual tactics. Devolution of power, decentralization, and even secession allow dissident groups to withdraw from oppressive central state control, thereby limiting political conflict with national government officials. Following the recommendations of such market theorists as Adam Smith, political leaders may enact policies that promote voluntary market exchanges and economic interdependence. Under a competitive market situation, protesters may seek 'private' solutions to their personal problems. This displacement of demands from an overloaded government to market mechanisms can lessen pressures on public policymakers and hence maintain an equilibrium between government resources and popular demands. Protesters pragmatically calculate that the costs of political disorder outweigh its benefits. From their instrumentalist perspective, reliance on free trade and market mechanisms, rather than on riots and rebellions, will produce more desirable concrete benefits. In contrast, structural–functional theorists such as Talcott Parsons stress the need for widespread normative commitments as the requirement for political order. Like Durkheim, he assumes that if people share cultural agreements about the purposes of political life and the rules of the political game, then order will ensue if these values and norms are accepted as morally legitimate by most individuals.[5]

Third, how do political structures make public policies that attain socioeconomic changes, especially changes in social stratification demanded by protest movements? Structural crises disturb the equilibrium among contending power centers and cause increased protests. Economic catastrophes (depressions, high inflation, greater poverty, falling world prices), geopolitical vulnerabilities (wars, foreign invasions, military defeats), and natural disasters lead to a changing balance of power among the state, social groups, political parties, and foreign institutions. Elite disunity generates pressures for more popular participation by dissident groups. Government agencies' ability to wield effective coercive and conensual power disintegrates. Policymakers respond by escalating repression against their opponents or by securing greater policy benefits for the mobilized protesters. As a result of the structural crises, conservative elites may maintain the old equilibrium and preserve the politicoeconomic status quo. Usually, however, various types of change emerge from this process. Evolutionary, incremental reforms may modify socio-political conditions. Less frequently, radical transformations produce a more equal distribution of political power, wealth, and status. Alternatively, reactionary elites try to restore the status quo ante. In short, the interactions between state and social groups explain the origins of change. Government paralysis, conflicts among elite groups, and a mobilized populace are the structural conditions that enable protest movements to implement their proposals for social change.[6]

Structural theorists view political life from an abstract perspective so that they can comprehend the general operation of the political system. By taking the position of an external observer who sees the political situation 'from above,' they ascertain the objective consequences of institutions and other concrete organizations on the performance of the whole political and social systems. Examinations of the interaction between state and society probe the ways that social group activities maintain or undermine political systems. Yet structural analysts, who live in a part of the whole, must infer general patterns by observing specific details. Hence, they face difficulties making the theoretical leap from the concrete to the abstract.

Most structural researchers rely on observation, elite questionnaires, and examination of written and visual records to ascertain the activities and consequences of concrete organizations. For example, government reports and international organization yearbooks include data on income distribution – a structural variable that often generates popular protests against exploitive elites. Newspapers feature stories about protest movements and police reactions to these movements. Television broadcasts, films, photographs, and videotapes present visual images of interactions among protesters and police. Police and court records describe the number of arrests for each one thousand participants as well as the length of sentences imposed on convicted protesters – two indicators that measure the degree of government repression. By joining a protest movement or remaining a detached observer, analysts can uncover the effectiveness of peer group sanctions in a protest organization, the money and weapons available to members, and the repressive tactics used by security forces. Elite interviews with protest activists may provide clues about the major decisionmakers in the movement. Because structural analysts can observe only a part of the whole situation, this partial perspective obviously confounds efforts to reach valid explanations about the entire context that shapes a political outcome, such as the success of protest movements in achieving their policy demands and the reasons for systemic changes.

Structural approaches toward social change assume that conflict and consensus generate pressures to maintain or transform the political system. Equilibrium theories emphasize consensus among the structural parts, such as government agencies, political parties, social groups, and foreign institutions. To press for gradual policy changes, these structures need to form coalitions. Constitutionalists posit a balance of power among contending agencies as the basis for political stability, incremental social change, and a 'dynamic equilibrium.' Like liberal pluralists, they seek an accommodation of diverse interests, an agreement on basic values, and especially procedural consensus on the rules that regulate conflict in the political game. Such a balance between normative consensus and interest group conflict will most effectively generate incremental, reformist changes. Marxist, Leninist, dependency, capitalist world-economy, and radical populist theories, however, assume that disequilibrium among conflicting structures causes social change. Instead of accommodating diverse interests, political organizations such as parties, unions, and protest movements should polarize the political situation. Rather than class coalitions, class struggles are needed to transform sociopolitical structures. Only by pitting radical protesters against oppressive elites can a society realize transformative changes. Protest movements most often emerge under conflictual conditions. Economic, ethnic, and religious cleavages are reinforcing, not overlapping or crosscutting. Political life revolves around struggles over abstract moral/spiritual values, not over compromisable interests. Political activists demonstrate a total loyalty to the organization that embodies their cause, rather than a partial commitment to several diverse groups. As a result of this polarization, radical changes often emerge.

Yet, as structural analysts recognize, a contradiction frequently occurs between the subjective intentions of political activists and the objective consequences of their behavior. The 'law of unintended consequences' or what Hegel called the 'cunning of reason' permeates political life. For instance, although government leaders usually expect that increased police repression will quash protests, greater coercion often stimulates moral outrage and higher participation in protest movements. Rather than producing increased political stability, government coercion unintentionally undermines system maintenance. Changes in the policy process may result from resistance to established government commands.[7]

Only by controlling powerful concrete structures can political leaders translate their policy preferences into binding government decisions. Government officials depend on effective organizations to either maintain or reform current conditions. Political dissidents need protest movements, political parties, and perhaps rebel armies, guerrilla bands, and popular militias to gain control over the policy process. Through an examination of nation-state institutions, political parties, domestic social groups, and transnational organizations, structural analysts hope to ascertain the agencies that wield dominant control over public policy-making. Observations of these concrete structures enable us to infer analytical structural dimensions that produce effective political power – such dimensions as cohesion, autonomy, flexibility, consensus, and coercion.

In sum, at the close of the twentieth century, the world has become more structurally complex. Government institutions and political parties perform several specialized activities. Particularly in constitutional democracies, the domestic legislative process involves diverse social groups – ethnic, religious, economic, civic action – as well as government bureaucracies and even transnational institutions. With the collapse of empires, the globalization of corporate capitalism, and the formation of regional economic networks like the European Union, states have grown so interdependent that national sovereignty erodes. Faced with all these structural complexities, protest movements arise to deal with such issues as who should rule, how order emerges, and what tactics will most effectively attain desired social changes. Part II probes these issues by focusing on four basic structures. Chapter 5 examines nation-state institutions and political parties. In Chapter 6 we analyze pluralist theories of social groups. Chapter 7 surveys theoretical approaches toward the world political system, especially the linkages between domestic structures and transnational institutions.

# 5 The Nation-State and Institutionalist Theories

Although Japanese elites regard the state as an instrument for promoting economic modernization, less powerful social groups believe that government policies bring undesirable social changes. During the last three decades, protests against the construction of the New Tokyo International airport represented a dramatic movement against the state. The cabinet, led by the dominant Liberal-Democratic Party, decided in the early 1960s to build a new airport outside Narita City. For the bureaucrats, corporate capitalists, and Liberal-Democratic politicians, the airport symbolized the Japanese commitment to rapid industrial growth, technological innovation, and export expansion. The construction of the airport involved the confiscation of land from small farmers, who organized a Farmers' League to protest this land expropriation. Along with militant students, the league staged demonstrations against the airport authority. Old women hurled human excrement at the police. Youths built fortresses, solidarity huts, watchtowers, and underground bunkers. A few young people attacked police with stones and bamboo spears. Molotov cocktails ignited construction machinery. Radical militants seized temporary control of the airport tower. For the farmers and youths in the protest movement, the new airport symbolized a corrupt, unresponsive state – a state dominated by bureaucrats, ruled by factions within the Liberal-Democratic Party, allied with large-scale Japanese capitalists, and committed to the United States war effort in Vietnam. The protest movement saw itself upholding communal agriculture, ecology, nuclear disarmament, peace, Japanese dignity, and the moral-spiritual values of the 'little people.' Neither the police nor the state officials remained passive against these challenges to their authority. Riot police used water cannons, tear gas, cranes, and power shovels against the students, farmers, watchtowers, and fortresses. In these confrontations, both policemen and protesters died. Backed by far greater power, the state triumphed. The Narita airport opened in

May 1978. Nevertheess, the protest movement scored partial gains. Committed to rational development and political order, the bureaucrats and Liberal Democratic Cabinet ministers came to perceive the disorderly consequences that occur when state officials remain unresponsive to the needs of unrepresented groups demanding greater citizen participation in the public policy process.[1]

## THE ENIGMA OF STATE POWER

In *The Enigma of Japanese Power*, Karel van Wolferen probes the elusive nature of state power in Japan.[2] Even though most foreign observers and even the Japanese themselves perceive that a powerful, unified state governs Japan, that conception is an illusion. Rather than run by the Liberal-Democratic Party, senior bureaucrats, and big business executives, the Japanese state from the early 1950s through the early 1990s operated in a more fragmented, uncoordinated, pluralist way. Government ministers in the cabinet did not govern. The prime minister rarely acted as a strong leader. The ruling Liberal-Democratic Party did not rule. The legislature did not legislate. Elections to the Diet ensured only limited popular accountability. Even though centralized in Tokyo, the governmental apparatus lacked a single center. The most influential policymakers – senior civil servants, corporate executives, top Liberal Democratic politicians – scarcely wielded monoithic power. Personal rivalries split their unity. Patron–client ties fragmented the policy process. Japan lacked a powerful state with ultimate sovereign authority to make binding decisions, especially policies that would implement fundamental change. Instead, Japanese officials in the public and private business sectors enacted marginal adjustments.

Not only Japan but most other societies reveal the enigma of state power. Political scientists need two hands to analyze the contradictory, paradoxical features of state institutions. On the one hand, a powerful state can surely repress people and secure outward behavioral compliance. On the other hand, its coercive power rarely translates into total control over society. Even so-called 'absolutist' rulers cannot guarantee obedience to all their decisions. Even 'totalitarian' party-states cannot implement fundamental changes in society. State coercion usually produces attitudinal resistance. When government repression declines, elite disunity surfaces. Citizens often cease their outward compliance. Protests emerge. The limits of state power become evident.

Structural theorists investigating the power of the nation-state have explored three basic issues. First, which agencies wield crucial decisionmaking power, and how do they control other people and societal outcomes? What mechanisms can citizens use to ensure responsive actions by key policymakers? In the policy process, do state institutions and social groups maintain independence, or do the 'public' and 'private' sectors reveal a fused relationship? Several patterns of political rule prevail among contemporary nation-states. A single individual may make binding policies. One organization whose members interact with each other can wield decisive influence. These organizations include the Communist Party's politburo, the cabinet in parliamentary regimes, and the armed forces' supreme military council. Often several autonomous agencies formulate crucial government decisions – for example, coalitions of diverse political parties, the president and the legislature, or the cabinet, civil service, military, and police.[3]

Second, how do political structures produce policies that realize socioeconomic changes, such as low unemployment, high economic growth, a clean environment, healthy living conditions, and extensive educational opportunities? What type of interaction among the nation-state, domestic groups, and foreign institutions will secure the greatest change? In statist societies like North Korea, government officials remain fairly independent from group and foreign pressures. Public policies reflect the preference of state leaders to either maintain the status quo or to institute change. In more pluralist societies such as Costa Rica, the operation of government institutions reflects the close involvement of dominant group leaders and perhaps representatives of foreign institutions, including the United States and multinational corporations. Under this condition, the nation-state wields limited autonomy. Public policies stem from the preferences of interest groups, protest movements, and foreign institutions as well as state officials.

Third, how do political institutions manage conflict and secure order? What are the bases of social order? Because people's interests and values conflict, some disorder prevails in all societies. If 'order' means the nonviolent management of conflicts, it can emerge in various ways. Agreement on shared values and norms promotes order. Political leaders rely on religion, nationalism, ideology, rituals, ceremonies, and myths to express concepts of political legitimacy that justify their right to shape the policy process. These symbols strengthen solidarity and provide meaning. Shared values also evoke agreement on laws and informal customs that regulate conflicts over scarce resources. By specifying the moral rights and obligations of personnel in role networks, procedures stimulate greater cooperation and predictability. Protesters rely on peaceful tactics. Political order thereby ensues.

Economic exchanges can create a functional interdependence based on mutual gains that arise in a market situation. Under these exchange conditions, political entrepreneurs negotiate bargains that satisfy diverse interests. Political institutions promote negotiation by establishing a national legal order, guaranteeing contracts, encouraging trade, upholding a stable currency, constructing a transportation/communications network, and ensuring widespread geographic labor mobility. Protest movements partially gain their policy preferences by forming coalitions with supportive government agencies that accommodate protesters' demands for concrete benefits.

Through wielding both consensual and coercive power, strong political institutions can also directly attain political order. Coercion and consensus designate the way that political leaders use resources. Denial of resources has a coercive impact. The granting of resources to others reflects a consensual strategy. Political leaders wield three types of coercive and consensual power. *Physical* coercion entails physical injury, imprisonment, torture, and loss of life. *Economic* coercion occurs when people lose their jobs, government benefits, tax credits, contracts, and subsidies. *Normative* coercion means that leaders, including state officials, label certain individuals and groups as morally impure, ideologically deviant, and unworthy of membership in the political community. Excommunication from political participation results. In contrast, under consensual power, people gain access to valued resources. Physical consensus secures personal safety. Economic consensus brings wealth in exchange for political support. Normative consensus denotes that the ruling elite bestows its moral approval on certain groups and individuals labeled as righteous members of the body politic. To gain compliance, political leaders do not always need to use their resources in a punitive or rewarding way. Threats of punishment often deter protesters from challenging government commands. The promise of future rewards may also secure obedience and order.

Especially when contemporary societies rapidly change, nation-state institutions – the cabinet, civil service, military, and police – try to integrate the population by using coercion and consensus. Protesters demand public policies that will effectively deal with industrial growth, urbanization, expanded educational opportunities, and income inequality. Under these changing conditions, expectations for government action usually rise. Discontented groups less readily accept political authority as legitimate. Political disorder mounts. Coercion may secure order by raising the costs of violent actions against the government. Consensual power encourages more voluntary compliance through the grants or promises of moral-material benefits. Strong consensual political institutions – durable, stabilized patterns of power – provide shared moral purposes, clear expectations about leaders' authority, and hence political order.[4]

These three issues provide useful guidelines for comparing diverse theoretical perspectives about the interaction between state and civil society. *Statist* perspectives assume that the state exerts primacy over society. National security strategists, Leninists, communal pluralists, and structural realists highlight the importance of state institutions in securing political order and social change. In contrast, *societal* perspectives such as constitutionalism, liberal pluralism, radical pluralism, Marxism, liberal institutionalism, and dependency theory stress the limits of state power. For them, diverse interest groups or dominant classes wield control over government institutions. Hence, the state cannot achieve fundamental societal change or political order unless powerful groups in civil society support these outcomes.

## The Power of the Nation-State: Statist Perspectives

Statist theories assert that the modern nation-state operates as the dominant structure throughout the world. It arose in sixteenth-century Western Europe, specifically England, Spain, France, and the Netherlands. With the disintegration of colonial empires first in Latin America during the early nineteenth century and after the Second World War in Asia, the Middle East, and Africa, nation-state institutions became the major center that made binding decisions over the society. The state centralizes control over a territory. It governs through complex, differentiated, specialized institutions, such as the cabinet, bureaucracy, military, police, legislature, and courts. Powerful states achieve autonomy from both domestic social groups and from foreign institutions, like other nation-states, multinational corporations, international organizations, and the Roman Catholic Church. Nation-states monopolize the authority to make binding laws for the society. Their scope of power extends to specifying rules and enacting decisions that regulate property rights, defend the society against foreign aggression, and manage conflicts so that order results.[5]

According to the statist perspective, powerful political institutions rule society. The cabinet, civil service, legislature, armed forces, police, and occasionally a dominant political party make binding decisions. These structures govern through hierarchical authority patterns. They operate in a cohesive way. Independent from both social groups and foreign organizations, political institutions express their own policy preferences and have the power to shape, even transform, societal demands.

The state brings order to a conflict-riven society. Political institutions, especially courts, express the normative rights and obligations that induce cooperative behavior in both society and government. Individuals internalize these norms so that procedural consensus results. Symbols, rituals, and myths communicate shared meanings that promote interpersonal trust. By articulating a general interest, the state helps reinforce social solidarity.

A powerful state can formulate and implement policies that produce social change. Conservative institutions provide strong, authoritative leadership. The reformist state upholds bargaining among civil servants and representatives of key interest groups. They negotiate, compromise, and stress technical competence. Change occurs through adaptation, incremental learning, conflicts between divergent interests, and innovative policies that meet future problems. The revolutionary state led by a powerful party or military destroys old institutions and creates new institutions designed to institute fundamental social changes. Whether guided by a conservative, reformist, or revolutionary state, change stems from a changing balance of power among government agencies.[6]

From a formalistic view, the dominant power of the contemporary nation-state to secure change and provide order derives from five structural aspects. First, its coercive agencies monopolize legitimate force. According to Max Weber:

> A state is a human community that (successfully) claims the *monopoly of the legitimate use of physical force* within a given territory. . . . The state is considered the sole source of the 'right' to use violence. Hence, 'politics' for us means striving to share power or striving to influence the distribution of power, either among states or among groups within a state.[7]

Weber assumes that the nation-state embodies the organization of legitimate coercion. The army and the police constitute its distinctive units. Even if they do not always exercise physical force, the threats to wield coercive power deter protesters from challenging state policies.

Second, the modern state governs through centralized control over a territorial society. Particularly in the industrialized societies, the state expands its central power over local life. As self-styled defenders of national integration, central government officials consolidate the power of the national armed forces. Committed to industrial growth, state leaders promote public policies that construct a national transportation–communications network of highways, railroads, postal service, and telephones for exchanging goods within a national economic market. Hence, local regions lose decisionmaking power to central government institutions.

Third, under a powerful nation-state, a single agency coordinates government activities. Originally from the sixteenth through the nineteenth centuries, European monarchs claimed to exercise 'sovereignty' – the ultimate legal right to make final decisions binding on the society. He and the royal bureaucracy coordinated government decisionmaking. When the king lost his dominant power during the late nineteenth and early twentieth centuries, the president, parliament, or dominant political party assumed the sovereign authority formerly wielded by the monarch. Today in most nation-states, single individuals and especially collective leadership unify the policy process. Usually cabinet ministers and senior civil servants perform this role. In most developing countries the military dominates the ruling elite.

Party and state bureaucrats coordinated government decision-making in the Communist Party-states.

Fourth, a strong nation-state maintains autonomy from domestic social groups and foreign institutions. Central government officials make decisions based on their own policy preferences, not on the preferences of ethnic groups, religious associations, social classes, multinational corporations, or other states. The nation-state possesses several key resources: legal authority, finances, information, bureaucratic expertise, and the loyalty of the military and police, who maintain control over the territory. By controlling the armed forces, police, security agencies, and mass media, state officials use their resources to repress the opposition, deter challengers, persuade dissidents, and maintain mass apathy. Hence, central government leaders have the power to see their policy preferences translated into binding decisions.[8]

Fifth, the modern nation-state wields an extensive scope of power; it performs a wide range of activities. Historically, central governments have implemented three types of programs: system-maintenance, construction of an economic infrastructure, and provision of social services to individuals. During the early stages, the nation-state concentrates on system maintenance – the preservation of its territorial integrity. Most public policies involve defense, internal order, export promotion, and the raising of revenues through levying taxes and printing a national currency. As the economic development process begins, the central government devotes greater attention to the construction of an economic infrastructure. Public policies stimulate public works, such as roads, railways, harbors, and dams. Postal, telephone, computer, and other communications services spread throughout the nation. By relying on state corporations, loans, subsidies, and tax credits, governments try to promote industrialization, agricultural productivity, and expanded commerce. During the twentieth century, particularly after the Second World War, the provision of social services to individuals has become an important government activity. Today in the most industrialized nations, public policies supply education, health care, family allowances (child benefits), day-care services, old-age pensions, and recreational facilities, such as public parks, museums, and artistic centers. All these services have increased the state's scope of power, thereby stimulating protests against public policy performance.[9]

## The Limits of State Power: Societal Perspectives

Despite the formal powers attributed to the modern nation-state, societal theorists assert that the state really exerts limited, not extensive, control over civil society. Empirical research about actual policy implementation indicates the limits of state power not only in constitutional governments but also in more dictatorial regimes. Indeed, political institutions show similarities in all areas, whatever the differences in systemic type. Only fuzzy boundaries separate state from society, the public realm from the private sector.

Society-centered theories view political power as diffused, fragmented, and incohesive, rather than monistic. Liberal pluralists assume that several diverse interest groups – economic, ethnic, religious, civic action – control the state. Marxists believe that dominant classes – landowners under feudalism, capitalists in a modern capitalist society – rule the nation. For some Marxists, including Ralph Miliband, powerful capitalists who head oligopolistic corporations wield decisive influence over government officials. For other Marxists such as Nicos Poulantzas, the state operates with greater autonomy. It preserves the long-term interests of the capitalist system, even if public policies do not always bring short-run advantages to particular corporate executives who control the means of production. Both Marxist perspectives assume that conflicting classes and class fractions permeate the policy process. Government decisions reflect the societal demands of dominant classes. According to pluralists, state officials respond not only to influential classes but more broadly to diverse interest groups.

Liberal pluralists and Marxists perceive political order arising from society, not the state. Under pluralist conditions, an efficient market secures mutually beneficial exchanges. Groups accept civil ties that uphold unity in diversity. Shared religious values induce cooperative interpersonal behavior. From the standpoint of Marxist theorists such as Antonio Gramsci, political order stems from a hegemonic culture. Through the mass media, advertisements, schools, and churches, the dominant capitalist class propagates its interpretations of basic cultural values. When fractions of the dominant class as well as the subordinate classes accept these interpretations, then political order emerges.

From the societal perspective, the state has limited power to achieve social change. Split by conflicting interest groups or class fractions, it lacks the cohesion to formulate, let alone implement, coherent public policies. If change-oriented government decisions do emerge, they stem from the success of political leaders in accommodating the conflicting preferences of classes, class fractions, and diverse interest groups. Public policies express an ad hoc consensus, not a coherent vision of the general interest determined by a unified state elite. Dynamic policies reflect a changing balance of power in society, not within the governmental apparatus. The state cannot easily transform social institutions or reshape human attitudes and behavior.[10]

Society-centered theories contrast the formal power of the nation-state with the limited capacity that the state actually possesses to secure social change and political order. First, the nation-state hardly monopolizes the legitimate use of coercive force. Although West European parliamentary governments have enacted strict gun control legislation, the United States has permissive laws about the importation, sale, and possession of firearms. Both the identification of guns with the populist assertion of authority against state control and the widespread availability of firearms lead to more extensive interpersonal violence than found in West Europe. In many less developed countries landlords, ranchers, urban businessmen, and drug lords maintain private armies and 'death squads' that repress their opponents. Urban and rural guerrillas carry on an armed struggle against incumbent government authorities.

Second, societal-centered theorists assume that throughout most parts of the modern world, actual policymaking shows decentralized, not highly concentrated, state power. Constitutional governments remain committed to a decentralized policy process. For example, even before the 1982–1986 laws that decentralized government decisionmaking in France, formal–legal centralization disguised the informal local autonomy wielded by mayors and prefects. Most Communist Party states, especially the less industrialized ones, experienced a gap between policy formulation in the capital city and policy implementation at the local level. Policies mandated from the central government were implemented in ways that diverged from the preferences of the top state officials. In the developing nations the extent of centralized power wielded by the state depends on military involvement in political life and on the level of industrialization. Particularly in agrarian societies where traditional leaders (chiefs, emirs, elders) retain influence, the central government wields only limited control over rural life. Most decisions affecting an individual, such as education, health care, and employment, originate within the village or region. In more industrializing states dominated by the armed forces, the state expands its central power over local activities. Nevertheless, even in these more economically developed countries, local leaders – landlords, military officers, party bosses, creditors, religious authorities – often implement central government policies. Their control over credit, land, employment opportunities, and some state revenue gives them extensive power to shape policy implementation as they bargain with national bureaucrats.

Third, the coordination of government activities appears fragmented in most nation-states. A single man or institution rarely coordinates all phases of the policy process. Nearly every regime reveals ambiguities about the rights and responsibilities of different agencies. Overlapping jurisdictions prevail. Authority to make specific decisions remains unclear. Officials within diverse government institutions, especially cabinet ministries and the civil service, hold no clear conceptions about their precise duties over specific policy domains. Particularly when governments perform a wide range of activities, the task of coordinating diverse state agencies becomes especially difficult. Factional conflicts fragment public policymaking. Policy struggles revolve around conflicts over personalities, rival groups, preferred government programs, and interpretations of ideology and law.

In Communist Party-states conflicts between party and government, within the state bureaucracy, and among competing party organs fragmented the policy process. For example, the Communist Party of the Soviet Union (CPSU) Politburo and Secretariat formulated general policies, which the Council of Ministers, the leading government organ, then implemented. At the regional and local level, party committees supervised government administration, monitored the behavior of state enterprise managers, tried to motivate higher productivity by the workers, and encouraged the local enterprises to fulfill their plan targets. Despite the formal coordinating role of the Communist Party, its actual performance revealed disunity, factionalism, competitive rivalries, and disorder. The rights and responsibilities of parallel party and state organs remained unclear. Often two party agencies, such as the Politburo and Secretariat, along with a state organization, the KGB (Committee of State Security), had charge of the same activity – ideological education. Although formally subordinate to the Administrative Organs Department of the CPSU Central Committee, the KGB retained extensive autonomy from tight party control. Within each city the factory management of a state enterprise, the government's economic ministries (both national and regional), the city soviet, the party committee, and the trade union committee assumed responsibility for the fulfillment of economic plans. Leaders from each organization often reached few agreements about the specific authority of the several party and state agencies. Factional struggles occurred about precise ways to implement centrally–formulated policies. Local party leaders became umpires and referees. The high centralization led to fear of punishment; local party cadres and government officials evaded their responsibilities. Hence, the CPSU faced difficulties realizing rapid, extensive changes in Soviet society.[11]

Fourth, rather than a monolithic institution controlling all social groups, most contemporary nation-states are pluralistic. Especially in constitutional regimes, groups exert considerable independence from state control. Churches, private business enterprises, labor unions, ethnic associations, and civic organizations shape policy formulation and participate in policy implementation. Throughout the developing nations, families, ethnic groups, churches, landed estates, domestic firms, and multinational corporations retain some autonomy. During the late 1980s in Eastern Europe, strike committees, trade unions, cooperatives, private trading firms, ethnic groups, churches, student organizations, intellectual clubs, ecological associations, and other 'unofficial' structures spontaneously emerged to challenge bureaucratic rule by the Communist Party.

Fifth, in most political systems, the nation-state wields only a limited scope of power. Central governments usually concentrate on system-maintenance activities – that is, the preservation of the state's territorial integrity and the right to make binding decisions over the society. The newly industrializing countries try to construct an economic infrastructure: public works, transportation facilities, and a communications network. During the 1980s, the highest expenditures for social service benefits – pensions, family allownces, public health care, unemployment compensation, public assistance – as a percentage of the national income went to individuals in the most industrialzed parliamentary regimes of northern Europe, including Sweden, Norway, Denmark, Belgium, the Netherlands, and France. Governments in the East European Communist Party-states allocated a lower proportion of their national income to these social services. In less developed countries expenditures for transfer benefits were relatively low. Generally, urban residents of the democratic, quasi-industrialized nations received more generous services than did people living in the agrarian dictatorial terriories.[12]

The following sections analyze different theoretical approaches toward the interactions between state and society, including the way that political institutions handle popular protests. Theorists of constitutional government take a pluralist perspective, assuming that social groups pressure government officials for reformist changes. Fearing the radical demands that arise from social mobilization, advocates of the national security state uphold powerful institutions that will secure political order. Marxists, Leninists, and dependency theorists perceive change arising from class conflict. They want to organize transformative institutions that will repress the counterevolutionary opposition and engineer radical changes in social stratification.

## CONSTITUTIONAL GOVERNMENT AND REFORMIST CHANGE

Theorists of constitutional government stress the limits of state power. According to Sheldon S. Wolin, constitutional systems reveal the following aspects:

> first, legal procedures for vesting authority among various office-holders; second, effective restraints upon the exercise of power; third, institutionalized procedures for insuring the responsibility and accountability of public officials; and fourth, a system of legal guarantees for enforcing the rights of citizens.[13]

Rather than using the term 'nation-state,' constitutionalists such as Herman Finer and Carl J. Friedrich focus on government as the dominant political institution. For them, government comprises the executive agencies that make binding decisions for a society. Representative government rests on a pluralist base of dispersed power and countervailing institutions. Coalitional parties, parliament, independent courts, a free press, and voluntary associations check executive power. One ruling majority party rarely controls both the executive agencies and the legislature. In most parliamentary regimes, several parties negotiate to form a coalition government. Presidential systems often confront a dispersed-power situation in which different parties control the presidency and the two houses of the legislature. Under this pluralist condition, competitive political parties give voters a choice of candidates who become legislators and execuive officials, such as president, governor, and mayor. By retaining the power to defeat elected leaders at the polls, citizens help make government officials accountable to the people.

Strengthening pluralism in constitutional governments, political parties play a key policy role. Constitutional systems ideally demonstrate a balance between conflict and consensus – between social change and political order. When competitive political parties promote both policy conflict and procedural consensus, they perform several activities that reinforce this needed balance. These activities revolve around party interactions with government, social groups, and the electorate.

First, competitive political parties help manage the government by recruiting government leaders and shaping public policies. In constitutional regimes, rival candidates openly compete for power. Since parties formulate consensual procedures to select leaders, they represent a convenient structure for regulating succession to such government offices as the prime ministership and the presidency. Under constitutional systems, one or more parties gain temporary responsibility for making key government decisions. Particularly in a multiparty parliamentary system where no single party gains a majority of legislative seats, the task of building an alliance among diverse parties becomes essential for the establishment of a coalition government. Even if partisan leaders wield little *structural* control over the cabinet ministers and senior civil servants who dominate the policy process, parties' *attitudinal* influence seems greater. In parliamentary regimes where parties control nominations for electoral candidates, they promote cohesive voting behavior in the legislature. By setting policy priorities, aggregating interests, and suggesting solutions to pressing social problems, political parties influence elected government leaders' policy positions.

Second, political parties reconcile the conflicting policy preferences of diverse social groups. Within a single party, group supporters often articulate divergent protest demands that represent their ethnic, regional, linguistic, religious, and economic interests. For example, partisan leaders try to reconcile the interests of factory workers and middle-class profesionals, dedicated Catholics and secularists, so that the party can produce a broad-based electoral alignment. Not only social group factions but factions based on opposing ideologies and personal leaders divide most democratic parties. To get its candidates elected and to formulate public policies after gaining executive authority, a party must bargain, negotiate, and compromise the different policy preferences held by the conflicting factions. Forming a coalition government among two or more parties also requires considerable political skills in the aggregation of conflicting interests.

Third, political parties educate voters about political issues and values. Party activists arouse political interest, inform citizens, and teach members the most effective ways to press their policy demands on the governent. Partisan leaders provide consensus by teaching their supporters the democratic rules of the game. When competing with other factions or party organizations, a party stimulates conflict and thereby strengthens voters' concern about policy positions, government performance, and electoral outcomes. Although opposition and governing parties may express conflicting policy preferences to the electorate, they agree to abide by constitutional procedures for managing the policy process.[14]

Not only political party operations but authority relations in constitutional governments ideally reveal the balance between conflict and consensus that produces political order. Constitutional restraints and a commitment to abide by the law provide political order. The leaders' right to make political decisions derives from the law. Legal principles also justify the right of individuals and social groups to challenge the leaders, their policies, and the government structure. Both rulers and ruled believe in due process – legal protection against arbitrary administrative actions (forced confessions, unwarranted detentions), unfair trial procedures, and vague, all-encompassing laws that give wide discretion to government officials. Ambiguous laws against disturbing the peace, failing to disperse, and opposing the government represent typical examples. The leaders and citizens also respect civil liberties – free speech, freedom to worship, right of assembly, and freedom to organize nonviolent opposition against the incumbent power wielders. These civil liberties usually produce conflict. Yet the rule of law also leads to consensus and political order. The law regulates disputes among groups as well as conflicts between protest movements and the government. It imposes moral obligations on the leaders to act according to due process. Procedural restraints curtail the arbitrary exercise of power by government agencies that wield coercion, especially the bureaucracy, military, and police. Applying impartially to all people, legal standards impose shared obligaions on the citizens. They, like government officials, have the duty to avoid injuring others and denying other groups their civil liberties. Nonviolent social movements rally citizens behind campaigns to limit the power of governments and private corporations to harm individuals.

Constitutional governments try to blend policy change with stable procedures for reconciling conflicts. Government officials, political party activists, and interest group leaders form coalitions that aggregate diverse interests. They support government programs committed to incremental, evolutionary social changes. The effectiveness of these reformist policies partly depends on the achievement of an equilibrium between government leadership and popular consent. Political leaders need the stable legal authority to make decisions. Yet in a constitutional government they must remain responsive to the citizenry. Hence, the dilemma arises about ways to limit arbitrary, repressive government power but still implement public policies that effectively cope with social changes, such as unemployment, industrialization, urbanization, deteriorating health conditions, and techological innovations.[15]

Constitutional theorists expect protest movements to advocate their demands for policy changes through the orderly processes of representative government. Rather than using disruptive tactics – riots, rebellions, sit-ins, mass demonstrations – protesters should seek redress of their grievances through such established institutions as competitive political parties, legislatures, executive agencies, bureaucracies, and courts. Two key policy variables shape protest strategies and the success of protest movements in attaining changes in the policy process as well as changes in society. One structural variable emphasizes policy formulation – the extent of institutional openness to protest groups. The other structural variable concentrates on policy implementation: its degree of coordination.

Open policy formulation and unified policy implementation lead to nonviolent accommodationist styles of attaining protest demands, policy innovations, and social changes such as more equal opportunities and economic conditions. Sweden represents the best modern example. Under Social Democratic rule (1932–1976, 1982–1991), diverse groups – trade unionists, youths, students, women, ecologists, homosexuals, immigrant workers, prisoners, tenants, and disabled people – gained varying degrees of access to political institutions, including the coalitional parties and legislature. The Cabinet coordinated the policy process, so that policy demands were transformed into binding government decisions. To accommodate the demands of these protest groups, central, regional, and local governments expanded their decision-making authority. Greater social equality emerged.

In contrast, the policy process operates through more fragmented patterns in federalist systems where independent courts wield extensive authority. Particularly in the United States and Germany, policy stalemates have led to political violence against subordinate ethnic, religious, and immigrant groups. As a system open to protest demands, the US government features an accommodationist policymaking style. Yet the weak political parties and the fragmented government institutions produce policy deadlocks. Protest groups that lack sufficient bargaining power to negotiate political compromises become violent or try to satisfy their demands through private institutions. In the Federal Republic of Germany, political parties are stronger yet more rigid than in the United States. Policy formulation structures remain more closed to protesters. Factions within the three major coalitional parties – Christian Democratic, Free Democratic, Social Democratic – powerful regional (Länder) governments, independent courts, and autonomous banks fragment the policy process. Stalemates result. Ideological groups form on the left (Baader–Meinhoff gang, Red Army Faction) and the right (neo Nazis) to challenge established government institutions. More violent confrontations ensue than in Sweden.

From the late 1950s through the early 1990s, the French and Japanese political systems experienced relatively closed policy formulation but coordinated policy implementation. Powerful bureaucratic agencies such as the Ministry of Finance unified the economic decision process. Yet rule by bureaucratic elites limited the access of small businesses and unions to institutions responsible for formulating economic policies. As a result of bureaucratic resistance, protest groups often relied on disruptive adversarial tactics to assert their policy demands. Few government initiatives emerged to transform society.[16]

Because theories of constitutional government lacked explanatory power, parsimony, and creativity, they failed to comprehend the profound sociopolitical changes that have occurred during the twentieth century. Rather than elucidate explanatory generalizations, constitutional theorists such as Herman Finer concentrated on describing formal–legal institutions but neglected to clarify actual power relationships within these government institutions. Detailed empirical descriptions of institutions' formal authority took precedence over explanations of institutional operations. Patron–client ties, informal networks, and factional bargaining received short shrift. Concerned to describe procedural regularities, these constitutionlists also downplayed the importance of individuals who hold formal government office. They ignored the values, attitudes, and behavior of government officials, especially their perceptions and meanings attributed to political events. Committed to the government of laws, not men, constitutionalist theorists never explicated the learning process by which government office-holders interpreted and internalized formal legal obligations. By underestimating the explanatory significance of political leaders and the informal power networks through which they governed, constitutionalists could not readily explain the downfall of quasi-democratic regimes such as Italy in 1922 and Weimar Germany in 1933. Greater attention to social group polarization and the powerful political personalities – Mussolini, Hitler – who commanded protest movements would have provided insights into these two systemic transformations.[17]

As a reaction against the descriptive specificity of formal–legal constitutional studies, neoinstitutionalists during the last two decades have formulated theoretical frameworks that better explain the structural interactions between state and society. Two different neoinstitutionalist approaches have influenced the analysis of public policymaking. As elaborated by James March, Johan Olsen, Theda Skocpol, Stephen Skowronek, and Rogers Smith, the political sociology variant explores the relations among political parties, government institutions, and diverse social groups: ethnic, religious, gender, and occupational. In contrast, the political economy version of neoinstitutionalism stresses the ways that institutions, especially courts, bureaucracies, and legislatures, interact with market mechanisms. Both these neoinstitutional approaches share some common assumptions with the older constitutional theorists. Normatively, they all advocate limited government, dispersed power, and rule by impersonal law, not arbitrary personalities. For all of them, order arises from procedural consensus and economic interdependence that prevails in a market system. Liberty can thrive only within institutional order. Social change stems from incremental reforms emerging from a 'dynamic equilibrium' among contending power centers that bargain for influence over the policy process. The most successful protest groups have gained the resources and mastered the bargaining skills needed to negotiate political compromises.

The political sociology interpretation of neoinstitutionalism makes certain assumptions about government decisionmakers, political order, and social change that diverge from the political economy approach. Who governs? According to political sociologists like Theda Skocpol, political institutions – legislatures, cabinets, bureaucracies, courts, political parties – make the key policy decisions independent of social group preferences. Rejecting the 'social determinism' of pluralist and class theories, she writes: 'Because states are authoritative and resourceful organizations – collectors of revenue, centers of cultural authority, and hoarders of means of coercion – they are sites of autonomous action, not reducible to the demands or preferences of any social group.'[18] From her perspective, state dominance over the policy process derives from its financial resources, bureaucratic expertise, territorial control, and alliances with powerful social groups and foreign institutions, such as other nation-states and multinational corporations. Given this control over resources, a powerful state can shape the success of protest groups in realizing their policy preferences. In contrast, political economy neoinstitutionalists, particularly those like Erich Weede who take a public choice view, express less confidence in a 'positive' state.

He assumes that market institutions, not government agencies, wield the greatest impact on efficiency, growth, and productivity. For him, discontented groups should satisfy their personal demands through the private market, rather than lobby government officials for subsidies, tax credits, high tariffs, or public assistance.[19]

What is the basis of political order? Political sociologists such as March and Olsen assume that order derives from normative commitments and institutional sanctions. According to them, institutions are bundles of rules that help resolve conflicts, define access to the decision process, and authorize sanctions against those who violate the rules of the political game. Order results not only from fear of sanctions but more importantly from voluntary agreements on procedures that specify moral obligations in specific political roles and outline routines for appropriate behavior toward other policy participants. Symbols, rituals, and myths also provide meaning, trust, and solidarity behind common political purposes. These values promote integration, even in a differentiated, pluralist society. In contrast, the political economists perceive order arising mainly from voluntary, impersonal exchanges in the market, which facilitates tradeoffs that bring reciprocal benefits. Formal laws and informal customs specify the rules of the political game, including property rights that indicate authority to use resources, exclude others from that use, produce goods, and derive income from their sale. Efficient government bureaucracies and independent courts need to enforce these rules of exchange in an impartial, neutral, nonarbitrary way. If entrepreneurs violate these procedures, then enforcement mechanisms must levy sanctions against the disobedient, so that order results.[20]

How does social change occur? According to political sociologists such as Theda Skocpol, Rogers Smith, James March, and Johan Olsen, the state plays a key role in forging social change. If protest groups want to realize changes through the policy process, their success depends on government agencies and political parties. The structure of these institutions shapes the opportunities for a group to organize effectively. In a fragmented, decentralized governmental system, disjointed policymaking occurs. Because many different institutions, such as legislatures, administrative agencies, and courts, assume responsibility for enacting decisions, a well-organized interest group can block or delay comprehensive programs that may provide assistance to the poor. Especially in presidential regimes with many weak parties, policy immobility often emerges; the president cannot form a coalition in the legislature to pass laws preferred by activist groups. Lacking legislative support, the president in many developing nations often rules by decree or relies on the armed forces to retain government power. These structural conditions in presidential systems thus hinder a viable constitutional democracy.

Institutional policies expand and narrow opportunities for group mobilization. Government agencies provide resources, such as subsidies, tax credits, licenses, contracts, information, and access to authority. By authorizing certain types of groups – ethnic, religious, economic – to participate in the policy process, institutions create and reinforce group identities. Political parties and legislative committees provide an arena for groups to deliberate political issues, so that the interpretation of group interests changes. As information about policies expands, protesters may mobilize to achieve their newly-defined demands. Government responsiveness toward groups' demands shapes their tactics and cultural attributions. Coercive policies often produce violent or disguised strategies. When a specific government institution – for example, the cabinet – assumes complete responsibility for a problem such as lowering unemployment, protesters know whom to blame if joblessness remains high. After policies are enacted, protest groups frequently organize coalitions to ensure that program implementation actually achieves their policy preferences. For example, the US Coalition of Citizens with Disabilities mobilized its supporters to protect disabled people's needs. Seeking equal status as full citizens, not subordinate subjects, this coalition demanded access to regular buses by the handicapped, rather than dial-a-ride taxi services. In these ways, political institutions and their policies shape protest group activities.[21]

The political economy approach toward neoinstitutionalism sketched by Douglass North and Thráinn Eggertsson assumes that social change derives from the interactions between government organizations and market mechanisms. They view political institutions as the formal laws and informal customs that define the scope of government organizations – the collective actors who make binding policies for a society. Compared with most political sociologists, these political economists place less faith in activist government to achieve intended changes, particularly sustained rapid growth. Government organizations fail to enact policies that facilitate a free market. They do not clearly define, monitor, and enforce contracts and property rights. Hence, voluntary exchanges on the market become difficult to transact. High transaction costs mar economic productivity. Entrepreneurs lack accurate information about options and their expected consequences. Neither formal laws nor especially informal customs offer positive incentives for the efficient use of resources. Economic growth occurs slowly because informal customs change more slowly than do formal laws. Even when the *ancien régime* disintegrates, groups with extensive resources often retain the bargaining power to block changes that endanger their economic privileges. After revolutionaries win government power, ideological commitments to transform society frequently wane as political activists seek concrete payoffs from public policies. Government inertia also mars attempts to transform social conditions. Historically, short-run decisions have long-term consequences. Routines that originally elicited high payoffs become difficult to modify when the situation changes. For these reasons, government organizations usually can achieve only evolutionary, incremental changes through the negotiation of diverse interests.[22]

The neoinstitutionalist approach toward social change fails to distinguish between normative judgments and empirical observations; it also downplays the importance of individual political behavior. Not only political economists but political sociologists make normative assumptions about the goals that government ought to pursue. March and Olsen want political institutions to attain shared purposes – the public good, integrity, competence. Political economists seek efficient government agencies that maximize productive efficiency, stabilize property rights, sanctify contracts, promote voluntary market exchanges, mitigate market imperfections, and uphold the rule of law. Compared with political sociologists, political economists such as North and Weede express less optimism that governments will actually realize these normative commitments. Yet neither camp investigates the behavior of government office-holders to ascertain the gap among policy intentions, actions to achieve these goals, and observable outcomes. Normative assumptions remain unexamined in specific historical contexts. For example, Weede claims, 'Politics may have been the opium for the people through the ages, and rent-seeking is the ever popular hard drug.'[23] Even though politicians often use government office to secure economic benefits for themselves, rather than to maximize general economic productivity, this assumption about political behavior needs empirical investigation across historical time and geographical space. Anecdotal impressions scarcely suffice. Illustrative material chosen to validate normative judgments about the superiority of the market over the state hardly explains systemic performance or change. Instead, neoinstitutionalists should probe more deeply into the processes by which individuals perceive the world, interpret the structural situation, and take actions to realize their policy preferences.[24]

## THE NATIONAL SECURITY STATE AND POLITICAL ORDER

Unlike most political economists who assume that rapid economic growth through market mechanisms will produce benign changes, Samuel P. Huntington takes a more pessimistic, conservative view about the outcomes of socioeconomic change. His most famous book *Political Order in Changing Societies* asserts the need for elites to establish powerful political institutions that will avert the political decay generated by uncontrolled social change.[25] In an earlier work, he linked conservatism to institutionalization. Conservatism means the defense of order against chaos: 'When the foundations of society are threatened, the conservative ideology reminds men of the necessity of some institutions and the desirability of the existing ones.'[26] Taking a statist orientation, Huntington assumes that the bureaucracy and military wield the dominant power in most societies. Competent bureaucracies organized along hier-archical patterns can supply order by efficiently implementing national government policies. A professionalized military based on hierarchy, obedience, and technical expertise can deter coups against civilian leaders. Besides these two administrative structures, a powerful political party can control political participation, promote political order, and bring stability to a situation of social group chaos.

Huntington's state-centered analysis challenges the pluralist views of constitutionalist theories. They regard the legislature, courts, and coalitional parties as the dominant institutions. He concentrates on the military and civil service as agencies that can secure domestic order and external security. Whereas constitutionalists highlight the need for procedural restraints on government power, Huntington assumes that the accumulation of government power takes priority over its dispersion. Particularly in the less developed countries, governments need more power, authority, and control to implement public policies. Rationalized authority means centralized governent power – the assertion of national sovereignty by government institutions that are unified, adaptable, complex (independent of a single person), and autonomous from social groups. Only strong institutions can restrain social conflicts, regulate succession among elites, expand the resources needed for implementing government decisions, and control the effects of destabilizing social change. Constitutionalists perceive that expanded educational opportunities, urbanization, extension of the mass media, and incipient industrialization promote adaptability, satisfy group demands, and restrain violent protests. In contrast, Huntington supposes that political disorder, chaos, and instability result from all these processes of social change. Rapid economic development leads to neither political stability nor political democracy. Instead, the expanded mass participation resulting from all these social changes causes popular alienation and violent protests, such as riots, rebellions, and mob actions. Political disorder ensues because citizens demand too much from their government and because government institutions lack the resources to satisfy people's expectations. 'Overloaded' governments can wield neither the sufficient consensual power to fulfill protesters' demands nor enough coercive power to quell popular disobedience.

Committed to a conservative, elitist stance toward social change, Huntington advocates a competitive elitist form of political democracy. He interprets democracy as a political system in which voters choose key decisionakers in competitive, free, and honest elections. It depends on extensive electoral participation, procedural guarantees, and elite accommodation of conflicting interests. Under his model, citizens should rarely participate in mass campaigns, protests, or 'extensive' opposition. Competing elites need to accept basic institutions: private property, a capitalist market, military autonomy, and privileges for established churches. To achieve political stability, leaders may have to compromise their populist promises and betray their followers' expectations. Huntington assumes that this brand of procedural elitist democracy will secure beneficial outcomes: stability, minimal violence, individual liberty, gradual social change, and international peace.[27]

Serving as coordinator of security planning for the National Security Council during the Carter administration and as director of the John M. Olin Institute for Strategic Studies at Harvard University, Huntington believes that a powerful government should protect a nation's security against foreign dangers. Taking a strategic realist viewpoint, he wants United States armed forces to defeat a military enemy quickly by reliance on superior technology – air power, tanks, and artillery. At the close of the twentieth century with the collapse of the Soviet Union, he sees the major future threat arising from a military 'connection' between China and Near Eastern Muslim states. To avert this threat, the United States government should maintain its military superiority, limit proposed arms reductions, and preserve its worldwide economic influence. According to Huntington, these strategies will enable the United States, Britain, Germany, Japan, and France to contain the rising power of China and Islamic states.[28]

Like the more liberal constitutionalists and neoinstitutionalists, Huntington downgrades the importance of the individuals who govern strong political institutions; hence, his explanations of social change remain limited. Focusing on the structural aspects of institutions – their unity, complexity, adaptability, and autonomy from social groups, – he gives less attention to leaders' personalities, goals, actions, and the actual consequences of their policies on groups and individuals within society. Yet the policies and their outcomes are more relevant for assessing the impact of social change than are the structural dimensions of political institutions. We need a clearer specification of the precise ways that different government institutions implement public policies and their effects on diverse social groups. Depending on the personalities of leaders, their political priorities, and the resources available for program implementation, the same 'strong' institutions in various societies may exert different consequences on social stratification.[29] Huntington's conception of strong institutions also needs greater clarification. Institutions that are cohesive and autonomous from social groups often lack flexibility, especially openness to information required for efficient policy-making. Downplaying the coercive tactics used by police and military forces to quash popular protests even in electoral democracies, he minimizes state restrictions on social group participation. Without the free flow of information from the general populace and interest groups, institutional elites remain unresponsive to citizens' policy prefernces. This lack of accountability hinders the performance of procedural democracies.[30]

## RADICAL INSTITUTIONALISM AND TRANSFORMATIVE CHANGE

Radical institutionalists – Marxists, Leninists, dependency theorists – challenge both the conservative views of Huntington and the liberal orientations of the constitutionalists. Rather than seeking minor modifications in sociopolitical stratification or liberal reforms, the radicals struggle for a transformed, egalitarian society – one with minimal class distinctions and relatively equal distribution of material wellbeing. For these radical institutionalists, classes constitute the basic structure. Class struggles and class alliances represent the most effective strategies to forge social change. Unlike the liberal constitutionalists and conservative institutionalists, the radicals draw a less sharp distinction between state and society. According to them, the polity and economy reveal only fuzzy boundaries; these twin sectors reciprocally interact to shape the policy process. Dominant social classes govern political institutions. Only protests by subordinate classes against the ruling elites will transform the society.

Making a radical critique of nineteenth-century European capitalism, Marx held that ruling social classes blocked opportunities for fundamental change. Economic elites who controlled the means of production also wielded decisive institutional power over the state. In the *Manifesto of the Communist Party*, he took an instrumentalist perspective. The state served as the instrument for capitalist class rule: 'The executive of the modern state is but a committee for managing the common affairs of the whole bourgeoisie.'[31] Large-scale capitalist corporations, especially the monopolies and oligopolies, controlled the state as their executive committee. In a work written twenty years later, however, Marx acknowledged that the state may wield greater autonomy from the dominant classes. According to *The Eighteenth Brumaire of Louis Bonaparte*, under Napoleon III, who governed France as a personal dictator from 1851 to 1870, the state seemed to wield autonomy from civil society. 'An adventurer' who ruled via a 'drunken soldiery,' Napoleon III claimed to represent the interests of the conservative peasantry and the lumpenproletariat, not the industrial bourgeoisie, which lost its political power in the 1851 coup d'état. Nevertheless, by creating a parasitic bureaucratic state dominated by the army, Napoleon III unintentionally 'created anarchy itself in the name of order.' State sponsorship of industry and trade preserved the capitalists' material power, thereby laying the foundation for their recapturing state control. Hence, Napoleon III sowed the seeds of his own destruction and prepared the way for the general capitalist class, if not specific factions of it, to regain political power.[32]

From Marx's standpoint, political order in capitalist society emerged from both coercive and consensual mechanisms. The capitalists controlled not only material production – factories, corporations, enterprises – but also institutions responsible for producing ideas, such as the media, schools, courts, and churches. Except in atypical situations like France under Napoleon III, the military and police usually protected capitalist interests, including the sanctity of private property. Social order resulted because capitalist bosses directly commanded the proletariat. State repression deterred and quelled proletariat uprisings. Through domination of communications media, the capitalists established ideological hegemony. They convinced subordinate classes that the interests of the capitalists equalled the general interests of everyone in society.

If the capitalists dominate the economic, political, and cultural systems, then how does revolutionary change emerge? Marx saw contradictions as the basis for transformative change. These contradictions or conflicts maintain a system in the short-run but produce systemic disintegration over the long-range period. Contradictions stimulate economic, political, and ideological mobilization by the proletariat. Economic contradictions between the productive forces (capital, labor power, raw materials, technology) and the relations of production (economic classes controlling investment, use of machinery, and workers) lead to economic collapse. Private capitalist class relations block ('fetter') capital accumulation or the rational use of capital to fulfill human needs. Toxic waste, pollution, ecological devastation, and human misery stem from capital accumulation under private ownership. As the profit rate falls, more small firms go bankrupt. Workers lose their jobs. As capitalist production becomes more social with larger factories and greater worker interdependence in the cities, profits go to fewer and fewer private capitalists. A contradiction arises between overproduction and underconsumption. Workers have too little money to purchase goods. High economic inequalities, class exploitation, and material deprivation generate alienation from the capitalist system. When workers gain control of the means of ideological production – mass media, schools, informal communications channels – capitalist ideological hegemony no longer atomizes the proletariat. These media transmit grievances, voice unifying symbols (interests of the exploited proletariat represent general societal interests), and increase feelings of political efficacy. As workers develop the socialist consciousness that the downfall of capitalism is inevitable, they become more politically efficacious about joining the class struggle. The development of solidary, autonomous sociopolitical networks among workers also raises their expectations about political success. Urbanized, numerous, and organized in large factories, workers gain the resources needed to wage the class struggle against the ruling capitalist class. The working class mobilizes behind unions, political parties, and armed militias. Rather than an accommodation of interests, political polarization emerges as the structural mechanism behind fundamental social change.[33]

Compared with Marx, Lenin took a more voluntarist stance toward achieving revolutionary change; he saw the need for ideology and a dominant party organization to shape decision-making, secure order, and construct a socialist society. Marx assumed that a successful revolution depends on both subjective conditions (the will of the proletariat to politically organize the class struggle against capitalism) and objective conditions, especially monopoly capitalism, high class exploitation, low economic growth, and the political power of a large urbanized factory working class. Spontaneous worker revolts against the capitalist system blended with the political organization of the class struggle by a socialist political party and allied unions. Marx warned against the tendency for socialist party leaders to regard the working class as too uneducated to liberate itself from capitalism. Lenin, however, assumed that only the party intelligentsia, along with a few 'enlightened workers,' possess the true political consciousness to lead the socialist revolution. Taking a Jacobin position, he asserted that a vanguard Communist Party of professional revolutionaries must wage revolution and begin the task of constructing socialism after it conquered government power.

Lenin proclaimed the dominance of political organization over social group spontaneity. Writing in 1902, fifteen years before the Bolshevik seizure of power in Russia, Lenin denounced both 'terrorism' and 'economism' for sacrificing political organization to social spontaneity. Perhaps remembering his brother Sasha, who participated in an abortive attempt to assassinate Czar Alexander III and was executed in 1887, Lenin condemned the Russian terrorists; their revolutionary intentions obscured the need to organize the masses for political victory. Although adopting a more peaceful strategy, the economists also fell prey to social spontaneity; their trade union activities reflected 'trade-union consciousness,' a primary concern to win higher wages and more favorable working conditions for the skilled factory working class. According to Lenin:

> The Economists and terrorists merely bow to different poles of spontaneity: the Economists bow to the spontaneity of the 'pure' working class movement, while the terrorists bow to the spontaneity of the passionate indignation of intellectuals, who lack the ability or opportunity to link up the revolutionary struggle with the working-class movement, to form an integral whole. It is difficult indeed for those who have lost their belief, or who have never believed that this is possible, to find some outlet for their indignation and revolutionary energy other than terror.[34]

Opposed to both terroristic and trade unionist spontaneity, Lenin campaigned for the development of a powerfully organized, centralized, elitist political party. It would educate the workers, raise their political consciousness, indicate primary political objectives, explain the tactics for achieving these goals, coordinate diverse activities, and lead the working classes toward a revolutionary seizure of power.

After the Bolsheviks gained control over the state in late 1917, they continued to maintain their power through a comprehensive political organization of Soviet society. Implementing state socialist policies, Communist Party bureaucrats and government officials played the leading role in political decisionmaking. As the self-proclaimed vanguard of enlightened rulers, party activists tried to create a new socialist person with transformed values and behaviors. Defining the general interest, the party elite imposed its interpretation of the public good on government officials, group leaders, and the populace. The party attempted to coordinate government decisionmaking. It recruited government officials, specified general policy goals, defined policy options, selected the final alternative, and monitored policy implementation. The key policy emphases revolved around developing heavy industry, educating the citizenry, and promoting mass health campaigns.

Particularly under Stalinist rule (1929–1953), the Communist Party of the Soviet Union wielded extensive, if not total, control over government and society. The exercise of power reflected a monistic structural pattern. The government ruled through hierarchical, centralized authority. Along with the armed forces and police, the party wielded pervasive physical, economic, and especially ideological coercion. The regime branded opponents as ideological 'deviants,' for example, counterrevolutionaries, traitors, and anti-Soviet capitalist reformers. The dominant leader and the party Politburo coordinated the policy process through the appointment of state officials (*nomenklatura*) and the organization of party structures that duplicated state structures at every government level. Few groups retained independence from party control. The party incorporated nearly all groups within its fold. Associations of trade unionists, farmers, writers, artists, old people, women, youths, and students functioned as transmission belts for the Party elite to mobilize the masses. The government exercised comprehensive power. Mobilization of the society for socialist construction involved the state in all aspects of life. Government institutions and economic agencies were tightly integrated, not separated. State ministries owned and regulated nearly all economic activities. Market mechanisms and private associations had little influence. This monistic, hierarchical pattern also prevailed in Eastern Europe from the late 1940s until the death of Stalin in 1953.[35]

Despite the powerful institutional rule by the Communist Party and state, why did Communist Party regimes collapse during the late 1980s throughout East-Central Europe? They disintegrated because they no longer fulfilled the essence of the Leninist model: a strong commitment to Marxist–Leninist ideology, rule by the vanguard party, and the operation of a centrally administered state socialist economy. As a set of universal principles that guided policymaking and mobilized the masses, Marxism-Leninism became illegitimate. Influential elites in the party, state administration, and party auxiliaries repudiated these abstract principles. The masses took a cynical view of Marxist–Leninist tenets, especially their relevance to actual political practices. More concrete particularistic values – nationalism, populism, ethnicity, religion – gained strength. The vanguard party as the agent of mobilization for socialist construction also disintegrated. Rather than mobilizing the masses, the party saw its role as providing order. The party's policy influence vis-à-vis the state declined. Lacking the power to control society, represent proletarian interests, or guide government decisionmaking, the party engaged in extensive corruption. Patron–client exchanges enabled key groups to gain favors from party cadres, who controlled access to key state resources. Most people withdrew from active political participation into their private lives, where families, ethnic groups, and religious associations fulfilled personal needs. As party control over government institutions, social groups, and citizens weakened, the state socialist centrally-planned economy collapsed. Powerful state bureaucratic agencies directed the production of armaments and heavy industrial goods but neglected food, consumer goods, and personal services. During the 1980s a thriving informal 'second' economy emerged to supply these products. State plans went unfulfilled. State enterprises lacked needed materials, advanced technological equipment, storage facilities, and distribution networks. Enterprise managers concealed information or reported inaccurate information about production capabilities, available supplies, and popular demands. Workers grew demoralized about consumer goods shortages and economic corruption. They transferred materials from the state factories to more lucrative private-sector activities in the informal private market economy. Hence, lower productivity resulted. By the late 1970s and early 1980s, economic stagnation plagued most East European societies.

Not only waning ideological legitimacy and economic stagnation but also decisions taken by USSR and West European governments accelerated the collapse of East European Leninist party states. In 1989 Soviet leader Mikhail Gorbachev accepted multiparty elections in Poland and renounced any USSR military intervention to maintain Communist Party monopolies throughout East Europe; that policy impeded Party elites' attempts to preserve their power and encouraged opponents to challenge these regimes. The West European experience further weakened the party's authority. Compared with East Europeans, West Europeans enjoyed greater civil liberties, owned more consumer goods, and used superior technological equipment, especially in electronics and information processing. Mass media from the core capitalist societies spread the messages of democracy and capitalist prosperity to East Europeans, who no longer expected Communist Party cadres to realize the Marxist–Leninist promises of socioeconomic equality and socialist abundance.

As structural ties with the Soviet Union weakened but contacts with West European institutions grew stronger, populist mobilization and elite accommodation undermined the Communist Party regimes. Dissident protesters from ethnic groups, religious associations, trade unions, and civic action groups staged strikes, mounted street demonstrations, and organized antiregime assemblies. Confronted by these popular pressures, the top Communist Party elites adopted an accommodating strategy. Subordinate to domestic party and USSR control, the armed forces refrained from impeding the movement toward democratization. Elite tolerance of opposition during the late 1980s stemmed from the perception that the costs of continued repression outweighed the benefits. Many Communist Party and state bureaurats gained control of privatized firms or continued managing state industries. Abandoning the Marxist–Leninist label, several ex-communist *apparatchiki* became nationalists or socialists. They continued to hold important government positions, including the civil service, security agencies, education administrations, health organizations, and local institutions. Only tepid efforts occurred to purge former Communist Party bureaucrats from government positions and prosecute them for their repressive actions. Hence, even though Communist Party regimes collapsed, the former party bureaucrats still wielded political power and enjoyed some economic privileges.[36]

Whereas Leninism represented a guide to government policy-making throughout Eastern Europe, dependency theory makes a radical critique of the world capitalist system by intellectual challengers outside formal government office. From Marx dependency theorists borrow concepts of the class struggle, class alliances, and the need for subordinate groups to mobilize against a divided ruling elite. These theorists, however, depart from Marx in extending the domestic class struggle to the world arena. Their interpretations of imperialism derive from Lenin. First published in 1917, his *Imperialism, the Highest Stage of Capitalism* linked imperial domination of the colonial areas to monopoly capitalism. These monopolies gain raw materials at a cheap price from the colonies, transform them into capital (coal, steel), and then export manufactured products at high prices. Monopoly profits result. Multinational financial oligarchies make political and economic institutions dependent on them for credit to expand capital accumulation. According to Lenin, only a socialist revolution can transform this 'parasitic,' 'moribund' form of international capitalism.[37]

Particularly during the late 1960s through the early 1980s, radical dependency theorists wielded their greatest intellectual influence when they challenged the liberal constitutionalist and conservative institutionalist approaches toward political development. The latter two approaches focus on the nation-state and social groups (communal, economic, civic) as the dominant decision-making structures. Political order emerges from shared normative commitments, procedural consensus, strong integrative political institutions, and economic interdependence in a competitive market economy. Evolutionary social change stems from structural differentiation (competitive political parties, widespread participation in voluntary associations), technological innovations, and the diffusion of modern cultural values such as achievement, secularity, and rationality. When modernizing structures like the mass media, factories, and public schools communicate these values, then active political participation rises.

According to dependency theorists, the main decisionmaking structure is the transnational capitalist class that controls the world capitalist economy. It wields influence through multinational corporations, intergovernmental agencies (International Monetary Fund, World Bank), and nation-states of the capitalist core, including the United States, Germany, Japan, Britain, and

France. Rather than group pluralism, class domination characterizes most underdeveloped countries. Primordial, religious, and economic groups hardly possess equal resources or share political power in dispersed institutions. Instead, the capitalist class – large-scale urban business enterprises and commercialized export agribusinesses – dominates the state and exploits the 'popular sector' of factory workers, peasants, and small businesspeople. Domestic economic inequalities fuse with inequalities in the world capitalist system. National capitalists in the agricultural periphery and especially the more industrializing semiperipheral nations manage subsidiaries of the multinational corporations headquartered in the core capitalist societies of Western Europe, North America, and Japan. In less developed countries, the state exerts limited independence from either the national capitalists or multinational corporate executives.

Political order in the capitalist core rests on a more consensual foundation than in the peripheral or semiperipheral zones. Ruling industrialized nations, government officials in the core possess greater state resources for financing social service programs. Unions and prolabor parties wield some policy influence. Class compromises and interclass alliances enable higher wages and more generous fringe benefits than in noncore areas. Widespread access to social service benefits and to opportunities for upward mobility legitimate the democratic and capitalist systems; hence, the state needs to rely on only limited coercion to secure compliance. Protesters use mainly nonviolent tactics. In contrast, in the peripheral and semiperipheral regions, political regimes govern through greater coercion. Bureaucratic–authoritarian states run by the armed forces, police, and security agencies quell popular protests against austerity policies. Burdened by scarce resources and high foreign debts, political leaders in underdeveloped nations give precedence to capital accumulation over such egalitarian consumption measures as high wages and generous social service benefits.

Rather than seeking incremental reformist change, radical dependency theorists who advocate a Marxist program struggle for a fundamental transformation of both the national and world capitalist systems. Marxist dependency theorists such as Andre Gunder Frank, Paul Baran, Samir Amin, Walter Rodney, Teotonio Dos Santos, and Arghiri Emmanuel assume that through a socialist state and dominant socialist party that mobilizes the popular sector, underdeveloped nations can transform domestic class relationships, abolish national class exploitation, redistribute wealth to the popular sector, and lessen the international inequalities separating the capitalist core societies from noncore nations. Eventually, dependency theorists hope to realize a world socialist system.

Even though dependence on the capitalist core stimulates popular grievances in the short run, over the long-range period these theorists expect that economic dependence will generate the opportunities for mobilization that lead to the downfall of capitalist regimes. Less developed countries depend on core societies for investment, trade, loans, and export sales. This dependence produces inequalities between the core and periphery. Popular protests by factory workers, agricultural wage-laborers, and even national capitalists often arise to challenge these unequal world exchanges, for example, high profits to the core but lower economic returns to the less developed countries. Class polarization within peripheral–semiperipheral societies also arises from dependency relations. Allied with the multinational corporations, the 'comprador bourgeoisie' struggles against the popular sector, which becomes marginalized. Excessive urbanization, a large service sector, a smaller manufacturing sector, and exploitation of agrarian smallholders, wage laborers, and subsistence farmers bring economic losses to unskilled factory laborers, peasants, and small businesspeople. Underemployment and low growth rates exacerbate economic inequalities. Dependency on the International Monetary Fund, World Bank, and multinational private financial institutions for loans leads to high foreign debts when noncore nations cannot stimulate rapid domestic growth or sell their exports overseas. As a result, the state enacts austerity policies: decreased wages, higher interest rates, reduced government employment, lower government subsidies for food, transportation, and housing. Urban riots protest these 'structural adjustment' programs. Economic grievances and inequalities heighten the motivation to transform dependency ties. Opportunities for mobilization derive from the structural conditions that accompany economic dependence on the capitalist core. Extensive trade and investment cause higher urbanization, greater formal education, extension of the mass media, and unionization in the multinational corporate subsidiaries. All these processes supply the resources that protesters may use to organize resistance against dependence on the capitalist core.[38]

The major limitation of these three radical institutionalist theories revolves around the gap between their transformative goals and the structural conditions needed to attain rapid social change. Their expectations about proletarian class solidarity and divisions among the ruling capitalist elite seem too optimistic; hence, societal change has occurred more slowly than desired by the radical institutionalists. For example, Marx underestimated the empirical constraints on securing proletarian class solidarity, forging the class struggle, and achieving polarization between workers and capitalists. He minimized the political importance of class differentiation, interclass alliances, and attachments based on ethnicity, religion, and gender; these latter ties fragment class unity. Particularly in the modern era, political struggles often revolve around cultural values and lifestyle issues, not just issues about economic production or distribution.

From 1917 through the late 1980s in Eastern Europe, Leninist regimes faced an incongruence between the ideological objective of socialist transformation and the more objective structural requirements that negated this vision. To construct socialism, Lenin relied on a powerful vanguard party and a strong state. The resulting bureaucratization of political life brought rigidities, bottlenecks, overlapping jurisdictions, and policy stalemates. Society changed more rapidly than did the rigid political system. Mass education, urbanization, extension of the mass media, and industrialization expanded the number of young professionals who sought a more consensual, decentralized, and pluralistic government. The centralized coercion needed to transform society and human behavior decreased the information required for efficient policymaking; the general populace, mass associations, and professionals feared sanctions if they reported information perceived harmful to political elites. Hence, political organizations never institutionalized the normative commitments for achievement and altruism. Rank-and-file citizens, even party cadres, failed to internalize the ideological requisites of socialism. As a result, these 'actually existing' socialist regimes never realized their ideological priorities of widespread social equality, economic abundance, the abolition of status distinctions, and the elimination of state oppression. By the end of the 1980s, the Communist Party regimes had sown the seeds of their own destruction.

Radical dependency theory fails to explain the gap between the goal of fundamental change and actual outcomes in most underdeveloped nations, where change has occurred more slowly than intended. According to dependency analysts, class cleavages, mobilization by leftwing organizations, and dependence on the capitalist core create the structural opportunities for systemic transformation of the world capitalist economy. Yet few developing countries, except some in Latin America like Chile and Uruguay, faced class cleavages. Group differentiation seems far more pervasive; family, gender, ethnic, regional, and religious groups remain powerful. Particularly in Africa, communal violence has outstripped any class struggles. Few peasant revolts or even workers' protests against austerity policies have occurred. Instead, most political violence stems from ethnic rivalries, weak political institutions (governments, parties), and leaders who seek to gain and maintain their power by intimidating their opponents. In only a few countries among the developing nations have leftwing unions and political parties mobilized the dispossessed. Dependence on the capitalist core has occasionally produced rapid industrial growth, particularly in such East Asian societies as South Korea, Singapore, and Taiwan. Even though the Korean and Taiwanese governents remained dependent on the capitalist core for military equipment, loans, and sales of their exports, these two states developed powerful bureaucratic institutions that controlled the use of foreign credit and limited multinational foreign private investment.

In short, dependency theorists underestimate the importance of political structures in forging social change. Concentrating on multinational corporations, national capitalists, and their ties with the capitalist core, they give less attention to informal structural conditions that have shaped the policy process in most developing countries. Personal rule, dynastic family traditions, patron-client relationships, bureaucratic factionalism, and army dominance all influence the degree of social change that government officials can implement. At the local level, chiefs, clan hierarchs, elders, wealthy landowners, traders, creditors, and army officers often serve as patrons to their clients. These patrons supply loans, jobs, contracts, licenses, and land to their followers in exchange for political support. Because the patrons dominate the local exchange network, they retain considerable power to influence national policy implementation and may block programs intended to achieve extensive social change. Not only multinational corporations, nationalist capitalist firms, and government institutions affect economic outcomes, such as growth and equality. Traders, moneylenders, and small-scale producers control informal markets, which the government cannot easily regulate. Neglecting the power of local political networks and informal markets, dependency theorists have downplayed these structural constraints on transformative change toward a socialist system.[39]

## CONCLUSION

This chapter has explored three basic issues. Which structures wield the greatest power over the policy process? In what ways do political organizations manage conflict and secure order? How do political institutions make public policies that produce social change? Liberal, conservative, and radical institutional theories formulate divergent assumptions about these issues.

Which institutions make the binding decisions? Constitutional theorists assign crucial authority to an elected prime minister or president, who chooses cabinet ministers. Senior civil servants help shape public policies. In these pluralist representative governments, elections, coalitional parties, parliament, independent courts, a free press, voluntary associations, and constitutional laws restrain executive power, so that the rulers become accountable to the citizens. Within the liberal neoinstitutionalist camp, political sociologists place greater emphasis on the power of government institutions and policies to shape social group activities; political economists, however, stress the impact of market structures, particularly economic entrepreneurs, on the policy process. Conservative institutionalists such as Samuel Huntington highlight the dominant role of the national security state, especially its military, civilian bureaucracy, and technocracy. Like Huntington, Leninists also concentrate on the policymaking importance of powerful state institutions, with Leninists upholding a vanguard Communist Party that controls the state. Marxists and dependency theories assume that domestic capitalist enterprises and multinational corporations wield the greatest policy influence; formal government institutions exert little independence from capitalist control.

What are the bases of political order? Constitutional theorists rely on procedural consensus to regulate conflict. Shared values of tolerance and civility – belief in the rule of law and concern for the general welfare – help produce political order. Guided by secure property rights enforced by the government, market mechanisms also secure peaceful exchanges. Conservative institutionalists perceive the need for state repression to ensure domestic order and security from external threats. Placing little faith in market mechanisms, Leninists used a strong state, security police, military, and vanguard party to secure order. The party tried to organize most individuals into mass associations that it controlled. Along with educational institutions, the armed forces, and mass media, these mass associations propagated Marxist–Leninist values intended to reinforce political solidarity. Marxists see order arising from ideological hegemony around capitalist values – the notion that capitalist interests concur with with the general interest. The capitalists use state repression to quash disobedience from dissidents who do not accept this ideological hegemony. Dependency theorists assume that in the noncore areas, both coercion and consent maintain order. A repressive bureaucratic–authoritarian state commanded by the military and police crush rebellions against the world capitalist economy. Economic payoffs go to the labor aristocracy and national capitalist class that agree to cooperate with subsidiaries of multinational corporations.

How do political institutions produce social change? Under pluralist conditions advocated by constitutional theorists, reformist social change emerges through relatively spontaneous mechanisms. Social group leaders, political party activists, and government personnel form coalitions to enact changes at the margins. They negotiate, bargain, and try to accommodate conflicting policy preferences. Technical experts and professional civil servants coordinate the implementation of reformist policies and may initiate some programs. Conservative institutionalists take a more pessimistic view about the possibilities of achieving peaceful change in a conflict-laden environment. From their Hobbesian perspective, powerful government institutions and a dominant political party, directed by strong leaders, must impose orderly change, so that rapid social mobilization does not threaten political paralysis and chaos. Leninists also placed limited faith in social spontaneity as a means of producing change. Rather than seeking minor modifications in the status quo, they struggled for a radical transformation of the social stratification system. Guided by Marxist–Leninist ideology, the vanguard Communist Party proposed social changes, selected the most approprite policies for attaining these changes, and monitored policy implementation. Through this party control of the state and mass associations, Leninists expected to construct a socialist society that diverged from the capitalist framework. Yet, as we have seen, bureaucratic bottlenecks impeded the efficiency of the state-planned economies. Marxist and dependency theorists anticipated that class struggle, populist mobilization, and socialist parties would engineer the overthrow of capitalism. Structural and ideological contradictions would alienate subordinate classes and fragment ruling class solidarity. Hence, the dispossessed would gain the opportunity to dislodge the capitalists from power and institute a more egalitarian sociopolitical system. Despite these optimistic expectations, structural constraints impeded social transformation. Instead of class polarization, social group differentiation seemed more pervasive. Patron–client ties and informal local networks hindered the power of a leftwing party or strong state to mobilize the populace behind radical social change.

# 6    Pluralist Theories and Social Groups

From the pluralist perspective, politics is a game. Competing teams of rival protest groups struggle for victory. Agreement on the rules of the game brings order. Players devise strategies to achieve success. They rely on both conflict and cooperation to win the game. Members of the same team need to coordinate their activities and cooperate with each other. Conflict occurs with the opposing team. When one side wins and the other side loses, the teams play a zero-sum game. Intense conflict results. Greater cooperation emerges under a positive-sum game; each side gains a victory. When both sides lose, a negative-sum game takes place. Because gains exceed losses for the two teams, their condition after the game seems worse than before the game started. Hence, conflict within and between teams intensifies.

The interpretation of pluralist politics as a game highlights three key issues of structural analysis. Who rules? What is the basis of political order? How does the public policy process produce social changes? These issues provide useful yardsticks for comparing the dominant types of pluralism in the world today. Where liberal pluralism prevails, economic and civic associations comprise the main groups. Competing teams view political life as a positive-sum game where all players can secure mutual gains. Protests against liberal pluralism emerge from communal and radical pluralism. Under communal pluralism, primordial and religious groups wield the greatest political influence. Politics resembles a zero-sum game; conflict between polarized groups hinders the accommodation of differences. Whereas communal pluralists restrict the political game to dominant ethnic and religious groups, radical pluralists seek expanded participation for more diverse groups, especially the weak, poor, and unorganized. They want to change the rules of the political game so that formerly-excluded groups become active participants in the policy process. Challenging the politico-economic elites with demands for greater equality, radical pluralism may unintentionally lead to a negative-sum game.

In the following sections, we compare liberal, communal, and radical pluralism by examining the power relationships among the state, social groups, and individuals. What are the structural interactions between the central government and the groups? What ties prevail among the diverse groups? How do group leaders relate to individual members? Table 6.1 summarizes the three types of pluralism.

## LIBERAL PLURALISM

Particularly in the United States, Canada, Australia, New Zealand, and Western Europe, liberal pluralism has permeated political life since the Second World War. Voluntary associations comprise the main types of groups. Intervening between the state and individual, these voluntary associations operate independently from direct state control, check government power, and try to satisfy the interests of individuals, who belong to a variety of groups with diverse memberships. Economic associations – business/professional organizations, labor unions, farm groups, consumer organizations – compete for influence. Civic associations such as the British Campaign for Nuclear Disarmament, the US Common Cause, and the Swedish KRUM (Association for the Humanizing of the Penal System) also actively press their policy demands on government officials. Ethnic and religious groups operate as voluntary associations that communicate their interest claims to government agencies. By articulating such interests as greater government subsidies for schools, expanded access to employment, and increased health-care facilities, ethnic and religious groups help transform their value cleavages into interest conflicts. Political compromise in the government arena hence becomes more possible. Under liberal pluralism, the state operates as the object of group demands, the preserver of the group equilibrium, and mediator of group differences. Government officials try to reconcile the divergent policy preferences voiced by various protest groups. If protesters cannot secure their rights through the legislative process, they press their claims in the courts, where matters of principle become reconciled with constitutional laws. If, however, a protest group seeks a concrete policy benefit that has strong public support, it pursues its goals

*Table* 6.1  Liberal, communal, and radical pluralism

| | Liberal pluralism | Communal pluralism | Radical pluralism |
|---|---|---|---|
| **Key decision-making structures** | | | |
| Government | Mediator of group differences | Agency for suppressing subordinate ethnic-religious groups and for securing policy benefits for dominant group | Decentralized, local self-governing agencies such as elected village and city councils |
| Groups | Powerful intermediary associations, especially economic groups and civic associations | Primordial (especially ethnic) and religious groups | Participation by the weak, poor, unorganized, and excluded people (youths, women, handicapped) against private and public bureaucracies |
| Individual | Member of several groups with diverse social backgrounds | Member of few groups with same ethnic-religious background | Member of several groups that encourage participants to perform diverse roles |
| Bases of Order | Competitive market economy; procedural consensus; shared civil values taught by coalitional parties, representative legislatures, independent courts, and comprehensive public schools | State repression and more consensual but ineffective mechanisms such as communal voting rolls, regional autonomy, and federalism | Expanded political participation by excluded groups in decentralized structures (town meetings, councils, cooperatives, communes) |
| Causes of social change | Coalitions formed between government officials and interest groups that press for marginal adjustments (incremental changes) | State repression by dominant communal (ethnic-religious) groups, violent protests by subordinate communal groups | Populist mobilization from below, which produces short-run changes in social stratification but leads to mass apathy and conservative elite opposition over the long-run |

through party politics and the legislature, where political entrepreneurs negotiate conflicting interests.

Even though dispersed government power and group pluralism expand protest movements' access to the policy process, the need to accommodate differences, make compromises, and moderate demands leads to slow social change through the policy route. Among movement activists, purists who articulate symbolic demands for fundamental change concentrate on public campaigns, citizen rallies, and demonstrations that attract media attention. Yet they operate on the margins of the policy process. In contrast, the pragmatists who stress accommodationist tactics become institutionalized. Relying on representative government agencies, they focus on raising funds and lobbying legislators for concrete, incremental benefits. High political stability results, but the fragmented decision process produces policy stalemates, not transformative social change.

Political order emerges from shared civil values, market interdependence, and the exercise of consensual power. Agreement on civil values and on the rules for regulating the political game facilitates a nonviolent group struggle. Political order stems partly from reasons of self-interest. To maximize their own group's gain and to promote a peaceful competition for resources, protest leaders abide by consensual procedures that ensure political liberty. The reliance on compromise, negotiation, and mutually beneficial payoffs characterizes a competitive market economy, where political entrepreneurs bargain to satisfy diverse interest groups. Through wheeling and dealing, political entrepreneurs strengthen economic interdependence, which further promotes political order.

According to liberal pluralists, dispersed power, peaceful competition, and mutually beneficial exchanges facilitate orderly change, which arises through a dynamic equilibrium. The political process resembles a market. In the economic sphere, individual buyers use money to demand goods that sellers supply through the market mechanism, which links buyers with sellers. The goal of the competitive market is to establish an equilibrium between supply and demand. Excessive demands or insufficient supplies disturb the equilibrium. By analogy, in the political sphere, individual citizens (buyers) with votes (money) demand public policies (goods and services) supplied by political officials (sellers) through legal institutions (market mechanisms). Representative structures, especially legislatures and coalitional political parties that include diverse interest associations, connect citizens with their leaders. Constitutional governments, coalitional parties, and voluntary associations try to secure an equilibrium between popular demands and public policies. Political disorder results when citizens demand too much from their government and government lacks the resources to meet group expectations. By transforming several partial interests into general public policies, political leaders temper demands for government payoffs. Group leaders, political party activists, and government officials also have the responsibility to encourage increased economic productivity, thereby enlarging the supply of resources.[1]

In a liberal pluralist system, protesters most effectively attain social change by forming coalitions with sympathetic government officials and interest group leaders. A social group's power over the policy process depends on its resources, organizational solidarity, relationships with other groups, and access to government officials. Protest groups with the greatest resources (wealth, information, technical expertise, legitimacy) can potentially wield the greatest political power; they have the ability to transform their preferences into binding public policies. If members share policy priorities, depend on the group, and comply with its obligations, group solidarity will increase, thereby strengthening its political power. Alliances with other groups for common political objectives become especially necessary for winning political victories. Close ties with supportive government officials and political party leaders who control executive power increase the probability that government institutions will implement a social group's policy preferences for social change. Because of the dispersed power in a pluralist system, social change usually takes place gradually and incrementally. Rather than securing comprehensive social transformations, pluralist policymakers have the power to attain reforms within specific sectors of society.

Civil norms and a strong group network produce effective, dynamic governments that implement innovative policies. Since 1970 the regional governments in northern Italy have demonstrated more effective institutional performance than have most southern regions. For example, in Emilia-Romagna, unlike Calabria, liberal pluralist practices have taken stronger root. Political activists adhere to civil norms: political equality, mutual reciprocity, trust, tolerance, compromise, concern for public policies, and the willingness to coordinate activities behind shared public goals. Citizens actively participate in diverse groups with overlapping memberships and crosscutting cleavages. These groups include not only political parties and voluntary unions but also cooperatives, literary societies, cultural associations, mutual aid groups, and guilds. Group leaders form coalitions to implement their policy preferences. As a result of these civil norms and participatory social networks, Emilia-Romagna during the 1980s showed higher economic growth and a more viable political democracy than did any southern region. The regional bureaucracy operated efficiently and responsively toward citizen demands. The regional council passed innovative programs for day-care centers, family clinics, health-care, and urban planning. As liberal pluralists assume, a strong civil society with egalitarian interactions and cooperative norms achieved an efficient market economy and a viable constitutional democracy that enacted innovative policies for reformist change.[2]

Since the Second World War three closely-related variants of liberal pluralism – polyarchy, democratic corporatism, consociationism – have functioned throughout the market economies of North America and Western Europe. All three reflect dispersed power, group bargaining, peaceful competition, and political compromise. As formulated by Robert Dahl, polyarchy – the rule of the many – combines extensive group competition with widespread political participation.[3] Through the electoral process, citizens check government power. Elected government officials decide public policies. Voters choose their government leaders at competitive elections. All adults have the right to vote, run for office, secure alternative sources of political information, and criticize leaders, public policies, political values, and government institutions. To press their demands on government institutions, citizens organize or join opposition political parties, voluntary associations, and social movements. Spontaneous groups emerge as new problems arise. Several groups articulate diverse interests and bargain with each other. Because most voluntary associations have decentralized and poorly coordinated structures, they cannot easily enforce political agreements among their members. Although business organizations exert stronger influence over the policy process than do labor unions, few business associations include all firms; their power remains decentralized, uncoordinated, and faction-riven. Similarly, the state operates as a fragmented institution divided by competing government agencies with conflicting policy preferences. This polyarchal model particularly applies to the United States, Canada, and Australia – federal systems with liberal political values.

Polyarchal theorists like Robert Dahl exaggerate the importance of social spontaneity and skillful use of resources as the main reasons for a group's policy effectiveness. Few groups emerge spontaneously. They need support from government agencies, nonprofit organizations (foundations, churches), profit-oriented business enterprises, professional associations, political parties, and wealthy patrons. State sanctions, laws, and court decisions also shape the mobilization of protests. In the United States business and professional associations comprise around four fifths of all interest groups; only 20 percent include social movements promoting general citizen causes. Because of their extensive financial-organizational resources, business-professional associations wield a greater impact on government decisionmaking than do other interest groups and show little inclination to support public policy benefits for the unemployed, such as government-provided jobs. Neither government institutions nor nonprofit organizations seem ready to mobilize the unemployed. Despite their economic deprivation, jobless persons and other low-income people remain politically inactive. As Jack Walker points out:

> The differential rates of political mobilization among social groups within any population are mainly a product of the structure of opportunities presented to each citizen by the legal, political, and organizational environment. Members of different social groups face entirely different sets of opportunities and obstacles to political activity. . . . Institutional and organizational variables are more important as determinants of political mobilization than the attitudes, feelings of political efficacy, or the political beliefs of individual citizens.[4]

Thus political activism in a polyarchal regime depends not only on individuals' motives or social background but on group access to organizational support.

Robert Dahl also underestimates the obstacles facing leftwing parties in achieving greater income equality in a pluralist system. Like business power, the policy influence of parties stems from numerous variables: their resources, centralization, structural cohesion, access to government office, attitudinal solidarity, and control over rival organizations. Even if governing parties influence policy contents, their effect seems less extensive than promised by partisan manifestos. Nearly every governing party in the industrialized capitalist societies has experienced factional rivalries based on divergent policy preferences, which need reconciliation. Although parties do shape the policy priorities of legislators and cabinet ministers, party activists exert only limited structural control over government officials. Particularly when a party controls the executive, government leaders dominate the party, rather than vice versa. Yet one party rarely governs alone; it usually must share power with other political parties in a coalition governent. Agencies other than parties and elected leaderships shape public policies. These organizations include foreign governments, intergovernmental institutions (International Monetary Fund, World Bank, Organization of Petroleum Exporting Countries), multinational corporations, domestic private business, labor unions, and the civil service. Because of this dispersed power in pluralist societies, socialist political parties face difficulties attaining a more egalitarian income distribution. Only when a social democratic party operates a centralized structure, establishes close alliances with powerful labor unions, wins support from the civil service, gains cooperation from corporate businesses, and holds government office for a long time period can it implement egalitarian public policies. These condiions remain most valid for Sweden and to a lesser extent Norway. Elsewhere, most other democratic capitalist nations have stronger conservative parties, more powerful business organizations, weaker unions, and more fragmented governments that give antiegalitarian groups the opportunity to impede income redistribution policies.[5]

Democratic corporatism prevails in northern European societies with a unified state, powerful social democratic parties, and centralized, coordinated, and inclusive interest groups. Particularly between 1960 and 1990, Austria, Sweden, and Norway represented the best examples of the corporatist version of liberal pluralism. With small, homogeneous populations, these three nations experienced few ethnic or religious cleavages. Major economic interest groups, especially business and labor, operated through centralized, coordinated, inclusive structures. Their leaders disciplined members and enforced agreements reached with the state and other dominant associations. Seeking cooperation from these economic associations, government agencies authorized businesses and unions to repreent group interests. Through legal recognition by the state, these 'peak associations' gained subsidies, tax concessions, access to government officials, and the authority to help implement public policies. Elite political bargaining occurred among government officials (cabinet ministers and particularly civil servants), heads of interest groups, and political party leaders. Closely aligned with powerful labor unions, Social Democratic parties actively participated in the cabinet. Government officials upheld the procedures that reconciled the decisions of corporate executives, union heads, and state bureaucrats. Dedicated to the pursuit of mutually beneficial gains, public policymakers in Austria, Sweden, and Norway secured comprehensive social service benefits, low unemployment, and labor peace from 1960 through 1990.[6]

Despite these policy successes of democratic corporatism in northern Europe, during the 1980s enthusiasm for the corporatist system waned. West European economies faced lower growth rates, rising unemployment, and greater international competition. As the industrialized manufacturing sector declined, the service sector became more important. Particularly in sectors like microelectronics, smaller units of production stressed individual skills and bargaining at the enterprise, not the national, level. Hence, national business associations and national unions wielded less control over collective bargaining. Economic stagnation weakened the social partnership among government civil servants, business executives, union activists, and political party leaders. Both business and labor showed greater policy divisions. Whereas some corporate executives preferred continued cooperation with unions and the socialist party, other business people supported tax cuts, lower social service expenditures, wage restraints, and reduced union influence in enterprise management, especially over investment decisions. Labor solidarity also declined as the wage equality issue split blue-collar workers from white-collar employees and also divided public unions from private unions. This fragmentation within business and labor impeded the accommodation of differences between the two sides. Centralized collective bargaining thus became less feasible than during the 1970s. Political parties also showed less willingness to compromise differences in a coalition government. Neoliberal austerity policies gained greater support among nearly all major parties, not just the nonsocialists. From 1960 through the late 1970s, governing Social Democrats had implemented Keynesian policies: an activist state, government regulation of aggregate demand, collective bargaining, cooperation among labor and capital, and programs to maintain low unemployment. During the 1980s, however, neoliberal policymakers wielded increased influence. They supported wage inequalities, deregulation, privatization, free trade, and policies that would promote higher productivity and greater international competition. Collective bargaining and expanded social services aroused little enthusiasm. All these neoliberal policies threatened the cooperative, accommodative spirit associated with strong Social Democratic parties, centralized unions, and the democratic corporatist model.

The consolidation of the European Union in 1993 further weakened democratic corporatism. Influenced by trade associations, multinational corporations, and technical experts, the pan-European market operated with little national government regulation. Labor and capital mobility took priority over workers' rights to expanded social service benefits or to representation in factory decisionmaking. Without powerful pan-European labor unions, collective bargaining became less important. The policy commitment to corporatism waned.[7]

Like democratic corporatism, the consociational variant of liberal pluralism also declined in importance during the 1980s. In smaller European democracies like the Netherlands, Belgium, and Switzerland, ethnic, linguistic, and religious cleavages divide the population. Under consociational democracy, these communal groups maintain their internal autonomy, often in a quasi-federal arrangement. The central government remains fragmented by ethnic/linguistic/religious diversities. Elite representatives of noneconomic groups share executive power in a coalition government and in various advisory councils. Negotiations among the elites help accommodate differences and secure some coordination over the policy process. Unlike corporatist systems, consociational democracies feature weaker Social Democratic parties but stronger Christian Democratic organizations – a reflection of the greater religious cleavages splitting these societies. Government expenditures and civil service positions accrue to each organized group on a proportional allocation formula. Rather than promoting majority rule, consociationism enables each primordial or religious group to wield a minority veto over important issues that affect its welfare. Examples include language rights, family programs, education, and government subsidies to religious schools. From the end of the Second World War through the mid-1970s, these consociational principles appealed to political elites in the Netherlands, Belgium, and Switzerland. After 1975, however, growth rates began to decline. Unemployment rose in Belgium and the Netherlands. Dutch society became more secularized. Catholics and Protestants no longer represented autonomous pillars. The pursuit of individual interests assumed increasing importance over family welfare or religious well-being. Individual citizens no longer showed high deference to the authority wielded by elites. Confronted by economic stagnation and joblessness, the Dutch and Belgian elites could not easily devise public policies that would resolve economic problems. The provision for minority vetoes reinforced political *immobilisme*. Swiss political order derived not so much from its consociational practices but from its low unemployment rate, price stability, secularization, economic differentiation, and extensive influence of Zurich-based financial institutions.

Even though Arend Lijphart, the leading advocate of consociational democracy, perceives it a 'realistic and feasible solution' for Third World societies such as South Africa, consociationism remains more an ideal hope than a feasible option for resolving communal cleavages. Ethnic diversity, religious polarization, economic stagnation, fragmented political institutions, and foreign interventions all impede elite attempts to secure the peaceful accommodation of group differences in most developing nations.[8]


## COMMUNAL PLURALISM

Although liberal pluralism remains the basis of political order in contemporary democratic societies, communal pluralism has recently become more widespread throughout the world, even in Western Europe. Particularly during the 1990s civil ties weakened. Politically-dominant ethnic groups showed less tolerance toward immigrants from Africa, Eastern Europe

(Yugoslavia, Romania, Bulgaria), Turkey, and Asia. Opportunities to gain political asylum in West European societies declined. Police and immigration officials secured greater power to harass non-European foreigners. Laws impeded the rights of children born in Europe to become national citizens. Both citizens and government officials took a less inclusive, universalist view of nationality. They perceived the nation dominated by a hegemonic ethnic group, rather than composed of diverse ethnic groups treated with equal value.[9]

Particularly in Eastern Europe, Africa, South Asia, the Caribbean, and the South Pacific, communal pluralism shapes the operation of the policy process. Whereas liberal pluralists view politics as a positive-sum game and seek expanded opportunities for diverse groups to gain political power, communal pluralists regard government decisionmaking as a zero-sum game. The major political objective focuses on controlling government, so that the dominant ethnic or religious group can obtain policy benefits, such as land, tax concessions, subsidies, licenses, contracts, university admissions, scholarships, and civil service positions. Through its government power, the dominant ethnic or religious group represses subordinate communal groups. They have only limited rights to participate in the policy process and hence receive few government payoffs.

Under communal pluralism, political order remains fragile; political leaders cannot easily resolve conflicts through nonviolent methods. Primordial and religious groups wield dominant influence. They maintain few links with other communal associations. An individual belongs to only a few groups, all of which have similar memberships. Permanently attached to these ascriptive groups, people cannot easily change their membership through achievement or persuasion. These rigid group ties contribute to the accumulation of communal and economic cleavages. When a single communal group dominates the government, coercion, not consensus, becomes a prime tactic for maintaining political order. Lacking peaceful options to reach their policy objectives, subordinate groups often resort to violent protest tactics. Hence, government coercion and violent protests pervade the policy process; social change rarely occurs through an accommodation of divergent group interests.[10]

Communal conflicts become violent because the political opportunity structures downplay ethnic tolerance, secular values, civil ties, and individual achievement. Ethnic hegemony takes precedence over empathy for other ethnic groups. Government officials reject equal rights before the law and equal access to educational opportunities and the labor market. Ascriptive considerations (ethnic or religious background), not individual merit, determine entrance to a university and employment in the civil service. As the dominant ethnic group centralizes government power, subordinate communal groups lose political rights and autonomy. As a result, younger, better-educated, alienated members of the repressed group often lead violent protests, such as riots, sabotage, terrorist acts, and guerrilla wars. Particularly when the national government either expands its coercive power over local communal groups or else yields some central control, the prospects for violent rebellion increase.[11]

Three societies – Northern Ireland, Sri Lanka, and Fiji – illustrate the difficulties of peacefully reconciling conflicts under communal pluralism. In each case, two communal groups compete for scarce resources. The politically dominant ethnic group uses government power to maintain or upgrade its economic position. Current political developments reflect the heritage of British rule, which strengthened domestic communal cleavages.

Political violence in Northern Ireland emerges from the reinforcement of ethnic, religious, and economic cleavages. Historical memories inflame contemporary passions between Catholics and Protestants. During the twelfth century, the British government conquered Ireland. Five centuries later Protestant English and Scottish settlers gained control over land and government. Catholic Irish held few political or economic rights. In the 1916 Easter Uprising, Irish Catholic nationalists compared their martyrdom with the sacrificial death of Christ. For them, the rebirth of the Irish nation resembled Christ's resurrection. Opposed to this Irish independence movement, the Presbyterians in Ireland viewed themselves as an elect people chosen by God to resist Catholic domination. Committed to maintain the covenant with God, they perceived Northern Ireland as the promised land and the Catholic Irish as the Canaanites. After the First World War the British government granted independence to the Catholic areas of Ireland. The six northern counties dominated by Protestants became incorporated into the United Kingdom in 1921. Today the Protestants represent two-thirds of the Northern Ireland population; most see themselves as British. Even though Catholics speak English, they identify with the Irish ethnic group. Educated in public Protestant schools, Protestants fear rule by the Catholics in the Irish Republic to the south. Most Catholic youths attend Catholic schools subsidized by the government. Economic inequalities reinforce the ethnic/religious cleavages. Protestants dominate larger industries, small businesses, and the security forces. They also comprise the skilled working class employed by shipbuilding, aircraft, and electrical industries. In contrast, Catholics work mainly as less skilled laborers. Areas with the highest ratios of Catholics generally contain the greatest unemployment rates. During the mid-1980s, over one-third of the Catholic male labor force but only 15 percent of Protestant male workers were unemployed.

Government institutions and policies strengthen the communal and economic inequalities. Protestants dominated the Northern Ireland government from 1921 through 1972; since then, the British administration has wielded direct rule. Protestants and English control law enforcement, courts, local government institutions, and access to public housing. Neither civil ties nor national integrating institutions bind the Protestant and Catholic communities together. Whereas most Protestants have supported the two Unionist parties (Ulster, Democratic), Catholics have voted for the Social Democratic and Labour Party as well as Sinn Fein, an ally of the Provisional Irish Republican Army. Nearly half the Protestants prefer integration between Northern Ireland and Britain; fewer want devolution with power-sharing or majority rule. Catholics, however, support devolution and shared power between the two religious communities. Around one fourth, especially young working class Catholics, favor a united Ireland. Over half the Catholic population rejects the Sinn Fein. Support for its program and the violent actions of the IRA comes mainly from unemployed young Catholics who remain committed to a union between the two Irelands and who participate with each other in male networks that pervade segregated neighborhoods. Some Catholics imprisoned for political violence perceive the British as Roman imperialists and view themelves as crucified martyrs. For example, Bobby Sands, who died in the 1981 prison hunger strike, saw himself as a Christ-like figure taking up the cross of national liberation so that others would gain redemption through his sacrifice.

The lack of civil values, shared cultural interpretations, and such national integrating institutions as political parties and comprehensive public schools has intensified communal violence. Militant Catholics and Protestants hold polarized interpretations about the political causes of deprivation and about the other group's motives. Magnifying differences with the outgroup, each side projects aggression on its 'enemy.' As a result, assassinations, armed robberies, bomb explosions, and high homicide rates have plagued Northern Ireland since 1969. Political violence has especially afflicted residents in North and West Belfast as well as in districts bordering the Republic of Ireland.[12]

Sri Lanka, another bicommunal society, has recently suffered from political violence. Religious cleavages intensify the primordial divisions. Sinhalese comprise 74 percent of the population; most practice Buddhism. Eighteen percent are Tamils, who form two groups. The indigenous Tamils arrived on the island nearly 2000 years ago; the 'Indian Tamils' came during the nineteenth century as workers on the coffee and tea plantations. Both Tamil groups are Hindu. Muslims from South India constitute the remaining ethno-religious group. British colonial rule in Ceylon (the former name of Sri Lanka) favored the minority Tamils in civil service recruitment and university education. Perceiving that the British administrators disriminated against the Sinhalese Buddhists, the Buddhist monks spearheaded the movement for national independence. After gaining independence from Britain in 1948, two Sinhalese-dominated parties – the United National Party (UNP) and the Sri Lanka Freedom Party (SLFP) – controlled government power. Under SLFP rule, Ceylon became the Republic of Sri Lanka in 1972.

Although the two Sinhalese parties disagreed over economic policies, both enacted programs that advanced Sinhalese values and interests at the expense of the Tamils. The government declared Sinhala the official language; Tamils who spoke Tamil or English faced difficulties gaining entrance to universities and securing civil service positions. Education and employment policies favored the Sinhalese. Whereas before the 1960s urban Sinhalese and Tamils attended the same English-language secondary schools, after 1956 the two ethnic groups experienced a different curriculum based on language, not on common linguistic or civil ties. A quota system for university admissions benefited the Sinhalese, especially in the prestigious science field. Tamils not only gained fewer opportunities for a university education but also faced discrimination in civil service appointments. Whereas before 1956 Tamils comprised around 30 percent of civil service jobs, today they hold only 5 percent. State nationalization of private industries, such as tea, rubber, and coconut, enabled Sinhalese to gain jobs as managers and other employees in the state corporations. Thus the educated Tamil minority lost access to university education and public sector employment. Although the Sinhalese suffered from an overall higher unemployment rate, secondary-school and university Sinhalese graduates faced lower joblessness than did similarly educated Tamils. Many from this group joined the Tamil United Liberation Front and guerrilla movements (for example, Liberation Tigers of Tamil Eelam), which seek political independence for the Tamil-dominated northern and eastern provinces. Sinhalese groups, especially the Janatha Vimukti Peramuna, conducted political violence against state officials, Tamils, and Indian government troops, who occupied Sri Lanka from 1987 through 1990. As a response to all these protests, the government implemented various authoritarian measures – martial law, curfews, censorship, electoral fraud, and restrictions on free association. Dominated by the Sinhalese, the army and police curtailed civil liberties.

The Sinhalese focus on ethnic hegemony and Buddhist values has subordinated economic conflicts to communal cleavages, which have inflamed violent protests and state repression. Buddhist monks perceive the Sinhalese as the 'lion race' destined to maintain 'Aryan' blood purity against the defiled 'Dravidian' Tamils. For them, the Sri Lankan motherland, the Sinhalese ethnic group, and the Buddhist faith all congeal. Buddhism has become the state religion, even though other churches retain freedom of worship. Economic disputes between the United National Party, which supports 'capitalist' business interests, and the Sri Lanka Freedom Party, which advocates a populist 'socialism,' assume a subordinate place in electoral appeals. Both parties, especially the SLFP, urge all Sinhalese, whatever their economic status, to back them against the minority Tamils. Thus primordial-religious values override more compromisable economic interests. Lacking powerful civil values and national integrating institutions, Sri Lanka experiences the political disorder linked to communal pluralism.[13]

The South Pacific islands of Fiji have also faced the destabilizing consequences of bicommunal pluralism. Like Ceylon, Fiji functioned as a British colony. The British government seized control in 1874 and ruled until 1970, when Fiji became independent. British colonial policies consolidated the power of the indigenous Fijians, who in 1986 comprised around 46 percent of the population. Through the indirect rule system, British officials recruited paramount chiefs and nobles into the Fijian administration. Fijians gained special land rights. Brought to Fiji by the British in the late 1800s, the Indians originally worked as indentured laborers on the sugar plantations; they gained little access to land ownership. Today Fijians hold 81 percent of the land; Indians own only 2 percent. (Europeans and the Crown possess the remaining land.)

The Indo-Fijians wield limited political power. Fijians control the civil service, the police, and the Royal Fijian Military Forces. Most political elites belong to the Great Council of Chiefs. Dominated by the paramount chiefs, the Alliance Party governed Fiji from 1970 until spring 1987. Communal voting arrangements strengthened the Alliance Party's control of government. According to these electoral procedures, Fijians, Indians, and Europeans each received a proportional number of seats in the fifty-two-member House of Representatives – 22 for Fijians, 22 for Indians, and 8 for Europeans. Because the Europeans always voted for the Alliance Party and most Fijians supported that party, it usually won the elections. Yet in the April 1987 election, low growth rates, rising unemployment, and wage reductions enabled a coalition of the multiethnic Fiji Labour Party and the Indian-dominated National Federation Party to win a majority of seats to the legislature. One month later, however, parliamentary democracy ceased. The Royal Fijian Military Forces, dominated by Fijians who comprise 97 percent of the personnel, staged a coup to restore the Alliance Party to government power. Later that September a second coup ended party rule and strengthened control by the army and police. Young retired Fijian veterans who had served overseas and then joined the Fijian administration spearheaded the two coups. Fearing lower military budgets, reduced personnel, and the entrance of numerous Indians into the army, these soldiers sought to protect the military's professional autonomy.

The military coups occurred against a backdrop of political polarization but economic differentiation. Divergent economic interests fragment each ethnic community. Among the Fijians, the aristocratic chiefs strive to retain their dominance over the commoners. Whereas the chiefs rule the eastern islands, more commoners live in the western islands – the site of sugar monopolies and poverty. Fijian aristocrats control most land and lease it to small-scale Fijian farmers. Other commoners work as wage laborers on the sugar plantations or in the cities. Recently, many Fijian chiefs have become urban commercial enterprisers. Even though the Indians came to Fiji during the late nineteenth century as indentured servants, today they have become wealthier than the Fijians. Yet like the Fijians, the Indians also are economically differentiated. They work as small sugar-cane farmers, skilled laborers, traders, and urban professionals, including civil servants, teachers, lawyers, and physicians. Along with the urban Fiji unemployed youths and west island Fiji commoners, these Indian groups backed the Fiji Labour Party in the April 1987 election. Led by unions of civil servants and teachers, the Labour Party advocated a nonethnic state with more equal opportunities for poorer Fijians and Indians. Its commitment to 'democratic socialism' actually reflected a policy preference for competitive capitalism, low interest rates, greater wage equality, and recruitment to the civil service on the basis of achievement criteria, not ethnic affiliation. Fearful of losing their power, the paramount chiefs and the military led by Colonel Rabuka staged the coup one month after the Labour Party gained office.

After seizing government control in 1987, the armed forces began implementing repressive policies that downplayed economic conflicts and exploited communal cleavages splitting the Fijians from the Indians. Even though the Fijians made up only 46-47 percent of the population, 'Fiji for the Fijians' became a rallying cry of the new military government. The 1990 Constitution legitimated the dominant power of the Fijians over government institutions. The constitution allocated over one-half the seats in the House of Representatives and at least 75 percent of Senate seats to Fijians. Electoral malapportionment procedures favored rural Fijians and the eastern region over urban and western residents, who form the major opposition against the Fiji aristocracy. The paramount chiefs choose the president; he then appoints the prime minister and members of the public service and police service commissions. Both the president and prime minister must be Fijian. Under quota provisions, Fijians secured over 60 percent of civil service positions. Indians gained fewer than two-fifths of government jobs. Education and economic policies strove to increase the Fijian elites' socioconomic status. Opposed to the wealthier, better educated, urbanized Indian proessionals, the government gave preferential treatment to Fijians who applied for admission to the University of the South Pacific. Aristocratic chiefs retained control over the allocation of land. Government contracts, licenses, subsidies, loans, and tax concessions went to Fijian chiefs who were moving into commercial enterprises. State repression helped implement these policies that increased Fijian elites' economic influence. Censorship, imprisonment, detainment, and internal security decrees restrained anti-government dissidents, whether Fiji commoners or Indians. Crackdowns on unions curtailed organized opposition to the military government's elitist policies. Civilian rule returned in early 1990; however, parliamentary elections did not occur until May 1992. At that election, the Fijian Political Party, established a year earlier by the Great Council of Chiefs, won 30 of the 70 seats to the House of Representatives. The FPP head, Major General Rabuka, became prime minister and formed a coalition with the second largest Indian party, the Fiji Labour Party, which secured 13 seats. In short, even though civilian govern ment ruled Fiji, military officers still played a key policy role. After consolidating Fijian control, Rabuka estabished a coalition with his former adversaries to gain a parliamentary majority. Agreements to repeal antilabor laws, abolish the value-added tax, and review the 1990 constitution for possible amendments secured legislative support from the Fiji Labour Party (FLP). Less than two years later, Prime Minister Rabuka lost this parliamentary ally when the FLP rejected his budget proposals. Yet in the February 1994 elections, the Fijian Political Party gained 31 out of 70 legislative seats. Allied with independents, Rabuka retained the prime ministership.[14] Under both liberal and even communal pluralism, coalition formation becomes an essential strategy to maintain government power.

As the Fiji case illustrates, the communal pluralist approach understimates the importance of economic differentiation within primordial and religious groups. Stressing the value cleavages between opposed communal groups, it minimizes the political–economic interest conflicts dividing each group. Class conflict pervades communal cleavages. Struggles between political elites and mass members pervade communal associations.

## RADICAL PLURALISM

Rejecting the elitism of both liberal and communal pluralism, radical pluralists protest unequal power relationships. According to the radical pluralists, in formally democratic societies, political parties, voluntary associations, and government institutions represent the interests of the wealthiest classes, who play the most active role in political life. Whereas powerless, disorganized individuals have few resources to shape public policies, politically powerful elites gain a veto over policies to transform the status quo. Liberal pluralism assumes that change emerges slowly through incremental means. Yet pluralist systems in North America and Western Europe seem plagued by deadlocked government, immobilism, and stalemate. The incrementalist strategy for piecemeal, marginal change produces extreme caution, for it relies on past solutions to meet present and future challenges. The resulting 'science of muddling through' often leads to inertia. Liberal pluralists perceive diverse groups competing for scarce resources. Although no single group secures all its demands, every group supposedly gains some satisfaction. Political settlements represent mutual adjustments. In the empirical political world, however, some groups never get any of their demands satisfied. To the powerless and their radical advocates, the rules of the liberal pluralist game appear as ways to maintain the privileges of the advantaged, who dominate the policy process through inordinate control over money, information, and organizational–communications skills. Even if citizens enjoy equality before the law, they endure unequal wealth and status. Rules regulating individual competition for scarce resources impede the pursuit of shared public goals that transcend self-interests. Why should outgroups accept rules that seem biased against their well-being? Societies operating under communal pluralism suffer greater political disorder than do liberal pluralist systems. Political elites deny ethnic and religious outgroups equal access to the public policy process and to policy benefits. Conflicts over material interests transform into deeper value conflicts. As a result, violent protests ensue. Political elites rely on state repression, including military coups, to maintain their power.

Radical pluralists seek a political system based on equality, decentralization, and widespread popular participation. Opposed to both the centralized bureaucratic state and to oligopolistic economic institutions, radical pluralists strive to organize the unorganized, empower the weak, and enrich the poor. Such populist structures as tenant rights' organizations, citizens' action groups, communes, syndicalist unions, workers' councils, ecological associations, antinuclear movements, producers' cooperatives, health clinics, and rape crisis centers expand participatory rights and government access to individuals formerly excluded from the policy process. These include women, youths, ecologists, renters, workers, consumers, and the disabled. Through local self-governing units like elected village and city councils, citizens cooperate with others to resolve pressing social problems: toxic waste, crime, bad housing conditions, inadequate schools. Local community control with a focus on mutual assistance takes precedence over reliance on a centralized state or elitist business enterprises. Mass political parties with democratic decision processes formulate general policies. Rather than striving merely to win elections, these parties organize mass participation. Factory committees, not bureaucratic unions, establish worker control of industry. Employees manage producers' cooperatives. In private and public jobs, clerks and managers share decisionmaking authority. Communes give rank-and-file citizens the opportunity to shape their destinies. Radical pluralists assume that each person can perform various different roles. A factory worker needs no managerial specialists to tell him how to perform his job. Although an office clerk may not have millions of dollars to press her demands on government policymakers, she has other potential assets – intelligence, political efficacy, a cooperative spirit – that can be used for shaping public decisions.

For radical pluralists, the ideal political system enables each person to realize equality with his or her fellows. Regardless of social status, all people gain the right to become actively involved in political decisionmaking. Radical pluralists assume that small-scale, decentralized structures will most effectively secure social change through spontaneous, consensual strategies. Widespread participation in egalitarian associations enables citizens to learn the norms of persuasion, cooperation, mutual obligation, and civic duty necessary for political order as well as social change.

Radical pluralistic movements exert greater policy influence at the local level than over the national arena. A coalition of leftist parties, including the Communist Party of India–Marxist and the Communist Party of India, governed the Indian state of Kerala from 1957 through 1991. Along with labor unions and peasant associations, the communist parties worked to secure greater land equality, higher literacy, and better health for the citizens. Despite its poverty (GNP per capita), Kerala by the early 1990s had secured a lower infant mortality rate, longer life expectancy, higher educational enrollments, more land redistribution, and greater opportunities for women than had India or most other less developed countries. Populist movements stimulated widespread citizen participation to attain these collective goals. For instance, the Kerala People's Science Movement mobilized local popular participation through health camps, literacy programs, village study classes, puppet shows, and theater troupes. These populist activities encouraged low-income people to press for mass education policies, maternal health centers, a cleaner environment, and methods to reduce AIDS fatalities.

Similarly, in several southern cities within Brazil, the *Partido dos Trabalhadores* (Workers' Party) has mobilized low-income individuals of the *favelas* (slums) behind policies to improve their living conditions. Neighborhood residents join committees, which then select members to *conselhos populares* (popular councils). These councils interact with city administrations governed by the Workers' Party to formulate and implement public policies about garbage collection, sewage treatment, health care, mass education, child care centers, paved streets, housing, and electricity. Through extensive popular participation, the administration of municipal public services becomes democratized.

In the United States groups such as the National People's Action (NPA) pressed Congress to implement policies that grant greater funds and decentralize more control to neighborhood programs like low-income housing, energy assistance, and drug prevention. Echoing the Kansas populist Mary Ellen Lease, who urged her followers during the late nineteenth century to 'raise less corn and more hell,' the NPA struggles to 'give the Democrats guts and the Republicans hell.' Yet it more effectively articulated proposals than secured the implementation of congressional programs. At the urban level, however, populist protesters increased the representation of diverse groups, enacted environmental impact reviews, secured some congressional block grants, and expanded social service activities like day-care, health, and legal counsel. Populist programs to achieve greater income redistribution, community planning, and regulation of capital fared less well.

However great the local influence of populist movements, radical pluralism remains more an ideal than a structural political reality at the national level. Hostile to organizational control mechanisms, radical pluralists often encounter problems of maintaining the viability of participatory, decentralized associations. The lack of strong political institutions and specific strategies impedes the generation of sufficient power to produce extensive change. Without the organizational means to implement populist preferences, the slogans of 'people vs profits,' 'health vs wealth,' and 'quality of life vs rapid economic growth' remain unfulfilled. Furthermore, many contemporary problems, like bad health, toxic waste, unemployment, and homelessness stem from decisions made outside the local community – at the national and even international level. Decentralized attempts to resolve these challenges face difficulties, particularly when conservative forces retain the national government power to block populist initiatives. Finally, extensive mass participation in public policymaking may so raise demands and deplete the supply of government resources that radical pluralists cannot easily attain their policy goals. Particularly when the consumption of present resources outstrips the investment of new resources, the political arena resembles a negative-sum game. Conservative elites fear losing their wealth, status, and political power. They perceive that popular spontaneity leads to political disorder and unwanted social changes. Marginals who fail to realize their demands become disillusioned with mass political participation. Popular apathy and conservative opposition enervate the policy process. As a result, the radical participatory structures become vulnerable to disintegration, accommodation with conservative interests, or overthrow by more bureaucratic, hierarchical institutions.[15]

## CONCLUSION

Liberal, communal, and radical pluralists play the political game in different ways. Voluntary associations, especially economic interest groups and civic action organizations, constitute the main players in the liberal pluralist game. Mediating between the central government and the individual, these associations represent group members' interests to public policymakers and also check government power. Coalitional political parties, representative legislatures, independent courts, and comprehensive public schools secure political order by upholding the value of civility and the rules of the political game. Through negotiations, bargains, tradeoffs, and coalition formation, these integrating organizations accommodate diverse interests and hence realize incremental social changes. Taking an optimistic view, liberal pluralists view politics as a positive-sum game where all players share some policy benefits.

In contrast, communal pluralists pessimistically assume that the political process resembles a zero-sum game where some communal groups gain at the expense of others. Primordial and religious groups represent the main players. Communal elites make the key decisions; rank-and-file members from divergent ethnic or religious groups maintain few political contacts with each other. Ethnic/religious and economic cleavages often accumulate. Lacking economic equality, shared consensual values, and national integrating institutions, communal pluralist societies face political disorder when the dominant communal group gains control over government institutions and represses subordinate groups. Despite efforts to disperse political power to primordial groups through such structural mechanisms as communal voting rolls, regional autonomy, and federalism, these techniques have rarely secured a peaceful management of conflicts. State repression by the dominant communal group and violent protests by subordinate groups constitute the major strategies for attaining social change. Especially when the economic growth rate declines, the scarce supply of resources means that the ruling communal leaders use their government power to reward members of their own ethnic/religious group with civil service jobs, university scholarships, licenses, contracts, subsidies, loans, and tax concessions. The excluded communal groups receive fewer policy benefits.

Attacking the economic elitism of liberal pluralism and the primordial–religious elitism of communal pluralism, radical pluralists attempt to expand the political game so that more diverse players participate. Even though they want youths, women, low-income persons, and the handicapped to play a greater role in political life, radical pluralist leaders themselves usually come from the 'new middle class' of professionals, intellectuals, white-collar employees, and university students. They optimistically assume that widened participation will promote, rather than impede, political order. Only through actively participating in such decentralized structures as city councils, town meetings, cooperatives, tenants' rights organizations, communes, worker-managed factories, and ecological associations will citizens learn the norms of cooperation, mutual assistance, and tolerance necessary for political order. Committed to socioeconomic equality, radical pluralists face difficulties framing public policies that will transform society. Mass members often become exhausted by protests and political mobilization. Particularly when policies do not secure concrete benefits, some citizens show disenchantment with radical pluralism. Others go along for the 'free ride,' ready to accept policy benefits but unwilling to bear the costs of time, taxes, and energy. In either case, political apathy results. Conservative elites who never supported efforts to expand political participation and social equality impede the radical pluralist policy process. They mount investment strikes, sabotage, and media defamation campaigns. Confronted by mass apathy and conservative opposition, the radical pluralist system usually collapses. For many players, politics has become a negative-sum game. Without the powerful organizations to coordinate mass activities and resist conservative elites, radical pluralists cannot easily transform society.

# 7 Theories of the World System

However appealing the radical pluralist vision of a small-scale, decentralized political system, today large-scale institutions in the world system make the crucial decisions that affect human lives. Protesters can no longer just think globally and act locally but must also consider the impact of transnational institutions on people everywhere. The major powers, along with minor regional powers, now possess nuclear weapons that can destroy millions in a catastrophic war. Investment decisions of multinational corporations determine employment opportunities and economic growth all over the world. Various intergovernmental agencies, such as the United Nations, its specialized agencies, the World Bank, the International Monetary Fund (IMF), and the Organization of Petroleum-Exporting Countries (OPEC), enact policies that shape nearly everyone's health, education, and economic well-being. Transnational social movements – for example, Amnesty International, Greenpeace International, the International Fellowship of Reconciliation, Disabled People's International, and Service for Peace and Justice in Latin America – play key roles on the world stage. As these movements interact with individual citizens, national government officials, and heads of international institutions, they struggle to prevent war, settle conflicts peacefully, and lessen the destructive consequences of rapid economic growth.

The exploration of political institutions in the world system focuses on three key issues. First, which agencies make the crucial decisions in the global arena? The interactions among the nation-state, domestic social groups, other states, intergovernmental organizations, and nongovernmental organizations shape the performance of the world system. To understand the international political power of each structure, we need to ascertain its resources, including military, diplomatic, economic, demographic, and informational capabilities. To what extent are these resources concentrated or dispersed among states, social groups, and international institutions? How do historical changes in resources among these structures affect the likelihood of warfare and rapid economic growth?[1]

Second, since the time of Thucydides' account of the Peloponnesian war between Athens and Sparta (431–404 BCE), political analysts have probed the causes of order (peace) and disorder (war) in the world system. Warfare represents a protest against the international status quo. What structural interactions among the state, domestic social groups, and transnational organizations escalate a conflict into warfare between states? By initiating a war or responding to a threat with military, rather than diplomatic means, government leaders make crucial policies that affect not only their own citizens but people beyond their borders. During the twentieth century the two world wars – 1914–1918 and 1939–1945 – brought more military and civilian casualties than any other wars in history. We probe the reasons for these two world wars and for the greater peace among the major powers after 1945.

A third issue revolves around the international causes of social change, especially economic growth. Even though domestic policies obviously influence the economic growth rates, government officials must frame their policies in light of world conditions. Hence, the interactions between a nation-state, on the one hand, and other states, multinational corporations, and intergovernmental agencies (IMF, World Bank, OPEC), on the other, affect national growth. What international structural conditions caused the higher national growth rates after 1945 than between the two world wars (1920–1940)?

Social scientists have formulated three theoretical approaches that explain international power relationships, war, and economic growth. Focusing on military power, structural realists perceive that in the contemporary world system each nation-state retains extensive independence from other states. More concerned with intergovernmental and nongovernmental organizations, the liberal institutional approach sees greater interdependence among nation-states, which primarily seek economic growth and material benefits for their citizens. By contrast, the capitalist world-economy interpretation of Immanuel Wallerstein assumes that capital accumulation and the search for profits override all other goals in the modern world-system. Wealth, particularly the control over physical and financial capital, comprises the key resource for wielding international power. The capitalist class in the core societies dominates the world market. Other areas – the semiperiphery and especially the peripheral zone – remain dependent on the capitalist core. Table 7.1 summarizes the general assumptions of the three theoretical approaches.

## STRUCTURAL REALISM

The realist perspective on world politics originated with the writings of Thucydides, who analyzed the Peloponnesian war during the fifth century BCE. For Thucydides, power constituted the basic element of international relations. The dominant Greek city-states of his time – Athens and Sparta – struggled to maintain and expand their power. Security and survival constituted the main drives motivating their leaders. Changes in the balance of power brought war between the two city-states. According to Thucydides, 'The growth of the power of Athens, and the alarm which this inspired in [Sparta], made war inevitable.'[2] A rising power, Athens challenged the hegemonic position of Sparta. Athenian ambition provoked fear among the Spartans. War ensued. In this war, power overrode all concepts of moral righteousness. Might made right. According to the Athenians, no third party could remain neutral in this bipolar struggle: 'Right, as the world goes, is only in question between equals in power, while the strong do what they can and the weak suffer what they must. . . . An intending ally does not rely on the goodwill of those who ask his aid but on a decided superiority of power for action.'[3] Even though the Melians tried to remain neutral between Athens and Sparta, Athenian leaders would not accept a neutral strategy. As the massacred Melians learned to their horror, military power transcended justice and ethical commitments.

At the start of the Renaissance, Machiavelli took a similar perspective about the primacy of interest and power in the world arena. During his lifetime, the modern nation-state began to emerge throughout West Europe. State rulers concentrated on securing, maintaining, and expanding political power. Amid this world of scarce resources and insatiable ambitions for greater power, wealth, property, and status, war became inevitable among states. Through imperialism and war, political rulers could maintain the state, cement national loyalty, promote military

200

*Table* 7.1  Structural theories of the world system

| | Structural realism | Liberal institutionalism | Capitalist world-economy |
|---|---|---|---|
| Key decisionmaking structures | Several unified nation-states with powerful armed forces and diplomatic staffs. | Pluralistic, fragmented nation-states; intergovernmental agencies; nongovernmental organizations. | World class system operating in world market economy; core/semiperiphery/periphery hierarchy; interstate system of unequally powerful and competing nation-states. |
| Causes of war and bases of peace | Peace depends on a stable balance of power. War stems from the uneven growth of power resources among competing states. | International institutions promote world cooperation based on free trade (World Bank, IMF, EC), improved socioeconomic conditions (UN specialized agencies), and democratic practices (Amnesty International). | Uneven development of capital accumulation produces conflict over scarce resources (raw materials, investment opportunities, trade) among competing core societies. This conflict leads to struggles between core states and peripheral zones. |
| Causes of economic growth | High growth stems from a powerful state that implements efficient domestic and international policies. Growth also derives from a hegemonic state that promotes free world trade and a stable world currency. | High growth stems from free trade, overseas-investment, and diffusion of ideas from industrialized countries to less developed societies. | Economic growth stems from union of agro-industrial, commercial, and financial sectors and from balance between high consumption and high production in the world market. |

courage, and enhance mass obedience to the new nation-states then arising in England, France, Spain, Portugal, the Nether-lands, and Italy.[4]

Contemporary realists divide into two camps: classical realism and neorealism. Both approaches assume that the world arena functions under anarchy; no transnational world government can regulate conflicts among nation-states. For both types of realists, the nation-state constitutes a key decisionmaking unit; it retains autonomy from any supranational organization. These nation-states pursue their own interests, defined as power, security, territorial control, and sovereign independence. The distribution of power (capabilities, resources) among nation-states shapes their tendency to initiate or expand a war. Operating in a dangerous, conflict-laden interational environment, nation-states function as unitary, rational actors. Prudence, strategic calculations, and skepticism about the possibilities of realizing world peace guide their foreign policies. World politics represents a zero-sum game. Confronting military threats to national security, statesmen can achieve only relative gains.

In other respects, however, classical realists and neorealists articulate different views of the world system. Like Thucydides and Machiavelli, classical realists – Hans Morgenthau, E. H. Carr, Raymond Aron, Arnold Wolfers – adopt an inductive approach that stresses historical changes, complexity, and empirical reality. They assert the dominance of politics and the nation-state over economic concerns. According to them, the maximization of power represents the dominant goal of national statesmen. War and social change stem from the actions of nation-states. In contrast, the neorealists or structural realists, especially Kenneth Waltz, take a deductive, axiomatic view of the international system – an approach that borrows assumptions about anarchy, self-interest, rationality, and utility maximization from neoclassical microeconomics. Focusing on two major variables – anarchical structure and interacting units (nation-states) – Waltz simplifies empirical reality in order to highlight theoretical explanations of the specific causes producing some effect like the outbreak of war. Rather than seek to maximize power as an end in itself, most national leaders regard power as a means to achieve greater security. Even though nations cause war, their actions derive not only from national structural conditions but more importantly from the structure of the world system –

that is, anarchy, the number of great powers (bipolarity vs multipolarity), the distribution of resources among states and alliances, and the degree of solidarity within each alliance.[5] In the following analyses, we will explore the assumptions made primarily by such neorealists as Waltz, Robert Gilpin, A. F. Organski, and Stephen Krasner.

From the neorealist perspective, nation-states operate as the dominant actors in the world political system. They seek to maintain or expand their power through military force, diplomacy, alliances, and geopolitical strategies. State leaders achieve unified control around their pursuit of sovereignty, security, and survival. Nation-states remain independent from control by national business firms, other domestic groups, and multinational corporations. Other institutions of the global system include intergovernmental organizations such as the United Nations, the Organization of American States, the Organization of African Unity, the Arab League, and the International Monetary Fund. All these organizations comprise nation-states, which retain sovereign authority. No world government operates to enforce a peaceful resolution of conflicts among independent nation-states. Instead, they live under a Hobbesian condition of international anarchy – a state of nature plagued by 'continual fear and danger of violent death' and by a 'restless desire of power after power that ceases only in death.'[6]

Structural realists (neorealists) perceive power relationships among nation-states as the major reason behind warfare. When power resources (military, economic, demographic) show an uneven growth among states, dominant states with declining capabilities feel threatened by insecurity and may fight the challenger that seeks a change in the international status quo. Challenging states with rising capabilities resent the dominant power that prevents them from playing a leading role; hence, they may resort to war, attempting to expand their power vis-à-vis the hegemonic state and to change the rules of the world system. As nation-states change their power positions, other states perceive greater insecurity to the political independence of their nation's territory. To counter the perceived threat, alliances expand. This external threat and the growth of military technology cause arms races to escalate. Nation-states polarize around opposition blocs. The resulting 'tight' alliances deter peaceful interactions and crosscutting ties among rival states in the two blocs. International politics becomes a zero-sum game. To the challenger that dominates one bloc, the costs of war seem low but the benefits from initiating a war appear higher. To the defender that leads the opposing alliance, the costs of yielding to the challenger outweigh the costs of fighting the adversary. In sum, world wars most likely erupt when several states with extensive resources become polarized in two major blocs with roughly equal resources.[7]

These structural conditions among states explain both the First and the Second World War. Before the First World War, Germany was increasing its military and economic capabilities vis-à-vis Britain, the declining hegemonic power. During the early twentieth century, alliances became more polarized. Imperial Germany allied with Austria–Hungary and Italy against Britain, France, and Russia. No widely accepted international agreements enforced agreements on rules for settling interstate conflicts between opposition blocs. A devastating war resulted. Similarly, during the 1930s two late industrializing nations – Nazi Germany and Japan – expanded their military and economic power against Britain, France, and the United States, which were suffering from the great depression. Germany wanted to conquer both West and East Europe. Japan sought conquest over China and Southeast Asia. These changing power positions heightened other states' insecurity. Neither the League of Nations nor the Permanent Court of International Justice wielded sufficient power to restrain aggressive behavior by Nazi Germany, Fascist Italy, and Japan. Domestic opposition in Britain and France impeded an alliance with the Soviet Union against the European Axis powers. Another world war began in 1939.

In contrast, after the Second World War, structural conditions produced a more peaceful era among the major powers. As the dominant victors in the Second World War, the United States and the Soviet Union competed against each other in a loose bipolar world system. Although the US attained a higher level of economic development, both superpowers maintained a military parity. Japan and Germany renounced military expansion and focused on increasing economic growth through export sales. The United Nations and its specialized agencies provided some institutional bases for cooperation between the two dominant nation-states. By maintaining a non-aligned position, a few influential Third World states such as India promoted a flexible bipolar situation. Given these structural conditions, the major powers felt little inclination to start wars with each other.[8] Instead, the major violent conflicts occurred in the developing nations.

Despite the plausibility of these propositions about the causes of war, the realist interpretation exaggerates the importance of structural interactions among states and downplays the impact of foreign policymakers' attitudes, perceptions, and expectations. As expected-utility (rational choice) theorists such as Bueno de Mesquita have pointed out, leaders within institutions make the crucial foreign policy decisions. These institutions pose constraints and opportunities to nation-state leaders, whose preferences, goals, expectations, and perceptions determine a state's policy to wage war. Government officials' responses to the world power situation, especially to changes in states' power positions, explain the decision to escalate a conflict into war.

Generally, if foreign policymakers show a strong willingness to take risks, they will more likely initiate a war than will risk-averse leaders. Risk-prone attitudes stem from the perception that the expected gains from war outweigh the expected benefits from peace and that the costs of peace exceed the costs of war. State leaders anticipate that victory will result from military actions; military success will bring desirable consequences. Dissatisfied with the international status quo, war-minded decisionakers retain an intense commitment to such policy priorities as territorial expansion, military dominance, or religious–ideological conversion. For them, war secures high international prestige. Rather than viewing war as irrational, these leaders glorify war, perceiving it as an inevitable struggle that invigorates the national character. This romantic concept morally justifies war. The decision to wage war also stems from the expectation that military actions will lead to victory. This expectation of success depends on the perception of states' intentions, capabilities, and actions. War usually results when state leaders exaggerate the hostile intentions of an enemy state, perceiving that an adversary will attack immediately. Since war appears inevitable, a first strike seems necessary. In rarer instances, government officials underestimate the hostile intentions of their adversaries and fail to prepare for an unexpected war. Decisions to wage war also emerge when risk-prone leaders underestimate an enemy's power capabilities but exaggerate their own military and economic resources. Because of this exaggeration, aggressive state leaders perceive that their adversaries have neither the power nor the will to retaliate if attacked. Thus the expected gains of waging war outweigh the expected punishment (retaliation) from committing an aggressive act. Furthermore, estimations about a state's own allies and its adversary's allies shape policies to instigate a war. War-prone leaders perceive a cohesive alliance for their own nation but a fragmented alliance among opponent states, which supposedly lack a shared preference for war. Hence, when military action erupts, the aggressor estimates that its allies will coalesce behind the war effort to a far greater extent than allies linked to the enemy nation.

In contrast, peaceful interactions among nation-states result when foreign policymakers assume risk-averse attitudes. Expected losses from military actions override the expected gains. War appears as undesirable – as an irrational way to attain goals. Policy priorities stress prosperity and economic growth, rather than territorial expansion, military aggrandizement, or religious–ideological conversion. Government leaders assume that war also represents a futile tactic for achieving their policy objectives. Calculating that war can be avoided through negotiation, they perceive that other national leaders have peaceful intentions. These risk-averse decisionmakers exaggerate the opponents' war capabilities but underestimate their own military and economic power. Policymakers seeking to challenge the status quo through military force view the defender's retaliatory power as credible. Deterrence policies succeed because the challengers perceive that the defender state has superior military/economic power and the will to retaliate against aggression. The alliance structure further reinforces the effectiveness of deterrence strategies. Leaders challenging the world status quo perceive tight alliances among opponent states but only loose alliances for their own states. Hence, policymakers contemplating military aggression maintain few expectations that their allies will support the escalation of a conflict into war. Instead, the challengers calculate that their adversary's allies will support retaliation against aggression. As a result, they adopt a risk-averse attitude, preferring negotiation and other peaceful strategies as the best way to secure their policy goals.

Unlike the situation before the First and Second World Wars, after 1945 these perceptual conditions largely contributed to the peaceful interactions among the major powers. Before the First World War, European state leaders, especially the Germans, viewed war as both inevitable and desirable. Taking a neo-Darwinian approach toward world politics, German elites perceived that warfare represented a necessary strategy for attaining national glory and for ensuring the survival of the fittest. Miscalculations and misperceptions about other states' intentions, capabiliies, and allied actions led to risk-prone policies. After that devastating war ended, most European leaders became disillusioned with war. Nevertheless, Hitler, Mussolini, and the Japanese generals retained the prewar conception of war as romantic, morally justified, and effective in realizing a state's objectives. All these aggressive leaders viewed warfare as invigorating the national race, promoting citizens' courage, and enhancing economic expansion. Leaders' perceptions about the benefits from war changed after the Second World War. During the postwar era, leaders of the two superpower blocs seemed risk-averse. For them, the costs of war outweighed its benefits. Second-strike nuclear capabilities held by the United States and the Soviet Union convinced their leaders that the prospects for victory in a nuclear war were dubious and that the costs of defeat were unbearable. Prosperity and economic growth became the major policy priorities for government officials. Thus peace prevailed among the major powers, if not within the less developed countries.[9]

Maintaining a statist orientation, structural realists assume that economic growth depends on a powerful state that implements efficient policies both domestically and internationally. A powerful state at home stimulates high productivity in land, labor, and capital. It supports rural development projects: irrigation facilities, land reclamation, rural electrification, roads. Extensive credits from state banks enable farmers to buy farm machinery, chemical fertilizers, and seeds that expand agricultural productivity. High prices for food encourage increased crop production. Public schools produce a highly skilled, technically trained, industrious labor force. Dedicated to economic growth and technological progress, state bureaucrats cooperate with private business managers to expand industrial capital investment. Through its control over loans from national banks and from multinational financial corporations, state policymakers encourage private enterprises to produce goods not only for the home market but especially for export. Multinational corporations, which supply needed capital, technology, and specialized innovative knowledge, remain subordinate to state control. They form joint ventures with either the national government or private business firms.

From the realist perspective, international structural conditions also facilitate rapid economic growth. Particularly when a hegemonic power committed to expanding the world market wields decisive influence over world economic transactions, then economic growth accelerates. Britain performed this hegemonic role from 1820 through 1914, when British financiers and traders dominated the world market. Even though Britain's hegemonic influence began to decline after 1890, economic growth rates of the industrialized capitalist societies remained fairly high. Between the two world wars, no hegemonic power maintained free trade and a sound currency. Protectionism, high tariffs, and economic nationalism caused economic stagnation and depression. After 1945, however, the United States assumed the hegemonic role, particularly from 1950 through 1973 – the years when the industrialized capitalist economies secured the highest growth rates during the 1820–1990 period. The US government promoted free trade, provided resources for international currency exchanges, and defended the world politico-economic system against challenges to its security. By upholding free trade and stable foreign exchange rates, several intergovernmental organizations influenced by the United States facilitated the market process throughout the world capitalist economy. These institutions included the Organization for Economic Cooperation and Development (OECD), the General Agreement on Tariffs and Trade, the World Bank, and the International Monetary Fund. They encouraged states to support low tariffs, technology transfers, guarantees for multinational investment, low taxes on foreign investment, and a 'sound' (not overvalued) currency that promoted export sales. According to the structural realists, these policies implemented by the United States, intergovernmental institutions, and other states contributed to the high growth rates immediately following the Second World War. When the United States' world economic influence began to decline after 1973, it could no longer guarantee free trade. International currency exchanges showed increasing volatility. Growth rates fell.[10]

# LIBERAL INSTITUTIONALISM

Whereas structural realists view the unified nation-state as the dominant actor in the world political system, liberal institution-alists take a more pluralist view of structural interactions. Several diverse interest groups and bureaucratic–political factions shape state policies. Instead of seeking just power and security, political leaders also strive for economic growth, prosperity, and material benefits for the citizenry. Physical capital, money, normative beliefs, and knowledge, not just military and diplomatic power, constitute key state resources. Besides the nation-state, other institutions like intergovernmental agencies and nongovernmental organizations play an influential role in the world arena. Influenced by the Enlightenment principles of Immanuel Kant, contemporary liberals believe that international law, a universal commitment to 'pure practical reason,' and international organizations of free states with representative institutions promote world peace.

Liberal institutionalists such as Robert Keohane, Joseph Nye, John Mueller, K. J. Holsti, and Richard Rosecrance define institutions to include organizations, practices, and permanent rules that guide international role behavior. Even though the nation-state remains primary, intergovernmental organizations such as the United Nations, its specialized agencies, the European Union, and the IMF have wielded extensive influence since the Second World War. Nongovernment organizations such as multinational corporations, the Roman Catholic Church, Green-peace, Oxfam, and Amnesty International also perform impor-tant functions. International rules comprise peace treaties, the General Agreement on Tariffs and Trade, the formal decisions reached by the International Court of Justice, the legal rights of sovereignty, and informal norms about reciprocal relations among states. Practices such as multilateral diplomacy and negotiations at peace conferences facilitate nonviolent interactions among states. All these institutions – organizations, rules, practices – promote interdependence within the world community. This interdependence leads to accommodation of national interests and to international cooperation. Unlike the structural realists, who stress the inevitable conflicts of interests among nation-states, liberal institutionalists take a more hopeful view about the possibility of forging cooperative links that unify diverse nations.

Even though pluralistic, the world system can realize some degree of peaceful order. Rather than a zero-sum game, world politics resembles a positive-sum game where all players secure mutual gains through cooperative endeavors.

From the liberal perspective, institutions attain a peaceful world by promoting international political cooperation, shaping socioeconomic conditions, and changing people's subjective attitudes. Power relationships within a nation and among nations affect cooperation and the occurrence of war. Dictatorial states usually wage wars of conquest. Democratic states, however, rarely fight each other. As the number of interactions among democratic states increases, the likelihood of war among them declines. Civil liberties encourage the peaceful settlement of domestic conflicts; fewer disputes escalate to war. Liberal pluralism vitalizes democratic societies. Autonomous media and organizations supporting world peace influence foreign policy-making. They communicate information about the material and human costs of lengthy wars. By belonging to several groups with different memberships, citizens become exposed to diverse opinions and express greater political tolerance. Diverse interests and crosspressures mitigate the intensity of group conflicts. National leaders hence feel less pressure to initiate aggressive policies against other societies as a way to alleviate domestic hostilities. Stressing the need to uphold conciliatory norms that peacefully reconcile conflicts, they rely on international mediation of disputes by other nation-states, intergovernmental organizations, and such transnational institutions as the Roman Catholic Church. Both national officials and citizens perceive that all democratic governments adhere to norms promoting cooperation, compromise, and accommodation of interstate disputes. Legal restraints on state officials' actions hinder violent actions against democratic states. Executive decisionmakers need to consult with various government agencies, especially legislatures. Civilian restrictions on autonomous actions by the armed forces also impede impulsive military actions against democracies. When nongovernmental organizations like Amnesty International uphold civil liberties throughout the world, they strengthen the prospects for peace.

Intergovernmental institutions also promote political cooperation among nations. International law, multilateral diplomacy, and organizations such as the United Nations, the European

Union, the Conference on Security and Cooperation in Europe, the Organization of African Unity, and the World Court perform several integrating functions. They communicate shared goals, specify procedures for conflict resolution, monitor compliance with international agreements, enforce verification schemes, facilitate mutual benefits, stabilize expectations about states' behavior, and reduce transaction costs so that mutual gains exceed a state's losses. Particularly during the 1950s and 1960s, the United Nations organization helped to lessen violence that erupted over decolonization movements in West Irian, Togo, British Cameroon, Zaire, Ifni, and the South African High Commission territories. Under these sitExpectations, the United States and the Soviet Union either supported the UN peace keeping activity or refrained from hindering its efforts. A coalition of independent nation-states within the UN rallied around the drive for national self-determination. The UN secretary-general and his secretariat strongly backed the drive for peaceful settlement of these conflicts in Asia and Africa. During the 1980s and 1990s, UN peace keeping agencies also played an important, but less effective, role trying to reconcile disputes in Lebanon, Israel, Iraq, Kuwait, Afghanistan, India, Pakistan, Cambodia, Cyprus, Somalia, Angola, Mozambique, El Salvador, and former Yugoslavia.

Liberal institutionalists assume that free trade on the world market facilitates peace. Within the European Union, the movement toward a single currency, one central bank, similar taxes, low tariffs, product standardization, and free mobility of labor and capital across the member-nations has strengthened political order. In the larger world arena, the General Agreement on Tariffs and Trade, the UN Conference on Trade and Development, the International Monetary Fund, and the World Bank all support expanded world trade. Since the early nineteenth century, nations highly involved in export trade as a percentage of their gross domestic product have shown a lower likelihood of going to war. When exports rapidly decline, as happened during the 1930s, the probability of warfare rises. Democratic political systems engaged in extensive export trade appear particularly unlikely to wage war.

Committed to an internationalist social service ethic, liberal institutionalists place a high faith in the UN specialized agencies to improve socioeconomic conditions that presumably divide nations and enhance war. The International Labor Organization, the World Health Organization, the Food and Agriculture Organization, the United Nations Educational, Scientific and Cultural Organization, and the Economic and Social Council tackle objective socioeconomic barriers to peace: poverty, income inequality, illiteracy, ill health, and labor exploitation. Despite serious obstacles – the need for major power support and the problems of overbureaucratized UN agencies – intergovernmental functional cooperation, however limited, helps lay the groundwork for the peaceful resolution of interstate conflicts.

The subjective attitudes of state decisionmakers also enhance the prospects for world peace. According to liberal institutionalists, peace requires changed attitudes. Policy leaders and citizen activists should hold mutual loyalties to their nation-state and to international organizations, especially the UN agencies. Rather than viewing world conflicts in zero-sum terms, leaders must begin seeing the international arena as a positive-sum game where cooperative policies produce mutually beneficial outcomes. Particularly when different state leaders share similar interpretations of the same values (democracy, freedom), pursue reconcilable issues, uphold common norms – agreement on international law and rules that restrain the use of force – and view other nations with empathy, these consensual attitudes mold the perceptions that promote peaceful conflict management.

Liberal institutionalists assume that the same conditions leading to world peace also produce high economic growth. When intergovernmental agencies such as GATT, the IMF, World Bank, and OECD support free trade, they strengthen greater economic efficiency, specialization, information flows, and technical cooperation among nations. Multinational corporations diffuse technical knowledge, transfer innovative technologies, and invest capital. Higher economic growth rates result. Since all nations gain mutual benefits from growth based on free trade and overseas investment, they have the incentive to cooperate. These conditions prevailed after the Second World War, when rapid growth occurred among the industrialized capitalist societies. Not only the United States but also West Germany, Japan, Britain, and France supported reduced tariffs, a common monetary system, and stable international currency exchanges. In contrast, during the 1930s depression, deflationary domestic policies, high protectionism, and economic nationalism led to low growth and eventually to war at the end of that decade. High tariffs accentuated economic scarcity. Market opportunities declined. To German, Italian, and Japanese leaders, war appeared a rational way to secure desired markets and raw materials from other less militarily powerful states. Adopting a zero-sum game outlook, officials from the Axis powers perceived that their economic gains occurred at the expense of other nations' losses. Given the weakness of international organizations to preserve peace and free trade, war erupted in Europe and Asia.[11]

## CAPITALIST WORLD-ECONOMY THEORY

Compared with the liberal institutionalists, capitalist world-economy theorists such as Immanuel Wallerstein express greater skepticism about the universal benefits of free markets, trade, and foreign investment. Rather than concentrating on the nation-state or intergovernmental agencies as the key decisionmakers, Wallerstein stresses the need to examine historical world-systems. All systems reveal patterns of social stratification based on a differential access to political power, economic wealth, and cultural status. Rather than empirically or even analytically autonomous sectors, the political system, economy, and culture comprise an interdependent whole. Wallerstein examines three world-systems that have dominated history. The reciprocal mini-systems functioned as stateless folk societies based on hunting, gathering, horticulture, fishing, or herding. Each small system shared similar cultural values about the division of labor in the production process. Because little economic surplus existed, minimal stratification occurred. These mini-systems fused one polity, one economy, and one culture. In contrast, tributary world-empires such as Rome and China featured one economy, one dominant state, and diverse cultures. Agriculture and trade became more prevalent. The economic surplus grew, which enabled a bureaucratic state to collect revenues and repress the subjects, mainly peasants. Since the sixteenth century the major world system has been the capitalist world-economy, which comprises many states, one economy, and several different cultures. Powerful states dominate the core societies, such as the United States, Japan, France, Britain, and Germany. The core capitalist class controls these nation-states, their national economies, and the world economy. The current world-economy operates primarily for the benefit of the core capitalist class, which gains profits through dominating subordinate classes at home and exploiting peripheral zones overseas. Non-capitalist classes in the semiperiphery and periphery suffer deprivation – that is, minimal political power, wealth, and status.

Different patterns of social stratification permeate the three zones of the contemporary world capitalist economy: the core, semiperiphery, and periphery. Within the core, a powerful state wields independence from external control and performs a wide range of activities. Controlled by the dominant capitalists, it extracts wage concessions from the workers, provides them social services, and socializes the labor force to accept capitalist values. The core state's military and diplomatic power helps multinational corporations expand throughout the world market. Government support for private property rights, legal contracts, an economic infrastructure, tax credits, and business subsidies strengthens capital accumulation. Formally democratic, the core political system gives citizens some organized opportunities to pressure public policymakers. Interclass alliances promote incremental policy changes. Political stratification remains flexible. Core societies are industrialized economies with capital-intensive production, a skilled labor force, a strong service sector, high role specialization, and a national market that enables poor people to buy goods. Economic stratification reflects moderate income equality and possibilities for upward social mobility. Internationally, core societies secure extensive economic independence. Their multinational corporations, especially financial institutions, wield immense economic power. Even though most trade and direct foreign private investment occur within the capitalist core, they dominate the world market. The multinationals can stage investment strikes, withhold credit, and reduce employment by moving from one country to another nation where labor costs are lower. They also control the world communications networks. From the cultural perspective, radio stations, television corporations, newspapers, magazines, publishing firms, and motion picture studios in the core societies determine what has high status throughout the world. These world mass media uphold capitalist values: hard work, labor discipline, instrumental rationality, efficiency, competitiveness, productivity. By legitimating these values, the media justify the need for entrepreneurs to pursue continual economic innovation and for subordinate groups to accept the inequalities of the capitalist system. The values of the capitalist core become equated with 'modernization.' People who fail to adopt these values resign themselves to economic backwardness and slow growth. Because of the pervasiveess of these specialized media, a minimal cultural gap separates elites and masses.

In contrast, the semiperipheral zone reveals more political, economic, and cultural stratification than does the core. In societies such as Brazil, Mexico, South Africa, Singapore, Indonesia, Thailand, and Malaysia, the political gap between rulers and ruled is rigid. Political inequalities split the centralized ruling elite from the masses. A powerful state faces strong opposition from student groups, newspapers, churches, unions, and occasionally peasant leagues. Military and police repression results. As a result of the politial coercion, polarization, and inequalities, protests take a violent form. Yet the bureaucratized state gives the ruling elite the power not only to suppress domestic internal opponents but to resist foreign military intervention. Economically, semiperipheral societies depend on the capitalist core for loans, physical capital, technology, and the sale of exports. Quasi-industrialized, these societies sell some manufactured goods to the core. Medium economic specialization prevails; few semiperipheral societies rely on the export of only one product. Despite the rapid economic growth, income inequalities divide rich and poor. The wealthy classes ally with the multinationals. The poor engage in small-scale trade, handicraft production, unskilled construction work, and subsistence agriculture. The rural population adheres to traditional religious and familial values. Most urban elites accept the core cultural values dominating the radio and television programs, movies, books, and magazines produced in the United States, Britain, France, and Spain. Demands for cultural autonomy arise from the more radical urban nationalist intellectuals who challenge core societies' economic exploitation, political domination, and cultural hegemony.

Peripheral societies reveal the greatest dependency on the capitalist core. The state exerts weak control over rural society. Military assistance from the core gives the central government the resources to coerce the opposition but not the power to transform society or resist foreign military intrusion. In peripheral countries most people work in subsistence agriulture, handicraft production, and small-scale informal trade. Exports comprise mainly oil, minerals, and food, usually one crop. With little economic diversity or industrialization, this zone depends on the core societies for trade, capital investment, loans, technical assistance, and personnel. Nearly all economic transactions occur through the core. Culturally, however, the peripheral zone experiences the least incorporation into the core's communication system. Patrons, elders, chiefs, marabouts, and landlords dominate the local communications network. For the village population, transistor radios provide the major link to the outside world, especially to the cultural messages transmitted from the core media.[12]

From the capitalist world-economy perspective, the interactions among the core, semiperiphery, and periphery constitute the major reasons for war and economic growth. Theorists such as Immanuel Wallerstein use concepts of Karl Marx and Fernand Braudel to explain military and economic changes in the capitalist world-economy. From Marxist theories Wallerstein derives such notions as class polarization, capitalist exploitation, and the need for revolutionary change to transform the world capitalist system. He assumes that dialectical contradictions explain fundamental change. 'Contradictions' imply that conflicts (competition among capitalists) produce short-term gains, such as technological innovation, but over the long-range period lead to economic stagnation as smaller firms go bankrupt or merge into conglomerates. Wallerstein relies on the historical methods of Braudel to explore the interactions among specific events, sociopolitical structures, and *conjunture* – that is, the cyclical rhythms of history. Like previous historical systems, capitalism over the last five hundred years has shown cycles of expansion and contraction. Caused by structural contradictions, these historical cycles explain the outbreak of wars among the core, semiperiphery, and periphery.

According to Wallerstein and Joshua Goldstein, war primarily stems from the capitalists' conflict over scarce economic resources. During the last four hundred years, core capitalists have relied on a militarily powerful state to secure raw materials, a cheap labor supply, markets, and outlets for capital investment. In the competitive world struggle for economic dominance, war represents a major means to secure scarce resources. Since the early seventeenth century, rivalries among core societies eventuated in world wars. The Thirty Years' War (1618–1648) saw the emergence of Dutch capitalism over the Hapsburg empire, Sweden, and France. As a result of the wars between 1792 through 1815, British capitalists triumphed over their French rivals and established world economic hegemony. During the twentieth century the Germans and Japanese threatened the economic dominance of the United States and Britain. This military-economic challenge provoked the two world wars. After the Second World War, the United States became the hegemonic world power that promoted capitalist expansion and maintained peace among the core societies.

Besides these world wars, regional conflicts pitted the core societies against militarily-weaker peripheral territories. During the late nineteenth century, the core capitalist states – Britain, France, the Netherlands, Belgium, Germany, the United States – used military force to conquer peripheral areas in Asia and Africa. These colonial conquests occurred at a time of economic stagnation (1873–1893), when economic growth, production, profits, and tax revenues fell throughout the core. The core states possessed the industrial strength and the military power to conquer areas lacking strong armies and national solidarity. Capitalist imperialism stimulated communist, socialist, and national liberation movements in the periphery. The communists in Russia and China fought civil wars to free their societies from internal exploitation and dependence on the core capitalist societies. Since the Second World War the United States has assisted its West European allies conduct limited wars in the periphery against 'national liberation movements' that mount armed struggles against colonial rule. The wars in Vietnam, Algeria, Angola, and Mozambique represent the most notable cases.

Unlike the liberal institutionalists, the capitalist world-economy theorists hold different assumptions about the linkages between economic growth and war. Liberal institutionalists assume that protectionism and economic depression lead to warfare among the major powers, which seek expanded markets, raw materials, and taxes. The world capitalist-economy approach, however, asserts that wars among core societies emerge during periods of rising economic production and international economic interdependence. On the economic upswing, core societies have the tax resources to finance warfare. Technological advances stimulate weapons production. Rapid growth leads to societal changes, which provoke international tensions. Hence, world wars erupt. The First World War seems to confirm this interpretation. From 1893 through 1914, Europe underwent an economic upswing, characterized by growth, prosperity, and economic interdependence. Nevertheless, a devastating war began in 1914. During the 1930s, the core, especially the United States, Britain, and France, suffered a severe economic depression. Even though economic growth increased slightly after 1932, substantial rises in production did not occur until 1940. After the Second World War ended, high growth rates lasted until the mid-1970s. Warfare prevailed mainly in the semiperipheral and peripheral areas of the Third World.[13]

For the world-economy theorists, economic growth in the capitalist core stems from actions by the multinational corporations and core nation-states that exploit the periphery. Unequal economic exchanges transpire between core and periphery. Rapid growth occurred when the capitalist class in core societies, such as Britain from 1820 through 1914 and the United States after the Second World War until the mid-1970s, efficiently united the agro-industrial, commercial, and financial sectors so as to maximize productivity. By controlling a relatively powerful state, these capitalists gained the enactment of policies that limited wage increases, gave some capitalist enterprises advantages over their competitors, enforced rules about private property rights, regulated the movement of capital and labor across national territorial boundaries, and brought outlying areas into the capitalist world-economy, either through colonial conquest or the acquisition of spheres of influence. After the Second World War, technological innovations (computers, electronics, biotechnology, information-processing equipment), postwar reconstruction, low unit labor costs, and the United States' economic hegemony stimulated rapid economic growth, particularly in the core capitalist societies and some semiperipheral countries such as South Korea, Taiwan, Singapore, and Brazil. Controlled by the core-based multinational banks and the US government, intergovernmental financial organizations – International Monetary Fund, World Bank – channeled investment loans into West Europe, Japan, and some newly industrializing countries (NICs) in Asia and Latin America. Multinational corporations headquartered in the United States, West Europe, and Japan invested physical and financial capital in such NICs as Singapore, Taiwan, South Korea, Hong Kong, the Philippines, Malaysia, Brazil, and Mexico.

Yet dependence on multinational corporations for investment capital and loans failed to produce long-term rapid growth in most peripheral societies. Even though a high infusion of new multinational foreign direct investment produced a faster growth in the short run (under six years), peripheral nations often experienced a capital loss over a longer-range period. When the technologically advanced machinery became outmoded, multinational corporations remitted most profits to the industrial core societies and no longer reinvested in the less developed country. The resulting decapitalization caused lower growth ten years after the initial investment. Investment in plants, equipment, and machinery required loans from multinational banks, but the high interest rates (especially from 1979 to 1984) aggravated the foreign debt. Large debt service ratios (payments on the foreign debt as a share of total export earnings) impeded additional expenditures for capital investment. Economic growth decelerated. Multinational financial corporations controlled the International Monetary Fund and the World Bank, which promoted austerity policies: lower real wage increases, decreased growth in the money supply, higher interest rates, and reduced expenditures for health care, education, and food subsidies. These policies deflated aggregate demand and lowered inflation rates; yet they also caused economic stagnation and growing income inequalities. Rather than achieving mutual benefits for all, the capitalist world market thus maximized rewards for some – the core capitalists and their allies in the NICs – but minimized benefits for small farmers, unskilled laborers, artisans, small traders, and the urban unemployed in the periphery.

By the mid-1970s even the capitalist core began to experience declining growth rates. From the capitalist world-economy perspective, the contradiction between overproduction and underconsumption explained this stagnation. By the 1970s the high aggregate demand stemming from postwar reconstruction had fallen. Fewer consumers needed private automobiles. Overproduction arose in automobiles, steel, ships, textiles, and petrochemicals. Faced with a declining growth of domestic demand and world export sales, governments in core societies enacted trade restrictions. Particularly during the 1980s, import quotas and 'voluntary restraint arrangements' became common policy tactics to reduce imports of automobiles, carbon steel, machine tools, textiles, and wearing apparel. These protectionist measures raised import costs and thus lowered consumption. In the semiperipheral NICs, hourly manufacturing wages totaled only between 10 percent and 20 percent of US wages. Although these low wages led to higher profits for the multinationals in the short term, over a longer-range period they reduced aggregate demand and lowered consumption for goods imported from the core societies. When production outstripped consumption, profit rates fell during the late 1970s and early 1980s. Direct private investment in physical capital – plants, machinery, equipment – declined. International financial investment rose. Multinational banks, brokerage firms, and insurance companies easily moved their financial capital across national boundaries. No state could restrict this flow. Debt escalated. Mergers and acquisitions became widespread. Financial speculation reinforced economic uncertainty. As trade and investment in physical capital decreased, growth fell in the core.[14]

## CONCLUSION

How plausible are these three theories' explanations of war and economic growth? Compared with the liberal institutionalist approach, the capitalist world-economy interpretation offers a more convincing explanation for the impact of the multinational corporations on economic growth in the Third World. True, as liberal institutionalists assume, during the period from the early 1960s through the early 1980s, extensive export trade and high domestic gross capital investment expenditures as a share of national income produced high growth rates. Nevertheless, lower growth resulted when multinational corporations controlled the export trade, direct foreign capital investment amounted to a high proportion of total energy consumption, and widespread capital outflow occurred.

Although their pessimistic assessments about the MNC effect on growth seem plausible, world-economy theorists exaggerate the involvement of core capitalist enterprises within the periphery.

Particularly after 1983, fewer loans and reduced direct foreign private investment went from the industrialized capitalist societies to less developed countries. Rising investment shares occurred in the industrialized countries, which had greater political stability, lower risks of expropriation, larger markets, a more adequate infrastructure (transportations, communications facilities), and a better-skilled labor force than did most Third World countries. Despite the higher wage rates, more powerful unions, and stronger social democratic parties in West European nations, US multinational corporations (excluding the oil industry) from 1950 through 1982 earned about the same profit returns there as in less developed countries. Moreover, most trade still occurs within the indusrialized core zone; trade flows between the developed economies and less developed nations have remained fairly constant since the Second World War. Whereas core societies used to import raw materials from the periphery, today core capitalist enterprises manufacture technological substitutes: synthetic fibers, plastics, corn syrup, and chemical food. In short, although the liberal institutionalists adopt a too sanguine view about the benign consequences of free trade and overseas investment, the capitalist world economy theorists downplay the importance of nationalism and state power in the semiperiphery.[15] Slow economic growth in the less-developed countries stems from variables other than just core exploitation and multiational investment. Powerful state institutions in East Asia have enacted pragmatic policies that secured rapid economic growth, despite their dependence on the capitalist core for trade and financial credit.

In probing the reasons for economic growth and war, structural realism and the world-economy approach overestimate the cohesive power of the ruling elites. Even though world-economy theorists recognize class 'fractions' and 'factions,' they exaggerate the solidarity of the world capitalist class, which actually remains divided by national loyalties, ideological orientations, economic interests, and policy views about the best ways to attain their goals. Given this weak cohesion, their control over government decisionmakers often seems limited. Structural realists assume that the nation-state operates as a unified actor. According to them, hegemonic states like Britain and the United States had the power to dominate the world system. Historically, however, few nation-states possessed either the cohesion or the combined military, economic, and informational resources needed to gain extensive general control over the world arena. Instead, their power extended to a region and to specific issues. Decisions to initiate a war often stemmed mainly from divisions within the national political elites, rather than from changing power relationships among cohesive dominant states. Transnational social movements of Islamic revivalists, environmentalists, and human-rights advocates have also secured social change. Liberal institutionalists adopt a more plausible assessment of the pluralist, faction-riven networks that comprise modern government bureaucracies as well as organizations within civil society. Compared with the structural realists, liberal institutionalists pay greater attention to the divergent bureaucratic pressures, social group demands, and domestic interest conflicts that often lead government policyakers into war.

Finally, all three structural theories minimize the attitudinal and behavioral variables that shape political leaders' decisions in the world arena. These structural approaches focus on power relationships among the nation-state, domestic social groups, and foreign institutions. Taking a structural determinist view, both neorealists such as Waltz and world-systems theorists such as Wallerstein equate power with the possession of resources, rather than with the skillful use of resources by individuals. Assuming that structural conditions determine personal attitudes, these theorists neglect the role of leaders in realizing changes in the world distribution of power. Liberal institutionalists best recognize the reciprocal impact between individual attitudes and sociopolitical structures. As we have seen, the decision to wage war or formulate particular economic policies depends on both objective structural conditions and the subjective beliefs of government officials – their policy priorities, motives, perceptions, and expectations.[16] Their assessment of structural opportunities and constraints determines public policies. Only by examining individual leaders' responses to structural conditions in the national and world environment can we comprehend war and economic growth in the modern era.

# Part III
# Behavior

# Introduction

Behavioral theorists study the people who participate in the political arena. Within every political institution or protest movement, specific individuals make decisions. Micropolitics involves persons' overt actions, skills, and subjective qualities like attitudes, motives, and perceptions. As active players in the political stage, participants shape culture and structure. When occupying government positions, they interpret cultural beliefs, enforce laws, operate agencies, formulate publicies, and implement government decisions. If acting as protesters outside the incumbent regime, individuals articulate demands for policy changes, try to rally support behind their cause, mobilize the discontented, coordinate the activities of formerly isolated persons, and struggle to overcome resistance so that they see their policy preferences translated into binding government programs. Rather than complying with government enforcement mechanisms, protest leaders organize disobedience to the incumbent regime. Instead of passively accepting the cultural interpretations transmitted by the dominant authorities, activists in protest movements seek to delegitimate existing cultural norms and to communicate new principles of legitimacy. Yet under more passive conditions, macropolitics often determines personal behavior; individuals fatalistically resign themselves to the political status quo. Cultural norms and structural constraints of the establishment guide attitude formation, information processing, and individual activities. Hence, protest leaders gain few opportunities to change the sociopolitical situation.

Exploring the interaction between political leadership and popular participation, behavioralists have probed three basic issues. First, how do individuals learn and change their political attitudes? In what ways do these attitudes influence personal choices to vote, refrain from electoral participation, become a political activist, and join a protest movement? Attitudes toward civil liberties wield an important impact on the opporunities for protest movements to articulate their policy demands. Second, why do people participate in political life, not only in electoral activities but also in protests and revolutions? What motivations influence their participatory behavior? How do perceptions of political events (definitions of the situation) shape the decision to participate? Political participation stems from both willingness and opportunities; behavioral theorists seek to explain the interaction between these two variables. Third, what personal qualities and sociopolitical conditions produce effective leadership both in formal government institutions and in revolutionary protest movements? From the behavioral perspective, the achievement of social change results from leaders' freedom of choice. Some effective leaders gain extensive opportunities to change sociopolitical structures and to reinterpret the meaning of cultural values. Others find themselves more constrained by small group norms and larger sociopolitical structures.

Psychodynamic, social learning, and cognitive theories suggest tentative explanations for attitude formation, political participation, and effective leadership. These theories formulate different conceptions of the interaction between individual characteristics (genetic endowments, thoughts, skills, emotions), personal actions, and the environment, which includes both cultural values and structural conditions. Psychoanalysts, especially the Freudians, assume that adult actions and attitudes stem mainly from biological drives (sex, aggression), unconscious impulses, and early parent child relationships. Individuals seek to defend their ego against threats. Punitive child-raising practices engender repressed hostility against the parents. Because the child cannot openly express disobedience, he often displaces aggression on outgroups such as atheists or homosexuals.

In contrast, social learning theorists explain interpersonal aggression as a result of environmental rewards and punishments. If peer groups bestow verbal approval on aggressive behavior, the individual will continue harming others deemed unworthy by the group. If state sanctions are uncertain and the person anticipates that the rewards of committing violence outweigh the costs, then she will engage in violent activities. Rejecting environmental determinism, cognitive learning theorists such as Albert Bandura stress the importance of subjective qualities: self-efficacy, self-imposed moral restraints, and expectations about the future consequences of one's present behavior. Persons learn by directly experiencing situations and by observing others. Their choices depend on perceived future punishments and more importantly on expected future gains. Nonaggressive behavior most likely occurs when individuals feel a strong moral imperative to act nonviolently and when the anticipated benefits of peaceful activities exceed the expected losses that may result from interpersonal aggression.

Cognitive theorists also focus on the reciprocal interaction between the individual and the cultural–structural environment. Rather than passively responding to environmental stimuli, the individual actively processes information and perceives the world as an active role-player. For example, rational choice theories examine how individuals reason about the political universe. They focus on expected consequences of behavior, including personal assessments of costs and benefits, expectations of success, and commitment to values and interests. From the rational choice perspective, cultural norms and sociopolitical structures both restrain individual choices and expand opportunities for goal attainment. Individual decisions mainly derive from cognitive processes. Persons interpret political life, attribute responsibility for social outcomes, process political information, and choose among perceived alternatives. According to these cognitive assumptions, an individual will join an antiregime protest movement if he expects a successful outcome, remains strongly committed to the movement's cause, holds unconventional attitudes, receives political information that highlights a public 'bad' (high unemployment), blames the incumbent government for the high unemployment, and perceives that new government decisionmakers will implement better policies about ways to lower joblessness.[1]

Most behavioral theorists, especially those using a social learning and cognitive approach, rely on logical–empirical methods to collect and analyze information about their hypotheses. They initially postulate a precise problem for explanation, for example, the decision to join a protest movement against high unemployment. Then behavioralists formulate an explanation for this outcome. General premises, axioms, and propositions guide the research. For example, a behavioral theorist may assume that rapidly deteriorating economic conditions create discontent with the national political system. This dissatisfaction strengthens protest movements. From these general assumptions derive more empirical hypotheses that can be tested. Hypotheses are if/then statements: if certain conditions occur, then certain consequences will result. For instance, if the unemployment rate rapidly escalates, then discontent with the incumbent government will increase. If people express strong dissatisfaction with the incumbent government's employment policies, opposition political parties and protest movements will gain greater support when they challenge existing policies for dealing with joblessness. To test the two hypotheses, the behavioralist devises operational indicators that measure such variables as unemployment rate, popular discontent, and support for opposition movements.[2]

Observations, oral interviews, questionnaires, sample surveys, quantitative content analyses, and laboratory experiments comprise the major techniques for gathering information. Through quantitative analyses of documents like letters, diaries, and speeches, behavioralists gain insights into the attitudes, perceptions, motives, and early socialization experiences of protest activists. Detached observation enables the behavioral theorist to learn about policy dissatisfactions, attribution of blame for personal miseries, expectations of success that may result from protest participation, and the intensity of commitment to ideological values or material interests. Oral interviews, questionnaires, and surveys of the general public provide data about individuals' overt actions, background characteristics (wealth, education, occupational experiences), and their subjective orientations. Behavioral theorists use sample surveys to measure protesters' incentives, political efficacy, causal attributions, and perceptions of established authorities and protest leaders.

Although laboratory experiments are the least widely used technique for collecting information, behavioralists rely on them for testing the causal validity of hypotheses. Assume that the dependent variable is participation in a protest movement seeking to upgrade the living conditions of the unemployed. The experimenter randomly selects subjects from students at a prestigious university and from individuals who reside in an adjacent low-income part of the city. These individuals are randomly assigned to two groups. The *experimental* group experiences some independent variable, such as watching a videotape in which the speakers claim that unemployment stems from an unjust political system and that government officials should enact job-creating public policies. The *control* group sees a television program 'Leave It to Beaver.' By randomizing the assignment of subjects to the two groups, the experimenter controls for extraneous variables (factors other than the independent variable) that affect an outcome like the decision to participate in a protest movement. The experimental and control groups are similar except that the experimental group becomes exposed to the independent variable – the inclination to blame the political system, not the individual, for unemployent. After a short time interval, the investigator measures the behavioral responses within the experimental and control groups. If the analysis of variance indicates a much stronger tendency for persons within the experimental group to join a protest movement than do control subjects, we assume that the 'blame-the-system' messages in the videotape cause the participation. Why? A high statistical association occurred between exposure to the videotape and decision to join the protest organization – an association greater than the relationship between socioeconomic background and participatory behavior. The independent variable came before the dependent variable. The random assignment of individuals to the control and experimental groups maximized their comparability, controlled for other extraneous variables affecting participation, and thus isolated the precise causal impact of the videotape that blames unemployment on unjust policies enacted by the political system.[3]

After collecting information, behavioral theorists probe causal explanations specifying the mechanisms by which certain conditions produce some outcome like participation in a protest movement. Both inductive and deductive methods help ascertain the causal status of the hypotheses. Using precise quantitative techniques, behavioral researchers try to estimate the extent to which changes in one variable (rising unemployment rate) generate changes in another variable (increasing participation in protest activities). Controls for third variables (socioeconomic status) ensure that no other factors 'explain away' the original strong correlation. Because many causes explain an effect, the behavioralist seeks to uncover those variables wielding the strongest impact on the effect – for example, the importance of motives (willingness) and structural conditions (opportunities) in explaining protest participation. The causal generalizations explain not only particular aspects of political life but also general human behavior. Axiomatic premises highlight the general laws that account for such activities as participation in protests. These inductive and deductive methods enable the analyst to refute some hypotheses and confirm others.

Behavioralists recognize the problems of accumulating a set of universally valid, objective generalizations. Unlike chemists or astrophysicists, social scientists must contend with larger numbers of more complex variables. Individual political actors with strong motives and clear perceptions can change such macrovariables as cultural values and sociopolitical structures. The limited opportunities to conduct controlled experiments and the numerous extraneous variables hinder the falsification and verification of hypotheses. The personal background and viewpoints of the behavioral theorist impede fully objective investigations. Nevertheless, by publicizing explicit methods, making data available to other analysts, and encouraging team research, behavioralists try to control for their personal biases. The stress on replication, the falsification of hypotheses, and the need for several political scientists with divergent values to conduct research on a specific topic promotes objectivity. Thus, compared with structural and particularly interpretive theorists, behavioral theorists retain greater confidence about gradually compiling an organized body of objective, cumulative generalizations that explain a specific outcome like political participation.[4]

Despite this sanguine perspective, the goal of accumulating causal generalizations remains elusive. In the political world, feedback processes occur. Rather than one independent variable producing changes in a dependent variable, the effect reciprocally influences the cause. Correlations between variables are usually fairly weak, especially in sample survey studies that probe individual attitudes. The analyst cannot control for all variables that produce some effect; misspecified equations cloud our understanding of political movements. No behavioralist can fully ascertain the interactions among all the variables causing an outcome. Assigning the precise weights to different structural, cultural, and attitudinal variables becomes difficult. Several types of error – random, measurement, sampling – impede the search for causal generalizations specifying all the necessary and sufficient conditions that produce an effect.

Because of these problems plaguing causal analysis, most behavioral theorists view their explanations as tentative probability statements, not as universal truths. The most plausible generalizations correspond with empirical observations under the highest proportion of conditions. Few social scientists assume that a causal explanation will likely hold true under all circumstances. A voluntarist orientation overrides any widespread belief in unchanging, deterministic laws. Individuals retain some opportunity to reinterpret cultural values and change the operation of political structures. Chance and randomly occurring events shape political outcomes. Exceptions to generalizations occur; for example, under exceptional circumstances, the poor become active participants in antistate protests. The exploration of such 'deviant cases' often highlights our understanding of causal processes. Thus, the behavior of individuals and the performance of political systems blend elements of personal choice and structural–cultural constraints. Generalizations undergo revision as culture, structures, and behavior change.[5]

According to the theory of political opportunity, individuals retain some free will to change structural conditions and formulate innovative reinterpretations of traditional cultural values. Of course, these macrophenomena also constrain personal behavior. Hegemonic cultural values that stress deference to established authority limit peoples' opportunities to protest against the status quo. Closed political systems with powerful repressive security agencies deter individuals from staging protests. Rigid social stratification prevents extensive upward mobility. Yet particularly in more open sociopolitical systems with pluralist values, individuals gain the incentives and the opportunities to participate in protest movements that may secure changes in public policies, political leaders, procedures, and structural arrangements. Innovative activists take advantage of existing structural opportunities. Motivated to achieve social and political change, they learn from past experiences. New cognitive understandings emerge about ways to attain reforms. Programmatic visions inspire individuals to make activist choices that facilitate change.[6]

By concentrating on individual actors, behavioral theorists elucidate the dynamic aspects of public policy processes. They probe the performance of government officials and activists who lead protest movements. Whether in government or a protest movement, leaders achieve the greatest success when they can effectively process information, learn necessary interpersonal skills, and display high self-esteem but low ego-defensiveness. With these personal qualities, an effective policymaker generates original ideas for policy solutions, supervises the implementation of policy options, attains support for government programs, and manages the conflict that inevitably ensues during the decision process. Protest activists who expect to influence public policies also need to demonstrate similar personal qualities. Like government officials, they need accurate, relevant, comprehensive information about the power, general values, and specific preferences of other participants in the policy process. Effective protest leaders make wise interpretations of the information they receive, so that they can adapt to unforeseen contingencies. Important interpersonal skills include the ability to communicate, persuade others, and wield coercion over opponents. High self-confidence and low ego-defensiveness also facilitate successful protest leadership. Naturally, the achievement of a leader's policy priorities depends on more than personal qualities. Dominant cultural norms may run counter to a leader's policy preferences. Situational obstacles, such as domestic group opposition or transnational institutions' antagonism, can impede goal attainment. Under these cultural–structural constraints, political leaders face difficulties achieving policy victories.[7]

In sum, Part III applies psychodynamic, social learning, and cognitive theories to explain political protests throughout the world. We explore three behavioral processes: the learning of political attitudes (Chapter 8), electoral participation (Chapter 9), and political leadership (Chapter 10). Cognitive development theories offer insightful explanations for the ways that individuals learn attitudes toward civil liberties – an attitude needed for the expression of protests against government policies, authorities, and institutional arrangements. Rational choice assumptions clarify the motives behind selecting a particular candidate or party. Particularly during the last decade, voters in many countries no longer support established parties but have opted for protest parties on the 'right' and 'left.' Chapter 9 suggests some reasons for citizens to back such new movements as the neofascists and greens. Finally, political leadership by incumbent officials and antiregime protesters partially explains the effectiveness of protesters in achieving their objectives. Psychodynamic, relative deprivation, and political opportunity theories stress the ways that leaders mobilize their resources behind revolutions. These theories elucidate the motivations that guide the participants, the tactics chosen to realize their goals, and their success in implementing social change.

# 8   The Learning of Political Attitudes

Nearly thirty years before the outbreak of the French Revolution, Jean-Jacques Rousseau in the *Social Contract* (1762) observed a major paradox of modern society: 'Man is born free, and everywhere he is in chains. . . . What man loses by the social contract is his natural liberty and an unlimited right to anything which tempts him and which he is able to attain; what he gains is civil liberty and the ownership of all that he possesses.'[1] Yet Rousseau saw few governments of his time guaranteeing civil liberty. Instead, the rich minority exploited the poor minority. Despots persecuted intellectuals. Just after the publication of the *Social Contract*, the French government in Paris banned its circulation and ordered Rousseau's arrest. Public officials in Geneva, Switzerland also burned the essay, fearing that its stress on liberty would provoke a revolution. If individuals were ever to realize their natural potential for liberty, Rousseau assumed that society should ensure certain structural and behavioral conditions. General laws must specify the rights and duties of citizens and policymakers, as well as procedures for regulating conflicts. Although guaranteeing the right to private property, the government should enact policies to narrow the gap between rich and poor. Government also needs to promote public education for all citizens, who learn consensual values of civic virtue, liberty, and equality under the law. Through this universal public education, individuals become socialized to participate as active citizens in a small-scale political system. By discussing political issues, debating others, voting, and disagreeing with majority views, citizens reconcile their private interests with the common good or general will of the political community. According to Rousseau, the general, impersonal principles of the common good maximize civil liberty, which he defined as 'obedience to self-imposed law.'[2]

A century later the American poet Walt Whitman affirmed the indispensability of political liberty. A self-styled 'rough' and 'kosmos,' Whitman assumed that poets are 'the voice and exposition of liberty. . . . The attitude of great poets is to cheer up slaves and horrify despots.'[3] To the nation-states of the world, he declared: 'Resist much, obey little.' Yet Whitman recognized that defiance provokes counterprotests. At the conclusion to 'Song of the Open Road,' he wrote:

> My call is the call of battle, I nourish active rebellion,
> He going with me must go well arm'd,
> He going with me goes often with spare diet, poverty, angry enemies, desertions.[4]

A prophet of the Enlightenment, Whitman championed freedom, social progress, equality between men and women, ethnic fellowship, spiritual solidarity, and individualism. A mystic but hardly a trinitarian, he rejected submission to conventional religious orthodoxy. A rebel and a philosophical anarchist, he preached the divine oneness of humankind and affirmed the sacredness of the 'body electric.' The children of Adam became the children of God. His focus on the holiness of both spirit and flesh naturally incurred opposition. The secretary of the Department of the Interior fired Whitman for authoring an 'indecent' book. During the early 1880s Anthony Comstock's Society for the Suppression of Vice urged the Boston district attorney to prosecute the publisher of Whitman's *Leaves of Grass*. Even though the Boston firm ceased printing the book after Whitman refused to delete offensive passages, another publisher in Philadelphia agreed to reissue a sixth edition. Ironically, the attempt to ban the book in Boston increased its sales and brought unexpected profits to the rebel poet.[5]

As Rousseau and Whitman asserted, civil liberty represents a basic policy issue that opposes state sanctions against challenges to government actions and conventional social mores. Governments take actions that expand or impede freedom. Cultural values – principles of freedom, equality, justice – imparted by political leaders through public schools, legal institutions, and the mass media prescribe the application of civil liberties to specific cases. Education becomes a primary mechanism for the transmission and learning of basic political attitudes. Institutional arrangements, such as the extent of decentralized government power and social pluralism, affect the degree of political freedom. This chapter probes the basic policy issues of civil liberties. First, why do some individuals hold more libertarian attitudes than do others? How do early childhood interactions with parents, later social learning experiences, especially in educational institutions, and the structure of thought processes shape people's support for civil liberties? Second, at the national level, to what extent does the degree of government coercion stem from elite attitudes, mass opinions, and a society's structural conditions?

Attitudes toward civil liberties assume particular importance because they highlight the relationship between the rulers and the ruled – the key interaction of political life. Attitudinal support for civil liberties means that individuals uphold nonviolent protests against political leaders, public policies, institutional arrangements, and basic values. People with the greatest political tolerance believe that all groups, no matter what their ideology or popularity, should have the rights to free speech, assembly, organization, and due process. Laws guarantee dissidents protection against arbitrary administrative actions (forced confessions, indefinite detentions), unfair trial procedures, and vague, all-encompassing decrees that give police broad discretion to repress citizens for 'disturbing the peace,' creating disorder, failing to disperse, and offending government officials. Individuals have the freedom to hold a job based on their occupational performance, not on their conformity to conventional or official political beliefs.[6] All these libertarian principles reflect a commitment to reformist methods for attaining social change. Particularly within democratic states, citizens' challenges against political authority represent opposition to specific leaders and their policies, rather than discontent with fundamental values and institutional arrangements. In dictatorial governments, dissidents demand more fundamental changes that challenge all aspects of political authority: elite interpretations of freedom and justice, institutional arrangements, specific policies, and particular leaders who formulate and implement these policies. Because democratic officials grant social science researchers the freedom to conduct sample surveys, most civil liberties studies since the Second World War have taken place in Western Europe, Canada, the United States, Australia, New Zealand, and Israel.

## DIMENSIONS OF POLITICAL ATTITUDES

Behavioral theorists view attitudes as cognitive representations
that evaluate some object, such as communists or fascists. As this
definition implies, attitudes reveal three basic dimensions:
cognitive, evaluative, and motivational. Political cognition refers
to the processing of information, that is, to the mental activities
that obtain knowledge, provide meaning, comprehend political
life, and offer coherent insights into political reality. The
processing of information about civil liberties encompasses
several phases. Individuals first *pay attention* to political stimuli,
including dominant interpretations of fundamental values such as
freedom and equality, constitutional procedures, the structure of
government power (especially the authority wielded by military
and police), and the policies of top governmental officials toward
civil liberties. Rather than concentrating on political stimuli, most
people pay primary attention to their immediate environment –
the concerns of their family, friends, neighbors, and workmates.
Most individuals thus view civil liberties for dissident groups as an
unimportant issue.[7]
  After paying attention to political issues, individuals then
*interpret* information about the political world. Few persons
interpret politics from an abstract, ideological cognitive perspective. They perceive the political system according to its impact on
national well-being or on specific groups, such as businesspeople,
workers, and farmers. Yet formally educated individuals, political
activists, and those preferring extensive changes in the system
think more abstractly, deductively, and systematically about such
issues as civil liberties. These ideologues link specific cases (rights
of communists) to general principles (political freedom, due
process), perceive concrete events in light of abstract ideas, and
deduce specific conclusions from general theoretical principles.[8]
According to sample survey research conducted in the United
States by Herbert McClosky, Paul Sniderman, and their
colleagues, causal attributions made by ideologues explain
support for civil liberties. 'Conservatives' perceive evil, lazy, and
undisciplined individuals as the cause of social disorder.
Pessimistic about human potentialities, they assume that a
person's laziness, drug addiction, and alcoholism cause both
personal and social problems. Affirming the need for order and
stability, 'conservative' ideologues adopt intolerant attitudes and

urge obedience to the dominant authority system. In contrast, 'liberals' show stronger support for civil liberties that challenge existing authority. They take a more optimistic view of human beings. 'Liberal' ideologues blame crime, poverty, and disorder on injustices in society, such as discrimination and lack of opportunities. They believe that government and social groups should help the disadvantaged. Expressing greater support for political freedom, 'liberals' want the political system to implement social reforms, rather than spend resources on maintaining order and defending society against exaggerated threats.[9]

When processing political information, individuals *assess* this knowledge for its accuracy, reliability, and credibility. They usually rely on family, friends, group leaders, and the media for their assessments. Particularly when the information about a dissident group seems far removed from their personal experiences, most individuals cannot easily appraise the informational accuracy of political communications. They defer to the messages of political authorities or media figures. The treatment of an unfamiliar or unconventional group in the media hence largely shapes the degree of popular tolerance for that group's dissident activities.[10]

Individuals *store and recall* political information. As we have seen, people recall information most comprehensible to them personally. For example, US citizens remember more information about government income tax or health care policies than about international monetary policy, arms control agreements, and civil liberties for the Socialist Workers Party.

The processing of political information involves *acting on* the knowledge and beliefs recalled from memory. Even individuals who believe in the general principles of political freedom and who hold extensive information about the political conditions of unconventional dissident groups will not necessarily act to uphold civil liberties for a specific group. Only if individuals place a high value on political freedom and expect that their libertarian actions will actually produce positive outcomes – innovation, institutional adaptability, social vitality – will they translate their attitudinal support for civil liberties into political action. Prospects for taking action seem particuarly strong when social group norms uphold civil liberties, people apply these general norms to specific dissident groups, and sanctions against political dissidence remain weak. Under these conditions, citizens perceive high benefits but low costs when they act to support protests from unconventional, unpopular, or unfamiliar organizations. For them, the expansion of political freedom becomes a public good.[11]

Political attitudes also reflect an evaluative component. Evaluations invoke a generalized concept of desirability – standards of right and wrong, good and evil, justice and injustice. Popular stands toward civil liberties for specific dissident groups involve evaluations about several attitudinal objects: political freedom, legal rights, government institutions (police, courts), and the dissident group. When an individual perceives conflicting obligations – for instance, the duty to preserve public order vs the responsibility to protect people's constitutional rights to civil liberties – moral principles evaluate competing claims and thus influence attitudes toward political freedom for an unpopular, unconventional organization. People who evaluate a dissident group as highly threatening express little tolerance for that group's right to campaign for elected office, make public speeches, hold rallies, talk on the radio, and teach in public schools.[12]

Political attitudes also involve a motivational dimension. Three motives seem important in shaping attitudes toward civil liberties. First, individuals need to defend themselves against threats that produce high anxiety. Identification with an authoritarian political leader often brings personal security. Defying a repressive political system may alleviate guilt. Second, the expression of certain attitudes enables an individual to interact with other people. When sharing the same attitudes with others in a small group, a person gains social approval for opposing a dissident political organization. Even though an individual may defy group norms by upholding civil liberties for atheists, that disapproval brings him attention. Rather than a punishment, disapproval appears as a reward. Thus both group approval and rejection shape personal attitudes toward civil liberties. Third, as the analysis of information processing suggested, political attitudes enable people to understand the political world, including the authority relationship between the rulers and ruled. Particularly during times of rapid social change and conceptual confusion, attitudes supply meaning to a complex, ambiguous political reality. They explain the relationship between political system performance and social disorder. By blaming 'communists' or 'fascists' for social turmoil, an individual labels such groups as threats to political order and hence justifies their suppression. More libertarian attitudes uphold the core values of political freedom and individual dissent; these values cognitively relate abstract principles to the need for government officials to expand civil liberties for dissident organizations. Assumptions about the proper functions of government also shape attitudes toward civil liberties. Individuals who assume that government has the primary responsibility to preserve order, stability, and national security express less enthusiasm for civil liberties than do citizens who believe that governent operates to provide social services, secure a clean environment, and attain world peace.[13]

## THEORIES OF ATTITUDE FORMATION AND CHANGE

Three general theories explain political attitude formation and change; each theory stresses a different motivation. Psychoanalysis views attitudes as a defense against personal threats. Unconscious motives originate in early childhood and determine adult political attitudes, which provide security and reassurance. Social learning theories assume that individuals learn attitudes when interacting with others – either in a face-to-face situation or through the mass media. Ties to membership and reference groups influence a person's attitudes. Group norms as well as the rewards (approval) and punishment (disapproval) emanating from the group shape the content of specific attitudes. Cognitive theories focus on information processing. Cognitive development theories emphasize that attitudes help individuals understand political reality, particularly their interactions with government authorities. Table 8.1 summarizes the three theories explaining support for civil liberties.

### Psychoanalytic Theories

Psychoanalytic theorists assume that unresolved, unrecognized personal conflicts about sex and aggression shape attitudes toward the political world. An individual who experiences anger against authorities and fear of personal weakness erects defense mechanisms against these threats. As Harold Lasswell postulated, a political actor displaces private motives – hatred of father – on political objects (the president, the czar) and rationalizes them in

Table 8.1  Theoretical explanations of support for civil liberties

| | Psychodynamic theories | Social learning theories | Cognitive development theories |
|---|---|---|---|
| General assumptions<br>Functions of attitudes | Defense against personal threats | Approval and disapproval from other people, both in membership and reference groups | Comprehension of political reality |
| Processes of attitude formation | 1. Unresolved personal conflicts unrecognized by self shape civil liberties' attitudes.<br>2. Political actor displaces unconscious private motives (fear, anger, low self-esteem) on political objects and rationalizes them in the public interest<br>3. Key defense mechanisms for coping with personal conflicts include rationalization, displacement, projection, and repression. | 1. Cultural norms (informal rights and obligations), small group pressures, and rewards and punishments of group leaders shape an individual's willingness to accept civil liberties for specific organizations.<br>2. Membership in tolerant groups and strong identification with libertarian reference groups increase support for civil liberties. | 1. Active participation in diverse role-playing activities increases tolerance.<br>2. Higher cognitive differentiation and integration raise support for civil liberties.<br>3. Attainment of higher levels of cognitive development increases support for civil liberties. |
| Processes of attitude change | Clinical interviews with psychotherapist lead to greater self-esteem, reassurance, and freedom from anxiety. | Small group leaders, political elites, and media figures articulate new norms of political tolerance and reinforce expression of tolerant attitudes. | Individuals gain new information about a dissident group and perceive that group as less threatening. |

| Hypotheses | 1. Attitudes of 'authoritarian personality' (one who shows conventionalism, submission toward established authority, and aggression toward outgroups) stem from inner, unresolved conflicts with parents and from punitive, domineering parents who cause children to feel hostile, unworthy, and fearful toward authority figures.<br>2. Ambivalent attitudes toward authority produce submissive obedience to establishment in-groups but antagonism toward outgroups. | 1. The higher the formal education, especially postsecondary education, the greater the support for civil liberties.<br>2. The more active the participation in 'fundamentalist' or 'orthodox' religious groups, the weaker the support for civil liberties.<br>3. The stronger the identification with movements that uphold the need for social reform and for an active government role in providing social services, the greater the political tolerance. | 1. Cognitively developed individuals with greatest formal education express highest political tolerance.<br>2. Individuals with high empathy and the cognitive ability to apply general principles of political freedom to concrete cases (specific unpopular groups) hold the most tolerant attitudes. |

terms of the public interest.[14] According to clinical interviews conducted by psychoanalysts Theodor Adorno, Else Frenkel-Brunswik, Daniel Levinson, and Nevitt Sanford, the 'authoritarian personality' employs several defense mechanisms. Rationalization occurs when altruistic reasons justify sadistic actions. For example, in Nazi Germany national self-righteousness – the belief in the moral superiority of the German people and the master Aryan race – condoned the extermination of the Jewish 'outgroup.' Authoritarian personalities resort to displacement when they blame their own failures on low-status groups or people labeled 'deviant' by political authorities. 'Projection' means that individuals condemn others for motives that they deny in themselves. They seek to coerce outgroups labeled as immoral, unclean, and guilty of sexual licentiousness. The repression of hostility appears a common feature of authoritarian personalities. Glorification of the parents disguises the children's repressed hatred of them. This repressed hostility toward parents then becomes displaced on weaker outgroups, such as the Jews in Nazi Germany.

The authoritarian personality ranks high on three beliefs: conventionalism, submission to established authority, and aggressiveness toward outgroups. Fearing chaos and a dangerous world, the authoritarian personality urges obedience to established authority figures: parents, government officials, and church hierarchs. Support for strong personal leadership accompanies an aversion to criticize dominant officials within society. Punitive, aggressive attitudes emerge toward unconventional, low-status, unpopular groups, who are viewed as repulsive and disgusting. Yet if societal leaders condemn higher-status people as 'deviant,' even these more prestigious groups become targets of aggression. To the authoritarian personality, corporal punishment, capital punishment, and strictly enforced laws represent policies for suppressing repulsive groups and establishing greater social order. The authoritarian personality also supports traditional, conventional norms, especially about women's role in society and acceptable patterns of sexual behavior. These norms dictate that children honor their parents, wives obey their husbands, citizens revere the flag, and laity follow the official teachings of the church hierarchs.

Psychoanalytic investigations into the authoritarian personality conclude that unsupportive attitudes toward civil liberties stem primarily from inner unresolved conflicts with parents. Punitive, domineering parents raise children who become authoritarian adults. Harsh treatment, especially by the father, produces fear, hostility, and low self-esteem in the children, who hold ambivalent attitudes toward parental authority. Even though vowing uncritical admiration for the parents, the children unconsciously feel anger about their unjust treatment. During adulthood these ambivalent feelings transform into submissive obedience toward dominant political authorities but intense antagonism toward less powerful, lower-status groups, such as religious and ethnic minorities – for example, Jews in Germany and blacks in the United States. Particularly among men, a glorification of virile masculinity masks latent feelings of personal vulnerability, which cause dependence on a powerful leader. Perceiving the world as threatening, the authoritarian personality upholds the need for unchallenged authority, which supposedly brings personal security to a dangerous, chaotic world. Intolerant of ambiguity and cognitively inflexible, authoritarian individuals dichotomize people into good and evil. They fail to differentiate the content of information from its source. For them, the prestige of the authority figure who issues a political message carries greater weight than substantive merits like logic, empirical accuracy, and relevance to a concrete situation. Even if psychoanalysts cannot change a child's parental upbringing, they assume that attitudinal change toward a more democratic personality will occur when adults gain greater self-esteem, reassurance, and freedom from anxiety. Through clinical interviews, the psychotherapist can help people develop more insight into their early childhood experiences, so that greater self-confidence emerges.[15]

How plausible are the psychoanalytical explanations for the authoritarian personality? Clinical interviews, experiments, and sample surveys conducted in the United States, Canada, West Europe, New Zealand, and Israel suggest that authoritarian individuals lack self-esteem, express ambivalence toward authority, and feel endangered by personal and environmental threats. Yet most research indicates that these orientations do not stem from either unconscious, latent motives or from early childhood experiences. Empirical investigators face difficulties finding any indicators of unconscious motivations. Although psychoanalysts can observe bodily actions and verbal responses to questions in a clinical interview, they cannot all agree on the precise significance of these behavioral patterns, especially the extent to which they tap unconscious fears and hostilities. Moreover, few psychoanalysts have conducted the longitudinal studies required to ascertain the impact of early childhood experiences on adult attitudes. The authors of *The Authoritarian Personality* exaggerated this impact. Other research suggests that individuals who score high on the 'F scale' measuring support for fascism do not necessarily have stern fathers and submissive mothers. Instead, most children, regardless of parental treatment, defer to fathers, mothers, and other authority figures. Attitudes toward authority usually crystallize during adolescence, when individuals become more independent and undergo diverse learning experiences. Compared with early parent–child interactions, adult learning in small groups and sociopolitical situations wields a greater impact on authoritarian attitudes.[16]

## Social Learning Theories

Social learning theories, not psychoanalytic studies, have engendered the more widely accepted explanations for attitudes toward civil liberties. These theories assume that individuals learn attitudes from cultural norms, small group pressures, and rewards and punishments of group leaders. Through participation in membership groups and identification with reference groups, people become exposed to certain norms about the desirability of allowing various organizations to exercise political freedom. As the classical liberal John Stuart Mill recognized, political dialogue that exposes participants to diverse viewpoints expands the opportunity for truth to emerge. Skepticism becomes a key virtue. Discussants learn to challenge orthodox opinions, reject arbitrary conventions, consider all sides of an issue, and tolerate eccentric individuals, dissident groups, and unpopular policies. By affirming the value of individual autonomy and social diversity, Mill sought to limit both state coercion and group conformity. Contemporary social learning theorists have discovered that when peer group members – relatives, friends, neighbors, workmates – debate diverse viewpoints and when leaders in the wider community support political freedom for unpopular organizations, then individuals exposed to these messages will likely take a libertarian attitude if they understand and accept the libertarian norm. The probability of acceptance increases when people in a membership group receive rewards (verbal approval) for expressing civil liberties attitudes and punishments (dispproval) for rejecting libertarian views. The rewarding outcomes represent reinforcements that strengthen the repetition of tolerant political attitudes. When individuals strongly identify with a reference group that articulates libertarian values, that identification will strengthen political tolerance. To increase support for civil liberties, group norms must change. Small group leaders, political elites, and media figures need to reinforce the expression of tolerant viewpoints.[17]

Educational institutions and churches, rather than occupational groups or political parties, wield the greatest impact on the learning of civil liberties norms. Education interacts with other social background variables to shape attitudes toward political freedom. People with a post-secondary education, especially those who have majored in the social sciences and humanities, express greater political tolerance than those with a secondary or primary education. Occupational differences seem less important. True, compared with farmers (a group with the least formal education), highly educated professionals – lawyers, judges, university faculty, teachers, journalists, writers – show more enthusiasm for civil liberties. Nevertheless, the attitudinal differences among other occupations such as managers, clerks, skilled workers, and craftspeople remain minimal, particularly when we examine employees with the same education. Identification with democratic socialist parties (for example, the New Democratic Party in Canada, the British Labour Party, the Australian Labour Party, the Dutch Labor party, the German Social Democrats) does raise support for civil liberties, particularly among highly educated activists. Yet only modest attitudinal differences separate partisans within the mass population of most nations.

Church membership more strongly influences civil liberties attitudes than does political party affiliation. Even after researchers control for educational background, in the United States and Canada members of Protestant fundamentalist churches – Baptist, Pentecostal, Church of God, Church of Christ – voice the least tolerance, especially toward issues of sexual behavior, abortion, homosexuality, pornography, obscenity, and women's role in society. Congregationalists, Episcopalians, Jews, and particularly individuals with no religious affiliation take the most libertarian stands. The fundamentalists' aversion to civil liberties stems not only from their limited formal education but also from their theological monism. They take an inerrant, literal interpretation of the Bible, view the world as polarized between a personal God and the Devil, and perceive that salvation stems from emotional ecstasy, not from a rational experience. Strengthened by the authoritarian norms of evangelical ministers, these monistic beliefs reflect a cognitive rigidity, particularly a tendency to dichotomize people into good and evil and to punish those who violate God's commandments.

In the United States ideological reference groups strongly influence political tolerance for all dissident organizations, whatever their beliefs or popularity. Individuals who identify with the 'liberal' movement express greater enthusiasm for civil liberties than do self-styled 'conservatives.' Besides ideological self-identifications, general ideological orientations also explain orientations toward political liberties. 'Liberals' who support social reform and prefer active government involvement in the economy, especially the provision of social services, favor the extension of civil liberties. In contrast, 'conservatives' who uphold tradition and express limited enthusiasm for government economic regulation, planning, and supply of social services take a more skeptical view of extending political freedom to unconventional organizations that may pose a danger to social order. Education combines with ideology to influence political tolerance. Highly educated liberals hold the most libertarian attitudes, followed by educated conservatives, uneducated liberals, and uneducated conservatives.[18]

Social learning, personality, and cognitive variables explain the sizeable impact of educational experiences on political tolerance. Acceptance of libertarian norms leads to tolerant orientations expressed by young, well-educated professionals. More than primary or secondary schools, universities uphold civil liberties norms. Professionals such as lawyers, judges, and journalists have majored in the social sciences and humanities – disciplines that encourage students to express diverse opinions, evaluate preferences, and formulate collective rules for reconciling conflicts. Their professional work also stresses the importance of legalistic principles and legal guarantees for all citizens. When evaluating an unpopular group, highly educated, well-informed political activists place greater emphasis on legal norms than on the undesirable characteristics of the group, such as nazis, fascists, or communists. Yet survey data from the United States suggest that if political elites express disagreement about civil liberties for specific groups, the strong correlation between high formal education and libertarian attitudes weakens. When courts, law firms, and the mass media cannot reach a consensus about upholding the freedom of abortionists, pornographers, prostitutes, and homosexuals, the best-educated, most informed, and politically active persons display lower political tolerance. Faced with ambiguous norms, young, highly educated individuals who perceive the need for social change favor civil liberties for an unconventional group, whereas educated people who affirm the desirability of the traditional order take an intolerant position, especially if they expect that the group granted political freedom will endanger their personal well-being.

Besides their greater exposure to group norms, educated people also have lower dogmatism. Those with a dogmatic personality think in polarized terms; they view themselves as unworthy, perceive the political world as dangerous, and thus affirm the need for absolute authority. In contrast, nondogmatic individuals show less conformity to conventional norms and instead rely on new sources of information when framing their political attitudes. Post-secondary education promotes certain cognitive abilities associated with an open mind: intellectual flexibility, comprehension of diverse ideas, and logical procedures for linking general principles like political freedom to specific cases involving a particular dissident group. Even if well-educated persons perceive a group as dangerous, they still tolerate its right to exercise political freedom.[19]

Although stressing the importance of group norms, social pressures, and reinforcements, social learning theory until recently downplayed the impact of cognitive processes on the formation of political attitudes. Viewing the individual as a passive spectator who acquiesces to social group rewards and punishments, it underestimated the active role that people play when responding to group stimuli. Whether in a small group or alone at home before a television set, most persons actively process political information. They interpret group norms to specific conditions, assign divergent meanings to rewards and punishments, and infer the likely consequences of expressing support for civil liberties. During the last decade, cognitive approaches have dominated the study of political attitudes.[20]

## Cognitive Development Theories

According to cognitive theories of political attitudes, individuals act rationally when processing political information. Rather than influenced solely by the rewards and punishments emanating from group leaders, people use their minds to define political problems, understand political reality, evaluate information, and take actions consistent with their political beliefs. Political attitudes depend on information about the political world, especially on the perceptions and assessments of this information. Attitudes toward civil liberties change when individuals gain new information about a dissident group and define the political situation in new ways – for example, perceive the group as less threatening. Education plays a crucial part in imparting new information and perceptions of political reality.

Cognitive development theorists assume that attitudes toward civil liberties derive from an individual's level of mental development. They formulate three general propositions about attitude formation and change. First, thinking occurs as the individual mind interacts with the social environment. Through cognitive processes, people come to know, define, order, and even change the political worlds. Individuals who play diverse roles in various environmental settings acquire the greatest political tolerance.

Second, political attitudes are structured. As persons cognitively develop, their thought structures become more complex – that is, differentiated and integrated. They can distinguish the self from the environment, symbols (the national flag) from the objects (the nation) to which they refer, hypothetical assumptions from empirical evidence, and viewpoints of the self from others' views. Instead of seeing political objects such as the United States and Iran from only one perspective – good versus evil – cognitively developed individuals can differentiate various aspects of the two nations: geography, economies, ethnic composition, popular attitudes, elite behaviors, and institutional performance. Higher cognitive differentiation brings greater support for civil liberties, mainly because of the ability to comprehend diverse ideas. People who think in differentiated ways can assume different viewpoints, empathize with others, and perceive aspects of a political situation beyond the immediate personal environment. A cognitively developed individual can also integrate complex information from the political world and relate core values – abstract principles of civil liberties – to concrete cases about specific dissident organizations. Rather than viewing political events in terms of concrete, immediate, familiar, and personal events, integrated thinkers perceive the world from the standpoint of more abstract, distant, unfamiliar, and impersonal principles. For them, freedom means not just the right to purchase a stereo, go bowling every Wednesday night, and take a long vacation. Instead, freedom refers to general procedures and abstract principles – notions of representative government, constitutional guarantees, and minority rights to express unconventional, unorthodox ideas in a peaceful forum. With their cognitive ability to discern the relationships between cause and effect, abstract, integrated thinkers can comprehend the societal impact of denying political freedom to a peaceful protest group. Abstract thought also enables individuals to envision patterns of authority relationships that diverge from established patterns; hence, at higher stages of cognitive development, they seem more willing to challenge political authority.

Third, thinking progresses through different stages. As a person's mental structures interact with environmental structures, the individual advances through stages. When the opportunities for role-taking increase, people become exposed to more diverse political stimuli. If greater conflict emerges between divergent cognitive elements, individuals attain higher stages of cognitive development. According to Lawrence Kohlberg, moral judgments rest on a rational, not an emotional, foundation. As individuals become more cognitively developed, they develop more advanced reasons for making moral choices about whether to obey or challenge political authority. At the lowest stage, obedience stems from a desire to avoid physical punishment by a powerful authority figure in the immediate environment. Stage 2 moral reasoning bases compliance on the wish to secure a concrete reward for the self. At stage 3, individuals seek trusting relationhips and social approval from peer group members; conformity to the small group norms of relatives, friends, and neighbors motivates obedient behavior. Respect for national traditions shapes attitudes toward authority for those who have attained stage 4; they seek to maintain social harmony and avoid institutional disorder. Individuals at stage 5 value laws made by free people who devised procedures for changing, not just maintaining, the operation of political institutions. Civil disobedience should occur when government officials violate the agreement to protect the legal rights of all people. At the highest stage of cognitive development, attitudes toward political authority derive from reverence for universal moral principles that regard each person as a free, autonomous being – an end, not a means. Viewing others with empathy, individuals feel a personal responsibility to care for all those who suffer injustices. People at stage 6 refuse to comply with rules and authorities that reject these principles of impartial justice and personal compassion.

Kohlberg's six stages reflect not only the emergence of different motives for making decisions but also a progression toward more differentiated, integrated structures of thinking. As individuals advance through the stages, they can better differentiate the commands of parents from the requests of friends, national traditions from consensually-made laws, and societal regulations from universal moral principles. Thoughts also become more integrated. At the lowest stage of cognitive development, people think mainly of themselves. Later they take into account the views of peer groups, national society, and its institutions. The most abstract thinkers make choices from a general, universal perspective that transcends any particular society. They take the view of humankind, a universe of rational moral individuals. According to the empirical research, persons who have attained the highest stages of cognitive and moral development – who interpret politics from a differentiated, integrated perspective – express the greatest support for civil liberties.[21]

Applications of Kohlberg's theory suggest that age and educational background interact with cognitive development to strengthen political tolerance. The freedoms to articulate political views, challenge incumbent leaders, and organize nonviolent opposition against government policies gain increasing support as people grow older, complete more years of formal education, and become more cognitively developed. Young children in the early years of US primary school perceive political leaders as infallible, believe that the law punishes bad actions, and link good citizenship to obeying the law. Unable to make cognitive differentiations, these young children fuse sacred objects with secular roles (God with the president) and equate the presidential role with the person occupying that office. Hence, challenges to government authority are unthinkable. In contrast, more cognitively developed individuals at higher educational levels take a more differentiated view of political life. From their perspective, government makes mistakes. Laws prescribe right behavior and prohibit undesirable actions. Citizens obey laws as well as participate more actively in political decisionmaking. Those at higher stages of cognitive development differentiate sacred values from secular roles – God from the president. They can distinguish between the presidential office and the incumbent leader who holds that office. For them, criticism of presidential policies does not mean disrespect for the institutional office or the fundamental constitutional values of the US political system. Particularly among university-educated, informed adults who have majored in the humanities and social sciences, their high level of cognitive development induces them to tolerate diverse groups – communists, atheists, racists, militarists, and homosexuals. They have learned empathy and insight – the ability to take the role of persons different from themselves. They can apply general rules about civil liberties to specific unpopular groups. They differentiate the assumptions of Marxist–Leninist ideology from the actual power of the Communist Party in the United States to threaten political freedom. All these cognitive abilities reflect a critical, rational, differentiated thought process that reinforces support for civil liberties.[22]

Critics of Kohlberg's theory of cognitive development claim that he has exaggerated the impact of mental structures and motives on political actions. Can the researcher really develop independent measures of cognitive structure and content? Although the analytical distinction between the two seems clear, social scientists devising empirical indicators of both dimensions must infer structure partly from content – the verbal responses made in personal interviews or on questionnaires. Content, not form, wields the greater impact on people's lives. Substantive decisions, rather than the mode of policyakers' reasoning, lead to behavioral consequences in the political realm. Kohlberg also stresses the motives for making moral judgments. Yet highly educated university graduates can justify their reasons better than those with less formal education. They can invoke 'good' reasons for taking actions that may harm others. Political actions stem not only from cognitive structures and moral intentions but also from the situational pressures that surround an individual.[23]

## MORAL ATTITUDES, COGNITION, AND POLITICAL ACTION

The impact of moral attitudes on political actions depends on both personal and situational variables. Individuals who hold certain personal beliefs will participate in peaceful demonstrations against government injustices. These beliefs include moral judgments, acceptance of group norms, and perceived political efficacy. Rather than merely justifying behavior, moral principles shape a person's commitment to action. They interpret the meaning of the political situation, draw inferences about one's responsibility to help others, evaluate the justice of government policies, and prescribe desirable conduct. Individuals at the highest stages of moral reasoning achieve greater consistency between their actions and ethical principles. They base their actions on general principles such as Kant's categorical imperative – treat each person as an end, not a means – or John Stuart Mill's utilitarian prescription to maximize social well-being and minimize suffering. Particularly when small group norms uphold such ethical principles and libertarian attitudes take priority over other values (order, security), individuals will feel a stronger motivation to act according to their tolerant orientations. The probability of acting on ethical principles also increases when people perceive they have the power to attain a successful outcome. Individuals will translate their moral principles into action if small groups support an activity, no powerful structures – churches, corporations, police, military – restrain actions, and the individual anticipates that desirable consequences will result from the action. Thus the motivation to act stems not only from moral judgments but also from structural opportunities and constraints. Whereas small group sanctions and high state repression often deter individuals from acting on their libertarian attitudes, peer group rewards and lenient police treatment may spur a person to translate support for civil liberties into peaceful political protests.

Students' participation in university protests has often stemmed from high stages of moral development. For example, University of California students, particularly women, who joined the 1964 Berkeley Free Speech Movement (FSM) were more likely than non-FSM participants to show higher moral stages – stage 5, rather than 3 or 4. During the 1970s leftwing student activists in three universities in England, Scotland, and France were interviewed about their degree of participation in such activities as attending rallies, demonstrating in the capital, contributing money, marching through city streets, collecting signatures for a petition, distributing literature, and engaging in civil disobedience. Students who expressed post-conventional moral principles (stages 5 and 6) showed the highest political participation. These student activists, who usually had leftwing parents, majored in the humanities or social sciences.[24]

Moral judgments also influenced a more dramatic form of libertarian political participation – actions to rescue Jews from their Nazi exterminators during the Second World War. The Nazis tried to deprive Jews not only of freedom but of life itself. These voluntary rescue activities emancipated Jews from the probability of death in concentration camps. During the early 1980s Samuel P. Oliner and Pearl M. Oliner supervised around 700 interviews of two groups: individuals who had taken high risks to rescue Jews and a matched sample of nonrescuers.[25] Most respondents lived in Germany, the Netherlands, France, and Poland. Compared with the nonrescuers, the rescuers displayed more of the attitudinal and situational characteristics associated with people at high stages of moral reasoning. From the situational perspective, rescuers had experienced warm and lenient relations with their parents, who explained the reasons for discipline. In contrast, the nonrescuers' parents had inflicted routine physical punishment. As adults, the rescuers maintained more contacts with Jews as friends, neighbors, and coworkers. Active in anti-Nazi resistance groups, they also participated in more democratic organizations, such as the German Social Democrats, the French Socialist Party, the Dutch Christian Democrats, and the Polish Socialist Party. From these parental and organizational experiences sprang the moral attitudes linked to individuals at the highest stage of ethical development. Committed to universal moral principles based on the need to help other people, the rescuers expressed high empathy, self-esteem, individual responsibility, integrity, political efficacy, and egalitarianism. They viewed all individuals as members of a universal family. Regardless of ethnicity, religion, or nationality, all people have similar human qualities and deserve dignified treatment. The nonrescuers, however, showed lower levels of moral judgment. They stressed the need to obey social conventions and take actions that would benefit the self. External rewards from others, not internal ethical standards, guided their behavior. Low self-esteem dissuaded the nonrescuers from feeling great empathy for those who suffered injustice. Fatalistic attitudes deterred them from taking personal responsibility to rectify collective injustices. Perceiving Jews and Gentiles as basically different people, the nonrescuers felt only a weak commitment to egalitarian values and the altruistic ethic of universal concern for the public good. Their disinclination to take risky actions that would rescue Jewish victims from extermination stemmed from a low level of moral developent.

## CONCLUSION

Both structural and attitudinal variables affect the degree of political freedom among different nations. The political attitudes of leaders and citizens, as well as structural conditions, explain crossnational rankings on civil liberty. According to national sample surveys, the inactive citizenry holds less tolerant attitudes than do political leaders. They receive more ideologically diverse messages, see a greater need to compromise policy positions, and can more accurately gauge the impact of repressive government actions. Nevertheless, certain elites pose a greater danger to civil liberties than do the rank-and-file public. To most citizens, political freedom for unpopular groups takes lower priority than unemployment, inflation, high taxes, and the personal rights to change jobs, attend church, and move from one residence to another. The unorganized mass population remains divided by conflicting values and interests. Elites, however, command greater financial, educational, and organizational resources to repress civil liberties. Particularly when leaders strongly believe in the norms of monistic classical conservatism, Marxism-Leninism, fascism, or fundamentalism, they will more likely implement repressive policies than if they hold classical liberal or democratic socialist views – ideologies that uphold individualism, secularism, and reformist change. Whatever their ideological orientations, most government officials have higher formal education than the mass population. Compared with tolerant citizens, intolerant educated elites more intensely fear real or imagined threats. They express greater willingess to take actions restricting disliked groups. When dissident organizations promote demands for change, these elites feel endangered, especially if the costs of tolerance seem to outweigh the benefits. With both the resources and the motivation to suppress dissident organizations, government officials enact repressive policies. To maintain political freedom, a society needs structural restraints on its leaders. Decentralized government institutions and liberal pluralism give numerous organizations the independent power to check the central state.[26] Yet intolerant leaders may head local governments and social institutions, including private corporate bureaucracies. Thus only when policymakers hold libertarian attitudes and citizens actively participate in politics to press for expanded freedom will a society become emancipated from its chains.

# 9  Electoral Participation

At the start of the twentieth century, women organized protest movements demanding the right to vote. The suffragettes originally hoped the suffrage would bring not only political power but higher status for women and greater economic equality with men.[1] Annie Kenney, a worker in a Lancashire textile factory and one of the early leaders of the women's suffrage movement, expected that a systemic transformation would result from women's enfranchisement: 'Poverty would be practically swept away; washing would be done by municipal machinery! In fact, Paradise would be there once the vote was won!'[2]

To attain these comprehensive goals, the suffragettes strove to organize a powerful protest movement that would mobilize the apathetic behind the cause, coordinate formerly isolated activities, and overcome the resistance of government leaders who opposed women's right to vote. From 1903 through 1918, the most important organization campaigning for the suffrage was the Women's Social and Political Union. Led by members of the Pankhurst family – Emmeline, the mother, and her two daughters, Christabel and Sylvia – the WSPU tried to rally support from various social groups. Although upper- and middle-class women played the dominant role in the organization, it also gained support from working-class women such as Annie and Jessie Kenney. Sylvia Pankhurst, a member of the upper-middle class, made special efforts to organize women in the East End of London, the poorest section of the city.

The tactics devised by the suffrage movement partly depended on the type of resistance that government leaders mounted. Initially, the tactics were relatively peaceful. As early as 1870, Dr Richard Pankhurst, Emmeline's husband, convinced a member of parliament to introduce a Women's Disabilities Removal Bill granting the suffrage to women. At that time, however, the governing Liberal Party of England refused to place the bill before parliament for a vote. After the WSPU was formed, women demonstrated in the streets, lectured at meetings, wrote magazine articles, published pamphlets, sent petitions to parliament, and negotiated with cabinet ministers in the government. Sylvia

Pankhurst designed calendars and banners emblazoned with WSPU slogans: 'Rebellion to Tyrants is obedience to God.' 'Grant the Womanhood the justice England should be proud to give.' 'Human Emancipation must precede Social Regeneration.' As expressive symbols, these banners urged WSPU supporters to rally behind the 'Votes for Women' cause as a way to secure their rights to dignity and freedom from oppression. The most popular banner portrayed a female angel blowing a trumpet for freedom.[3]

Despite these attempts to mobilize political support behind the feminist cause and to unify diverse suffragette activities behind a common movement, England's male leaders still refused to accommodate women's demands. When the Pankhurst family members peacefully demonstrated outside the House of Commons, the police arrested them and judges sent them to prison. After hunger strikes in prison, forced feeding ensued. The police also raided WSPU offices. Encouraged by the police in its crackdown on civil liberties, mobs attacked suffragettes trying to question England's political leaders about voting rights.

Reacting to this government's resistance, the WSPU implemented more militant tactics. Women in prison went on hunger strikes. Suffragettes outside prison smashed windows. Some set fire to theaters. Others planted bombs in public buildings. In 1913 at the Derby, Emily Wilding Davison, a graduate of London University and a former honors student at Oxford University, threw herself in front of King George's horse and died with the WSPU colors sewn inside her coat. But English government officials still denied women the vote.

At the start of the First World War, a split erupted in the suffrage movement. In 1914 Emmeline and Christabel Pankhurst extended their support to the government in its war efforts against Germany. They assumed that if women played an equal role with men in winning the war, the government would have to grant women the franchise after hostilities ceased. Sylvia Pankhurst, however, remained more committed to pacifist, internationalist, and socialist ideals. In her view, English participation in the war threatened to bring even greater deprivation to the poor people of London's East End. As early as 1906 Christabel and Sylvia had disagreed over the relationship among socialism, democracy, and universal suffrage. Christabel wanted only the 'strongest and most intelligent' women to lead the suffrage movement as generals command an army. Winning the vote took precedence over rallying workers behind the socialist and suffragette cause. In contrast, Sylvia encouraged both poor men and poor women to play a participatory role in the campaign for the vote. During the war, she worked in the East End to provide free meals for the poor, to uphold civil liberties, and to institute a health clinic, day nursery, and Montessori school. Organizing the Workers' Suffrage Federation in 1916, Sylvia Pankhurst changed its name two years later to the Workers' Socialist Federation. Under her guidance, the WSF struggled for the cause of socialism, workers' councils, international workers' solidarity, and participatory democracy. From her perspective, not only male factory employees but housewives were 'workers.'

After the war ended in 1918, the electoral objectives of the suffrage movement triumphed over Sylvia Pankhurst's socialist ideals. Fearful of postwar WSPU militancy and recognizing women's wartime contributions, the English parliament granted voting rights to women over thirty who met certain property qualifications. A decade later the government enfranchised all women aged twenty-one and above. Through the activities of the WSPU and other feminist organizations, women had gained greater electoral equality, higher status as citizens, and perhaps more equal economic opportunities. Yet the more comprehensive policy priorities of the suffrage movement remained unfulfilled. Enfranchisement hardly brought paradise or the abolition of poverty, as Annie Kenney had anticipated. Contrary to the aspirations of Sylvia Pankhurst, poor people still experienced an inferior status, economic deprivation, unequal access to political power, and only limited opportunities to shape the public policy process.

Working through protest movements, social groups, and political organiations, later generations continued the struggle for egalitarian social change. For example, during the 1980s women's committees pressured local councils governed by the Labour Party to finance health clinics, rape crisis shelters, and feminist collectives. National movements such as the Rights of Women, the National Abortion Campaign, and Women against Pit Closures articulated women's policy demands. Yet, as during the first decade of the twentieth century, the tensions between socialism and feminism remained. Whereas some women's organizations allied with the unions in their struggle for more socioeconomic equality, other feminist groups rejected male patriarchy, preferring instead to concentrate on mobilizing only women. Along with Conservative Party opposition, this fragmentation of the women's movement has impeded the implementation of government programs that increase gender equality.[4]

Although American women gained the right to vote in 1920, Southern state governments denied blacks the suffrage until the mid-1960s; Fannie Lou Hamer played a leading role staging protest movements against electoral repression. Unlike Sylvia Pankhurst, Mrs Hamer hardly came from an upper-middle class, well-educated family. Born in 1917 the youngest child of African-American parents with nineteen other children, she worked most of her early life as a sharecropper picking cotton in the Mississippi Delta. Until her death in 1977, she remained poor, sick, and formally uneducated. Yet she possessed an indomitable spirit, a great singing voice, a knowledge of the Bible, and the will to overcome adversity.

Like Sylvia Pankhurst, Fannie Lou Hamer was an Enlightenment prophet determined to realize greater political, social, and economic equality. For her, a favorite scriptural passage was Matthew 5:14–16: 'You are the light of the world. . . . Let your light shine before others, so that they may see your good works and give glory to your Father in heaven.' In church and at protest marches, she loved to sing the African-American spiritual 'This little light of mine, I'm goin'-a let it shine.' Encouraged by the Student Nonviolent Coordinating Committee, she attempted to register to vote in 1962 and the next year. Her participatory efforts led to loss of job, eviction from her home, imprisonment, severe beatings in prison, and hypertension. Yet she persisted. In 1964 Mrs Hamer helped found the Mississippi Freedom Democratic Party as an alternative to the state Democratic party that prevented African-Americans from voting. The MFDP challenged President Lyndon Johnson and his decision to escalate US involvement in the Vietnam War. Partly as a result of the civil rights movement, President Johnson signed the Voting Rights Act in 1965. Nevertheless, Southern state government repression against black voters continued. Mrs Hamer maintained her protests against several injustices: electoral oppression, curtailment of antipoverty programs, and efforts to eliminate Head Start educational plans. She also organized several egalitarian projects that fed the poor, healed the sick, and provided job training. Six years before her death, she became a founding member of the

National Women's Political Caucus. Despite all the odds against her, why did Fannie Lou Hamer take such risks? The drive for social justice, equality, freedom, and dignity certainly motivated her participation. And, as her tombstone in Ruleville, Mississippi read, she became 'sick and tired of being sick and tired.'[5] Even though her protests helped secure the franchise and greater civil liberties for Mississippi blacks, the struggle to realize greater socioeconomic equality in the United States still continues.

In the following sections, we probe two general sets of questions about electoral participation. First, what motives shape the choice of certain parties and candidates? How do cultural values – ideology, religion, nationalism – and structural conditions affect these motivations? To what extent do voters' choices represent a protest against incumbent government officials, their policies, and the socioeconomic situation at election time? Second, what policy consequences emerge from electoral decisions? Under what conditions can the individual wield an impact on elections, public policies, and their outcomes? Most electoral research has occurred in the United States, Canada, West Europe, Japan, Australia, and New Zealand since the Second World War. Hence, in answering the two questions, we will concentrate on these areas.

## RATIONAL CHOICE PERSPECTIVES ON ELECTORAL BEHAVIOR

Rational choice theories offer a useful guide for exploring the motivations, processes, and outcomes of electoral participation. They examine how individuals reason about the political world and make evaluations of the incumbent government, its policy performance, governing parties, opposition parties, and candidates running for legislative or presidential office. Two competing approaches contend for influence as the most efficient framework for explaining why people vote or abstain from voting and why individuals choose one political party over alternative parties. The neoclassical *public choice* approach elaborated by Anthony Downs, James Buchanan, Gordon Tullock, William Riker, Peter Ordeshook, and Dennis Mueller assumes that individuals are motivated to vote mainly by their economic self-interests. They seek personal advantages from government policies and choose those candidates and parties that will supply desired concrete benefits. In contrast, the *rational choice structuralist* approach relies on sociological concepts such as values, norms, and structures to explain voting behavior. Formulated by George Homans, Michael Hechter, Karl-Dieter Opp, Aaron Wildavsky, Dennis Chong, and Daniel Little, this perspective assumes that cultural beliefs (values, norms) and sociopolitical structures influence voting intentions. Rather than seeking just their private interests, individuals also have concern for the wellbeing of other people. Even though individuals play an active role processing political information and evaluating perceived alternatives, their decisions are scarcely autonomous. Instead, structural opportunities facilitate personal choices; structural constraints impede them. We will first explore the neoclassical approach, critique it, and then justify the greater explanatory power of the rational choice structuralist perspective.

The neoclassical public choice approach makes three closely related assumptions about electoral behavior. First, these theorists adopt a methodological individualist position. According to them, individuals, not groups, institutions, or society, comprise the main unit of analysis. Only individuals act and made choices. Individual goals, preferences, beliefs, expectations, perceptions, and motivations explain electoral participation. The individual retains extensive independence to make her choices, free of cultural and structural constraints. Society is an aggregate of interacting individuals, not a holistic entity that shapes personal voting decisions.[6]

Second, individuals act rationally in political life. Their actions are prudential, calculating, utilitarian, and strategic. For public choice theorists, rationality means an instrumental orientation. The individual has the motivation and the cognitive capacity to seek efficient means to attain her ends. Rationality thus refers to a process; only means are rational, not ends. Rational behavior occurs when individuals can clearly rank order their goals, especially concrete tangible benefits. For example, many rational voters expect government officials to place highest priority on low taxes, regard increased expenditures for public education as less important, and rank foreign assistance to Malawi at the bottom of policy priorities. A voter with these ordered preferences will vote for the candidate most strongly supporting reduced taxation. Rational voters can also identify options to achieve their goals. They can accurately estimate the costs and benefits of each option, evaluating each alternative for its feasibility and desirability. This assumption implies that the voter has accurate, complete information about the policy positions taken by competing candidates. He can anticipate the likelihood that the preferred candidate will gain office, actually support the desired policy (tax reductions), and ensure that lower taxes will produce a favorable outcome like less unemployment. The probability of goal attainment also depends on strategic considerations. Rational political actors need complete, reliable information about the strategies and payoffs of other players in the electoral game. What are the opportunities and constraints that shape the moves made by competing political parties? How likely will they achieve success at the polls? What value do they place on alternative outcomes? Strategic decisionmaking thus entails weighing the comparative advantage of alternative actions to the self and to other participants in the electoral arena.[7]

Third, rational choice theorists assume that voters seek to maximize their utility, so that benefits exceed costs. An individual's electoral decisions stem from both value preferences (desired satisfactions, expected benefits) and the probability of realizing these preferences. Voters will select a party or candidate whose policy stands congrue with their own issue positions. In the past, the preferred party has implemented policies that brought more extensive gains but fewer losses than competing parties. In the future, voters expect that if their party achieves significant influence over the policy process, the personal costs to them will be lower than such benefits as economic wellbeing.

What are the comparative advantages and disadvantages of the neoclassical perspective? As a deductive, axiomatic theory, this public choice approach shows considerable parsimony and logical consistency. Its proponents have generated counterintuitive, innovative propositions about political participation – for example, about the problems of transforming individual preferences into collective political action. General propositions explain behavior in situations that transcend specific historical contexts. Despite these virtues, the empirical evidence collected about electoral participation often contradicts theoretical assumptions. Neoclassical axioms about politicoeconomic man as selfish, hedonistic, acquisitive, competitive, and calculating fail to explain the behavior of such individuals as Sylvia Pankhurst and Fannie Lou Hamer who experienced far greater personal losses than benefits when they struggled for universal suffrage. The neoclassical view of individuals is too atomistic, instrumentalist, and economistic.[8] Hence, its explanations remain empirically inadequate.

As methodological individualists, neoclassical theorists take an atomistic view that downplays the importance of collective public goods transcending individual preferences. Political institutions and social groups shape personal intentions. Rather than just satisfy individual interests, political organizations define the moral purposes of the community. They educate people about values and norms. Cultural norms – shared, stable expectations about rights and obligations in particular roles – both constrain and facilitate personal choices. Some norms are instrumentally rational. Credible commitments – rules about keeping one's promises – increase the efficiency of interpersonal transactions. Others norms are expressive; individuals perceive them as ends in themselves. For example, the choice of nonviolent tactics, regardless of the consequences, reflects an expressive norm. Rather than passive recipients of group norms, individuals actively interpret them, rank order divergent norms, and apply them to specific historical conditions. Cultural beliefs also shape the structural conditions affecting electoral participation. The decision to vote stems not only from actual structural constraints (state repression) and opportunities (automatic registration by government officials) but from causal attributions transmitted through communications networks. If political messages stress the desirability and feasibility of voting, then individuals will feel a greater incentive to vote. From this cultural–structural perspective, politics becomes a collective game shaped by sociopolitical institutions, organizations, and groups. An individual's partisan identity, ideological preferences, and conceptions of the public good assume meaning only in a societal context.

Neoclassical theorists also exaggerate the instrumental rationality of voters. Few voters choose their candidates in as calculating way as the model supposes. Their goals are often ambiguous, unstable, and intransitive; policy priorities display no clear order. Information to assess the possible outcomes of alternative choices remains incomplete, inaccurate, unreliable, and inaccessible. Individuals lack the cognitive skills to estimate the actual costs and benefits of selecting one party's candidates over the opposition. Hence, an incongruence emerges among goals, efficient means, and outcomes. Rather than acting rationally, many voters make nonrational and irrational decisions. Their choices derive from nonrational criteria: habit, custom, emotional impulses, unconscious desires, astrology, or deference to influential authority figures. Some voters behave irrationally; they choose an option that blocks the attainment of desired goals. For instance, they may vote for a candidate who promises to reduce income taxes but who helps enact higher taxes after election to legislative office. Rather than judging individuals as either rational or irrational, we should regard rationality as an ordinal variable and examine which individuals make the most rational choices under what specific conditions.[9]

The neoclassical approach toward expected utility assumes too economistic a view. Perceiving individuals as self-interested egoists, it defines expected utility as personal material gain. Voters prefer the party that will secure for them the most tangible benefits: lower taxes, higher transfer payments, or greater business subsidies. Yet people seek goals other than just economic gains for the self. They pursue not only material interests but also moral/spiritual/ideological values. According to rational choice theorist George Homans, two dominant motives guide personal decisions: the value attached to the goals (intended outcomes) and the expected probability of successful goal attainment.[10] The choice of a particular party or candidate depends on the intensity of the value preferences times the strength of the individual's political efficacy. 'Purists' participate in politics to affirm the intrinsic value of certain moral/spiritual/ideological principles. Dedicated to an ethical cause, participants such as Sylvia Pankhurst and Fannie Lou Hamer perceive electoral participation as a way to assert demands for justice, equality, freedom, and dignity. Motivated by group loyalties and organizational identifications, they seek to enhance the wellbeing of the larger collectivity. Empathy, sharing, and cooperation become valued political attributes. In contrast with the purists, 'pragmatists' anticipate that their votes will lead to a successful outcome. Less committed to idealistic principles, they seek to maximize their benefits but minimize their costs. Pragmatists assume that electoral participation will secure greater material benefits – for example, lower taxes, reduced tuition, and expanded access to health services. Empirical investigations of voting behavior can ascertain the relative proportions of purists and pragmatists participating in the electoral process. In general, purists most often operate as educated activists and political leaders who show willingness to take risks. Pragmatists, however, are usually found among the more risk-averse followers who join the bandwagon when electoral success appears imminent.

In sum, the rational choice structuralist (RCS) approach offers a more empirically valid analysis of electoral participation than does the neoclassical economic perspective. Even if less parsimonious, RCS theories posit a more complex understanding of the interactions among goals, means, and outcomes. Neoclassical theorists assume that both the political system and the market involve self-interested actors who seek to maximize their personal concrete benefits. Political parties form coalitions to negotiate bargains among conflicting interests. They aggregate the divergent preferences of partisan supporters. Party leaders function as sellers who offer concrete policy benefits in exchange for votes (dollars). Voters behave as consumers of present payoffs or as producers who invest their resources (electoral support) to attain future policy satisfactions. According to the criterion of Pareto optimality, an efficient outcome occurs when the electoral game makes some people better off than before without making anybody worse off. In contrast, the RCS approach perceives politics as the discussion, formulation, and implementation of shared values. Such public goods as trust, empathy, and justice become key civic virtues. Individuals seek both material interests as well as communal values for the self and the society. Means to realize these goals include deliberation, dialogue, education, and participation in the electoral process, where people learn how to cooperate with others. Political parties integrate conflicting interests into a general decision that expresses shared purposes.[11] In the following sections, we use these general assumptions of RCS theorists to formulate tentative explanations for electoral choices, particularly citizens' inclination to protest the incumbent government by voting for opposition parties.

## VOTING BEHAVIOR AND THE PROCESSING OF POLITICAL INFORMATION

According to rational choice theorists, an individual's vote depends on the perceived value of public goods – policies, policy outcomes, leadership – and on her expectations about competing parties' success in achieving these goods. When making judgments, the voter processes information about six key political objects: social groups, political parties, ideology, policy issues, policy performance, and candidates. These six objects constitute 'cognitive schema' that citizens use to comprehend, interpret, and evaluate political life.[12] Individuals evaluate parties according to cognitive criteria. What consequences (benefits vs costs) will result from voting for a preferred party, rather than for opposition parties? To what extent will that party realize beneficial outcomes for the self, particular social groups, and the larger community? These expected benefits include the enactment of specific policy measures, the attainment of desirable policy outcomes, and the manifestation of leadership qualities (competence, integrity, character) in candidates running for office. Voters with strong party loyalties who frequently receive consistent partisan messages from homogeneous information networks – relatives, friends, neighbors, churches, voluntary associations, mass media – choose the same party at election time. Generally, the most informed citizens base their electoral choices on the perceived congruence between their own policy positions and the policy stands of the preferred party's candidates. By assigning responsibility for such political outcomes as high inflation, war, and corruption, ideological interpretations and party images shape voting behavior.

Electoral outcomes largely derive from the interaction between political party leaders and voters. Parties try to raise expected benefits for their supporters but to lower transaction–information costs. Partisan leaders focus on persuading the voter that support for their party will increase the policy benefits accruing to a membership group – for example, a church, union, business, or ethnic association. Campaign appeals highlight the congruence among personal, group, and party interests. One party links its policy benefits to 'deserving' groups and associates opposition parties with groups labeled as 'undeserving.' Through personal contacts, electoral campaigns, rallies, and advertising over the media, parties lower the information and transaction costs of voting. They strengthen partisan loyalties, attachments, and identifications. Party labels become 'brand names' that simplify voters' judgments about candidates' personal qualities, their policy views, images of policy performance by competing parties, and the links among a party's positions, its past performance in government office, and its anticipated future ability to satisfy a voter's policy expectations. By monitoring the behavior of elected politicians, parties reduce the transaction costs to voters. Legislators who display high party cohesion receive prized committee assignments and money for campaigns. Through these monitoring techniques, party leaders make legislators more accountable to the citizenry. The ideologies articulated by political party activists influence voters' value preferences about freedom, equality, and justice. Partisan interpretations of these abstract values then shape general attitudes and specific policy positions toward diverse issues: government involvement in the economy, governmental responsibility for promoting ethnic, occupational, and gender equality, and proper government restraints on cultural lifestyles. Communications from political parties also affect voters' perceptions of policy outcomes and candidates' qualities. Retrospective judgments made by party spokesmen focus on the costs and benefits of the incumbent government's performance, particularly on causal responsibility for policy successes and failures. Prospective voting revolves around the estimated future consequences of the incumbent parties versus challengers. Naturally, a party will make optimistic prognoses of its own expected performance but render pessimistic assessments about opposition parties. By highlighting the positive attributes of its candidates running for parliament or the presidency, party leaders try to convince voters that its candidates will demonstrate competence, ethical behavior, and empathy in office.[13]

Party strategies toward social groups partly determine an individual's voting behavior. In heterogeneous societies, political party leaders first must decide which groups to target for electoral support and then devise campaign strategies that will maximize the party's appeal to these groups. For example, during the 1960s the Democratic Party concentrated on winning black votes; the civil rights laws passed by the Democratic Congress and President Lyndon Johnson represented a commitment to secure equal rights for all citizens, including the newly enfranchised Southern blacks. In contrast, the Republican strategy stressed the need to gain votes from Southern whites. To further expand its electoral base, the Republican leaders also appealed to middle-income Catholics and skilled trade unionists – groups that used to support the

Democrats. In Western Europe both the socialists and the Christian Democrats have broadened their campaign appeals to include more diverse groups. As the proportion of skilled factory workers in the labor force has declined, the Social Democratic Party has tried to attract more middle-class voters, especially professionals and salaried employees. Campaign appeals stress the need for full employment policies and comprehensive public services that accrue to all citizens, not just the poor or factory workers. Abandoning its opposition to established churches, Social Democratic leaders also target Catholics and other church attenders. When the Christian Democratic parties uphold the social service state and union demands for representation in economic decisionmaking, they gather votes from factory workers, Protestants, and even some individuals who remained uninvolved in any church. Hence, if party strategists advocate policy issues that transcend the interests of class and religion, the linkage between social group membership and electoral behavior weakens. The declining impact of both religious and especially occupational cleavages on electoral behavior reflects the calculated strategies of party leaders to gain support from diverse social groups.[14]

Not only party strategies but a social group's influence over individual behavior guides electoral choices. If a group maintains high solidarity based on shared political preferences and on a tightly organized communications network, its likelihood of shaping a citizen's vote increases. Under these conditions, the member becomes dependent on the group for political cues about voting; particularly in small groups, leaders can control their members' behavior. Those who accept certain policy views earn rewards (group approval), but individuals who reject issue stands linked to a preferred party receive disapproval. Close ties between group leaders (church, union, business) and political party activists increase the group's power over electoral choices. Members will likely conform to group leaders' recommendations. For example, during the post-Second-World-War era, class voting reached the highest levels in countries such as Sweden where the Social Democratic Party and allied trade unions established the strongest base of power and the closest working relationships. These two organizations taught norms – civic duty, political efficacy, concern about electoral outcomes – important to electoral behavior. By encouraging people to vote and promising increased policy benefits (higher pensions, increased child care, expanded health-care services) for choosing the Social Democrats, organizational leaders helped swing their membership behind the party at election time. Similarly, in Britain group norms and incentives transmitted by the Labour Party and trade unions persuaded industrial workers employed in the public sector to support the Labour Party. Workers who identified with the working class, supported close ties between unions and the Labour party, and took a positive view toward union power most often voted for Labour candidates to the House of Commons. In nations such as Belgium, the Netherlands, Germany, and Italy, the Christian Democratic parties stressed religious appeals. Whereas Roman Catholics who frequently attended Mass selected Christian Democrats, the less religiously involved citizens chose more secular parties, such as Socialist or Liberal.[15]

Throughout West Europe, North America, and Japan, party images, identification with a political party, and the perceived closeness to a party emerge as the most important cause of a person's vote. In the United States the more strongly an individual identifies with a party, the greater the tendency to choose that party's candidates at the polls. For example, 'strong' democrats and particularly 'strong' Republicans select their party's nominee for president more often than do voters who weakly identify with a party or see themselves as 'independents.' Governor William Clinton defeated President George Bush in the 1992 election partly because a higher proportion (80 percent) of Democratic Party identifiers chose Clinton than Republican Party identifiers (70 percent) selected Bush. Clinton also gained slightly greater support from independents. In Europe and Japan citizens who feel closest to a party and hold favorable images of their party most frequently vote for it. Subjective attachments to a party and the decision to support the party at election time bring certain expressive benefits – self-satisfaction – that may supplement or even transcend the more tangible rewards such as group approval that ensue from participation in a party organization. Political party identifications also influence the vote because they shape an individual's evaluation of candidates, national policy performance, specific issues, and general ideological orientations.

Like party preference, ideological self-designation helps determine electoral choices. If a US citizen perceives himself as 'very conservative,' he will probably vote Republican. Those viewing themselves as 'very liberal' choose the Democratic candidate for president. Similarly, in Europe people who place themselves at the 'left' end of the ideological scale usually vote for Socialist parties. In contrast, self-designated 'right-wingers' select the Conservative or Christian Democratic Party at the polls. Educated voters who actively participate in their party's organization most consistently think in abstract terms and link their ideological orientations to specific policy issues.[16]

If the policy preferences of the voter congrue with the policy stands of a specific party, then the citizen will select that party's candidates. Since the Second World War political parties have taken conflicting policy positions on two general types of ideological orientation: *economic* issues and *cultural* issues. Established parties disagree about economic issues related to government management, role of unions, government provision of social services, and government policies to reduce income inequality. Parties on the 'left' – Labor, Social Democrat, Socialist, US Democrats – show greater enthusiasm for government regulation of privately-owned firms, active union participation in a business, extended provision of social services (health care, pensions, day care facilities, family allowances), and egalitarian public policies. In contrast, 'rightwing' parties – European Conservatives, Christian Democrats, some Liberals and Free Democrats (Germany, Austria, Italy, the Netherlands), Japanese Liberal Democrats, and US Republicans – prefer managerial control in private enterprises, want to maintain or restrict government-provided social services, and reject government efforts to secure greater equality of income. Voters who take a rightist economic stand on these issues and correctly identify the party articulating these ideological viewpoints will generally vote for that party. Whereas factory workers and educated professionals in the public sector generally prefer the leftist parties, employees in private businesses (especially wealthier managers and owners) as well as younger working-class individuals prefer rightwing parties.

On issues linked to cultural values, voters' ideological positions derive mainly from age and education. Youths, especially highly-educated professionals in the public sector, take libertarian or 'leftist' stands on cultural issues. They uphold civil liberties and expanded popular participation in decisionmaking, especially for youths, women, ethnic minorities, and immigrant workers. Holding a secular view of morality, the cultural leftists support abortion, divorce, and homosexual rights. Opposed to nuclear energy, they favor slow-growth policies and government decisions promoting a nonpolluted environment. Disarmament assumes a high priority. Green and ecological parties throughout Western Europe most fervently back these cultural leftist issues. Socialists show somewhat less enthusiasm for cultural liberalism. Conservative and Christian Democratic parties adopt the most rightwing stands toward these issues. They prefer societal order, back punitive policies for lawbreakers, and reject women's rights for greater equality. Upholding the traditional sacred values of established churches, they oppose abortion, divorce, and homosexuality. For them, rapid economic growth, military preparedness, and nuclear power take priority over government efforts to secure a 'clean' environment or a disarmed world. Older and less formally educated supporters of the rightwing parties particularly articulate these culturally conservative positions.

Compared with less-well-educated party followers, political party activists and highly educated voters take more polarized positions toward both economic and cultural issues. Just as leftwing party leaders voice more leftist stands than does their mass base, so rightwing activists articulate more conservative orientations than do their supporters. Although this tendency holds true for all countries, the stronger, more ideological parties in Sweden produce greater attitudinal differences among the citizenry than occurs in the United States. Unlike American voters, Swedes can choose several different ideological alternatives: the Left Party, the Social Democrats, Ecologists, Liberals, Center, Conservatives, and Christian Democratic Union. These parties articulate clear issue positions. Hence, Swedish citizens, whatever their education, vote for the party that upholds preferred policy preferences. One's ideology – whether 'left' or 'right' – influences voting behavior and stands on specific policy issues. In contrast, the two major US political parties voice less divergent ideological messages. Neither the mass media nor local party organizations provide detailed information to the electorate about candidates' positions on specific issues. Even though party activists and college-educated individuals make their electoral choices according to the ideological congruence between their policy preferences and the candidates' policy stands, few other Americans interpret electoral campaigns through an ideological prism or can articulate the meaning of 'liberalism' and 'conservatism.' Most Americans who use these ideological concepts define them as a relative commitment to social change. 'Liberals' equate liberalism with support for change, especially securing more equality for disadvantaged groups. 'Conservatives' feel more ideologically intense about conservatism, which they interpret as a lower scope of government authority over economic decisionmaking. For them, conservatism means lower taxes and expenditures. Unlike these ideological activists, most other US voters – over 80 percent – lack detailed information about complex issues, hold vague policy preferences, and change their positions over time. This pattern probably holds for most other Western democratic countries as well, with Sweden representing an exceptional case. Because specific issues remain unimportant, incomprehensible, or too complex, citizens base their vote on evaluations of the government's policy performance in securing desirable national outcomes.[17]

Electoral choices mainly rest on citizens' retrospective and prospective judgments – on the past policy competence of the incumbent parties and on expected future policy achievements. If a citizen positively evaluates an incumbent party's performance, she will vote for that party because of its success in securing such favorable national outcomes as peace, low unemployment, minimal inflation, and large increases in real disposable income. Whereas satisfied voters choose the incumbent party, dissatisfied individuals select opposition parties. If voters expect the governing party to wield beneficent outcomes on future national developments, the optimists will remain with the incumbent party. Compared with the issue voting model, this cognitive approach to retrospective and prospective voting assumes that the electorate holds less political information. Rather than ascertaining the candidates' detailed, esoteric policy positions, citizens need know only about certain outcomes: national economic conditions, foreign policy results (war, peace), and government integrity as evidenced by the lack of corruption and scandal. Voters protest the incumbent regime by voting for opposition parties.

Instead of selecting candidates who will most likely maximize a voter's economic *self*-interests, most citizens base their electoral decisions on perceptions of *national* conditions. If an individual perceives that the incumbent party has secured national well-being, that government policies have contributed to societal improvements, and that opposition parties lack the ability to perform better, she will back the incumbent party. Two mediating variables – causal attributions and issue hierarchies – intervene between a voter's personal economic situation and electoral choices. Consider an unemployed individual. He can blame his jobless status on fate, himself, big business, labor unions, foreign competitors, OPEC, and government policies. Only if he blames government for his jobless status, assumes that the governent can implement programs that will actually lower unemployment, and perceives the opposition parties as more competent to resolve economic problems will he support the opposition. Moreover, not all unemployed persons rank economic issues at the top of their issue hierarchy. When a jobless voter ranks noneconomic issues (interpersonal violence, 'moral decay,' national honor, legality of abortion) as the highest importance to country and self, that voter may still choose the incumbent party's candidate. In short, issue priorities and causal attributions of personal problems shape a rational voter's evaluation of the relative costs and benefits of governents' policy outcomes.

The electoral impact of specific economic conditions depends on the cohesion of the political system, national cultural expectations, and social group interests. As we have seen, if the national economic situation deteriorates, then the incumbent party or parties face the prospects of electoral defeat. Particularly when a single party and one government institution like the cabinet coordinate the policy process, voters can clearly allocate responsibility for policy performance. Knowing whom to blame for high unemployment or rising inflation, they can make accurate retrospective judgments. In New Zealand, Britain, Canada, Japan, and Sweden from 1970 through the late 1980s, one party usually controlled executive power in the cabinet. The lower house of parliament made the key decisions; legislative committees exerted limited influence over policy formulation. Votes on legislative bills showed fairly high party cohesion. Under these conditions, voters could hold one party accountable for the economic mess. Under a more dispersed power situation, however, several different parties share authority in making government decisions. For example, Switzerland, Norway, Denmark, and Germany have featured coalition governments. Two or more different parties held cabinet ministries. In countries such as Germany with a bicameral, federal system, opposition parties controlled the upper house; a different party coalition dominated the lower chamber. Powerful legislative committees provided representation for opposition party members. In the United States, Italy, and Switzerland, legislative voting behavior reflected party fragmentation. This diffusion of responsibility meant that citizens could less easily identify the parties accountable for economic decline. Hence, incumbent parties did not suffer such a sizable loss of electoral support as they did under a more coordinated government.

Diverse groups react differently to the national economic situation. Younger, low-income voters who prefer leftwing parties appear sensitive to high levels and rapid rises in unemployment. Particularly under unified government institutions, center and leftist parties that control the executive face waning electoral support when joblessness rises to high levels. In contrast, wealthy people, old persons on a fixed income, and supporters of conservative parties react against an incumbent rightist or leftist government failing to halt inflation only when these voters blame the governing parties and perceive that the opposition can lower the inflation rate. Whereas Swedes and Canadians seem particularly concerned with the unemployment rate, Germans accept higher joblessness if the inflation rate remains fairly low.

Whatever the country, the effect of inflation, personal income, and unemployment on voting behavior varies according to their level and rate of change. Especially when prices rise rapidly to double-digit figures, unemployment rates escalate beyond 10 percent, and citizens' real disposable income sharply falls, then voters with weak partisan and ideologial ties will switch from their normal allegiances to vote the 'rascals' out of power. Under the opposite conditions – falling joblessness, declining inflation, and rising real disposable income – the incumbent party will retain support from the centrist, nonpartisan voters influenced by national economic conditions.

Attitudes toward risk shape retrospective and prospective judgments of competing parties. In US presidential elections, retrospective assessments have occurred most often when an incumbent president runs again, as happened during the 1980, 1984, and 1992 elections. When faced with a deteriorating economic situation, voters become risk-averse to economic losses and punish the incumbent candidate, as they did in 1980 and 1992. Prospective voting becomes more significant when two nonincumbent candidates compete for the presidency. Voters feel less certain about the future consequences of each candidate's policy performance. More prone to take risks, they expect that their preferred candidate will achieve greater policy benefits than losses.[18]

Particularly in countries electing a powerful president, such as the United States and France, citizens base their electoral choices on images of the candidates' personalities. The mass media stress the personal qualities of the presidential candidates – their warmth, humor, sincerity, and honesty. Specific stands on complex issues assume less importance over television. Hence, American and French voters assess presidential candidates on their technical competence, moral character, and personal warmth. Competence involves strength, decisiveness, dependability, efficiency, intelligence, knowledge, comprehension of issues, and effective problem-solving. Moral character includes such virtues as courage, honesty, trustworthiness, integrity, and the ability to inspire people with an ethical vision. Personal warmth implies compassion, kindness, understanding, empathy, friendliness, likeability, and humor. For example, Governor Clinton won the 1992 presidential election because his supporters perceived him, not President Bush, as a stronger, more compassionate leader who would implement expanded public programs for social services like health care. In most parliamentary systems, voters select legislators from a particular geographic constituency. Members of parliament then choose the prime minister. During recent years the television media have focused attention on the competing parties' leaders who will likely become prime minister; Canada, Britain, and New Zealand represent notable examples. Nevertheless, the evaluations of legislative candidates' personalities still wield less impact on electoral behavior in parliamentary systems than in regimes dominated by a nationally elected president.[19]

In summary, party identification and evaluations of the government's policy performance largely shape voters' choices throughout most Western democratic societies. Candidates' images and their policy positions on specific economic issues seem less important to the general electorate. Ideological principles carry the greatest weight with well-educated partisan activists. Protest voting against established parties reveals the importance of weak party identifications, retrospective judgments, and cultural values on electoral choices.

## PROTEST VOTING

During the 1980s and 1990s political alienation led to greater protest voting for antiestablishment parties, especially the greens and neofascists. A conflict emerged between voters' general normative principles and their perceptions of government performance. For example, ecologists interpreted justice to mean liberty from environmental degradation and greater equality for women, immigrants, and the poor. Neofascists, however, perceived justice as less social equality but more freedom for private entrepreneurs to challenge bureaucratic state regulations. Inequity of allocation generated protest votes for parties that challenged a fragmented, paralyzed government unable to remedy perceived socioeconomic problems.[20]

Despite their shared opposition to the central bureaucratic states, electoral support for the green and neofascist parties stems from divergent reasons. They assume different attitudes toward social groups, political parties, personal leaders, ideology, issues, and evaluations of government's policy performance. Whereas green parties reflect a radical pluralist stance, the neofascist movements in France, Italy, Germany, Austria, and Belgium lean toward communal pluralism, under which the West European majority dominates people from Africa, the Middle East, Asia, and East Europe. Ecological parties reflect the views of young, well-educated professionals employed by the public and social service sectors. Women give these green parties strong support, especially if they work as teachers, social service personnel, or health practitioners. In contrast, neofascist parties such as the French *Front National* appeal to a multiclass constituency of small shopkeepers, unskilled workers, and private-sector professionals. Young men gravitate toward the neofascists more than do young women. The pro-nazi *Republikaner* Party attracts disproportionate support from Germans with only a primary education.

Even though both protest movements rally voters with weak ties to established parties, the greens and neofascists take different orientations toward the personal leader. Opposed to party bureaucracies, the ecologists prefer collegial decisionmaking and widespread participation in discussing political issues. With their more authoritarian attitudes, the neofascists long for a powerful dominant leader who will rescue the nation from policy paralysis, corruption, and interpersonal crime.

Ideologically, whereas the greens identify with the left, neofascist voters label themselves as 'rightwingers.' Their issue positions reveal divergent positions toward freedom and equality. Ecologists uphold equality for women, disadvantaged economic groups, ethnic minorities, and immigrants. Supporting civil liberties, green voters perceive the central bureaucratic state as an institution that stifles spontaneity. They seek liberation from government policies that produce environmental pollution and enhance the profits of multinational corporations. Opposed to national particularism, the greens affirm a pan-European identity based on multicultural diversity. In contrast, the neofascist voters reject libertarian and egalitarian values. Taking an ethnocentric, xenophobic stance, they support a homogeneous nation-state free from immigrants who come from the Maghreb (Algeria, Tunisia, Morocco), Africa, the Middle East, Asia, and East Europe, especially Bulgaria, Romania, and Albania. Closed borders and repatriation become rallying cries against the established parties. Fearful of growing personal crime, the neofascists demand that the police and army implement punitive policies against lawbreakers. Elitist attitudes fuse with this authoritarian outlook. Male patriarchy takes precedence over gender equality. Support for private entrepreneurs assumes greater priority than redistribution measures that will secure more income equality. Opposition to the social service state reflects a belief that it brings too many policy benefits to the 'undeserving poor,' especially immigrants and non-European ethnic minorities.

The neofascists and greens offer different evaluations of European policy performance. Neofascist voters make retrospective judgments. They blame the incumbent government and established parties for 'excessive' numbers of immigrants, for high unemployment, and for rising interpersonal crime. Green voters blend retrospective with prospective evaluations. Less dissatisfied with democratic procedures, they express greater optimism about the possibilities of changing the status quo. Both conventional tactics – lobbies, petitions, litigation – and more unconventional tactics such as demonstrations and civil disobedience represent ways to protest past policies and pressure government officials to attain greater socioeconomic equality, increased civil liberties, enhanced international cooperation, a more peaceful world, and a cleaner environment.[21]

## PARADOXES OF ELECTORAL PARTICIPATION

Voting behavior in North America, West Europe, and Japan suggests two paradoxical results about the roles of active partisans and more apathetic citizens. First, electoral outcomes depend on the less actively involved citizens, not on the better-informed, more ideologically aware participants. Political party identification influences learning from social groups and the processing of political information. The correlation between social group affiliations (ethnicity, religion, occupation) and voting behavior declines when researchers control for the strength of attachment to a party. Party identification shapes an individual's policy preferences, perceptions of the incumbent party's policy performance, and images of partisan candidates. Hence, 'strong' party identifiers are less influenced than 'weak' identifiers by campaign personalities and sociopolitical conditions – the national economic situation, war and peace, and government scandals. Regardless of the candidates' personal qualities and the 'nature of the times,' a strong partisan will always vote for her party's candidates. Ideological identifications also mold party preferences, stands on specific issues, evaluation of the incumbent government's policy performance, assessments of the candidates, and the vote. Whereas individuals who view themselves as very 'conservative' or 'rightist' vote for the conservative party, self-designated 'liberals' and 'leftists' support the leftwing party at the polls. Hence, individuals with weak ideological or partisan ties determine electoral outcomes. To gain the most votes, party leaders must maintain the support of committed partisans and attract the allegiance of moderately informed voters who swing from one party to another during different elections.

Second, even though passive swing voters account for parties' electoral success, party leaders who wield government power represent the views of political activists more than passive voters. Rank-and-file citizens wield limited influence over policy formulation and implementation. Political analysts have sketched three models of representation. According to the 'mandate' model, the voters communicate detailed policy preferences to their representatives, who then implement these policy views in specific legislation. The 'trustee' approach assumes that representatives make their own judgment about the best policies to pursue. Under the 'party loyalist' model, representatives follow the policy preferences of their party's leaders in the legislature. Whereas most voters adhere to the mandate approach, legislators usually follow the cues of party leaders. Legislative party elites take the policy initiative; they set the political agenda, strongly influence legislative voting behavior, and shape mass attitudes toward specific issues. Votes in the legislature reflect the policy preferences of party activists more than the views of party identifiers or the general electorate. Because the voting public holds divergent, vague, and contradictory stands on specific issues, an election rarely produces a clear policy mandate. Electoral returns indicate the proportion of voters selecting a candidate, not their information about party programs, their policy preferences, and particularly the intensities of these preferences. Coalition governments usually rule continental European nations. One party rarely secures 51 percent of the parliamentary seats; two or more parties wield executive power in the council of ministers. Even in the two-party US political system, different parties often control the legisative and executive branches. Hence, in neither Europe nor the United States can the electorate hold one party responsible for any perceived policy failures. Under these coalition conditions, parties forming the government enjoy broad discretion to frame policies. Most often, the chosen policies about egalitarian redistribution measures follow the mandates of partisan activists, business group leaders, and professionals, rather than the preferences of a national majority. Because political elites are wealthier, more formally educated, better informed, and more ideologically polarized than the general electorate, they articulate more detailed policy preferences and preciser instructions to government officials. As a result, government leaders – presidents, prime ministers, cabinet ministers, legislators – remain more accountable to sociopolitical elites than to the mass public.[22]

Under these elitist conditions, what impact do antiestablishment protest movements wield over the public policy process? Despite their small proportion of the general electorate, the ecological and neofascist parties have realized some policy influence. Neofascist activists have pressured incumbent parties to support punitive legislation that curtails immigrants' rights to residency, citizenship, health care, education, housing, and employment. Green activists have increased government officials' concern about environmental issues, especially the deleterious effects of nuclear power. Incumbent leaders established environmental ministries. Greater government regulation of air and water pollution occurred. Recycling efforts expanded. Antinuclear activists helped delay or stop the construction of new nuclear plants. Government-mandated safety standards facilitated healthier working conditions.[23] Even if these two protest parties rarely secured more than 15 percent of the vote during elections, their demands did secure at least partial satisfaction from government elites.

## CONCLUSION

This chapter has probed two general questions about voters' behavior. First, why do individuals vote for specific candidates and parties? Rational choice structuralist theorists assume that both motives and structural conditions shape a person's decision to participate. Some participants – the 'purists' – remain committed to certain moral/spiritual/ideological values, such as justice, dignity, and freedom. They support elected officials who uphold these values but oppose authorities whose policies deny these 'ultimate ends.' More pragmatic individuals, however, select a party because they expect to realize certain concrete benefits – lower taxes, higher government expenditures, lower inflation, increased scholarships, and better health care. Electoral decisions depend not only on individual attitudes but on structural opportunities and constraints. Peer groups, political parties, the mass media, and government institutions affect how people vote. By transmitting certain information and evaluations about candidates, parties, issues, and policy performance, these structures shape citizens' choices. Particularly if social networks and parties can monitor an individual's electoral behavior, dispense sanctions, and provide rewards, their electoral influence rises.[24]

Second, what policy consequences arise from participating in elections? In the democratic countries of North America, Western Europe, and Japan since the Second World War, the mandate theory of voting has limited applicability. Elected legislators make policy decisions that reflect the preferences of senior civil servants, party leaders, and heads of powerful social groups, especially business and professional spokesmen. When elite preferences contradict the goals of a majority of voters, especially on such issues as income distribution and austerity programs, legislators usually follow the policy priorities of organized leaders. The success of a protest party depends on the flexibility of government officials, their policy priorities, and their perceptions about the need to accommodate protest activists as a way of securing greater electoral support.[25]

# 10   Political Leadership

What makes great leaders? At the beginning of the seventeenth century, Shakespeare wrote in his play *Twelfth Night*: 'Some are born great, some achieve greatness, and some have greatness thrust upon them.'[1] At a time of political conflict and the emergence of the absolutist state in England, Shakespeare chronicled the wars among royal families, landlords, Church officials, and foreign powers. Succession crises created a violent political life. Only those leaders who showed ruthlessness, decisiveness, shrewdness, and calculation triumphed over their adversaries.[2] Politics expressed the will to power.

Shakespeare's aphorism implies that great leadership depends on an interaction between personal qualities and the socio-political situation. Individual characteristics include cognitive abilities, emotional attributes, and interpersonal skills. Some leaders are born with an ability to process political information; political learning enables them to develop this cognitive potential. Emotional attributes such as self-confidence, tolerance for stress, and control over anger also stem from the interaction between inheritance and environmental learning. Through participating in political life, individuals develop the needed interpersonal skills, including coalition formation, persuasion, communication, and mastery over others. However important these personal qualities for effective leadership, some people never manifest their potential abilities until the political situation demands great leadership. Particularly during times of political change – economic crisis, war, the founding of new states, revolutions – effective leadership becomes necessary. Under this unstable situation of popular protests, weak institutions, and ambiguous cultural norms, political leaders with strong motives, keen perceptions, and political skills have the greatest opportunity to act decisively.

Whether in stable or changing situations, political leaders wield a crucial impact over the policy process. They interpret cultural values and operate sociopolitical structures. Government officials formulate and implement public policies. Activists in protest movements and revolutions seek to translate their policy preferences into binding government decisions for a society. Along with the opportunities and constraints of the environental context, the behavior of political elites shapes the life experiences of citizens everywhere. According to Plato, the political leader plays an analogous role to the captain of a ship. Just as the captain steers the ship toward a safe port in a rough sea, so the leader steers the political system to certain objectives in a turbulent environment.[3] Of course, political leaders may not steer the ship toward its intended destination. Policy consequences often diverge from stated goals. As George Bernard Shaw observed in *Man and Superman*, although the pilot wants to reach the destination safely, he may land on the rocks or even fail to keep the ship afloat. Poking fun at Plato's analogy between the philosopher-king and the navigator, Shaw imagines the following exchange between Don Juan and the Devil:

*Don Juan*: Does a ship sail to its destination no better than a log drifts nowither? The philosopher is Nature's pilot. And there you have our difference: to be in Hell is to drift: to be in Heaven is to steer.
*The Devil*: On the rocks, most likely.[4]

Effective leadership thus implies successful collective goal attainment. Yet the actual exercise of power by political leaders often brings divergent outcomes than intended. Some navigators drift around a turbulent sea and never reach a safe port. Others steer so poorly that the ship of state sinks.

Political leaders effectively attain their policy goals when certain personal qualities blend with aspects of the political situation, including a leader's relations with followers, the nature of the political system, and the severity of crises facing a society. Constraints and opportunities vary from one context to another. Skills that bring success in one situation may produce failure under different circumstances.

By viewing political life as a drama, we can best understand the conditions that produce effective leadership. In Shakespeare's *As You Like It*, Jacques draws an analogy between life and the theater:

> All the world's a stage,
> And all the men and women merely players.

> They have their exits and their entrances,
> And one man in his time plays many parts.[5]

According to this metaphor, political actors play several different roles. Particularly during revolutionary situations, the major players divide into protagonists and antagonists. A charismatic revolutionary leader may blend the roles of star, playwright, and director. To the audience he articulates a discourse about the unjust power relationships plaguing the incumbent political regime. The bit players rally support for political dissidents. Stage hands prepare the props for the insurgent drama; they circulate antigovernment leaflets, distribute pamphlets, stage guerrilla theater performances, and gather resources for the revolutionary struggle. All these activities reflect a drive to gain a favorable response from members of the audience, who comprise alienated elites and more passive spectators. To win support from the audience, an effective director needs to demonstrate the power of the revolutionary movement, especially its solidarity, adherence to group norms, disciplined role-playing, and sensitivity to unforeseen contingencies. For example, absent players, a hostile audience, and attempts by government officials to close the performance impede goal attainment. Flexible directors can overcome these obstacles by changing the script, recruiting new actors, or targeting a different audience. The performance succeeds when audience members ascribe the same interpretation to political events as do the players. Particularly if the drama relates to the viewers' cultural heritage – traditions, customs, myths – and to their personal experiences, the revolutionary performance will most likely mobilize supporters and neutralize opponents.[6]

This chapter explores three general questions about the ways that leaders use resources. First, under what cultural, structural, and personal conditions will leaders most effectively deal with a crisis situation? How can incumbent government officials prevail against opponents? How can revolutionary leaders mobilize resources, rally popular support, and overthrow an established regime? Second, what motivations impel individuals to follow a revolutionary leader or remain loyal to governing elites? Third, what policy consequences emerge from a successful revolution? Why do policy outcomes often diverge from the promises of fundamental social change articulated by revolutionary actors?

## TYPES OF POLITICAL LEADERSHIP

Following the approach of Max Weber, we can distinguish five types of political leadership: traditional, charismatic, legalistic, entrepreneurial, and technocratic. The first three types correspond to Weber's analysis of legitimate authority, that is, the principles used to justify political leaders' right to rule and followers' duty to obey.[7] When rule becomes legitimate, followers comply with the commands of their leader because they accept his right to issue orders as morally binding. Whereas charismatic heroes and political entrepreneurs play the greatest role in revolutionary movements, traditional, legalistic, and technocratic leaders usually identify with established governments (Table 10.1).

Traditional leaders claim past practices, customs, and precedents as the major bases behind their authority. A master/subject relationship regulates interactions between the ruled and such rulers as kings, patriarchs, sultans, chiefs, emirs, elders, and priests. The traditional ruler retains some discretion when wielding power. Although he needs to abide by sacred customs, he retains some arbitrary authority to interpret these customs to present circumstances. Traditional authority has disintegrated throughout most of the contemporary world. Nevertheless, traditional leaders still perform important activities, especially at the local government level where they serve as patrons to

*Table* 10.1   Types of political leadership

| Leader | Source of authority | Relation between rulers and ruled |
| --- | --- | --- |
| Traditional | Custom, tradition, habit, precedent | Master/subject |
| Charismatic | Extraordinary personal qualities – the 'gift of grace' | Prophet/disciple |
| Legalistic | Laws, formal rules | Government official/citizen |
| Entrepreneurial | Tangible payoffs, concrete benefits, mutual gains | Seller/buyer |
| Technocratic | Expertise, technical knowledge, specialization | Expert/amateur |

their client followers. For example, in sub-Saharan Africa chiefs interact with subchiefs, who receive service and protection in exchange for support. Islamic religious leaders – marabouts and emirs – offer the promise of salvation to their disciples; often these marabouts wield considerable influence as landlords, traders, and local government officials. Throughout some rural areas of Latin America, local landowners and peasants interact in the same patron–client relationship that used to link nobles with serfs.[8]

Breaking with established traditions, charismatic leaders justify the right to rule on the basis of their extraordinary personal qualities, heroism, and gift of grace. The charismatic leader appears as a prophet to his disciples, who obey him because of his exemplary personality that he demonstrates in his mission to change society. Articulating transformative values in a conflict-riven environment, charismatic leaders challenge both traditional and bureaucratic authority. They embody the *conscience collective* of the new society. The follower shows them supernatural awe or secular enthusiasm for a short period before their charisma wanes.

The most important charismatic roles include the prophet, ideologue/sage, warrior, and party politician. Prophets such as Mohandas K. Gandhi, who led India toward political independence from British bureaucratic rule, played a charismatic role. Called by his disciples 'Mahatma' (Great Soul), he perceived his mission as a struggle to bring hope, salvation, and redemption to society. Political sages articulate a new programmatic ideology and try to teach their pupils a higher moral character. Julius Nyerere, the leader who guided Tanzania to national independence from Britain, exemplified the ideological charismatic leader. Known as 'mwalimu' (teacher), President Nyerere taught the principles of African socialism to the rural masses.

Charismatic warriors lead both nationalist and revolutionary movements. Their authority rests on strategy and risk-taking – on their ability to overcome obstacles, wage successful battles, and eventually realize military victories. Fidel Castro and Che Guevara began their political careers as guerrilla warriors fighting to overthrow established bureaucratic authority in Cuba during the 1950s. Even though Sukarno, the first president of independent Indonesia, never fought any military battles, he did lead the nationalist movement against the Dutch colonial rulers. Many Indonesians saw him as a mythic warrior, a reincarnation of the Javanese warrior hero Bima – 'King of the Warriors' and

'Constant Victor.' Most charismatic leaders have also acted as party organizers mobilizing the masses for national independence, triumph in a revolutionary civil war, or success in the battle to industrialize the economy. Appealing to youths, women, farmers, and factory workers, their charisma rests on their skill at communicating general political concerns that evoke widespread popular support.

Mao Zedong not only led the Chinese Communist Party but also played the roles of prophet, sage, and warrior. As a prophet, he urged his disciples to sacrifice their individual material interests for the moral redemption of Chinese society. As a political educator, he became the 'Great Helmsman,' the political navigator who led the Chinese peasants out of the wasteland through the turbulent seas of civil war into the socialist society of the People's Republic. As an ideologue/sage, Mao enlightened the masses in the caves of Yenan, where he applied the abstract principles of Marxism-Leninism to concrete Chinese realities. As a military leader within the People's Liberation Army, Mao and his comrades directed the successful revolutionary war against the bureaucratic Kuomintang regime.[9]

Associated with the modern bureaucratic state, legalistic officials perceive impersonal rules established by rational procedures as the source of their authority. Legislators, judges, and civil servants obey an impersonal rule – the law – not the person who issued the order. Citizens who interact with these government officials expect to secure equal treatment under the law.

The behavior of bureaucratic leaders usually diverges from the rational–legal model sketched by Weber. According to the model, bureaucracies operate in rational ways; leaders calculate efficient means to attain specific ends. Bureaucrats perform functionally specialized roles with clearly defined responsibilities. Impersonal rules govern their behavior. Within the administrative hierarchy, centralized authority patterns prevail. Decisionmaking takes place according to stable, routine procedures. The actual behavior of bureaucratic leaders, however, often departs from this rational–legal model. Unclear role expectations lead to indecision and lack of responsibility. Strong personal loyalties to family, relatives, and friends guide political decisionmaking. Although supposedly centralized and cohesive, the bureaucracy is faction-riven; local administrators implement policies that diverge from centralized plans. Rather than routinization, randomness often characterizes the policy process; bureaurats make decisions according to personal whim. Instead of planned, centrally directed change, political instability and drift result. To overome this drift, a powerful personality emerges at the top of the bureaucratic hierarchy to provide innovation, flexibility, and guidance. Unlike bureaucrats, legislators and judges occupy weaker leadership positions in most states throughout the world. Autonomous court justices and legislators rarely wield substantial influence over the policy process. They remain subordinate to bureaucratic officials and technocrats, who dominate the modern administrative state.[10]

Whether in modernizing societies or nations at a high level of modernization, technocrats and managers play a crucial policy role. Such technocratic leaders as engineers, industrial managers, economists, planners, scientists, agronomists, architects, cyberneticists, and computer specialists not only implement but also help formulate government decisions. Their political authority derives from the expertise and technical knowledge that promote modernization. Relations with subordinates involve those of expert and amateur. Technocrats uphold achievement, pragmatism, specialization, and professionalism as demonstrated by university credentials, examination performance, and achievement on the job. For them, the major policy task revolves around devising the most efficient techniques to achieve rapid economic development, a modern administrative state, and scientific advance. Even at high levels of industrialization, technocrats continue to dominate political life, for they specialize in the processing of information through computer networks. Although committed to social stability, technocrats often bring sociopolitical change. Their stress on economic productivity, efficiency, pragmatic flexibility, and scientific developments upsets traditional or routinized ways of handling political issues. Unintended social change often ensues.[11]

Particularly in societies where exchange relationships link leaders with their followers, political entrepreneurs play a key political role. They justify their right to rule on their ability to supply diverse groups with mutual gains – for example, material benefits, protection, opportunities for upward mobility, and access to power and status. In exchange for these tangible payoffs, followers give support, loyalty, and service. Making astute bargains, political entrepreneurs revel in the compromises that the political marketplace promotes. Entrepreneurial leaders act as sellers and brokers who negotiate deals, facilitate cooperation, form coalitions, and coordinate resources. They offer policy benefits in exchange for political support from their customers. Policies try to accommodate the divergent interests of followers, who function as buyers of public goods. Compliance with leaders' demands occurs when net gains exceed costs.[12]

A leader's effectiveness partly depends on the type of political system. Traditional leaders, especially elders and priests, thrive in a folk or theocratic system, where they interpret past customs and sacred norms to their followers. Charismatic leaders organize popular participation in mobilizaion systems, which seek fundamental transformations of society and government. Particularly when a society faces catastrophes – wars, depressions, natural disasters, foreign conquest, political disorder – a charismatic leader often emerges who embodies a moral example of transformaive principles. By identifying with this magnetic leader, followers gain higher self-esteem, empowerment, and solidarity with a collective cause, such as national independence, revolutionary victory, and societal modernization.[13] Administrators and technocrats dominate bureaucratic–authoritarian systems. Often allied with military officers, civilian bureaucrats not only administer specific programs but also assume general responsibilities for central planning and coordination of public policies. Neither the legislature nor political parties controls bureaucratic decisionmaking.[14] Political entrepreneurs and two types of legalistic officials – legislators and judges – function most effectively in a reconciliation system. Linked to constitutional governments where legal norms and dispersed power shape public policymaking, autonomous courts and legislatures wield substantial influence over the reconciliation process. Within the legislature, negotiators bargain with other representatives, the prime minister, or the president to secure mutually satisfactory agreements. Judges adjudicate differences and formulate binding common rules that reconcile the conflicting interests of the diverse policy participants. Aggregating particularistic demands, political entrepreneurs combine special interests into general public policies. Skilled at formulating deals in the political marketplace, they exchange favors, make reciprocal tradeoffs, and form short-term coalitions.

The severity of crises facing a society influences the type of leader who will most effectively resolve social problems. Committed to sacred norms, precedents, and customary ways of handling political routines, traditional leaders operate most effectively during stable, peaceful situations. Legalistic leaders also achieve their greatest successes under political stability. Based on rational–legal authority, the modern administrative state relies on settled ways of conducting political affairs. Conformity to impersonal laws and bureaucratic regulations often brings political stasis – an inability to respond to crisis situations with innovative policies. Commitent to tactical efficiency supersedes the formulation of new goals and flexible ways to attain policy objectives. This rigidity of government policymaking often produces personal leadership at the top of the administrative hierarchy. A 'presidential monarch' articulates new policy priorities, institutes new government agencies, and thereby tries to cope with sociopolitical crises.

Although preferring political stability, technocrats often gain extensive policy influence when economic crises erupt. If inflation skyrockets, growth rates fall, the foreign debt soars, and production collapses, economists, planners, professionals, computer specialists, and engineers try to redirect the economy toward increased growth. Leading the drive for efficient modernization, they stress the need to depress consumption and increase investment. Policies to deal with the economic recession often lead to unintended social changes – for example, higher unemployment, greater income inequality, deteriorating educational opportunities, and lower economic growth.

Even though political entrepreneurs wield some power in a revolutionary setting, they perform most effectively under a stable, peaceful situation. In nations such as Vietnam and China, revolutionary entrepreneurs exemplified a moral vision that motivated their followers to make sacrifices for the collective cause. Linking the national objectives to local concerns, they supplied concrete benefits to the village peasantry, who gained land, food, employment, loans, health care, and educational opportunities in exchange for support. Yet political entrepreneurs especially thrive in more pluralistic conditions that promote marginal, incremental changes. Entrepreneurial leaders uphold continuity in the rules that regulate the political game. For them, efficiency means adherence to Pareto optimality – that is, political tradeoffs that improve the material position of some individuals without hurting any others. Particularly under inegalitarian conditions where a wide gap separates the privileged from the deprived, few negotiators can ever formulate public policies that improve poor people's wellbeing without leaving some of the wealthy worse off. Although effective at accommodating interest conflicts, political entrepreneurs can less easily deal with the value conflicts that usually arise during sociopolitical crises.

Charismatic leaders have generally played the most significant role during turbulent times, when people perceive the need for drastic changes in society and the political system. Civil wars, wars with a foreign power, national liberation movements, revolutions, and struggles for rapid industrialization often give rise to charismatic leaders who break with traditional and legalistic authority. Although these charismatic heroes portray a vision of a transformed political system, the waning of their charisma poses problems of how to institutionalize new norms. Without the institutionalization ('routinization') of charisma, the political system may revert to customary patterns based on habitual routines.[15]

## POLITICAL CHARISMA AND MOVEMENTS FOR SOCIAL CHANGE

Charismatic leaders dominate movements for social change because they fulfill certain cognitive, interpersonal, and ego-defensive needs during sociopolitical crises. Wars, economic depressions, natural disasters (floods, droughts, hurricanes, earthquakes), and extensive political violence alienate people from the existing political system. These deteriorating social situations generate cognitive confusion. Failing to understand the meaning behind the political crisis, individuals cannot discover effective ways to surmount their personal problems. Skilled at rhetoric, the charismatic sage communicates an ideology that offers explanations for rapid change, interpretations of daily experiences, and priorities for political action. Transmitting these understandings to their followers, charismatic ideologues help citizens perceive the reasons for active participation in movements attempting to change the political system.

Charismatic heroes also respond to the interpersonal needs for group identity and social solidarity. During adolescence young people face identity and solidarity crises. Separation from the family weakens emotional ties to parents. Youths often feel unsure of their identities. They long for a persistent 'self-sameness' to their ego and seek to share this essential character with others. Environmental catastrophes, industrialization, upward social mobility, and geographic migration from rural areas to the city weaken social solidarity. By embodying shared values, the charismatic leader links an individual's personal identity with the collective identity proclaimed by a revolutionary, religious, or nationalist movement. He tries to convince individuals that attainment of their personal needs for identity and solidarity depends on the success of a transformative political movement. Concentration on external and internal threats to the national or revoluionary movement mobilizes aggression against outgroups. Idealization of the charismatic leader and anger toward the outgroup reinforce the fusion of the personal identity with the collective identity. Particularly when the state disintegrates and established authority collapses, the charismatic hero can specify new political role relationships and recreate social solidarity based on shared symbols.[16]

Under conditions of widespread personal anxieties, a charismatic leader may provide self-esteem, personal efficacy, and hope to his followers. According to such psychoanalysts as Heinz Kohut, early childhood experiences may accentuate personal stress, fear, anxiety, and threats to self-esteem. Children feel hostile and ambivalent toward parents. During adolescence biological maturation often heightens personal anxieties. Environmental crises, such as war, economic deterioration, and disintegration of state authority, reinforce the personal stress. Individuals long for an effective leader who will solve their problems and take control of the catastrophic situation. By challenging traditional values about the need for subordination to established elites, charismatic prophets provide faith in political salvation. By emphasizing the need to overcome feelings of personal futility, they strengthen their disciples' self-esteem, dignity, and morale. Through various defense mechanisms – repression of anger, sublimation of guilt, projection of hostility – negative emotions originally focused on parents or other kin are redirected toward established political authorities.[17]

The political careers of Juan and Eva Perón illustrate the role of charismatic leaders in securing social change. Juan Perón dominated Argentinian political life from 1943 through 1955. Before the coup that brought him to power in 1943, economic depression, rule by a conservative agrarian elite, and the Second World War had exacerbated political alienation. Backed by the army, urban industrialists, and the Roman Catholic Church, Perón promised greater economic independence, nationalism, populism, and social justice. Appealing primarily to organized laborers and the urban poor who had migrated from the countryside into Greater Buenos Aires, Perón provided his supporters – *las masas descamisadas* (the shirtless masses) – both symbolic dignity and concrete policy benefits. As a charismatic leader, he claimed to embody *el pueblo* against *la oligarquía*. Perón condemned the oligarchy for its corruption, luxurious lifestyle, elitist behavior, and ties to foreign powers (Britain, the United States). He praised the people for their purity, simplicity, egalitarianism, and national authenticity. His disciples regarded *El Líder* as a saint who dwelled close to God. His wife Evita represented the Madonna, the Blessed Mother, the *Dama de la Esperanza* (Lady of Hope), and the *Abanderada de los Humildes* ('Standard Bearer of the Poor'). As a former actress, she played the role of a humble follower who remained devoted to her master. Because of these symbolic appeals, both Juan and Evita Perón brought greater self-esteem to their supporters. Concrete policy rewards supplemented the expressive benefits. Even though the state controlled the major union, the Confederación General del Trabajo (CGT), workers gained higher real wages, inexpensive housing, larger pensions, and access to hospitals, health clinics, and vacation resorts. Greater income equality and lower unemployment resulted. As head of the Eva Perón Foundation, Evita presided over the opening of new housing projects, schools, hospitals, and clinics. Besides organizing the distribution of food to the poor, she also held weekly audiences with petitioners. At her instigation, women won the right to vote in 1947. When Evita died of cancer in 1952, many of her followers wept for the loss of the martyr who had brought political redemption to both *los descamisados* and *las descamisadas*. After her death, President Perón's popular support declined; slow economic growth and high inflation led to protests by unions and urban entrepreneurs. His repressive tactics increased. In 1955 an alliance of armed forces officers, agrarian exporters, urban businessmen, and Catholic Church hierarchs dislodged Perón from government power. The Peronist Party and the CGT continued the struggle for sociopolitical change.

Yet Perón's charisma never became institutionalized; during the period from 1955 until the early 1980s, Argentina suffered from economic stagnation, high inflation, popular protests, extensive political violence, coercive rule, and frequent *golpes de estado*. Military domination alternated with governance by civilian authorities. Perón granted generous social service benefits and established high tariffs that protected national industrialists manufacturing consumer goods. These policies led to large domestic fiscal debts, falling export sales, high trade deficits, and low growth. After 1950 real wage increases failed to match factory workers' gains secured during the late 1940s.[18] Even though concrete policy benefits did not meet workers' expectations, Perón raised their political awareness and gave them dignity. As one labor leader affirmed: 'Before Perón I was poor and I was nobody; now I am only poor.'[19]


## LEADERSHIP AND PARTICIPATION IN REVOLUTIONS

What strategies do revolutionary leaders use when mobilizing support for the overthrow of an incumbent government? Revolutionaries perceive the government as unwilling to grant any significant concessions, especially a share in decisionmaking. Rather than seeking partial changes in the political system, they struggle for a fundamental transformation of the system, including its policy priorities, structural relationship between rulers and ruled, and the behavioral interactions that link political leadership with mass participation. Because the demand for structural transformations generates resistance, revolutionary leaders usually employ extensive violence to gain and maintain government control. Violent tactics seem necessary to rouse the masses from their apathy and to overcome the opposition of those counterelites who reject fundamental, rapid changes.[20]

Relative deprivation and resource mobilization theorists have tried to explain the reasons for participation in revolutionary protest movements. Whereas the relative deprivation approach focuses on motives for political participation, the resource mobilization framework stresses the structural conditions – the opportunities and constraints – that shape an individual's decision to join a revolutionary organization.

Based on the psychoanalytic paradigm, relative deprivation theories assume that parental restraints against the display of aggression may lead individuals to redirect their anger against the political system when they become youths or adults. Violent protesters who join a revolutionary movement displace their private frustrations and anger on political objects, such as the government and its officials. Personal conflicts become politicized. When an abrupt economic decline occurs, high deprivation results. Individuals who suffer a loss feel a wide gap between their attainments and their just entitlements. The deprived compare their present situation with their own past accomplishments, with the conditions of more favored groups, and with their expectations of distributive justice. Political anger focuses on institutions, policies, and officials assumed responsible for personal deprivation. According to the 'J-Curve' hypothesis of James Davies, revolutionary protests most likely emerge when a sharp decline follows an extended period of rapid growth and prosperity. The growth rate raises expectations, but the economic deterioration frustrates them. The gap between higher expectations and lower satisfactions leads to widespread deprivations, which motivate aggrieved groups to launch protests against the incumbent government.

Despite the popularity of relative deprivation theories, they fail to explain the specific conditions under which revolutions will actually emerge. Every society experiences popular discontents, deprivations, frustrations, and grievances. Not all societies, however, face revolutionary protest movements. Several cognitive variables must intervene for personal deprivations to produce political violence. Individual protesters view the political system as unjust and illegitimate. Politically alienated, they blame the government, not the self, nonpolitical groups, or fate, for unfulfilled goals. They use ideological principles or instrumental arguments to justify political violence. Occasionally, a totalistic ideology rationalizes violence against 'evil' people as ethically righteous. More often, because the government and powerful social groups block opportunities for the peaceful solution of personal problems, protesters feel that violence represents a functionally useful tactic to attain a concrete benefit. Without these intervening variables, relative deprivation scarcely leads to political violence but to other behavioral responses, such as geographic migration, self-improvement projects, personal stress, homicide, suicide, and withdrawal into alcohol, drugs, or religious communes.[21]

Focusing primarily on grievances, relative deprivation theorists downplay the structural political conditions and political leadership that channel these grievances into revolutionary political action. The specific grievances that motivate an individual to use violent tactics remain unclear. What is the relative importance of economic inequalities, stagnant growth, limited mobility opportunities, and especially political repression? According to most crossnational studies of revolutionary violence, deprivation wields less impact on political aggression than do such structural conditions as political exclusion, government coercion, and the balance of power between the incumbent regime and the revolutionary organizations. Political leadership also plays a fundamental part in organizing discontented individuals behind a revolutionary cause and highlighting the illegitimacy of established authorities. As James S. Coleman indicates, few revolutions emerge spontaneusly from 'an aggregation of individual actions.' Instead, leaders organize revolutionary actions. At best, the relative deprivation approach can explain 'the responsiveness of a population in general to an opportunity to revolt, an opportunity that is ordinarily created by an organized leadership.'[22]

Unlike relative deprivation theories that concentrate on popular grievances, resource mobilization explanations place greater emphasis on the structural opportunities that cause individuals to rally behind a revolutionary movement. If revolutionaries have access to a high number of resources – money, weapons, communication channels, general information, technical expertise, authority, leadership – and can skillfully use their resources, then prospects for goal attainment increase. When exploited groups achieve autonomy, gain cohesion, and live in a small geographic area, revolutionary leaders can more easily mobilize them behind an ideological cause. If peer group members (relatives, neighbors, friends, coworkers) encourage participation in a revolutionary organization, if powerful leaders ally with the dissidents, and if sociopolitical elites take a disunified stand toward antigovernment protests, individuals will likely support the revolutionary struggle. Political entrepreneurs and charismatic leaders organize their followers behind a cause. Whereas charismatic prophets sketch a vision of a purified political system, political entrepreneurs negotiate the exchanges required for popular support. For example, if a repressive state seizes land from peasants and wields arbitrary coercion against them, they may rally behind revolutionary entrepreneurs in exchange for land and sanctuary against punitive acts by soldiers and police. Under opposite conditions, structural restraints deter individuals from joining a revolutionary movement. It has access to only to few resources. Peer groups discourage participation by threatening disapproval or ostracism. Sociopolitical elites stand united in their opposition to the protesters. No charismatic hero articulates a political discourse that reformulates personal and collective interests behind the need for fundamental systemic transformation. Revolutionary political entrepreneurs lack the power to organize and coordinate activities.

Even if widely used to analyze protest movements, the resource mobilization framework offers an incomplete explanation for popular participation in revolutionary organizations. Focusing on objective structural conditions, it downplays the motives for mobilization, especially such expressive needs as spiritual values and emotional impulses. Through expressive symbols and rituals, revolutionary leaders rally popular enthusiasm – a key political resource often minimized by mobilization theorists. Ambiguities remain about the resources and organizing strategies that produce the greatest success in overthrowing an established political system. Effectiveness of various resources – money, weapons, expertise, leadership authority, organizational skills – may depend on specific historical conditions only partially understood by resource mobilization theorists.[23]

Compared with relative deprivation and resource mobilization theories, the theory of political opportunities provides a clearer explanation for the interaction between political leadership and popular participation in revolutionary movements. Unlike other approaches, it clarifies the relationships among cultural values, sociopolitical structures, and individual actions. According to political opportunity theory, revolutionary leaders raise morale, coordinate organizational activities, and shape attitudes, perceptions, and motives so that supporters gain the power to challenge the incumbent regime.

During the revolutionary struggle intellectuals play a crucial role communicating a new political discourse about the need for transformative change. Throughout history Jewish prophets, Christian priests, Confucian literati, Islamic ulama, and more secular, autonomous intellectuals have sketched a vision of the mundane world transformed according to transcendental ends. These intellectuals highlight the desirability of transforming the world so that economic exploitation, political oppression, and status degradation no longer prevail. Collective values assert communal solidarity and blame the political system for widespread personal problems. Articulation of moral-spiritual principles – the righteousness of the revolutionary cause – fuses with a commitment to secure greater economic equality and tangible material benefits, such as land, housing, and health care. Although ideologues demand more equal economic conditions and increased equality of social interaction, they uphold the need for political elitism, especially submission to the revolutionary leader. By raising enthusiasm for the revolutionary cause, intellectuals hope that these values will inspire their followers to take advantage of the structural opportunities for collective political action.[24]

Participation in a revolutionary movement increases when the structural opportunities for political action become more favorable. Leaders of the central government, political parties, social groups, and transnational institutions either facilitate or impede the prospects for effectively mobilizing popular support. When state repression declines, incumbent leaders change, and factional conflicts fragment ruling elite coalitions, opportunities for antiregime actions rise. A personalized regime that remains closed to social groups appears more vulnerable than a system based on collegial leadership that can adapt to catastrophic conditions, such as wars, natural disasters, and economic crises. If revolutionaries control a strong political party, guerrilla band, or rebel army and if the incumbent government lacks powerful structures to control the populace, antiregime forces can more easily overthrow the incumbent regime.

Cohesive, autonomous small group networks expand the space for revolutionary political mobilization. Autonomy emerges when members of the subordinate groups (for example, peasants) have a high degree of interaction among their own group but remain isolated from other groups, such as landlords. Particularly when peasants live in areas outside state control, such as mountainous regions, revolutionaries have greater opportunities to organize and educate them. Pervasive interactions within the group, combined with segregation from opposing groups, produce high cohesion. Neither state officials nor landlords provide protective services. Small group members become dependent on each other for the satisfaction of personal and collective benefits. Group leaders possess the control capacities to ensure that participants comply with the revolutionary movement's obligations. If low occupational and ethnoreligious status reinforce each other, if exit from the group is difficult, and if the incumbent state officials lack the power to crush the revolutionary movement, this high group autonomy and solidarity strengthen the prospects for widepread participation behind the revolutionary cause. Especially when a social elite (landlords) rely on the state to repress a subordinate group (peasants) and this state power declines, members of the oppressed group often join a revolutionary organization that aims to overthrow the state and its social allies.

Foreign support for a revolutionary movement gains importance mainly after the domestic balance of power has shifted against the incumbent regime. If a foreign state withdraws backing from an established government and if revolutionaries secure resources from a transnational institution, then their prospects for success grow brighter. Particularly when established authorities remain corrupt, vacillating, isolated from key social groups, and overly dependent on foreign governments, they become vulnerable to overthrow by a powerfully organized revolutionary movement.[25]

Although structural conditions pose opportunities and constraints, a person's choice to back a revolution more directly stems from individual attitudes, perceptions, and motivations. Two general motives shape the decision to participate: the intensity of commitment to a public good and the probability of attaining that good. If people perceive that a revolutionary movement upholds desirable moral–spiritual–ideological values and that their participatory actions will secure valuable expressive or material benefits, they are likely to join the movement. Dissatisfied with the incumbent regime's policy performance, they expect that the benefits of participation will outweigh such costs as loss of resources, time, personal freedom, or life if state repression crushes the dissidents. Antiregime entrepreneurs supply concrete benefits. They recruit followers, coordinate activities, promote cooperation, pool resources, and link local to national concerns. The more ideological revolutionaries – the 'purists' – sketch a moral vision that inspires people to endure suffering and sacrifice for eventual victory. These leaders – usually students, intellectuals, professionals, party activists, clergy – teach new values and norms about the desirability of participating in a collective action to overthrow an established regime. New normative principles of justice reinforce orientations about the need for change. Revolutionary ideologues convince their followers that inequity of allocation by government officials has produced mass misery and that individual participation in the revolutionary struggle will lead to valued outcomes, such as greater income equality, restoration of lost goods (land), or enhanced social justice.

Alienation from the existing political system, combined with allegiance to the revolutionary cause, stimulates the political consciousness that heightens participation in a revolutionary struggle. Through leadership activities, members of the oppressed group focus their discontent on the incumbent regime. Alienation stems from both material and moral grievances. High taxes, land expropriation, low wages, and food shortages illustrate typical material deprivations. Revolutionary leaders enhance sentiments of moral outrage against ruling elites, who are charged with violating ethical rights, normative standards, justice, and reciprocity. This moral anger justifies and directs revolutionary behavior. Participation in the revolutionary organization intensifies these moral and material grievances. Attacking the corruption and moral laxity of incumbent authorities, revolutionary challengers promise to implement greater economic equality and a purified political system. These activists expect that participation in the revolutionary movement will bring greater expressive and material benefits than political abstention.

If individuals blame their personal problems on a collective source (the government) and seek a collective solution to their grievances, they are more likely to rally behind a revolutionary movement than if they blame fate, themelves, or a nonpolitical group for their discontents. Supporters of revolution perceive that government policies have produced unbearable costs caused by indifference to the poor, failure to provide equal opportunities, and alliances with a corrupt wealthy elite. Integration into a revolutionary movement strengthens the incentive to rebel, lowers risks, increases resources, and raises expectations that revolutionaries will actually conquer state power. Revolutionary mobilization highlights the dominance of public concerns. Effective mobilizing leaders teach individuals to link their self-interests with the fate of the revolutionary organization, so that they expect personal improvements will result from a systemic transformation. Participants learn that individual benefits depend on cooperative behavior and that consensual procedures facilitate collective solutions to personal problems. Political activists envision an alternative society structured differently than the existing sociopolitical system. This vision of a revolutionary utopia motivates people to endure present hardships for a future public good and raises their political efficacy about future success.

If individuals overcome their apathy, resignation, and fatalism and demonstrate political efficacy, participation in a revolutionary organization increases. Their high political effectiveness enhances the expectation that their revolutionary political actions will lead to a successful outcome. A heightened sense of political efficacy particularly emerges when government leaders can neither form alliances with sympathetic groups nor efficiently use coercion against revolutionaries. Government repression may both deter and facilitate support for the revolutionaries. On the one hand, a high level of coercion applied consistently over time deters opposition. Both opportunities for peaceful protest and the prospects for success remain low. Even if people feel angry toward the regime, they fear punitive costs if they participate in a resistance movement. Pragmatists – those who back the revolution for concrete rewards – seem especially constrained by coercion. On the other hand, if the military and police employ a moderate level of arbitrary, random coercion inconsistently over time, political stability becomes endangered. As coercive force fluctuates, anger toward the government mounts. Yet the temporary decline of repression reduces fear of punishment. When coercion declines and defections from the armed forces and police mount, opportunities for revolutionary organization rise. Expectations of successful action against an unresponsive, repressive regime increase. If war, economic collapse, succession crises, and natural disasters cause government's coercive power to disintegrate, individuals may mobilize behind a revolutionary movement. Viewing the incumbent government as morally illegitimate and regarding peaceful protests as ineffective, these pragmatists perceive political violence as the most feasible way to secure social change. By forming alliances with supportive groups and by using coercion against their opponents, revolutionary leaders gain the opportunity to seize state power and establish a transformed political system.[26]

The theory of political opportunities explicates contrasting peasant support for revolutionary movements in China and Afghanistan. During the 1930s and 1940s Mao Zedong, the Chinese Communist Party (CCP), and the People's Liberation Army (PLA) transformed the political system because of favorable structural, cultural, and behavioral conditions. The large peasant class was fairly homogeneous. Neither ethnic nor religious divisions split the peasants. Few opportunities existed for upward social mobility. Particuarly after 1937, the peasants in the interior mountainous regions remained isolated from extensive supervision by landowners, Nationalist government bureaucrats, and Chiang Kaishek's army. The civil war and the Japanese invasion led to the collapse of state power in the rural areas; this declining state coercion facilitated the organization of the revolutionary movement. Low morale among Nationalist government soldiers, defections from the armed forces, and recruitment of troops into the PLA weakened the incumbent regime. In contrast, the PLA demonstrated higher morale, greater discipline, and tighter unity – resources that overcame its lack of technologically advanced armaments.

The CCP and PLA stimulated a strong political consciousness among the peasants, especially tenant farmers, hired hands, landless squatters, migrant farm laborers, and herders. They sought similar interests: lower rents, decreased taxes, reduced interest rates, lower salt prices, land redistribution, grain relief, expanded trade opportunities, mass education, improved health care, and greater security against bandits, warlord oppression, and the ruling officials in the Kuomintang (KMT – National People's Party). When the invading Japanese armies allied with some landowners against the poor farmers, the national struggle reinforced the class struggle. The CCP leaders convinced the peasants that their individual and family fate depended on the fate of the collective revolutionary struggle.

Even though the CCP began with a rural constituency, it eventually established a multiclass coalition. Students, professionals (doctors, lawyers, journalists, teachers), and even some businesspeople rallied behind the revolutionary movement. These urban residents protested the KMT adminisration's repressive, corrupt policies. Nearly all Chinese felt betrayed by Chiang Kaishek's use of defeated Japanese troops to fight Chinese communist forces after the end of the Second World War. Faced with these severe problems, Chiang never articulated a set of moral–spiritual values that legitimated his Nationalist regime among either the urban or rural populations. Its major backers after 1945 included a faction-riven coalition of landed gentry, financial speculators, some bankers, provincial army officers, and regional KMT activists.

Without powerful coercive control or cohesive group alliances, the Nationalist government could not maintain power through United States assistance. The US Truman administration provided Chiang Kaishek with extensive military and economic resources. Over 50,000 US marines helped protect Beijing and other northern cities against a PLA-directed attack. US naval and air forces transported Nationalist troops to fight the CCP in North China. In 1947, however, US marines withdrew from China. A year later, the US government refused to supply the Nationalist army the weapons needed for the defense of the Yangtze river. Because the domestic power balance had shifted toward the CCP and the PLA, they conquered the mainland in 1949.

As a charismatic leader, Mao Zedong played a leading role in forging the revolutionary victory. A prophet, ideologue, warrior, and party head, he explicated political objectives, linked general ideological values to people's specific needs, and offered hope for a better future. Rather than stressing abstract Marxist–Leninist themes, Mao appealed to the rural populace on a nationalist, populist program. He sketched a vision of a transformed society based on an egalitarian reinterpretation of Chinese peasant traditions, such as village autonomy, voluntarism, cooperation, and opposition to the agrarian state bureaucracy. A narrator of the revolutionary struggle, he reformulated folk tales to link traditional peasant insurrections with modern armed resistance against Japanese invaders and Nationalist troops. As creator of symbolic capital, he articulated the discourse that mobilized the masses behind the new political culture. His disciples viewed him as the 'great savior' who redeemed China from foreign imperialists and domestic enemies opposed to the communist revolution. Through the CCP, PLA, and mass organizations – rural unions, peasant leagues, youth associations, women's groups – the revolutionary leaders carried out their mobilizing activities. Organizational mobilization strengthened the peasants' political consciousness. For literate people, leaflets, bulletins, newspapers, pamphlets, and books carried the revolutionary message. Art, plays, operas, and dances conveyed new political norms about the need for collective sacrifice, moral redemption, ideological renewal, economic equality, and societal transformation. By building on such traditional structures as family, village, and mutual aid groups, Communist Party leaders secured cooperation among the peasants. Often traditional agencies became transformed into party auxiliaries. All these organizational activities helped mobilize segments of the Chinese peasantry behind the revolutionary overthrow of the Kuomintang government.

Subordinate CCP leaders included both purists and pragmatists. At the beginning of the Chinese civil war, individuals who joined the revolutionary movement usually held an intense commitment to the socialist ideological cause; these purists were willing to risk government coercion for the sake of their ideals. As the CCP and PLA gained strength, pragmatic recruits became more numerous. With heightened political efficacy, these pragmatists expected that their participatory activities would help the movement seize state power and implement desired policy objectives. During the late 1930s and early 1940s, the CCP established regional administrations in north China that implemented several activities associated with a civilian government. CCP leaders distributed land, settled disputes, supervised educational programs, created health centers, levied progressive taxes, prosecuted the civil war, provided protection against Nationalist government repression, supplied security against the Japanese, and expanded opportunities for upward personal mobility. All these concrete policy benefits granted by CCP pragmatists created the foundations for revolutionary victory in 1949.[27]

In contrast, Afghanistan during the 1980s lacked the favorable conditions needed for revolutionary success. The ruling People's Democratic Party of Afghanistan (PDPA) failed to mobilize the peasantry behind the revolutionary cause. The peasants, who constituted 80 percent of the population, were more fragmented than in China. Village autonomy, ethnic divisions (Pushtun, Tajik, Uzbek, Hazara), linguistic differences (Persian, Pushtu, Turkic), religious cleavages (85 percent Sunni vs 15 percent Shiite), tribal rivalries, and clan factionalism within each tribe weakened class and national solidarity. Neither the central government nor the Islamic rural resistance remained cohesive. Plagued by personal, ideological, ethnic, and religious cleavages, the PDPA lacked a charismatic leader who could surmount this factionalism. The central government wielded limited power over the rural areas. Landlords, tribal elders, and Muslim ulama dominated the peasantry. Unlike the Chinese Communist Party, the PDPA never developed a rural base; instead, its main support came from city residents, students, intellectuals, the armed forces, and especially the Soviet Union. In 1979 the Soviet military entered Afghanistan to support the PDPA and fight a guerrilla war against the rural population. Hence, in Afghanistan, unlike China, the urban revolutionaries allied with a foreign power. The rural guerrillas rallied around the banner of Islam and opposition to Soviet domination. Under these structural conditions, the peasants lacked a powerful class consciousness. Even though they felt alienated by extensive land inequality, high unemployment, and massive illiteracy, attitudinal solidarity remained weak. Riven by personal and ideological factions, dependent on the USSR military, and concentrated in the cities, PDPA leaders never gained sufficient power to mobilize the rural masses, to teach them new values, expand educational opportunities, improve health-care conditions, redistribute land, and secure greater social equality, especially for women. Instead, landlords, clan heads, tribal elders, and Muslim clergy retained the support of most subsistence farmers and even the agricultural wage-laborers who worked on the few commercialized farms. For most Afghani peasants, the costs of supporting the revolutionary government seemed to outweigh the benefits. With military assistance from the United States, Pakistan, Iran, and Saudi Arabia, the Islamic resistance finally conquered Kabul, the capital city, in early 1992. Three years after the withdrawal of Soviet troops and three months after the USSR's disintegration, the PDPA government fell. Lacking charismatic leaders, powerful party-government structures, and cultural legitimacy from an Islamic society, the Marxist–Leninist government never developed the power to institutionalize its revolutionary programs.[28]

## CONCLUSION

In this chapter we have examined three issues about political leaderhip in crisis situations. First, how do effective leaders mobilize resources and rally popular support behind their cause? Conflicts between rival elites often generate systemic disintegration. Incumbent government officials cannot effectively process political information. Isolated from influential social groups and subordinate policy administrators, they fail to receive accurate, relevant information about pressing problems. Usually, these incompetent leaders can neither interpret information nor evaluate it according to feasible policy options. Unable to coordinate and supervise the behavior of subordinates, top officials do not gain the feedback required to modify original decisions or to change goals. Government programs remain unclear, vacillating, and arbitrary. They cannot cope with war, foreign invasions, economic depressions, and natural disasters. Revolutionary elites promise to institute a transformed political system that will remedy personal problems. These leaders voice plausible explanations for social dislocation, clarify priorities for political action, and specify effective strategies for goal attainment.

Revolutionary leaders gain state power when they undermine the legitimacy of established authorities. Incumbent officials cannot communicate the expressive or instrumental beliefs that would justify their right to rule. Their policies generate insufficient material benefits to consolidate widespread support among citizens and aspiring elites. No moral–spiritual–ideological message convinces skeptics about the need to undergo sacrifice for an ultimate cause linked to the incumbent regime. In contrast, revolutionary dissidents attract greater legitimacy. Purists expect that a revolutionary government will uphold just principles. They fuse supposedly opposite values: sacred and secular, populist and elitist, traditional and modern, collectivist and individualist. The pragmatists perceive that participation in the revolutionary movement will bring concrete benefits – land, jobs, upward occupational mobility – that exceed the costs of defying established government authority or remaining politically inactive.

By organizing a multiclass coalition and building on informal small-group networks, revolutionary leaders establish a powerful structural base for dismantling the incumbent regime. Small group associations form the basis of political networks. Group members frequently interact. Peer group pressures – the fear of members' disapproval – monitor compliance with revolutionary leaders' strategies. Under these structural conditions, protesters secure high solidarity. They persuade supporters to link their self-interest with the fate of the revolutionary movement. Particularly when revolutionary activists convince discontented individuals from various social classes that the incumbent regime bears the blame for personal grievances, a systemic breakdown of the *ancien régime* becomes more probable. Antiregime leaders persuade alienated groups that only a new political system will solve their current problems.[29]

Second, why do individuals participate in revolutionary movements? According to the theory of political opportunities, cultural values, structural conditions, and personal motives interact to shape the decision to participate. The purists maintain their faith in certain moral–spiritual–ideological values, such as freedom, dignity, justice, and equality. They support government officials who uphold these values but reject authorities whose policies deny these 'ultimate ends.' The purists thus view participation as the way to affirm their ethical commitments. More pragmatic activists participate because they expect to realize concrete benefits – lower taxes, more land, better health care, increased schooling. They will most likely join a revolutionary struggle when the prospects of success appear brightest. Structural opportunities and constraints affect individuals' political efficacy. Peer group disapproval can deter aggrieved persons from joining a revolutionary movement. State repression usually exerts a stronger deterrent effect on the pragmatists than on the purists. If the policy and government armed forces wield consistently high coercion, these sanctions dissuade dissidents from participating in revolutions. Yet if state coercion declines, the prospects for success increase and so does participation behind the revolutionary cause. Rather than arousing fear among purists, greater state repression strengthens their attitudes of injustice toward political authorities and provokes increased antiregime activity, despite the higher risks of punishment. Dedicated to a cause, the purists view government's punitive treatment as an opportunity to demonstrate their moral commitments: courage, perseverance, and concern for the public good. For them, sacrifice becomes a benefit, not a cost.[30]

Third, what policy consequences resulted when revolutionaries conquered state power? The outcomes of their policies frequently diverged from promises made to supporters. Some adherents to the revolutionary movements in Russia, China, Vietnam, Cuba, and Iran originally joined the struggle because of their populist opposition to a repressive bureaucratic state. When the revolutionary leaders seized control over the government, however, they strengthened coercive institutions, especially the military and police. Greater national freedom from outside control and more socioeconomic equality prevailed than under the *ancien régime*. Popular access to educational opportunities and health-care facilities expanded. Through gaining a technical education and joining the dominant party (or religious association in Iran), persons from low-status families gained upward mobility. Nevertheless, male elites, particularly managers, technocrats, and ideologues, dominated the policy process; they enjoyed the greatest political power, wealth, and status. Factory workers, small-scale businesspeople, the urban dispossessed, poor farmers, and women held fewer rights and privileges. Hence, fundamental social changes lagged behind the revolutionary gospel originally articulated by protest activists. The pursuit of social group freedom, personal liberty, and political equality assumed a low policy priority.

The gap between transformative ideological objectives and actual policy achievements not only stemmed from a nation's resources, level of economic development, and incorporation into the world capitalist economy but also derived from the dominant governing style of the revolutionary rulers. Viewing nonviolent participation as ineffective and political authority as illegitimate, revolutionary activists had perceived violence as a morally appropriate, effective tactic to gain government office. Once in control over the policy process, the revolutionary elites continued to rely on coercion as a way to consolidate their power. As normative, economic, and physical coercion increased, they lost needed information from the general public, group activists, and technical experts. Subordinates feared communicating unwanted information that would displease their superiors. In the bureaucratic hierarchy that emerged after the revolutionary takeover, a disjunction arose between policy goals formulated at the top and policy implementation at the bottom. Viewing the programmatic objectives as undesirable or infeasible, lower-level administrators felt no strong incentive to implement the policies decided by central elites. Bureaucratic bottlenecks and policy stalemates developed. Despite their apparent centralized control over the policy process, governing revolutionaries proved unable to realize the fundamental social changes originally promised by the radical protest movement.[31]

# Epilogue

This book has used the theory of political opportunities to explain the origins, tactics, and outcomes of protests. A simple 'middle-range' theory, it helps us understand the complexities of political life at the close of the twentieth century. We assume that cultural values, sociopolitical structures, and individual behaviors explain protest movements and their impact on social change. Individuals become important because they guide organizations, interpret cultural values, and thereby expand the opportunities for political action against social injustice. These cultural and structural conditions also shape individuals' motives, perceptions, attitudes, skills, and hence their choices. By highlighting feasible and desirable alternatives, cultural norms and sociopolitical organizations influence the strategies chosen for political action. From this viewpoint, the historical context affects the opportunities and constraints that face contemporary protesters. For example, the French Revolution of 1789, which upheld the nation as the primary source of popular loyalty and urged people with a distinctive cultural identity to control the state, invigorated modern nationalism over the next two centuries. The ethnonationalist movements now struggling for political independence in East-Central Europe, South Asia, and sub-Saharan Africa proclaim themes voiced by French revolutionaries two hundred years ago. The campaign for expanded human rights – civil liberties, representative government, popular participation in the policy process – reflects liberal reformist priorities that enlivened political discourse in Western Europe during the mid-nineteenth century. Current workers' strikes, land seizures, and opposition to bureaucratic state regulations recall earlier protests at the beginning stages of industrialization. The modern green movements advocating a clean environment, political decentralization, and harmonious settlement of disputes not only represent a postmodern impulse but also resemble the traditional Confucianist orientation toward harmony with nature.

Historical investigations reveal that the 'new' social movements retain important continuities with past experiences. Institutional practices and cultural norms inherited from previous generations facilitate as well as constrain political actors today. Like past movements, contemporary protests reject a subordinate status based on political oppression, economic exploitation, and public humiliation. Affirming the moral values of dignity and equality, ethnic groups, religious revivalists, liberation theologians, peasant leagues, unions, ecologists, and feminists assert new group identities. Yet the rigid social stratification system often impedes the struggle for more dignified, egalitarian treatment. Similar to their predecessors, modern protesters make public policy demands on government institutions for expanded politico-economic rights. Private businesspeople seek greater freedom from bureaucratic regulations. Unions demand the rights to strike and to bargain collectively for higher wages, improved working conditions, and increased fringe benefits. Government policymakers have the power to limit or grant all these rights. Women's movements press for nondiscriminatory treatment, reproductive freedom, day-care centers, health-care programs, and more government finances for these social services. Protesting environmental devastation, toxic wastes, and acid rain, ecological organizations advocate stricter government standards to curtail air and water pollution. Yet the need for rapid economic growth to supply the revenues for government programs often constrains the implementation of environmental preservation policies.

Unlike the pre-twentieth-century protesters, modern protest movements benefit from mass media technologies that expand the opportunities for communicating their political message. Before 1900 most domestic media were local, oral, informal, and personalized. Influential patrons dominated the local communications networks. Today, however, mass media are mainly national, urban, written, formal, and depersonalized. Protest activists rely on radio, television, tape recorders, videocassettes, fax machines, and E-mail to transmit grievances. These modern media enable protesters to define key political problems, reinterpret group identities, transmit tactical information, and cement personal ties with supporters not only in a nation but throughout the world. By publicizing shared discontents and aspirations, technologically-advanced media increase a movement's political power, especially its opportunity to place a key problem on the political agenda. Nevertheless, if the mass media portray the protesters' goals as unworthy and their tactics as illegitimate, a public backlash may result, thereby hindering the movement's prospects for political success.[1]

The theory of political opportunities offers plausible explanations for the three general issues raised in this book. First, what motivations lead people to join nonviolent protests, rebellions, and revolutionary movements? We assume that participation stems from a commitment to a public good and the expectation of success. If individuals feel strongly dedicated to a valued outcome – for example, human rights, justice, freedom, equality, dignity – and if they perceive that their participation will help ensure goal attainment, they will participate in protest activities. Dissatisfaction with policy performance, combined with anger toward the sources of injustice, stimulates their involvement.

Protesters seek both personal and collective benefits. Some groups seek rewards for their members. Examples include the Canadian Swine Breeders' Association and the Wildlife Legislative Fund of America, which represents the policy preferences of hunters and trappers. In contrast, other groups advocate the interests of nonmembers. Protesting the carriage horse trade, the Ecological Forces of Animal Liberation struggles to influence the Guadalajara city government in Mexico. The Animal Legal Defense Fund wants the legal status of animals changed from 'property' to 'persons.' As these examples indicate, most participants link their personal benefits to public policy goals. If the protest movement gains political power, some activists may secure government positions. Others may gain a concrete reward like lower taxes, more land, cheaper credit, higher wages, increased housing, or expanded educational opportunities. These pragmatic supporters perceive that the tangible gains from alliance with the protest movement exceed the losses suffered under the established political system.

Not only concrete rewards but symbolic benefits stimulate political participation in protests. Many individuals join a movement because they find its activities educational, interesting, and enjoyable. Purists perceive that political involvement helps assure the triumph of an ideological or spiritual cause. Particularly under a rigid, polarized situation, material interests become transformed into moral principles. For example, the novel *Germinal* by Émile Zola depicted a coal miners' strike that occurred during the late 1860s in northern France. Union strikers who heard their leader Étienne Lantier call for higher wages and healthier working conditions envisioned a dramatic transformation in their personal lives. Those down in the pits of the capitalist social heap – the 'wage-slaves' – would rise up as masters of their fate. According to Zola: 'They were uplifted in a religious ecstasy, like the feverish hope of the early Christians expecting the coming reign of justice. . . . What a wonderful dream! To be the masters and suffer no more! To enjoy life at last!'[2]

Cultural values shape both the commitment to a public good and individuals' feelings of political efficacy. Ideologies, religious doctrines, and nationalist beliefs communicate general value priorities – justice, freedom, equality, human dignity – that shape more specific policy goals explicating the scope of government authority. By highlighting the saliency of certain problems, such as air pollution or high taxes, cultural messages justify the issues that ought to appear on the political agenda. Value-laden communications not only sketch desirable conditions but also transmit norms of feasibility. Causal attributions elucidate ways that the policy process operates and indicate effective solutions to key problems. By raising or lowering expectations of success, cultural norms affect protesters' political efficacy. For example, classical liberal and democratic socialist ideologies perceive reformist change as desirable and feasible. Through education and reason, political activists can uplift social conditions. Marxists assume that socialist intellectuals and the proletariat can achieve the class efficacy needed to transcend capitalism and realize a communist system. Classical conservatives, however, remain skeptical about the possibilities for transforming society. From their perspective, political change brings perverse, unintended, or insignificant consequences. Taking a fatalistic viewpoint, many conservatives believe that no public policy can change the status quo: 'You always have the poor with you.' Deference to a traditional hierarchical order dissuades individuals from challenging the incumbent regime, since change will undoubtedly worsen the existential situation. Conservatives also expect that policy changes lead to unintended outcomes; since the costs outweigh the benefits, innovative government programs endanger the achievements secured by the family, church, or private business firm. All these causal assumptions made by conservative ideologues weaken the expectations about successful outcomes of protest activities.[3]

The power of sociopolitical organizations influences conceptions of the public good and degrees of political efficacy. Particularly when one powerful institution – the government, private corporation, church – establishes hegemonic control over communications media, it can more easily secure support for its value priorities than under pluralist conditions. A powerful, coercive state also determines the feasibility of goal attainment. When government agencies remain cohesive and implement consistently high repressive sanctions, this extensive state control deters pragmatic protesters from resisting the incumbent regime. The numbers and particularly the commitments of supportive organizations influence protesters' political efficacy. If the protest movement can rally enthusiastic members, attract allies outside the movement, and gain the backing of structures beyond the nation – for example, the United States, Russia, the Vatican, the European Union, Amnesty International – then expectations of success increase. As the costs of state repression fall, dissent rises. If peer groups encourage protest actions, individuals feel less guilty about defying government authority. Particularly when external shocks – wars, military invasions, economic depression, natural disasters – weaken state control, fragment elite cohesion, and rally diverse groups around an opposition movement, opportunities for antiregime political action expand. The political efficacy of protesters hence increases.[4]

Second, why do protest movements choose particular tactics to attain their goals? Both expressive and instrumental reasons shape this choice. Some activists uphold the need for accommodationist tactics as ends in themselves; for them, alliance formation, nonviolence, litigation, and reliance on legal procedures have expressive value. Others view violent confrontation as a purifying strategy against an evil, unjust situation. Violence brings expressive benefits that come from challenging an exploitative, oppressive, and degrading system. For instance, in his novel *Germinal*, Zola portrayed the anarchist Souvarine as a follower of the Russian anarchist Mikhail Bakunin, who advocated revolutionary terrorism as a way to destroy all existing political, economic, and religious institutions. Attacking the effectiveness of evolutionary, reformist, legalistic tactics as a way to change the capitalist system, Souvarine urged the striking miners to view violence as a purifying tactic that would 'horrify the rulers and awaken the people':

Don't talk to me about evolution! Raise fires in the four corners of cities, mow people down, wipe everything out, and when nothing whatever is left of this rotten world perhaps a better one will spring up. . . . Everything must be destroyed or else hunger will start up again. Yes, anarchy, the end of everything, the whole world bathed in blood and purified by fire.[5]

Unlike Souvarine, most protesters regard tactics as useful means for attaining their policy preferences. These pragmatists switch tactics when a new strategy becomes more effective. This decision partly stems from the response of group allies and government officials to the protest movement's actions. If allies and officials respond favorably to nonviolent, accommodationist, carefully planned tactics, protesters will use them. When, however, accommodation meets with indifference or rejection, violent confrontational tactics may grow more popular. Yet protest activists face a tactical dilemma. On the one hand, extensive political violence attracts media attention but often generates a populist or counterelite backlash. On the other hand, pragmatic coalitions with established parties and interest groups gain the protesters access to the policy process but fail to realize the movement's fundamental goals, particularly changes in social stratification.[6]

Third, under what conditions do protest movements succeed in attaining their policy objectives? The theory of political opportunities assumes that policy success depends on effective leadership, committed participants, and a structural situation where the power of protesters overwhelms the power of the incumbent government. If protesters can skillfully use their resources to mobilize supporters, coordinate activities among diverse groups, and overcome resistance from the opposition, then the prospects for goal attainment appear favorable. Certain structural conditions magnify these prospects. The protest movement must demobilize opponents, secure autonomy from state control, reinforce internal solidarity, and form alliances with supportive interest groups, political parties, and government agencies. When government institutions wield sufficient power to coalesce with sympathetic elites, mobilize followers, monitor the protesters' activities, and maintain high solidarity, protest tactics usually prove futile. Effective leadership also contributes to policy success. Articulating clear policy priorities, successful protest activists reinterpret dominant cultural values so that they congrue with movement demands. They process information to ascertain the linkages among goals, tactics, and outcomes. These leadership skills expand their opportunities for rallying committed supporters. Dedication to the movement seems more crucial than group size. Whereas a large movement can convince others of its political efficacy, members often hold diverse values and interests; hence, coordination becomes difficult. A smaller-sized group, however, can achieve greater solidarity. Its leaders can more easily control members' behavior.[7] Yet especially in constitutional democracies, the limited membership hinders the opportunity for protest activists to help enact public policies that secure fundamental social change.

# Notes and References

## 1 Introduction

1. James C. Scott, *Domination and the Arts of Resistance: Hidden Transcripts* (New Haven, CT: Yale University Press, 1990).
2. For analyses of political opportunity structures, see Sidney Tarrow, *Power in Movement: Social Movements, Collective Action and Politics* (New York: Cambridge University Press, 1994), 17–18, 81–99; Herbert P. Kitschelt, 'Political Opportunity Structures and Political Protest: Anti-Nuclear Movements in Four Democracies,' *British Journal of Political Science*, 16 (January 1986): 57–85; J. Craig Jenkins and Kurt Schock, 'Global Structures and Political Processes in the Study of Domestic Political Conflict,' in *Annual Review of Sociology 1992*, vol. 18, ed. Judith Blake and John Hagan (Palo Alto, CA: Annual Reviews, 1992), 172–75; Kurt Schock, 'Political Opportunities and Social Movements: A Comparative Approach,' *States and Societies*, 10 (Spring 1993): 2–4.
3. George C. Homans, 'Behaviourism and After,' in *Social Theory Today*, ed. Anthony Giddens and Jonathan Turner (Stanford, CA: Stanford University Press, 1987), 58–81; Reinhard Wippler and Siegwart Lindenberg, 'Collective Phenomena and Rational Choice,' in *The Micro-Macro Link*, ed. Jeffrey C. Alexander, Bernhard Giesen, Richard Münch, and Neil J. Smelser (Berkeley: University of California Press, 1987), 135–52; Dennis Chong, *Collective Action and the Civil Rights Movement* (Chicago: University of Chicago Press, 1991).
4. Eric Rambo and Elaine Chan, 'Text, Structure, and Action in Cultural Sociology,' *Theory and Society*, 19 (October 1990): 635–48; Mark Warren, 'Ideology and the Self,' *Theory and Society*, 19 (October 1990): 599–634; Richard Harvey Brown, 'Rhetoric, Textuality, and the Postmodern Turn in Sociological Theory,' *Sociological Theory*, 8 (Fall 1990): 188–94; Seymour Martin Lipset, *Revolution and Counterevolution: Change and Persistence in Social Structures* (New York: Basic Books, 1968), 159–69; Albert Bandura, 'Selective Activation and Disengagement of Moral Control,' *Journal of Social Issues*, 46, no. 1 (1990): 27–46; Herbert C. Kelman and V. Lee Hamilton, *Crimes of Obedience* (New Haven, CT: Yale University Press, 1989), esp. 261–338.
5. Charles Tilly, *From Mobilization to Revolution* (Reading, MA: Addison-Wesley, 1978); Charles Tilly, 'Models and Realities of Popular Collective Action,' *Social Research*, 52 (Winter 1985): 717–47; Doug McAdam, John D. McCarthy, and Mayer N. Zald, 'Social Movements,' in *Handbook of Sociology*, ed. Neil J. Smelser (Newbury Park, CA: Sage Publications, 1988), 695–729; Mayer N. Zald, 'Looking Backward to Look Forward: Reflections on the Past and Future of the Resource Mobilization Program,' in *Frontiers in Social Movement Theory*, ed. Aldon D. Morris and

Carol McClurg Mueller (New Haven, CT: Yale University Press, 1992), 326–48; James B. Rule, *Theories of Civil Violence* (Berkeley: University of California Press, 1988), 170–99; James B. Rule, 'Rationality and Non-Rationality in Militant Collective Action,' *Sociological Theory*, 7 (Fall 1989): 145–60; Daniel R. Sabia, Jr., 'Rationality, Collective Action, and Karl Marx,' *American Journal of Political Science*, 32 (February 1988): 50–71; Michael Hechter, *Principles of Group Solidarity* (Berkeley: University of California Press, 1987); Jonathan H. Turner, 'The Misuse and Use of Metatheory,' *Socioogical Forum*, 5, no. 1 (1990): 37–53; Scott, *Domination and the Arts of Resistance*, 108–35, 218–27.

6.  George C. Homans, 'The Present State of Sociological Theory,' *Sociological Quarterly*, 23 (Summer 1982): 285–99. For the distinction between 'purists' and 'pragmatists,' see James DeNardo, *Power in Numbers: The Political Strategy of Protest and Rebellion* (Princeton, NJ: Princeton University Press, 1985), 87–105.

7.  See Karl-Dieter Opp, *The Rationality of Political Protest: A Comparative Analysis of Rational Choice Theory* (Boulder, CO: Westview Press, 1989).

8.  See Edgar Kiser and Michael Hechter, 'The Role of General Theory in Comparative-historical Sociology,' *American Journal of Sociology*, 97 (July 1991): 1–30; Randall Collins, 'Sociology: Proscience or Antiscience?', *American Sociological Review*, 54 (February 1989): 124–39; Charles E. Lindblom, *Inquiry and Change: The Troubled Attempt to Understand and Shape Society* (New Haven, CT: Yale University Press, 1990), esp. 135–74; Guillermina Jasso, 'Principles of Theoretical Analysis,' *Sociological Theory*, 6 (Spring 1988): 1–20; Guillermina Jasso, 'Notes on the Advancement of Theoretical Sociology (Reply to Turner),' *Sociological Theory*, 7 (Spring 1989): 135–44; William A. Harris and Henry A. Walker, 'Theory Construction and Development in Sociology: An Appropriate Framework,' *Sociological Theory*, 10 (Spring 1992): 111–17; Tim Futing Liao, 'Theory Construction and Development in Sociology: A Reply to Willer and to Harris and Walker,' *Sociological Theory*, 10 (Spring 1992): 118–21.

## Part I

1.  James M. Jasper, 'The Politics of Abstractions: Instrumental and Moralist Rhetorics in Public Debate,' *Social Research*, 59 (Summer 1992): 315–44.

2.  See Talcott Parsons, *Essays in Sociological Theory*, 2d ed. rev. (Glencoe, IL: The Free Press, 1954), 54; Marjorie L. DeVault, 'Novel Readings: The Social Organization of Interpretation,' *American Journal of Sociology*, 95 (January 1990): 886–921; Aaron Wildavsky, 'Can Norms Rescue Self-Interest or Macro Explanation Be Joined to Micro Explanation?', *Critical Review*, 5 (Summer 1991): 301–23; Nils Karlson, 'Bringing Social Norms Back In,' *Scandinavian Political Studies*, 15, no. 3 (1992): 249–68; Karl Mannheim, *Ideology and Utopia: An Introduction to the Sociology of Knowledge*, trans. Louis Wirth and Edward Shils (New York: Harcourt, Brace and World, 1961), 192–263.

3.  David I. Kertzer, *Ritual, Politics, and Power* (New Haven, CT: Yale University Press, 1988).

4.  Daniel Little, 'Rational-Choice Models and Asian Studies,' *Journal of Asian Studies*, 50 (February 1991): 35–52; Michael Hechter, 'Should Values Be Written Out of the Social Scientist's Lexicon?', *Sociological Theory*, 10 (Fall 1992): 214–30; Robert Wuthnow, *Meaning and Moral Order: Explorations in Cultural Analysis* (Berkeley: University of California Press, 1987), 66–185, 265–98; James G. March and Johan P. Olsen, *Rediscovering Institutions: The Organizational Basis of Politics* (New York: The Free Press, 1989), 21–52; Roger Friedland and Robert R. Alford, 'Bringing Society Back In: Symbols, Practices, and Institutional Contradictions,' in *The New Institutionalism in Organizational Analysis*, ed. Walter W. Powell and Paul J. DiMaggio (Chicago: University of Chicago Press, 1991), 232–63.

5.  For analyses of political culture, see Gabriel A. Almond and Sidney Verba, *The Civic Culture: Political Attitudes and Democracy in Five Nations* (Princeton, NJ: Princeton University Press, 1963); Gabriel A. Almond and Sidney Verba, eds., *The Civic Culture Revisited* (Boston: Little, Brown, 1980); Gabriel A. Almond, *A Discipline Divided: Schools and Sects in Political Science* (Newbury Park, CA: Sage Publications, 1990), 138–56; Harry Eckstein, *Regarding Politics: Essays on Political Theory, Stability, and Change* (Berkeley: University of California Press, 1992), 265–303; Lucian W. Pye, 'Political Culture Revisited,' *Political Psychology*, 12 (September 1991): 487–508; Ronald Inglehart, *Culture Shift in Advanced Industrial Society* (Princeton, NJ: Princeton University Press, 1990); Seymour Martin Lipset, *The First New Nation* (New York: Basic Books, 1963); Seymour Martin Lipset, *Continental Divide: The Values and Institutions of the United States and Canada* (New York: Routledge, 1990). Philip Converse has done the classic analyses of 'belief systems.' See his 'The Nature of Belief Systems in Mass Publics,' in David E. Apter, ed., *Ideology and Discontent* (New York: The Free Press of Glencoe, 1964), 206–61.

6.  See Josef Bleicher, *Contemporary Hermeneutics* (London: Routledge and Kegan Paul, 1980), 11–13, 257–59; Judith N. Shklar, 'Squaring the Hermeneutic Circle,' *Social Research*, 53 (Autumn 1986): 449–73; Sheldon S. Wolin, 'Contract and Birthright,' *Political Theory*, 14 (May 1986): 179–93; Terence Ball, 'Deadly Hermeneutics; or *SINN* and the Social Scientist,' in *Idioms of Inquiry: Critique and Renewal in Political Science*, ed. Terence Ball (Albany: State University of New York Press, 1987), 95–112; Gregory Leyh, ed., *Legal Hermeneutics: History, Theory, and Practice* (Berkeley: University of California Press, 1992); Nancy C. Much, 'The Analysis of Discourse as Methodology for a Semiotic Psychology,' *American Behavioral Scientist*, 36 (September 1992): 52–72; Marc W. Steinberg, 'Rethinking Ideology: A Dialogue with Fine and Sandstrom from a Dialogic Perspective,' *Sociological Theory*, 11 (November 1993): 314–20; Joseph Schull, 'What Is Ideology? Theoretical Problems and Lessons from Soviet-Type Societies,' *Political Studies*, 40 (December 1992): 728–41; John Street, 'Review Article: Political Culture – from Civic Culture to Mass Culture,' *British Journal of Political Science*, 24 (January 1994): 95–114; Kathleen Stewart, 'On the Politics of Cultural Theory: A Case for "Contaminated" Cultural Critique,' *Social Research*, 58 (Summer 1991): 395–412; Robert D. Benford, 'Dramaturgy and Social Movements: The Social Construction

and Communication of Power,' *Sociological Inquiry*, 62 (February 1992): 36–55; Richard A. Couto, 'Narrative, Free Space, and Political Leadership in Social Movements,' *Journal of Politics*, 55 (February 1993): 57–79; Robin Erica Wagner-Pacifici, *The Moro Morality Play: Terrorism and Social Drama* (Chicago: University of Chicago Press, 1986); Robert Wuthnow, *Communities of Discourse: Ideology and Social Structure in the Reformation, the Enlightenment, and European Socialism* (Cambridge, MA: Harvard University Press, 1989); Hank Johnston, *Tales of Nationalism: Catalonia, 1939–1979* (New Brunswick, NJ: Rutgers University Press, 1991); James C. Scott, *Domination and the Arts of Resistance: Hidden Transcripts* (New Haven, CT: Yale University Press, 1990); Daniel Little, *Varieties of Social Explanation: An Introduction to the Philosophy of Social Science* (Boulder, CO: Westview Press, 1991), 68–87; Paul Diesing, *How Does Social Science Work? Reflections on Practice* (Pittsburgh, PA: University of Pittsburgh Press, 1991), 104–45; Richard Harvey Brown, 'Cultural Representation and Ideological Domination,' *Social Forces*, 71 (March 1993): 657–76; Wendy Griswold, 'Recent Developments in the Sociology of Culture: Four Good Arguments (and One Bad One),' *Acta Sociologica*, 35 (December 1992): 323–28; Stephan Fuchs, 'Three Sociological Epistemologies,' *Sociological Perspectives*, 36 (Spring 1993): 23–44; John McClure, *Explanations, Accounts, and Illusions: A Critical Analysis* (Cambridge, England: Cambridge University Press, 1991), 13–24, 67–101; Larry J. Griffin, 'Narrative, Event-Structure Analysis, and Causal Interpretation in Historical Sociology,' *American Journal of Sociology*,98 (March 1993): 1094–1133.

7. Andrew M. Greeley, 'Bricolage among the Trash Cans,' *Society*,30 (January/February 1993): 74.

8. David E. Apter, 'Democracy and Emancipatory Movements: Notes for a Theory of Inversionary Discourse,' *Development and Change*, 23 (July 1992): 139–73; David E. Apter and Nagayo Sawa, *Against the State: Politics and Social Protest in Japan* (Cambridge, MA: Harvard University Press, 1984); David E. Apter, *Rethinking Development: Modernization, Dependency, and Postmodern Politics* (Newbury Park, CA: Sage Publications, 1987), 226–58; Mansoor Moaddel, 'Ideology as Episodic Discourse: The Case of the Iranian Revoluion,' *American Sociological Review*, 57 (June 1992): 353–79.

9. See Robert D. Benford, 'Frame Disputes within the Nuclear Disarmament Movement,' *Social Forces*, 71 (March 1993): 677–701; David A. Snow and Robert D. Benford, 'Master Frames and Cycles of Protest,' in *Frontiers in Social Movement Theory*, ed. Aldon D. Morris and Carol McClurg Mueller (New Haven, CT: Yale University Press, 1992), 133–55; Jürgen Gerhards and Dieter Rucht, 'Mesomobilization: Organizing and Framing in Two Protest Campaigns in West Germany,' *American Journal of Sociology*, 98 (November 1992): 555–95; Gary Alan Fine and Kent Sandstrom, 'Ideology in Action: A Pragmatic Approach to a Contested Concept,' *Sociological Theory* 11 (March 1993): 21–38; Charles F. Andrain, *Politics and Economic Policy in Western Democracies* (North Scituate, MA: Duxbury Press, 1980), 31–38; David E. Laitin, *Hegemony and Culture* (Chicago: University of Chicago Press, 1986), 11–20, 23–24, 97–108, 171–83; Deborah A. Stone, 'Causal Stories and the Formation of Policy Agendas,' *Political Science Quarterly*, 104 (Summer 1989): 281–300.

## 2  Political Philosophies, Ideologies, and the Quest for Meaning

1.  See Karl Mannheim, *Ideology and Utopia: An Introduction to the Sociology of Knowledge*, trans. Louis Wirth and Edward Shils (New York: Harcourt, Brace and World, 1961), 71–75; John B. Thompson, 'Ideology,' in *The Oxford Companion to Politics of the World*, ed. Joel Krieger (New York: Oxford University Press, 1993), 409–10; Daniel Bell, *The End of Ideology*, new rev. ed. (New York: Collier Books, 1962), 393–407; John B. Thompson, *Ideology and Modern Culture* (Stanford, CA: Stanford University Press, 1990), 28–44; Banu Helvacioglu, 'The Thrills and Chills of Postmodernism: The Western Intellectual Vertigo,' *Studies in Political Economy*, no. 38 (Summer 1992): 7–34; Patrick L. Baker, 'Chaos, Order, and Sociological Theory,' *Sociological Inquiry*, 63 (May 1993): 123–49; John McClure, *Explanations, Accounts, and Illusions: A Critical Analysis* (New York: Cambridge University Press, 1991), 18–34; Charles F. Andrain, *Foundaions of Comparative Politics: A Policy Perspective* (Monterey, CA: Brooks/Cole, 1983), 103–68.
2.  Carl J. Friedrich, *Man and His Government: An Empirical Theory of Politics* (New York: McGraw-Hill, 1963), 89–90; Gary Alan Fine and Kent Sandstrom, 'Ideology in Action: A Pragmatic Approach to a Contested Concept,' *Sociological Theory*, 11 (March 1993): 21–38.
3.  John Maynard Keynes, *The General Theory of Employment, Interest and Money* (London: Macmillan, 1936), 383–84.
4.  Robert Wuthnow, *Meaning and Moral Order: Explorations in Cultural Analysis* (Berkeley: University of California Press, 1987), 145–85, 265–98; Michael Hechter, *Principles of Group Solidarity* (Berkeley: University of California Press, 1987), 40–58.
5.  Jaroslav Pelikan, *Jesus through the Centuries: His Place in the History of Culture* (New Haven, CT: Yale University Press, 1985), 17–70.
6.  Dino Bigongiari, ed., *The Political Ideas of St. Thomas Aquinas* (New York: Hafner, 1953); Vernon J. Bourke, *The Pocket Aquinas* (New York: Washington Square Press, 1960), 184–259; St Thomas Aquinas, *On Politics and Ethics*, ed. and trans. Paul E. Sigmund (New York: W. W. Norton, 1988), 13–66; James M. Blythe, 'The Mixed Constitution and the Distinction between Regal and Political Power in the Work of Thomas Aquinas,' *Journal of the History of Ideas*, 47 (October–December 1986): 547–65.
7.  Immanuel Kant, 'An Answer to the Question: "What Is Enlightenment?"', in Hans Reiss, ed., *Kant's Political Writings*, trans. H. B. Nisbet (London, England: Cambridge University Press, 1970), 54.
8.  Baron d'Holbach, 'A Materialist View of Nature,' in *Main Currents of Western Thought*, 4th ed., ed. Franklin Le Van Baumer (New Haven, CT: Yale University Press, 1978), 408.
9.  See Immanuel Wallerstein, 'Should We Unthink Nineteenth-Century Social Science?', *International Social Science Journal*, 40 (November 1988): 525–31; Immanuel Wallerstein, 'Typology of Crises in the World-System,' *Review*, 11 (Fall 1988): 581–98; Alain Touraine, 'Modernity and Cultural Specificities,' *International Social Science Journal*, 40 (November 1988): 443–57; Loren E. Lomasky, 'Socialism as Classical Political Philosophy,' *Social Philosophy and Policy*, 6 (Spring 1989): 112–38; Karl W. Deutsch, *The Nerves of Government* (New York: The Free Press, 1966), 22–79; David E. Apter,

*Introduction to Political Analysis* (Cambridge, MA: Winthrop, 1977), 75–136; Margaret C. Jacob, 'The Enlightenment Redefined: The Formation of Modern Civil Society,' *Social Research*, 58 (Summer 1991): 475–95.

10. Andrain, *Foundations of Comparative Politics*, 117–24.

11. See Thomas Hobbes, *Leviathan*, Parts One and Two (New York: Liberal Arts Press, 1958); Thomas Hobbes, *Leviathan*, ed. Richard Tuck (New York: Cambridge University Press, 1991), xviii–xxvi; Gregory S. Kavka, *Hobbesian Moral and Political Theory* (Princeton, NJ: Princeton University Press, 1986); Sheldon S. Wolin, *Politics and Vision: Continuity and Innovation in Western Political Thought* (Boston, MA: Little, Brown, 1960), 239–85; Sheldon S. Wolin, 'Hobbes and the Culture of Despotism,' in *Thomas Hobbes and Political Theory*, ed. Mary G. Dietz (Lawrence: University Press of Kansas, 1990), 9–36; Ronald Beiner, 'Machiavelli, Hobbes, and Rousseau on Civil Religion,' *Review of Politics*, 55 (Fall 1993): 624–31; Joshua Mitchell, 'Luther and Hobbes on the Question: Who Was Moses, Who Was Christ?', *Journal of Politics*, 53 (August 1991): 676–700; Andrzej Rapaczynski, *Nature and Politics: Liberalism in the Philosophies of Hobbes, Locke, and Rousseau* (Ithaca, NY: Cornell University Press, 1987), 17–111; Mark Hartman, 'Hobbes's Concept of Political Revolution,' *Journal of the History of Ideas* 47 (July–September 1986): 487–95.

12. John Locke, *Two Treatises of Government*, ed. Thomas I. Cook (New York: Hafner, 1947); Richard Ashcraft, *Revolutionary Politics and Locke's Two Treatises of Government* (Princeton, NJ: Princeton University Press, 1986); Richard Ashcraft, 'Liberalism and the Problem of Poverty,' *Critical Review*, 6, no. 4 (1993): 493–516; Rapaczynski, *Nature and Politics*, 113–217; Michael H. Hoffheimer, 'Locke, Spinoza, and the Idea of Political Equality,' *History of Political Thought*, 7 (Summer 1986): 341–60; Herman Lebovics, 'The Uses of America in Locke's *Second Treatise of Government*,' *Journal of the History of Ideas*, 47 (October–December 1986): 567–81; David McNally, 'Locke, Levellers and Liberty: Property and Democracy in the Thought of the First Whigs,' *History of Political Thought*, 10 (Spring 1989): 17–40; Richard J. Ellis, 'Radical Lockeanism in American Political Culture,' *Western Political Quarterly*, 45 (December 1992): 825–49.

13. Adam Smith, *An Inquiry into the Nature and Causes of the Wealth of Nations*, ed. R. H. Campbell, A. S. Skinner, and W. B. Todd (Oxford: Clarendon Press, 1979), 456, 687–815; John A. Hall, *Liberalism: Politics, Ideology and the Market* (Chapel Hill: University of North Carolina Press, 1987), 35–59; James Farr, 'Political Science and the Enlightenment of Enthusiasm,' *American Political Science Review*, 82 (March 1988): 51–69; Ashcraft, 'Liberalism and the Problem of Poverty,' 510–11.

14. Jeremy Bentham, *The Principles of Morals and Legislation* (New York: Hafner Press, 1948), 3.

15. See Hanna Fenichel Pitkin, 'Slippery Bentham: Some Neglected Cracks in the Foundation of Utilitarianism,' *Political Theory*, 18 (February 1990): 104–31.

16. John Stuart Mill, *Utilitarianism*, ed. George Sher (Indianapolis, IN: Hackett Publishing Company, 1979), 10.

17. John Stuart Mill, *On Liberty*, ed. Currin V. Shields (New York: Liberal Arts Press, 1956); John Stuart Mill, *Considerations on Representative Government*, ed.

Currin V. Shields (New York: Liberal Arts Press, 1958); David Held, *Models of Democracy* (Stanford, CA: Stanford University Press, 1987), 85–104; O. Kurer, 'John Stuart Mill on Government Intervention,' *History of Political Thought*, 10 (Autumn 1989): 457–80.

18. See Friedrich A. Hayek, *The Constitution of Liberty* (Chicago: University of Chicago Press, 1960); Kari Polanyi-Levitt and Marguerite Mendell, 'The Origins of Market Fetishism,' *Monthly Review*, 41 (June 1989): 11–32; Robert Nozick, *Anarchy, State, and Utopia* (New York: Basic Books, 1974); Daniel M. Hausman and Michael S. McPherson, 'Taking Ethics Seriously: Economics and Contemporary Moral Philosophy,' *Journal of Economic Literature*, 31 (June 1993): 703–04; David Rubinstein, 'The Concept of Justice in Sociology,' *Theory and Society*, 17, no. 4 (1988): 527–50; Steven E. Rhoads, *The Economist's View of the World: Government, Markets, and Public Policy* (New York: Cambridge University Press, 1985); William C. Mitchell, 'Virginia, Rochester, and Bloomington: Twenty-Five Years of Public Choice and Political Science,' *Public Choice* 56 (February 1988): 101–19; William C. Mitchell, 'The *Calculus of Consent*: Enduring Contributions to Public Choice and Political Science,' *Public Choice*, 60 (March 1989): 201–10; Gordon Tullock, 'The Costs of Rent Seeking: A Metaphysical Problem,' *Public Choice* 57 (April 1988): 15–24; William H. Riker, *Liberalism against Populism* (Prospect Heights, IL: Waveland Press, 1988), esp. 233–53.

19. John Rawls, *A Theory of Justice* (Cambridge, MA: Harvard University Press, 1971); John Rawls, *Political Liberalism* (New York: Columbia University Press, 1993); Philip Selznick, *The Moral Commonwealth: Social Theory and the Promise of Community* (Berkeley: University of California Press, 1992); Bruce A. Ackerman, *Social Justice in the Liberal State* (New Haven, CT: Yale University Press, 1980); Ronald Dworkin, *A Matter of Principle* (Cambridge, MA: Harvard University Press, 1985), esp. 190–213; David C. Paris, 'The "Theoretical Mystique": Neutrality, Plurality, and the Defense of Liberalism,' *American Journal of Political Science*, 31 (November 1987): 909–39; Stephen Holmes, 'The Liberal Idea,' *The American Prospect*, no. 7 (Fall 1991): 81–96; Stephen Mulhall, 'The Theoretical Foundations of Liberalism,' *European Journal of Sociology*, 28, no. 2 (1987): 269–95; Michael J. Sandel, 'Democrats and Community: A Public Philosophy for American Liberalism,' *New Republic* 198 (22 February 1988): 20–23. Stephen Holmes, *The Anatomy of Antiliberalism* (Cambridge, MA: Harvard University Press, 1993), defends egalitarian liberalism against its illiberal critics. Drawing on the insights of Locke, Adam Smith, Montesquieu, Kant, and John Stuart Mill, Holmes stresses the liberal commitment to public liberties of discussion and criticism, individual autonomy, secularism, impartiality, equality before the law, legal restraints on state power, and the separation of the public from the private realm.

20. Francis Fukuyama, *The End of History and the Last Man* (New York: The Free Press, 1992), 48. For a critique of the contradictions in Fukuyama's Hegelian perspective, see Stephen Holmes, 'The Scowl of Minerva,' *New Republic*, 206 (23 March 1992): 27–33.

21. Ian Roxborough, 'Neo-Liberalism in Latin America: Limits and Alternatives,' *Third World Quarterly*, 13 (September 1992): 421–40.

22. For diverse interpretations of democratic socialism, see Derek L. Phillips, *Toward a Just Social Order* (Princeton, NJ: Princeton University Press, 1986); Derek L. Phillips, 'Fundamental Rights and the Supportive State,' *Theory and Society*, 17, no. 4 (1988): 571–88; Michael Harrington, *Socialism: Past and Future* (New York: Arcade Publishing Company, 1989); Joshua Cohen, 'The Economic Basis of Deliberative Democracy,' *Social Philosophy and Policy*, 6 (Spring 1989): 25–50; Philip Pettit, 'Towards a Social Democratic Theory of the State,' *Political Studies*, 35 (December 1987): 537–51; David Miller, 'A Vision of Market Socialism,' *Dissent*, 38 (Summer 1991): 406–14; Roy Hattersley, 'The Unheroic Truth about the Market,' *New Socialist*, 55 (May/June 1988): 22–23; Kjell-Olof Feldt, 'What Shall We Do with Capitalism?' *Inside Sweden* (July 1989): 3–5; Anna Lindh, 'The Social Demoratic Party: A Clever 100–Year-Old Lacking in Self-Confidence,' *Inside Sweden* (May 1989): 10–11; Leif Blomberg, '. . . But Are the Social Democrats Still on the Side of the Workers?', *Inside Sweden* (May 1989): 8–9; Pat Devine, 'Market Mania of the Left,' *Marxism Today*, 32 (June 1988): 34–35, 37, 39; Pat Devine, 'Economy, State and Civil Society,' *Economy and Society*, 20 (May 1991): 205–16; Ian Gough, Len Doyal, and the Sheffield Group, 'Conclusion: Socialism, Democracy and Human Needs,' in *The Social Economy and the Democratic State: A New Policy Agenda*, ed. Pete Alcock, Andrew Gamble, Ian Gough, Phil Lee, and Alan Walker (London: Lawrence and Wishart, 1989), 246–75.

23. Göran Therborn, 'The Life and Times of Socialism,' *New Left Review*, no. 194 (July–August 1992): 17–32; David Marquand, 'After Socialism,' *Political Studies*, 41, Special Issue (1993): 43–56; Noel O'Sullivan, 'Political Integration, the Limited State, and the Philosophy of Postmodernism,' *Political Studies*, 41, Special Issue (1993): 21–42; Hans Keman, 'Theoretical Approaches to Social Democracy,' *Journal of Theoretical Politics*, 5 (July 1993): 291–316; George Ross, 'Turning Technocratic: Euro-Socialists and 1992,' *Socialist Review*, 21 (April–June 1991): 133–57; W. Rand Smith, 'Nationalizations for What? Capitalist Power and Public Enterprise in Mitterrand's France,' *Politics and Society*, 18 (March 1990): 75–99; Alain Claisse, 'Question of Rolling Back the State in France,' *Governance: An International Journal of Policy and Administration*, 2 (April 1989): 152–71; Donald Share, 'Spain: Socialists as Neoiberals,' *Socialist Review*, 18 (January–March 1988): 38–67; Donald Share, 'Dilemmas of Social Democracy in the 1980s: The Spanish Socialist Workers Party in Comparative Perspective,' *Comparative Political Studies*, 21 (October 1988): 408–35; David Feikhert, 'The Kiwi Tendency,' *New Socialist*, no. 55 (May/June 1988): 19–21; Francis G. Castles, 'Australian Welfare State Expenditure Revisited: Some Implications for Change,' *Australian Journal of Political Science*, 25 (November 1990): 251–72.

24. Karl Marx, *Political Writings*, vol. 2: *Surveys from Exile*, ed. David Fernbach (New York: Vintage, 1974), 146. See too Karl Marx, *Capital*, vol. 1, trans. Ben Fowkes (New York: Vintage Books, 1977), 91; Kai Nielsen, 'Marx and the Enlightenment Project,' *Critical Review*, 2 (Fall 1988): 59–75; Andrzej Walicki, 'Karl Marx as Philosopher of Freedom,' *Critical Review*, 2 (Fall 1988): 10–58; J. C. Glass and W. Johnson, 'Metaphysics, MSRP and

Economics,' *British Journal for the Philosophy of Science*, 39 (September 1988): 313–29.

25. See the following works of Karl Marx: *Early Writings*, trans. Rodney Livingstone and Gregor Benton (New York: Vintage, 1975), 257, 419–20; *Political Writings*, vol. 1: *The Revolutions of 1848*, ed. David Fernbach (New York: Vintage, 1974), esp. 62–98, 319–30; *Political Writings*, vol. 3: *The First International and After*, ed. David Fernbach (New York: Vintage, 1974), 270–72, 333–75. See too Richard Schmitt, *Introduction to Marx and Engels: A Critical Reconstruction* (Boulder, CO: Westview Press, 1987), 171–204; Hal Draper, *The 'Dictatorship of the Proletariat' from Marx to Lenin* (New York: Monthly Review Press, 1987); Julie Mostov, 'Karl Marx as Democratic Theorist,' *Polity*, 22 (Winter 1989): 195–212; Paresh Chattopadhyay, 'The Economic Content of Socialism: Marx vs Lenin,' *Review of Radical Political Economics*, 24 (Fall and Winter 1992): 90–110.

26. See V. I. Lenin, *What Is to Be Done?* (Peking: Foreign Languages Press, 1973); V. I. Lenin, *Selected Works* (New York: International Publishers, 1971); Alfred B. Evans, 'Rereading Lenin's *State and Revolution*,' *Slavic Review*, 46 (Spring 1987): 1–19; Robert Mayer, 'Marx, Lenin and the Corruption of the Working Class,' *Political Studies*, 41 (December 1993): 636–49.

27. Lenin, *Selected Works*, 294–336, 379, 417, 501–5, 599.

28. Carl Boggs, *Social Movements and Political Power* (Philadelphia, PA: Temple University Press, 1986), 21–79; Fedor Burlatsky, 'The State after Stalin,' *Marxism Today*, 32 (July 1988): 30–33; Marta Harnecker, 'Democracy and Revolutionary Movement,' *Social Justice*, 19 (Winter 1992): 60–73.

29. Georges Sorel, *Reflections on Violence*, trans. T. E. Hulme and J. Roth (New York: Collier Books, 1961); Michael Tager, 'Myth and Politics in the Works of Sorel and Barthes,' *Journal of the History of Ideas*, 47 (October–December 1986): 625–39; E. J. Hobsbawm, 'Inside Every Worker There Is a Syndicalist Trying to Get Out,' *New Society*, 48 (5 April 1979): 8–10; Carl Boggs, Jr., 'Revolutionary Process, Political Strategy, and the Dilemma of Power,' *Theory and Society*, 4 (Fall 1977): 359–93.

30. For analyses of conservatism, see Noel O'Sullivan, *Conservatism* (New York: St. Martin's Press, 1976); Philip W. Buck, ed., *How Conservatives Think* (Baltimore, MD: Penguin Books, 1975); Samuel P. Huntington, 'Conervatism as an Ideology,' *American Political Science Review*, 51 (June 1957): 454–73; Ivor Crewe and Donald D. Searing, 'Ideological Change in the British Conservative Party,' *American Political Science Review*, 82 (June 1988): 361–84; David Marquand, 'Richesse Oblige: The New Tory Wave,' *New Statesman*, 115 (3 June 1988): 21–22; Glen C. Dealy, 'The Pluralistic Latins,' *Foreign Policy*, no. 57 (Winter 1984–1985): 108–27; Kenneth P. Langton, 'The Church, Social Consciousness, and Protest?', *Comparative Political Studies*, 19 (October 1986): 317–55; James Conniff, 'Burke and India: The Failure of the Theory of Trusteeship,' *Political Research Quarterly*, 46 (June 1993): 291–309; Randall Collins, 'The Rise and Fall of Modernism in Politics and Religion,' *Acta Sociologica*, 35, no. 3 (1992): 171–86; Gøsta Esping-Andersen, 'Power and Distributional Regimes,' *Politics and Society*, 14, no. 2 (1985): 223–56; Gøsta Esping-Andersen, *Three Worlds of Welfare Capitalism* (Princeton, NJ: Princeton University Press, 1990), 26–138.

31. See John H. Garvey, 'Introduction: Fundamentalism and Politics,' in *Fundamentalisms and the State*, ed. Martin E. Marty and R. Scott Appleby (Chicago: University of Chicago Press, 1993), 13–27; Hans G. Kippenberg, 'Revolt against Modernism: A Note on Some Recent Comparative Studies in Fundamentalism,' *Numen*, 38 (June 1991): 128–33; Robert Wuthnow, 'American Democracy and the Democratization of American Religion,' *Politics and Society*, 15, no. 2 (1986–1987): 222–34; Gerald M. Platt and Rhys H. Williams, 'Religion, Ideology, and Electoral Politics,' *Society*, 25 (July/August 1988): 38–45; Richard Rodriguez, 'A Continental Shift,' *Los Angeles Times*, 13 August 1989, Part V, pp. 1, 6; Nazih N. M. Ayubi, 'The Politics of Islamic Movements in the Middle East,' *Journal of International Affairs*, 36 (Fall/Winter 1982–1983): 271–83; Asher Arian, *Politics in Israel: The Second Generation* (Chatham, NJ: Chatham House Publishers, 1985), 135, 216–25; Bruce B. Lawrence, *Defenders of God: The Fundamentalist Revolt against the Modern Age* (San Francisco: Harper and Row, 1989).

32. Quoted in S. J. Woolf, 'Italy,' in *European Fascism*, ed. S. J. Woolf (New York: Vintage, 1969), 44.

33. See *Readings on Fascism and National Socialism*, ed. members of the Department of Philosophy, University of Colorado (Chicago: Swallow Press, 1952); Adolf Hitler, *Mein Kampf*, trans. Ralph Mannheim (Boston: Houghton Mifflin, 1943); Adolf Hitler, *The Speeches of Adolf Hitler, April 1922–August 1939*, vol. 1, ed. Norman H. Baynes (London: Oxford University Press, 1942); Adolf Hitler, *My New Order*, ed. Raoul de Roussy de Sales (New York: Reynal and Hitchcock, 1941); Andrain, *Foundations of Comparative Politics*, 141–51, 161; Milton Rokeach, *The Nature of Human Values* (New York: The Free Press, 1973), 165–211.

34. Klaus von Beyme, 'Right-Wing Extremism in Post-War Europe,' *West European Politics*, 11 (April 1988): 1–18; Hans-Georg Betz, 'The Two Faces of Radical Right-Wing Populism in Western Europe,' *Review of Politics*, 55 (Fall 1993): 663–85; Tony Bunyan and Liz Fekete, 'Jeux sans Frontières: It's a Lock-Out,' *New Statesman and Society*, 6 (5 November 1993): 23–26; Jürgen W. Falter and Siegfried Schumann, 'Affinity towards Right-Wing Extremism in Western Europe,' *West European Politics*, 11 (April 1988): 96–110; Jim Sidanius, 'Social Attitudes and Political Party Preference among Swedish Youth,' *Scandinavian Political Studies*, 10, no. 2 (1987): 111–24; Pierre-André Taguieff, 'The Doctrine of the National Front in France (1972–1989): A "Revolutionary" Programme? Ideological Aspects of a National-Populist Mobilization,' *New Political Science*, nos. 16–17 (Fall/Winter 1989): 29–70; Roger Eatwell, 'Towards a New Model of Generic Fascism,' *Journal of Theoretical Politics*, 4 (April 1992): 161–94.

35. See Sidney Verba, et al., *Elites and the Idea of Equality: A Comparison of Japan, Sweden, and the United States* (Cambridge, MA: Harvard University Press, 1987); Robert Y. Shapiro and John T. Young, 'Public Opinion and the Welfare State: The United States in Comparative Perspective,' *Political Science Quarterly*, 104 (Spring 1989): 59–89; Leslie Holmes, *Politics in the Communist World* (New York: Oxford University Press, 1986), 76–95; Rachel Walker, 'Marxism-Leninism as Discourse: The Politics of the Empty Signifier and the Double Bind,' *British Journal of Political Science*, 19 (April 1989): 161–89; Piero Melograni, 'The Cult of the Duce in

Mussolini's Italy,' *Journal of Contemporary History*, 11 (October 1976): 221–37; Edward R. Tannenbaum, *The Fascist Experience: Italian Society and Culture, 1922–1945* (New York: Basic Books, 1972).

36. Wallerstein, 'Should We Unthink Nineteenth-Century Social Science?', 525–31; Michael Mann, 'Ruling Class Strategies and Citizenship,' *Sociology*, 21 (August 1987): 339–54; Robert L. Heilbroner, *The Nature and Logic of Capitalism* (New York: W. W. Norton, 1985), 78–105; Charles F. Andrain, 'Capitalism and Democracy Reappraised,' *Western Political Quarterly*, 37 (December 1984): 652–64.

37. Ross Terrill, *R. H. Tawney and His Times: Socialism as Fellowship* (Cambridge, MA: Harvard University Press, 1973), 178. Max Weber took a similar view. Contrasting the ethic of ultimate ends with the ethic of responsibility for consequences, Weber doubted that the coercive, violent means used by political leaders would ever realize ultimate ends: the salvation of one's own soul and others' souls. See H. H. Gerth and C. Wright Mills, eds., *From Max Weber: Essays in Sociology* (New York: Oxford University Press, 1946), 117–28.

## 3   Religion and Political Vision

1. Albert Hirschman, *The Passions and the Interests: Political Arguments for Capitalism before Its Triumph* (Princeton, NJ: Princeton University Press, 1977), 117.

2. Sheldon S. Wolin, *Politics and Vision: Continuity and Innovation in Western Political Thought* (Boston: Little, Brown, 1960), 17–21; S. N. Eisenstadt, 'Frameworks of the Great Revolutions: Culture, Social Structure, History and Human Agency,' *International Social Science Journal*, 44 (August 1992): 385–401; Dimitris J. Kyrtatas, 'Revelation Revised,' *New Left Review*, no. 190 (November–December 1991): 131–37; David E. Aune, 'Revelation,' in *Harper's Bible Commentary*, ed. James L. Mays (San Francisco: Harper and Row, 1988), 1300–19. During the turmoil of seventeenth-century English political life, Thomas Hobbes wrote two books with titles from the great beasts of Revelation. *Leviathan* called for a powerful state that would provide security against the violent deaths brought by civil wars. In *Behemoth: The Long Parliament*, Hobbes charged the parliament with causing the civil war (1642–1649) by rebelling against King Charles I.

3. For analyses of the functions of religious values, see Clifford Geertz, *The Interpretation of Cultures* (New York: Basic Books, 1973), 87–125; Andrew Greeley, 'Protestant and Catholic: Is the Analogical Imagination Extinct?', *American Sociological Review*, 54 (August 1989): 485–502; Ole Riis, 'The Role of Religion in Legitimating the Modern Structuration of Society,' *Acta Sociologica*, 32, no. 2 (1989): 137–53; Ronwyn Goodsir Thomas, 'Hermeneutics and Liturgy,' *The Month*, 19 (October 1986); 264–67, 79; N. J. Demerath III, 'Religious Capital and Capital Religions: Cross-Cultural and Non-Legal Factors in the Separation of Church and State,' *Daedalus*, 120 (Summer 1991): 21–40.

4. See David E. Apter, *The Politics of Modernization* (Chicago: University of Chicago Press, 1965), 266–356.

5. Clarke E. Cochran, Jerry D. Perkins, and Murray Clark Havens, 'Public Policy and the Emergence of Religious Politics,' *Polity*, 19 (Summer 1987): 595–612.
6. Donald Eugene Smith, *Religion and Political Development* (Boston: Little, Brown, 1970); Robert Wuthnow, *Meaning and Moral Order: Explorations in Cultural Analysis* (Berkeley: University of California Press, 1987), 265–66; Michael Hechter, *Principles of Group Solidarity* (Berkeley: University of California Press, 1987), 1–58; Eugen Schoenfeld, 'Militant and Submissive Religions: Class, Religion and Ideology,' *British Journal of Sociology*, 43 (March 1992): 111–40.
7. For analyses of the impact of religious beliefs on modernization, protest movements, and social change, see Kenneth Thompson, 'Secularization and Sacralization,' in *Rethinking Progress: Movements, Forces, and Ideas at the End of the 20th Century*, ed. Jeffrey C. Alexander and Piotr Sztompka (Boston: Unwin Hyman, 1990), 161–81; Mario Diani, 'Themes of Modernity in New Religious Movements and New Social Movements,' *Social Science Information*, 32 (March 1993): 111–31; John A. Hall, *Powers and Liberties: The Causes and Consequences of the Rise of the West* (Berkeley: University of California Press, 1986); John A. Hall, 'Religion and the Rise of Capitalism,' *European Journal of Sociology*, 26, no. 2 (1985): 193–223.
8. Reinhard Bendix, *Max Weber: An Intellectual Portrait* (Garden City, NY: Anchor Books, 1962), 98–141; John King Fairbank, *The United States and China*, 4th ed., enlarged (Cambridge, MA: Harvard University Press, 1983), 53–79; Zi Zhongyun, 'The Relationship of Chinese Traditional Culture to the Modernization of China: An Introduction to the Current Discussion,' *Asian Survey*, 27 (April 1987): 442–58.
9. Charles F. Andrain, *Political Change in the Third World* (Boston: Unwin Hyman, 1988), 91–93; Tzong-biau Lin, 'International Competition: A Challenge from the Asian Pacific Rim,' *Political Economy*, 3, no. 2 (1987): 161–79; Winston Davis, 'Religion and Development: Weber and the East Asian Experience,' in *Understanding Political Development*, ed. Myron Weiner and Samuel P. Huntington (Boston: Little, Brown, 1987), 221–80; Marion J. Levy, Jr., 'Confucianism and Modernization,' *Society*, 29 (May/June 1992): 15–18; Tu Wei-Ming, 'The Search for Roots in Industrial East Asia: The Case of the Confucian Revival,' in *Fundamentalisms Observed*, ed. Martin E. Marty and R. Scott Appleby (Chicago: University of Chicago Press, 1991), 740–81.
10. Robert Eric Frykenberg, 'Hindu Fundamentalism and the Structural Stability of India,' in *Fundamentalisms and the State*, ed. Martin E. Marty and R. Scot Appleby (Chicago: University of Chicago Press, 1993), 233–55; Daniel Gold, 'Organized Hinduisms: From Vedic Truth to Hindu Nation,' in *Fundamentalisms Observed*, ed. Marty and Appleby, 531–93; Susanne Hoeber Rudolph and Lloyd I. Rudolph, 'Modern Hate,' *New Republic*, 208 (22 March 1993): 24–29; Bendix, *Max Weber*, 142–99; Robert L. Hardgrave, Jr. and Stanley A. Kochanek, *India: Government and Politics in a Developing Nation*, 4th ed. (New York: Harcourt, Brace, Jovanovich, 1986), 157–81; Cynthia Keppley Mahmood, 'Sikh Rebellion and the Hindu Concept of Order,' *Asian Survey*, 29 (March 1989): 326–40; T. N. Madan, 'Religion in India,' *Daedalus*, 118 (Fall 1989): 115–46.

11. Martin Stuart-Fox, 'Marxism and Theravada Buddhism: The Legitimaion of Political Authority in Laos,' *Pacific Affairs*, 56 (Fall 1983): 428–54; Clayton Jones, 'Will Burma's Monks Enter the Political Fray?' *Christian Science Monitor*, 6 October 1988, pp. 7–11; Smith, *Religion and Political Development*, 39–45, 70–75, 148–50, 195–200, 258–65.

12. Steven Grosby, 'Religion and Nationality in Antiquity: The Worship of Yahweh and Ancient Israel,' *European Journal of Sociology*, 32, no. 2 (1991): 229–65; Michael Walzer, *Exodus and Revolution* (New York: Basic Books, 1985); H. Mark Roelofs, 'Hebraic-Biblical Political Thinking,' *Polity*, 20 (Summer 1988): 572–97; H. Mark Roelofs, 'Church and State in America: Toward a Biblically Derived Reformulation of Their Relationship,' *Review of Politics*, 50 (Fall 1988): 561–81; Peter H. Davids, 'God and Caesar: Part I,' *Sojourners*, 10 (April 1981): 12–15; David J. Levy, 'Israel and Judah: Politics and Religion in the Hebrew Kingdoms,' *Continuity: A Journal of History*, no. 10 (Spring 1985): 47–62; Eliezer Schweid, 'Jewish Messianism: Metamorphoses of an Idea,' *The Jerusalem Quarterly*, no. 36 (Summer 1985): 63–78; Jeremiah Unterman, 'Covenant,' in *Harper's Bible Dictionary*, ed. Paul J. Achtemeier (San Fransisco: Harper and Row, 1985), 190–92; Bernhard W. Anderson, 'Covenant,' in *The Oxford Companion to the Bible*, ed. Bruce M. Metzger and Michael D.Coogan (New York: Oxford University Press, 1993), 138–39; Richard Elliott Friedman, *Who Wrote the Bible?* (New York: Summit Books, 1987), 33–49, 234–45.

13. David Biale, *Power and Powerlessness in Jewish History* (New York: Schocken Books, 1987); Asher Arian, *Politics in Israel: The Second Generation* (Chatham, NJ: Chatham House Publishers, 1985), esp. 1–24, 71–154, 216–25; Walzer, *Exodus and Revolution*, 136–41; Myron J. Aronoff, 'The Failure of Israel's Labor Party and the Emergence of Gush Emunim,' in *When Parties Fail: Emerging Alternative Organizations*, ed. Kay Lawson and Peter H. Merkl (Princeton, NJ: Princeton University Press, 1988), 309–37; Gideon Aran, 'Jewish Zionist Fundamentalism: The Bloc of the Faithful in Israel (Gush Emunim),' in *Fundamentalisms Observed*, ed. Marty and Appleby, 265–344.

14. See Ched Myers, *Binding the Strong Man: A Political Reading of Mark's Story of Jesus* (Maryknoll, NY: Orbis Books, 1988), esp. 290–353, 413–47; John P. Meier, *A Marginal Jew: Rethinking the Historical Jesus* (New York: Doubleday, 1991), 205–19; Doron Mendels, *The Rise and Fall of Jewish Nationalism: Jewish and Christian Ethnicity in Ancient Palestine* (New York: Doubleday, 1992), 227–29, 259–63, 309–10; E. P. Sanders, *Jesus and Judaism* (Philadelphia, PA: Fortress Press, 1985); James H. Charlesworth, *Jesus within Judaism* (New York: Doubleday, 1988); Irving M. Zeitlin, *Jesus and the Judaism of His Time* (Cambridge, England: Polity Press, 1988), esp. 129–83; John D. Levenson, *The Death and Resurrection of the Beloved Son: The Transformation of Child Sacrifice in Judaism and Christianity* (New Haven, CT: Yale University Press, 1993), 200–32; Ian Wilson, *Jesus: The Evidence* (San Francisco: Harper and Row, 1984); Marcus J. Borg, *Jesus: A New Vision* (San Francisco: Harper and Row, 1987), esp. 79–185; Thomas Sheehan, *The First Coming* (New York: Random House, 1986); Robert N. Bellah, 'Resurrecting the Common Good,' *Commonweal* 114 (18 December 1987): 736–41.

15. James G. Williams, 'The Sermon on the Mount as a Christian Basis of Altruism,' *Humboldt Journal of Social Relations*, 13 (Fall/Winter and Spring/ Summer 1985/1986): 89–112; Alan F. Segal, *Paul the Convert: The Apostolate and Apostasy of Saul the Pharisee* (New Haven, CT: Yale University Press, 1990), 134–38.

16. Peter H. Davids, 'God and Caesar: Part II,' *Sojourners*, 10 (May 1981): 24–28; Alan F. Segal, *Rebecca's Children: Judaism and Christianity in the Roman World* (Cambridge, MA: Harvard University Press, 1986), 68–116; Segal, *Paul the Convert*, 34–183, 254–84; Hugh J. Schonfield, *The Original New Testament* (San Francisco: Harper and Row, 1985), 199–415.

17. Joseph M. Bryant, 'The Sect-Church Dynamic and Christian Expansion in the Roman Empire: Persecution, Penitential Discipline, and Schism in Sociological Perspective,' *British Journal of Sociology*, 44 (June 1993): 303–39.

18. St Augustine, *The City of God*, trans. Henry Bettenson (New York: Penguin Books, 1984), 593.

19. Wolin, *Politics and Vision*, 121–31; Alasdair MacIntyre, *Whose Justice? Which Rationality?* (Notre Dame, IN: University of Notre Dame Press, 1988), 146–63.

20. Cited in Robert A. Packenham, *The Dependency Movement: Scholarship and Politics in Development Studies* (Cambridge, MA: Harvard University Press, 1992), 147–48.

21. Michael Legris, 'Exclusif: Le Nouveau Catéchisme de l'Église Catholique,' *L'Express*, no. 2158 (20 November 1992): 26–40; Pope John Paul II, *The Pope Speaks to the American Church: John Paul's Homilies, Speeches, and Letters to Catholics in the United States*, ed. Cambridge Center for the Study of Faith and Culture (San Francisco: Harper Collins,1992), esp. 206–221; Glen C. Dealy, 'The Pluralistic Latins,' *Foreign Policy*, no. 57 (Winter 1984–1985): 108–27; Victor Kiernan, 'Marx and the Undiscovered Country,' *New Left Review*, no. 190 (November–December 1991): 99–118; Penny Lernoux, 'The Pope and Medellín: Casting out the "People's Church," ' *The Nation*, 247 (27 August/3 September 1988): 161–65; Penny Lernoux, *People of God: The Struggle for World Catholicism* (New York: Viking, 1989), 28–75.

22. Eric O. Hanson, *The Catholic Church in World Politics* (Princeton, NJ: Princeton University Press, 1987), 125–61; Harold L. Wilensky, 'Leftism, Catholicism, and Democratic Corporatism: The Role of Political Parties in Welfare State Development,' in *The Development of Welfare States in Europe and America*, ed. Peter Flora and Arnold J. Heidenheimer (New Brunswick, NJ: Transaction Books, 1981), 345–82; Harold L. Wilensky, Gregory M. Luebbert, Susan Reed Hahn, and Adrienne M. Jamieson, *Comparative Social Policy: Theories, Methods, Findings* (Berkeley: Institute of International Studies, University of California at Berkeley, 1985), 22–29.

23. Brian J. Shaw, 'Praxis, Hermeneutics, and the Kingdom: Marx and Latin American Liberation Theology,' *Rethinking Marxism*, 5 (Winter 1992): 62–88; Enrique Dussel, 'Liberation Theology and Marxism,' trans. Irene B. Hodgson and José Pedrozo, *Rethinking Marxism*, 5 (Fall 1992): 50–74; Ernesto Cardenal, *The Gospel in Solentiname*, vol. 1, trans. Donald D. Walsh (Maryknoll, NY: Orbis Books, 1978); Philip J. Williams, 'The Catholic Hierarchy in the Nicaraguan Revolution,' *Journal of Latin American Studies*, 17 (November 1985): 341–69; Michael Dodson, 'The Politics of Religion in

Revolutionary Nicaragua,' *Annals of the American Academy of Political and Social Science*, 243 (January 1986): 36–49; Penny Lernoux, 'In Common Suffering and Hope: The Base Comunity Movement in Brazil,' *Sojourners*, 16 (December 1987): 22–28; Lernoux, *People of God*, 79–152, 365–405; Daniel H. Levine and Scott Mainwaring, 'Religion and Popular Protest in Latin America: Contrasting Experiences,' in *Power and Popular Protest*, ed. Susan Eckstein (Berkeley: University of California Press, 1989), 203–40; Daniel H. Levine, 'Assessing the Impacts of Liberation Theology in Latin America,' *The Review of Politics*, 50 (Spring 1988): 241–63; Daniel H. Levine, 'Popular Groups, Popular Culture, and Popular Religion,' *Comparative Studies in Society and History*, 32 (October 1990): 718–64; H. Mark Roelofs, 'Liberation Theology: The Recovery of Biblical Radicalism,' *American Political Science Review*, 82 (June 1988): 549–66; Pablo Richard, 'Religion and Democracy: The Church of the Poor in Central America,' *Alternatives*, 13 (July 1988): 357–78.

24. Jean-Pierre Bastian, 'The Metamorphosis of Latin American Protestant Groups: A Sociohistorical Perspective,' *Latin American Research Review*, 28, no. 2 (1993): 33–61; Edwin Eloy Aguilar, José Miguel Sandoval, Timothy J. Steigenga, and Kenneth M. Coleman, 'Protestantism in El Salvador: Conventional Wisdom versus Survey Evidence,' *Latin American Research Review*, 28, no. 2 (1993): 119–40; Richard Rodriguez, 'A Continental Shift,' *Los Angeles Times*, 13 August 1989, Part V, pp. 1, 6; Sergio Spoerer, 'Pentecôtisme et Religiosité Populaire au Chili,' *Problèmes d'Amérique Latine*, no. 81, no. 3 (1986): 97–109; Lernoux, *People of God*, 153–64; David Stoll, *Is Latin America Turning Protestant? The Politics of Evangelical Growth* (Berkeley: University of California Press, 1990).

25. T. N. Madan, 'Secularism in Its Place,' *Journal of Asian Studies*, 46 (November 1987): 747–59; John L. Esposito, 'Islam in the Politics of the Middle East,' *Current History*, 85 (February 1986): 53–57, 81; John L. Esposito, 'Political Islam: Beyond the Green Menace,' *Current History*, 93 (January 1994): 19–24; John L. Esposito, *The Islamic Threat: Myth or Reality?* (New York: Oxford University Press, 1992); Robin Wright, 'The Islamic Resurgence: A New Phase?' *Current History*, 87 (February 1988): 53–56, 85–86; Robin Wright, 'Islam's New Political Face,' *Current History*, 90 (January 1991): 25–28, 35–36; Nazih N. M. Ayubi, 'The Politics of Militant Islamic Movements in the Middle East,' *Journal of International Affairs*, 36 (Fall/Winter 1982/1983): 271–83; Bernard Lewis, 'State and Society under Islam,' *Wilson Quarterly*, 13 (Autumn 1989): 39–51.

26. Fouad Ajami, 'The Silence in Arab Culture,' *New Republic*, 196 (6 April 1987): 31.

27. Thomas Hodgkin, 'The Revolutionary Tradition in Islam,' *Race and Class*, 21 (Winter 1980): 221–37; Bassma Kodmani, 'L'Islam dans le Monde,' *Politique Étrangère* 48 (Winter 1983): 953–64; Jane I. Smith, 'Islam,' in *Women in World Religions*, ed. Arvind Sharma (Albany, NY: State University of New York Press, 1987), 235–50; Arnold Hottinger, 'Iran: From Revolution to Holy War,' *Swiss Review of World Affairs*, 35 (January 1986): 13–19; Mehdi Mozaffari, 'Changes in the Iranian Political System after Khomeini's Death,' *Political Studies*, 41 (December 1993): 611–17; Fouad Ajami, 'Iran: The Impossible Revolution,' *Foreign Affairs*, 67

(Winter 1988/1989): 135–55; Said Amir Arjomand, 'History, Structure, and Revolution in the Shi'ite Tradition in Contemporary Iran,' *International Political Science Review*, 10 (April 1989): 111–19; Said Amir Arjomand, 'Shi'ite Jurisprudence and Constituion Making in the Islamic Republic of Iran,' in *Fundamentalisms and the State*, ed. Marty and Appleby, 88–109; Shahla Haeri, 'Obedience versus Autonomy: Women and Fundamentalism in Iran and Pakistan,' in *Fundamentalisms and Society*, ed. Martin E. Marty and R. Scott Appleby (Chicago: University of Chicago Press, 1993), 181–98; Majid Tehranian, 'Islamic Fundamentalism in Iran and the Discourse of Development,' in *Fundamentalisms and Society*, 341–73; Richard Cottam, 'Inside Revolutionary Iran,' *Middle East Journal*, 43 (Spring 1989): 168–85; Andrain, *Political Change in the Third World*, 252–79.

28. John A. Coleman, 'Civil Religion,' *Sociological Analysis*, 31 (Spring 1970): 67–77; Clarke E. Cochran, *Religion in Public and Private Life* (New York: Routledge, Chapman, and Hall, 1990); Rhys H. Williams and N.J. Demerath III, 'Religion and Political Process in an American City,' *American Sociological Review*, 56 (August 1991): 417–31.

29. See Jack A. Goldstone, *Revolution and Rebellion in the Early Modern World* (Berkeley: University of California Press, 1991), 444–50; Apter, *Politics of Modernization*, 81–122, 266–312; Samuel P. Huntington and Jorge I. Domínguez, 'Political Development,' in *Handbook of Political Science*, vol. 3: *Macropolitical Theory*, ed. Fred I. Greenstein and Nelson W. Polsby (Reading, MA: Addison-Wesley, 1975), 18–22; Eisenstadt, 'Frameworks of the Great Revolutions,' 388–98.

## 4 Nationalism and Political Identity

1. Bernard Shaw, *Saint Joan* (Baltimore, MD: Penguin Books, 1951), 59–61. For accounts of the role played by Joan in creating a French national identity, see Jules Michelet, *Joan of Arc*, trans. Albert Guerard (Ann Arbor: University of Michigan Press, 1957); Ingvald Raknem, *Joan of Arc in History, Legend and Literature* (Bergen, Norway: Scandinavian University Books, 1971).

2. Adam J. Lerner, 'Transcendence of the Nation: National Identity and the Terrain of the Divine,' *Millennium: Journal of International Studies*, 20 (Winter 1991): 407–27.

3. Liah Greenfeld, *Nationalism: Five Roads to Modernity* (Cambridge, MA: Harvard University Press, 1992), 187–88.

4. See Jack David Eller and Reed M. Coughlan, 'The Poverty of Primordialism: The Demystification of Ethnic Attachments,' *Ethnic and Racial Studies*, 16 (April 1993): 183–202; Kenneth Thompson, 'Secularization and Sacralization,' in *Rethinking Progress: Movements, Forces, and Ideas at the End of the 20th Century*, ed. Jeffrey C. Alexander and Piotr Sztompka (Boston: Unwin Hyman, 1990), 161–81; Paul R. Brass, *Ethnicity and Nationalism: Theory and Comparison* (New Delhi, India: Sage Publications, 1991), esp. 13–68, 245–99; Greenfeld, *Nationalism*, 3–21; Edward Shils, 'Primordial, Personal, Sacred, and Civil Ties,' *British Journal of Sociology*, 8 (June 1957): 130–45; Edward Shils, 'The Virtue of Civil Society,' *Government and Opposition*, 26 (Winter 1991): 3–30; Charles F. Andrain,

*Political Life and Social Change*, 2d ed. (Belmont, CA: Duxbury Press, 1975), 59–64; James Anderson, 'On Theories of Nationalism and the Size of States,' *Antipode* 18 (September 1986): 218–32; Anthony D. Smith, 'The Myth of the "Modern Nation" and the Myths of Nations,' *Ethnic and Racial Studies*, 11 (January 1988): 1–26; Philip Selznick, *The Moral Commonwealth: Social Theory and the Progress of Community* (Berkeley: University of California Press, 1992), 390–92, 409–27. Selznick contrasts civil values with communal ties based on primordial and sacred attachments. Civility is cooler, more detached, and more inclusive. 'In civility respect, not love, is the salient value,' p. 391.

5.  Peter Worsley, *The Three Worlds: Culture and World Development* (Chicago: University of Chicago Press, 1984), 235–95; Michael Hechter, 'Nationalism as Group Solidarity,' *Ethnic and Racial Studies* 10 (October 1987): 415–26.

6.  John H. Schaar, 'Legitimacy in the Modern States,' in *Power and Community: Dissenting Essays in Political Science*, ed. Philip Green and Sanford Levinson (New York: Vintage Books, 1970), 323.

7.  Anthony H. Richmond, 'Ethnic Nationalism: Social Science Paradigms,' *International Social Science Journal*, 39 (February 1987): 3–18; Ernst B. Haas, 'What Is Nationalism and Why Should We Study It?' *International Organization*, 40 (Summer 1986): 707–44; Fred W. Riggs, 'What Is Ethnic? What Is National? Let's Turn the Tables,' *Canadian Review of Studies in Nationalism*, 13 (Spring 1986): 111–23; Ivo D. Duchacek, 'Antagonistic Cooperation: Territorial and Ethnic Communities,' *Publius: The Journal of Federalism*, 7 (Fall 1977): 3–29; Charles F. Andrain, *Political Change in the Third World* (Boston: Unwin Hyman, 1988), 215–51.

8.  Walker Connor, 'The Nation and Its Myth,' *International Journal of Comparative Sociology*, 37 (January–April 1992): 48–57; Simon Taylor, 'Symbol and Ritual under National Socialism,' *British Journal of Sociology*, 32 (December 1981): 504–20.

9.  See Brian M. du Toit, 'The Far Right in Current South African Politics,' *Journal of Modern African Studies*, 29 (December 1991): 627–67; Heribert Adam and Kogila Moodley, 'Political Violence, "Tribalism", and Inkatha,' *Journal of Modern African Studies*, 30 (September 1992); 485–510; Patrick Laurence, 'Finding Common Ground,' *Africa Report*, 38 (May/June 1993): 25–27; Robert M. Price, *The Apartheid State in Crisis: Political Transformation in South Africa 1975–1990* (New York: Oxford University Press, 1991).

10. Miroslav Hroch, 'From National Movement to the Fully-Formed Nation: The Nation-Building Process in Europe,' *New Left Review*, no. 198 (March–April 1993): 3–20; Steven L. Burg, 'Nationalism Redux: Through the Glass of the Post-Communist States Darkly,' *Current History*, 92 (April 1993): 162–66; Pierre Béhar, 'Central Europe: The New Lines of Fracture,' *Géopolitique*, no. 39 (Autumn 1992): 42–45; Diane Flaherty, 'Socialism and Nationalism: Ethnicity, Class, and Civil War in Yugoslavia,' *Rethinking Marxism*, 6 (Summer 1993): 127–39; Dusko Sekulic, Garth Massey, and Randy Hodson, 'Who Were the Yugoslavs? Failed Sources of a Common Identity in the Former Yugoslavia,' *American Sociological Review*, 59 (February 1994): 83–97.

11. Fyodor Dostoyevsky, *The Possessed*, trans. Andrew R. MacAndrew (New York: New American Library, 1962), 237–39. See too *Letters of Fyodor*

*Michailovitch Dostoevsky to His Family and Friends*, trans. Ethel Colburn Mayne (New York: Horizon Press, 1961), 257–59.

12. John A. Coleman, 'Civil Religion,' *Sociological Analysis*, 31 (Spring 1970): 67–77; Andrain, *Political Life and Social Change*, 61–62, 75–81; Alexander Hamilton, James Madison, and John Jay, *The Federalist Papers*, ed. Clinton Rossiter (New York: The New American Library, 1961), 38.

13. Sheldon S. Wolin, *Politics and Vision* (Boston: Little, Brown, 1960), 95–140; Emil L. Fackenheim, *What Is Judaism?* (New York: Summit Books, 1987), esp. 60–127.

14. See Niccolò Machiavelli, *The Prince* and *The Discourses*, trans. Luigi Ricci and E. R. P. Vincent (New York: Random House Modern Library, 1950); Wolin, *Politics and Vision*, 195–238; Ronald Beiner, 'Machiavelli, Hobbes, and Rousseau on Civil Religion,' *Review of Politics*, 55 (Fall 1993): 621–24.

15. Charles Elkins, 'Chapter and Verse: The Bible and the English Revolution,' *California Sociologist*, 9 (Winter–Summer 1986): 167–97; Michael Walzer, *The Revolution of the Saints: A Study in the Origins of Radical Politics* (Cambridge, MA: Harvard University Press, 1965); Wolin, *Politics and Vision*, 141–94.

16. Charles F. Andrain, *Foundations of Comparative Politics: A Policy Perspective* (Monterey, CA: Brooks-Cole, 1983), 290–310; Sheldon Wolin, 'Postmodern Politics and the Absence of Myth,' *Social Research*, 52 (Summer 1985): 217–39; Mark A. Noll, 'The American Revolution and Protestant Evangelicalism,' *Journal of Interdisciplinary History*, 23 (Winter 1993): 615–38.

17. Alexis de Tocqueville, *The Old Régime and the French Revolution*, trans. Stuart Gilbert (Garden City, NY: Doubleday Anchor, 1955), 12–13.

18. Lynn Hunt, *Politics, Culture, and Class in the French Revolution* (Berkeley: University of California Press, 1984); James Mayall, '1789 and the Liberal Theory of International Society,' *Review of International Studies*, 15 (October 1989): 297–307; Benjamin R. Barber, 'The Most Sublime Event,' *Nation*, 250 (12 March 1990): 351–60; François Furet, 'The French Revolution Revisited,' *Government and Opposition*, 24 (Summer 1989): 264–82; Crane Brinton, *The New Jacobins* (New York: Macmillan, 1930), 175–221; Lerner, 'Transcendence of the Nation,' 419.

19. Crane Brinton, *The Shaping of the Modern Mind* (New York: New American Library, 1953), 203–11; Nina Tumarkin, *Lenin Lives! The Lenin Cult in Soviet Russia* (Cambridge, MA: Harvard University Press, 1983); Nina Tumarkin, 'Myth and Memory in Soviet Society,' *Society*, 24 (September/October 1987): 69–72; Thomas O. Cushman, 'Ritual and Conformity in Soviet Society,' *Journal of Communist Studies*, 4 (June 1988): 162–80; Frederic Lilge, 'Lenin and the Politics of Education,' in *Power and Ideology in Education*, ed. Jerome Karabel and A. H. Halsey (New York: Oxford University Press, 1977), 556–72; N. H. Gaworek, 'Education, Ideology, and Politics: History in Soviet Primary and Secondary Schools,' *History Teacher*, 11 (November 1977): 55–74.

20. David E. Apter, 'Mao's Republic,' *Social Research*, 54 (Winter 1987): 691–729; Jean C. Robinson, 'Mao after Death: Charisma and Political Legitimacy,' *Asian Survey*, 28 (March 1988): 353–68; Li Cheng and Lynn White, 'The Thirteenth Central Committee of the Chinese Communist Party,' *Asian Survey* (April 1988): 371–99; Theodore Hsi-en Chen, 'The

Maoist Model of Education: Origins and Ideology,' *Asian Affairs*, 3 (July–August 1976): 384–400; R. F. Price, 'Chinese Textbooks, Fourteen Years On,' *China Quarterly*, no. 83 (September 1980): 535–50.

21. Yim Chae-wan, 'Approach to the North Korean System in Terms of Political Culture,' *Vantage Point*, 7 (September 1984): 1–9; Bruce Cumings, *The Two Koreas*, Headline Series no. 294 (New York: Foreign Policy Association, 1990), 53–62; Sung Chul Yang, 'The Kim Il-sung Cult in North Korea,' *Korea and World Affairs*, 4 (Spring 1980): 161–86; Yong Soon Yim, 'Language Reform as a Political Symbol in North Korea,' *World Affairs*, 142 (Winter 1980): 216–35.

22. B. E. Aguirre, 'The Conventionalization of Collective Behavior in Cuba,' *American Journal of Sociology*, 90 (November 1984): 541–66; Andrain, *Political Change in the Third World*, 127–44.

23. John Charles Chasteen, 'Fighting Words: The Discourse of Insurgency in Latin American History,' *Latin American Research Review*, 28, no. 3 (1993): 83–111.

24. See Gabriel A. Almond and Sidney Verba, *The Civic Culture: Political Attitudes and Democracy in Five Nations* (Princeton, NJ: Princeton University Press, 1963); Gabriel A. Almond and Sidney Verba, eds., *The Civic Culture Revisited* (Boston: Little, Brown, 1980); Craig Calhoun, 'Nationalism and Civil Society: Democracy, Diversity and Self-Determination,' *International Sociology*, 8 (December 1993): 387–411.

25. Ashutosh Varshney, 'Contested Meanings: India's National Identity, Hindu Nationalism, and the Politics of Anxiety,' *Daedalus*, 122 (Summer 1993): 227–61; Praful Bidwai, 'Window of Opportunity,' *New Statesman and Society*, 7 (January 1994): 12–13; Yogendra K. Malik and Dhirendra K. Vajpeyi, 'The Rise of Hindu Militancy: India's Secular Democracy at Risk,' *Asian Survey*, 29 (March 1989): 308–25; Subrata Kumar Mitra, 'Desecularising the State: Religion and Politics in India after Independence,' *Comparative Studies in Society and History*, 33 (October 1991): 755–77; Achin Vanaik, 'Reflections on Communalism and Nationalism in India,' *New Left Review*, no. 196 (November–December 1992): 43–63; Robert Eric Frykenberg, 'Hindu Fundamentalism and the Structural Stability of India,' in *Fundamentalisms and the State: Remaking Polities, Economies, and Militance*, ed. Martin E. Marty and R. Scott Appleby (Chicago: University of Chicago Press, 1993), 233–55.

26. Ronald Takaki, *A Different Mirror: A History of Multicultural America* (Boston: Little, Brown, 1993), 425, 428. See too Ronald Takaki, *Strangers from a Different Shore: A History of Asian Americans* (Boston: Little, Brown, 1989); John C. Mohawk and Oren R. Lyons, eds., *Exiled in the Land of the Free: Democracy, Indian Nations, and the U.S. Constitution* (Santa Fe, NM: Clear Light Publishers, 1992); Michael Paul Rogin, *Ronald Reagan, the Movie, and Other Episodes in Political Demonology* (Berkeley: University of California Press, 1987), 134–68; Mario Barrera, *Beyond Aztlan: Ethnic Autonomy in Comparative Perspective* (New York: Praeger, 1988); Everett Carll Ladd, 'Secular and Religious America,' *Society*, 24 (March/April 1987): 63–68; *Public Opinion*, 10 (July/August 1987): 21–39; Seymour Martin Lipset, *Revolution and Counterrevolution: Change and Persistence in Social Structures* (New York: Basic Books, 1968), 31–63; Benjamin I. Page and Robert Y. Shapiro,

*The Rational Public: Fifty Years of Trends in Americans' Policy Preferences* (Chicago: University of Chicago Press, 1992), 67–90; Trin Yarborough, compiler, 'What's Good about America – and Southern California?' *Los Angeles Times*, 12 July 1993, p. B4.

27. Seymour Martin Lipset, *Continental Divide: The Values and Institutions of the United States and Canada* (New York: Routledge, Chapman, and Hall, 1990); Joseph F. Fletcher, 'Mass and Elite Attitudes about Wiretapping in Canada: Implications for Democratic Theory and Politics,' *Public Opinion Quarterly*, 53 (Summer 1989): 225–45; *Maclean's*, 102 (3 July 1989): 48–50; Brian Bergman, 'A Nation of Polite Bigots?' *Maclean's*, 106 (27 December 1993): 42–43; *World Opinion Update*, 13 (August 1989): 89–90; *World Opinion Update*, 16 (April 1992): 48; V. Seymour Wilson, 'The Tapestry Vision of Canadian Multiculturalism,' *Canadian Journal of Political Science*, 26 (December 1993): 645–69; Andrew E. Kim, 'The Absence of Pan-Canadian Civil Religion: Plurality, Duality, and Conflict in Symbols of Canadian Culture,' *Sociology of Religion*, 54 (Fall 1993): 257–75.

28. See Mattei Dogan, 'Comparing the Decline of Nationalisms in Western Europe: The Generational Dynamic,' *International Social Science Journal*, 45 (May 1993): 177–98; Ronald Inglehart, *Culture Shift in Advanced Industrial Society* (Princeton, NJ: Princeton University Press, 1990), 408–21; John Pinder, 'Economic Integration versus National Sovereignty: Differences between Eastern and Western Europe,' *Government and Opposition*, 24 (Summer 1989): 309–26; *World Opinion Update*, 13 (July 1989): 74–76; *World Opinion Update*, 13 (August 1989): 86; *World Opinion Update*, 17 (June 1993): 62–64; Max Kaase, 'Political Alienation and Protest,' in *Comparing Pluralist Democracies: Strains on Legitimacy*, ed. Mattei Dogan (Boulder, CO: Westview Press, 1988), 114–42; Stuart Hall, 'Our Mongrel Selves,' *New Statesman and Society*, supplement 5 (19 June 1992): 6–8; Nora Räthzel, 'Germany: One Race, One Nation?' *Race and Class*, 32 (January–March 1991): 31–48. Several generalizations in this paragraph about ethnic tolerance in Western Europe derive from analyses of survey data that came from Karlheinz Reif and Anna Melich, Euro-Barometer 30; Immigrants and Out-Groups in Western Europe, October–December 1988 [computer file], conducted by Faits and Opinions, Paris. ICPSR ed. Ann Arbor, MI: Inter-university Consortium for Political and Social Research [producer and distributor], 1991. The original collector of the data, ICPSR, and the National Science Foundation bear no responsibility for uses of this collection or for interpretations and inferences based upon such uses.

29. Crawford Young, *Ideology and Development in Africa* (New Haven, CT: Yale University Press, 1982); Richard L. Sklar, 'Beyond Capitalism and Socialism in Africa,' *Journal of Modern African Studies*, 26 (March 1988): 1–21; Ernest J. Wilson III, 'Strategies of State Control of the Economy: Nationalization and Indigenization in Africa,' *Comparative Politics*, 22 (July 1990): 401–19.

30. David I. Kertzer, *Ritual, Politics, and Power* (New Haven, CT: Yale University Press, 1988); Robert Wuthnow, *Meaning and Moral Order: Exploraions in Cultural Analysis* (Berkeley: University of California Press, 1987), 97–144.

**Part II**

1. See Gabriel A. Almond, Scott C. Flanagan, and Robert J. Mundt, '*Crisis, Choice, and Change* in Retrospect,' *Government and Opposition*, 27 (Summer 1992): 345–67.
2. Marion J. Levy, Jr., *Modernization and the Structure of Societies*, 2 vols. (Princeton, NJ: Princeton University Press, 1966), 175–340, 654–73.
3. Douglas V. Porpora, 'Cultural Rules and Material Relations,' *Sociological Theory*, 11 (July 1993): 212–29; Charles F. Andrain, *Foundations of Comparative Politics: A Policy Perspective* (Monterey, CA: Brooks/Cole, 1983), 178–81.
4. Randall Collins, *Theoretical Sociology* (San Diego, CA: Harcourt Brace Jovanovich, 1988), 403–07, 435–47; T. David Mason, 'Nonelite Response to State-Sanctioned Terror,' *Western Political Quarterly*, 42 (December 1989): 467–92; Dipak K. Gupta, Harinder Singh, and Tom Sprague, 'Government Coercion of Dissidents: Deterrence or Provocation?', *Journal of Conflict Resolution*, 37 (June 1993): 301–39.
5. Pauline Vaillancourt Rosenau and Harry C. Bredemeir, 'Modern and Postmodern Conceptions of Social Order,' *Social Research*, 60 (Summer 1993): 337–62.
6. Jack A. Goldstone, *Revolution and Rebellion in the Early Modern World* (Berkeley: University of California Press, 1991), esp. 1–62, 459–97; Collins, *Theoretical Sociology*, 45–147.
7. Robert Grafstein, *Institutional Realism: Social and Political Constraints on Rational Actors* (New Haven, CT: Yale University Press, 1992), 1–59; James B. Rule, *Theories of Civil Violence* (Berkeley: University of California Press, 1988), 54–90, 119–99; William H. Sewell, Jr., 'A Theory of Structure: Duality, Agency, and Transformation,' *American Journal of Sociology*, 98 (July 1992): 1–29.

## 5 The Nation-State and Institutionalist Theories

1. David E. Apter and Nagayo Sawa, *Against the State: Politics and Social Protest in Japan* (Cambridge, MA: Harvard University Press, 1984); David E. Apter, *Rethinking Development: Modernization, Dependency, and Postmodern Politics* (Newbury Park, CA: Sage Publications, 1987), 226–58.
2. Karel van Wolferen, *The Enigma of Japanese Power: People and Politics in a Stateless Nation* (New York: Alfred A. Knopf, 1989); Karel van Wolferen, 'Interview: Japan in the Age of Uncertainty,' *New Left Review*, no. 200 (July/August 1993): 15–40.
3. Charles F. Andrain, *Foundations of Comparative Politics: A Policy Perspective* (Monterey, CA: Brooks/Cole, 1983), 178–81; Margaret G. Hermann and Charles F. Hermann, 'Who Makes Foreign Policy Decisions and How: An Empirical Inquiry,' *International Studies Quarterly*, 33 (December 1989): 361–87.
4. Jon Elster, *The Cement of Society: A Study of Social Order* (New York: Cambridge University Press, 1989); Samuel P. Huntington, *Political Order in Changing Societies* (New Haven, CT: Yale University Press, 1968), 1–92;

Jeffrey C. Alexander, 'Social-Structural Analysis: Some Notes on Its History and Prospects,' *Sociological Quarterly*, 25 (Winter 1984): 5–26.

5. Michael Mann, *The Sources of Social Power*, vol. 1: *A History of Power from the Beginning to A.D. 1760* (New York: Cambridge University Press, 1986), esp. 1–32, 416–517; Michael Mann, *The Sources of Social Power*, vol. 2: *The Rise of Classes and Nation-States, 1760–1914* (New York: Cambridge University Press, 1993), 55–63; Bertrand Badie and Pierre Birnbaum, *The Sociology of the State*, trans. Arthur Goldhammer (Chicago: University of Chicago Press, 1983), 25–64; Randall Collins, *Theoretical Sociology* (San Diego, CA: Harcourt Brace Jovanovich, 1988), 131–37; Gianfranco Poggi, *The State: Its Nature, Development and Prospects* (Stanford, CA: Stanford University Press, 1990), 19–105.

6. See Gregory Hooks, 'From an Autonomous to a Captured State Agency: The Decline of the New Deal in Agriculture,' *American Sociological Review*, 55 (February 1990): 29–43; Eric A. Nordlinger, *On the Autonomy of the Democratic State* (Cambridge, MA: Harvard University Press, 1981); Eric A. Nordlinger, 'Taking the State Seriously,' in *Understanding Political Development*, ed. Myron Weiner and Samuel P. Huntington (Boston: Little, Brown, 1987), 353–90; John Dearlove, 'Bringing the Constitution Back In: Political Science and the State,' *Political Studies*, 37 (December 1989): 521–39; James G. March and Johan P. Olsen, *Rediscovering Institutions: The Organizational Basis of Politics* (New York: The Free Press, 1989); Ove K. Pedersen, 'Nine Questions to a Neo-institutional Theory in Political Science,' *Scandinavian Political Studies* 14, no. 2 (1991): 125–48; Ernst B. Haas, *When Knowledge Is Power: Three Models of Change in International Organizations* (Berkeley: University of California Press, 1990); Michael M. Atkinson and Robert A. Nigol, 'Selecting Policy Instruments: Neo-Institutional and Rational Choice Interpretations of Automobile Insurance in Ontario,' *Canadian Journal of Political Science*, 22 (March 1989): 107–35.

7. Max Weber, 'Politics as a Vocation,' in *From Max Weber*, ed. H. H. Gerth and C. Wright Mills (New York: Oxford University Press, 1946), 78.

8. See Theda Skocpol, 'Bringing the State Back In: Strategies of Analysis in Current Research,' in *Bringing the State Back In*, ed. Peter B. Evans, Dietrich Rueschemeyer, and Theda Skocpol (New York: Cambridge University Press, 1985), 3–37; Eric A. Nordlinger, 'The Return to the State: Critique,' *American Political Science Review*, 82 (September 1988): 875–85.

9. Richard Rose, 'On the Priorities of Government: A Developmental Analysis of Public Policies,' *European Journal of Political Research*, 4 (September 1976): 247–89.

10. See Inis L. Claude, Jr., 'Myths about the State,' *Review of International Studies*, 12 (January 1986): 1–11; Fred Halliday, 'State and Society in International Relations: A Second Agenda,' *Millennium: Journal of International Studies*, 16 (Summer 1987): 215–29; Joel S. Migdal, 'Strong States, Weak States: Power and Accommodation,' in *Understanding Political Development*, 391–434; Paul Cammack, 'Review Article: Bringing the State Back In?', *British Journal of Political Science*, 19 (April 1989): 261–90; Martin Carnoy, *The State and Political Theory* (Princeton, NJ: Princeton University Press, 1984), 65–127; G. William Domhoff, *The Power Elite and the State:*

*How Policy Is Made in America* (New York: Aldine de Gruyter, 1990), 6–15, 187–95; March and Olsen, *Rediscovering Institutions*, 69–116; Richard Lachmann, 'Elite Conflict and State Formation in 16th- and 17th-Century England and France,' *American Sociological Review*, 54 (April 1989): 141–62. In his analysis of the evolution of West European and the U.S. nation-states from 1760 to the First World War, Mann, *The Rise of Classes and Nation-States*, 735, refers to the 'polymorphous' incohesive states riven by divergent factional elites and groups.

11. Bert A. Rockman, 'Minding the State – Or a State of Mind? Issues in the Comparative Conceptualization of the State,' *Comparative Political Studies*, 23 (April 1990): 25–55; Vivien A. Schmidt, 'Unblocking Society by Decree: The Impact of Governmental Decentralization in France,' *Comparative Politics*, 22 (July 1990): 459–81; Timothy J. Colton, 'Approaches to the Politics of Systemic Economic Reform in the Soviet Union,' *Soviet Economy*, 3 (April–June 1987): 145–70; Charles H. Fairbanks, Jr., 'Jurisdictional Conflict and Coordination in Soviet and American Bureaucracy,' *Studies in Comparative Communism*, 21 (Summer 1988): 153–74; Philip G. Roeder, *Soviet Political Dynamics: Development of the First Leninist Polity* (New York: Harper and Row, 1988), 196–230; Philip G. Roeder, *Red Sunset: The Failure of Soviet Politics* (Princeton, NJ: Princeton University Press, 1993).

12. International Labour Office, *The Cost of Social Security: Thirteenth International Inquiry, 1984–1986* (Geneva: International Labour Office, 1992), 79–85.

13. Sheldon S. Wolin, *Politics and Vision: Continuity and Innovation in Western Political Thought* (Boston: Little, Brown, 1960), 388.

14. Andrain, *Foundations of Comparative Politics*, 259–69; Jon H. Pammett, 'A Framework for the Comparative Analysis of Elections across Time and Space,' *Electoral Studies*, 7 (August 1988): 125–42; Michael Hechter, *Principles of Group Solidarity* (Berkeley: University of California Press, 1987), 78–103; Alan Ware, *Citizens, Parties and the State: A Reappraisal* (Princeton, NJ: Princeton University Press, 1987).

15. See David E. Apter, *Introduction to Political Analysis* (Cambridge, MA: Winthrop, 1977), 139–212; Carl J. Friedrich, *Man and His Government* (New York: McGraw-Hill, 1963), 267–84; Michael Laver and Kenneth A. Shepsle, 'Divided Government: America Is Not 'Exceptional,' *Governance*, 4 (July 1991): 250–69; Gabriel A. Almond and Sidney Verba, *The Civic Culture: Political Attitudes and Democracy in Five Nations* (Princeton, NJ: Princeton University Press, 1963), 476–79; Stephen L. Elkin, 'Constitutionalism: Old and New,' in *A New Constitutionalism: Designing Political Institutions for a Good Society*, ed. Stephen L Elkin and Karol Edward Søltan (Chicago: University of Chicago Press, 1993), 20–37; Karol Edward Søltan, 'Generic Constitutionalism,' in *A New Constitutionalism*, ed. Elkin and Søltan, 70–95.

16. Herbert P. Kitschelt, 'Political Opportunity Structures and Political Protest: Anti-Nuclear Movements in Four Democracies,' *British Journal of Political Science*, 16 (January 1986): 57–85; Sidney Tarrow, *Democracy and Disorder: Protest and Politics in Italy 1965–1975* (Oxford, England: Clarendon Press, 1989), 8–27; Peter Hall, *Governing the Economy: The Politics of State*

*Intervention in Britain and France* (New York: Oxford University Press, 1986), 139–283; van Wolferen, 'Japan in the Age of Uncertainty,' 19–40; Takashi Inoguchi, 'Japanese Politics in Transition: A Theoretical Review,' *Government and Opposition*, 28 (Autumn 1993): 443–55.

17. Herman Finer, *Theory and Practice of Modern Governments*, rev. ed. (New York: Henry Holt, 1949); David E. Apter, 'Institutionalism Reconsidered,' *International Social Science Journal*, 43 (August 1991): 463–70; Wolin, *Politics and Vision*, 388–93.

18. Theda Skocpol, *Protecting Soldiers and Mothers: The Political Origins of Social Policy in the United States* (Cambridge, MA: The Belknap Press of Harvard University Press, 1992), 42.

19. Erich Weede, 'Ideas, Institutions and Political Culture in Western Development,' *Journal of Theoretical Politics*, 2 (October 1990): 369–89.

20. March and Olsen, *Rediscovering Institutions*, 21–52; Johan P. Olsen, 'Modernization Programs in Perspective: Institutional Analysis of Organizational Change, *Governance*, 4 (April 1991): 125–49; Douglass C. North, *Institutions, Institutional Change and Economic Performance* (New York: Cambridge University Press, 1990), 27–69; Christer Gunnarsson, 'What Is New and What Is Institutional in the New Institutional Economics?' *Scandinavian Economic History Review*, 39, no. 1 (1991): 43–67.

21. Skocpol, *Protecting Soldiers and Mothers*, 41–60; Theda Skocpol, 'State Formation and Social Policy in the United States,' *American Behavioral Scientist*, 35 (March/June 1992): 559–84; Theda Skocpol, *States and Social Revolutions: A Comparative Analysis of France, Russia, and China* (New York: Cambridge University Press, 1979); March and Olsen, *Rediscovering Institutions*, 95–142; Rogers M. Smith, 'If Politics Matters: Implications for a "New Institutionalism,"' *Studies in American Political Development*, 6 (Spring 1992): 1–36; Paul Pierson, 'When Effect Becomes Cause: Policy Feedback and Political Change,' *World Politics*, 45 (July 1993): 595–628; Scott Mainwaring, 'Presidentialism, Multipartism, and Democracy: The Difficult Combination,' *Comparative Political Studies*, 26 (July 1993): 198–228; Alfred Stepan and Cindy Skach, 'Constitutional Frameworks and Democratic Consolidation: Parliamentarianism versus Presidentialism,' *World Politics*, 46 (October 1993): 1–22.

22. Douglass C. North, 'Towards a Theory of Institutional Change,' *Quarterly Review of Economics and Business*, 31 (Winter 1991): 3–11; North, *Institutions, Institutional Change and Economic Performance*, 73–140; Douglass C. North, 'Institutions and Credible Commitment,' *Journal of Institutional and Theoretical Economics*, 149 (March 1993): 11–23; Thráinn Eggertsson, *Economic Behavior and Institutions* (New York: Cambridge University Press, 1990); Thráinn Eggertsson, 'The Economics of Institutions: Avoiding the Open-Field Syndrome and the Perils of Path Dependence,' *Acta Sociologia*, 36, no. 3 (1993): 223–37; Elinor Ostrom, *Governing the Commons: The Evolution of Institutions for Collective Action* (New York: Cambridge University Press, 1990).

23. Weede, 'Ideas, Institutions and Political Culture in Western Development,' 385.

24. Jan-Erik Lane, *The Public Sector: Concepts, Models and Approaches* (London: Sage Publications, 1993), 166–89; Apter, 'Institutionalism Reconidered,'

472–78; Jack Knight, *Institutions and Social Conflict* (New York: Cambridge University Press, 1992), 108–22.

25. Huntington, *Political Order in Changing Societies*, 1–92, 397–461.
26. Samuel P. Huntington, 'Conservatism as an Ideology,' *American Political Science Review*, 51 (June 1957): 460–61.
27. Samuel P. Huntington, *The Third Wave: Democratization in the Late Twentieth Century* (Norman: University of Oklahoma Press, 1991).
28. See the following works by Samuel P. Huntington: *Political Order in Changing Societies*, esp. 1–92, 142–44, 192–98, 262–63, 344, 401; *The Soldier and the State: The Theory and Politics of Civil-Military Relations* (Cambridge, MA: Harvard University Press, 1957); *American Military Strategy* (Berkeley, CA: Institute of International Studies, University of California at Berkeley, 1986); 'Transnational Organizations in World Politics,' *World Politics*, 25 (April 1973): 334–68; 'The U.S. – Decline or Renewal?' *Foreign Affairs*, 67 (Winter 1988/89): 76–96; 'The Goals of Development,' in *Understanding Political Development*, ed. Weiner and Huntington, 3–32; 'The Clash of Civilizations?' *Foreign Affairs*, 72 (Summer 1993): 22–49; 'The Islamic-Confucian Connection,' *New Perspectives Quarterly*, 10 (Summer 1993): 19–23.
29. Huntington, *Political Order in Changing Societies*, 24–32.
30. For critiques of Huntington's institutionalist approach, see David E. Apter, *Political Change: Collected Essays* (London: Frank Cass, 1973), 167, 195–96, 198, 208; Cal Clark and Jonathan Lemco, 'The Strong State and Development: A Growing List of Caveats,' *Journal of Developing Societies* 4 (January–April 1988): 1–8.
31. Karl Marx, *Political Writings*, vol. 1, *The Revolutions of 1848*, ed. David Fernbach (New York: Vintage Books, 1974), 69.
32. Karl Marx, *Political Writings*, vol. 2, *Surveys from Exile*, ed. David Fernbach (New York: Vintage Books, 1974), 236–49.
33. See Collins, *Theoretical Sociology*, 79–91; Erik Olin Wright, 'Explanation and Emancipation in Marxism and Feminism,' *Sociological Theory*, 11 (March 1993): 39–54.; Terry Boswell and William J. Dixon, 'Marx's Theory of Rebellion: A Cross-National Analysis of Class Exploitation, Economic Development, and Violent Revolt,' *American Sociological Review*, 58 (October 1993): 681–702.
34. V. I. Lenin, *What Is to Be Done?* (Peking: Foreign Languages Press, 1975), 93.
35. See Ken Jowitt, *New World Disorder: The Leninist Extinction* (Berkeley: University of California Press, 1992), esp. 1–120; Bartłomiej Kamiński and Karol Sołtan, 'The Evolution of Communism,' *International Political Science Review*, 10 (October 1989): 371–91; Leslie Holmes, *Politics in the Communist World* (Oxford, England: Oxford University Press, 1986); Jeffrey W. Hahn, 'Power to the Soviets?', *Problems of Communism*, 38 (January–February 1989): 34–46; Don van Atta, 'The USSR as a "Weak State": Agrarian Origins of Resistance to Perestroika,' *World Politics* 42 (October 1989): 129–49; Graeme Gill, 'Ideology, Organization and the Patrimonial Regime,' *Journal of Communist Studies*, 5 (September 1989): 285–302; Patrick Flaherty, 'Class Power in Soviet Society,' *New Politics*, 2 (Winter 1990): 157–77; Zhores Medvedev, 'Soviet Power Today, *New Left Review*, no. 179 (January–February 1990): 65–80.

36. Stephen White, 'What Is a Communist System?' *Studies in Comparative Communism*, 16 (Winter 1983): 247–63; Stephen White, John Gardner, George Schöpflin, and Tony Saich, *Communist and Postcommunist Political Systems: An Introduction*, 3d ed. (New York: St. Martin's Press, 1990), 4–6; Bartłomiej Kamiński, *The Collapse of State Socialism: The Case of Poland* (Princeton, NJ: Princeton University Press, 1991); Grzegorz Ekiert, 'Democratization Processes in East Central Europe: A Theoretical Reconsideration,' *British Journal of Political Science*, 21 (July 1991): 285–313; John Higley and Jan Pakulski, 'Revolution and Elite Transformation in Eastern Europe,' *Australian Journal of Political Science*, 27 (March 1992): 104–19; Zoltan D. Barany, 'Civil-Military Relations in Comparative Perspective: East-Central and Southeastern Europe,' *Political Studies*, 41 (December 1993): 594–610; Barbara A. Misztal, 'Understanding Political Change in Eastern Europe: A Sociological Perspective,' *Sociology*, 27 (August 1993): 451–70; Leslie Holmes, *The End of Communist Power* (New York: Oxford University Press, 1993); Bogdan Denitch, 'The Crisis and Upheaval in Eastern Europe,' *Social Text*, 8, no. 2 (1990): 117–31; Shlomo Avineri, 'Reflections on Eastern Europe,' *Partisan Review*, 58 (Summer 1991): 442–48; Ernest Mandel, 'The Roots of the Present Crisis in the Soviet Economy,' in *Socialist Register 1991*, ed. Ralph Miliband and Leo Panitch (London: Merlin Press, 1991), 194–210; Kazimierz Poznanski, 'An Interpretation of Communist Decay: The Role of Evolutionary Mechanisms,' *Communist and Post-Communist Studies*, 26 (March 1993): 3–24.

37. V. I. Lenin, *Selected Works* (New York: International Publishers, 1971), 169–75, 259–63.

38. See Peter B. Evans, 'Dependency,' in *The Oxford Companion to Politics of the World*, ed. Joel Krieger (New York: Oxford University Press, 1993), 231–33; Viviane Brachet-Márquez, 'Explaining Sociopolitical Change in Latin America: The Case of Mexico,' *Latin American Research Review*, 27, no. 3 (1992): 91–122; J. Craig Jenkins and Kurt Schock, 'Global Structures and Political Processes in the Study of Domestic Conflict,' in *Annual Review of Sociology*, vol. 18, ed. Judith Blake and John Hagan (Palo Alto, CA: Annual Reviews, Inc., 1992), 175–81; Syed Faiid Alatas, 'Theoretical Perspectives on the Role of State Élites in Southeast Asian Development,' *Contemporary Southeast Asia*, 14 (March 1993): 368–95; Philip McMichael, 'Rethinking Comparaive Analysis in a Post-Developmentalist Context,' *International Social Science Journal*, 44 (August 1992): 351–65; Kevin Neuhouser, 'Foundations of Class Compromise: A Theoretical Basis for Understanding Diverse Patterns of Regime Outcomes,' *Sociological Theory*, 11 (March 1993): 96–116; Robert A. Packenham, *The Dependency Movement: Scholarship and Politics in Development Studies* (Cambridge, MA: Harvard University Press, 1992); Cristóbal Kay, 'Reflections on the Latin American Contribution to Development Theory,' *Development and Change*, 22 (January 1991): 31–68; Ronald H. Chilcote, 'A Question of Dependency,' *Latin American Research Review*, 13, no. 2 (1978): 55–68; Ronald H. Chilcote, *Theories of Development and Underdevelopment* (Boulder, CO: Westview Press, 1984); Joseph L. Love, 'The Origins of Dependency Analysis,' *Journal of Latin American Studies*, 22 (February 1990): 143–68; Alvin Y. So, *Social Change and Development: Modernization, Dependency, and World-System Theories*

(Newbury Park, CA: Sage Publications, 1990), 91–165. So contrasts the classical dependency analyses and the new dependency studies, which place greater emphasis on the interaction between foreign economic control and internal class conflicts.

39.  Leonard Binder, *Islamic Liberalism: A Critique of Development Ideologies* (Chicago: University of Chicago Press, 1988), 44–62; Apter, *Rethinking Development*, 25–31; Apter, *Political Change*, 201–05, 209; David E. Apter and Carl G. Rosberg, 'Changing African Perspectives,' in *Political Development and the New Realism in Sub-Saharan Africa*, ed. David E. Apter and Carl G. Rosberg (Charlottesville: University of Virginia Press, 1994), 28–33; Adrian Leftwich, 'States of Underdevelopment: The Third World State in Theoretical Perspective,' *Journal of Theoretical Politics*, 6 (January 1994): 55–74; Andre Gunder Frank, 'Latin American Development Theories Revisited: A Participant Review,' *Latin American Perspectives*, 19 (Spring 1992): 125–39; Gerardo L. Munck, 'Capitalism and Democracy: The Importance of Social Class in Historical Comparative Perspective,' *Journal of Interamerican Studies and World Affairs*, 34 (Winter 1992–93): 225–44; Terry Nichols Clark and Seymour Martin Lipset, 'Are Social Classes Dying?' *International Sociology* 6 (December 1991): 397–410; Paresh Chattopadhyay, 'The Economic Content of Socialism: Marx vs. Lenin,' *Review of Radical Political Economics*, 24 (Fall and Winter 1992): 90–110; Roeder, *Red Sunset*, 3–20, 210–53; Joel S. Migdal, *Strong Societies and Weak States: State-Society Relations and State Capabilities in the Third World* (Princeton, NJ: Princeton University Press, 1988), esp. 206–77; Joshua B. Forrest, 'The Quest for State "Hardness" in Africa,' *Comparative Politics*, 20 (July 1988): 423–42; Henry Bienen, 'Leaders, Violence, and the Absence of Change in Africa,' *Political Science Quarterly*, 108 (Summer 1993): 271–82; Robert H. Jackson and Carl G. Rosberg, 'The Political Economy of Personal Rule,' in *Political Development and the New Realism in Sub-Saharan Africa*, ed. Apter and Rosberg, 291–322; James A. Caporaso, 'Global Political Economy,' in *Political Science: The State of the Discipline II*, ed. Ada W. Finifter (Washington, DC: American Political Science Association, 1993), 468–76.

## 6  Pluralist Theories and Social Groups

1.  David E. Apter, *Introduction to Political Analysis* (Cambridge, MA: Winthrop, 1977), 336–39; Charles F. Andrain, *Foundations of Comparative Politics* (Monterey, CA: Brooks/Cole, 1983), 294; David S. Meyer, 'Institutionalizing Dissent: The United States Structure of Political Opportunity and the End of the Nuclear Freeze Movement,' *Sociological Forum*, 8 (June 1993): 157–79; Thomas R. Rochon and Daniel A. Mazmanian, 'Social Movements and the Policy Process,' *Annals of the American Academy of Political and Social Science*, 528 (July 1993): 75–87.

2.  Apter, *Introduction to Political Analysis*, 293–375; Michael Hechter, *Principles of Group Solidarity* (Berkeley: University of California Press, 1987), 1–58. From 1970 through 1989 Robert D. Putnam, with Robert Leonardi and Raffaella Y. Nanetti, investigated the twenty regional governments of

Italy. See *Making Democracy Work: Civic Traditions in Modern Italy* (Princeton, NJ: Princeton University Press, 1993).

3. See the following works by Robert A. Dahl: *Polyarchy: Participation and Opposition* (New Haven, CT: Yale University Press, 1971); *Dilemmas of Pluralist Democracy: Autonomy vs. Control* (New Haven, CT: Yale University Press, 1982); *Democracy and Its Critics* (New Haven, CT: Yale University Press, 1989), esp. 213–98; *Modern Political Analysis*, 5th ed. (Englewood Cliffs, NJ: Prentice-Hall, 1991), 71–94.

4. Jack W. Walker, Jr., *Mobilizing Interest Groups in America: Patrons, Professions, and Social Movements* (Ann Arbor: The University of Michigan Press, 1991), 186. See too 1–40, 187–96 and Sidney Verba, Kay Lehman Schlozman, Henry Brady, and Norman H. Nie, 'Citizen Activity: Who Participates? What Do They Say?', *American Political Science Review*, 87 (June 1993): 303–18.

5. Dahl, *Dilemmas of Pluralist Democracy*, 174–75; Andrain, *Foundations of Comparative Politics*, 229–69. According to Erich Weede ('Democracy, Party Government and Rent-Seeking as Determinants of Distributional Inequality in Industrial Societies,' *European Journal of Political Research*, 18 (September 1990): 515–33), during the post-Second World War period, governing conservative parties more effectively protected the share of national income held by the wealthiest 20 percent than social democratic or labor parties redistributed income to the poor.

6. See Alexander Hicks, 'National Collective Action and Economic Performance: A Review Article,' *International Studies Quarterly*, 32 (June 1988): 131–53; Frederic L. Pryor, 'Corporatism as an Economic System: A Review Essay,' *Journal of Comparative Economics*, 12 (September 1988): 317–44; Göran Therborn, 'Does Corporatism Really Matter? The Economic Crisis and Issues of Political Theory,' *Journal of Public Policy*, 7 (July–September 1987): 259–84; Alan Cawson, 'In Defence of the New Testament: A Reply to Andrew Cox, "The Old and New Testaments of Corporatism",' *Political Studies*, 36 (June 1988): 309–15; Bo Rothstein, 'Corporatism and Reformism: The Social Democratic Institutionalization of Class Conflict,' *Acta Sociologica*, 30, nos. 3/4 (1987): 295–311; Arend Lijphart and Markus M. L. Crepaz, 'Corporatism and Consensus Democracy in Eighteen Countries: Conceptual and Empirical Linkages,' *British Journal of Political Science*, 21 (April 1991): 235–46; Markus M. L. Crepaz, 'Corporatism in Decline? An Empirical Analysis of the Impact of Corporatism on Macroeconomic Performance and Industrial Disputes in 18 Industrialized Democracies,' *Comparative Political Studies*, 25 (July 1992): 139–68; Jenny Stewart, 'Corporatism, Pluralism and Political Learning: A Systems Approach,' *Journal of Public Policy*, 12 (July–September 1992): 243–55; Bruce Western, 'A Comparative Study of Corporatist Development,' *American Socioogical Review*, 56 (June 1991): 283–94.

7. Philippe C. Schmitter, 'Corporatism Is Dead! Long Live Corporatism!', *Government and Opposition*, 24 (Winter 1989): 54–73; Wolfgang Streeck and Philippe C. Schmitter, 'From National Corporatism to Transnational Pluralism: Organized Interests in the Single European Market,' *Politics and Society*, 19 (June 1991): 133–64; Peter Gerlich, Edgar Grande, and Wolfgang C. Müller, 'Corporatism in Crisis: Stability and Change of

Social Partnership in Austria,' *Political Studies*, 36 (June 1988): 209–23; James Fulcher, 'Labour Movement Theory versus Corporatism: Social Democracy in Sweden,' *Sociology*, 21 (May 1987): 231–52; Jonas Pontusson, 'Radicalization and Retreat in Swedish Social Democracy,' *New Left Review*, no. 165 (September–October 1987): 5–33; Agne Gustafsson, 'Rise and Decline of Nations: Sweden,' *Scandinavian Politial Studies*, 9 (March 1986): 35–50.

8. See Arend Lijphart, *Democracy in Plural Societies: A Comparative Exploration* (New Haven, CT: Yale University Press, 1977); Arend Lijphart, *Power-Sharing in South Africa: Policy Paper in International Affairs, no. 24* (Berkeley: Institute of International Studies, University of California at Berkeley, 1985), esp. 6–9, 83–135; Jürg Steiner, 'Consociational Democracy as a Policy Recommendation: The Case of South Africa,' *Comparative Politics*, 19 (April 1987): 361–72; Jürg Steiner, *European Democracies* (New York: Longman, 1986), 201–18; Kees van Kersbergen and Uwe Becker, 'The Netherlands: A Passive Social Democratic Welfare State in a Christian Democratic Ruled Society,' *Journal of Social Policy*, 17 (October 1988): 477–99; Peter L. Hupe, 'Beyond Pillarization: The (Post-) Welfare State in the Netherlands,' *European Journal of Political Research*, 23 (June 1993): 359–86.

9. Stephen Games, 'The Asylum-Seeker: Persecuted and Unwanted in Europe,' *Los Angeles Times*, 15 August 1993, pp. M1, M6; John Darnton, 'Western Europe Is Ending Its Welcome to Immigrants,' *New York Times*, 10 August 1993, pp. A1, A6.

10. Charles F. Andrain, *Political Life and Social Change*, 2d ed. (Belmont, CA: Duxbury Press, 1975), 120–27; Pierre L. van den Berghe, 'Social and Cultural Pluralism,' in *Political Life and Social Change: Readings for Introductory Political Science*, ed. Charles F. Andrain (Belmont, CA: Wadsworth, 1971), 104–15; Ivo D. Duchacek, 'Dyadic Federations and Confederaions,' *Publius: The Journal of Federalism*, 18 (Spring 1988): 5–31; Erich Weede, 'Dilemmas of Social Order: Collective and Positional Goods, Leadership and Political Conflicts,' *Sociological Theory*, 3 (Fall 1985): 46–57.

11. See Thomas Hylland Eriksen, 'Ethnicity versus Nationalism,' *Journal of Peace Research*, 28, no. 3 (1991): 263–78; Ted Robert Gurr, 'Why Minorities Rebel: A Global Analysis of Communal Mobilization and Conflict since 1945,' *International Political Science Review*, 14 (April 1993): 161–201; Myron Weiner, 'Peoples and States in a New Ethnic Order?', *Third World Quarterly*, 13 (June 1992): 317–33; Rita Jalali and Seymour Martin Lipset, 'Racial and Ethnic Conflicts: A Global Perspective,' *Political Science Quarterly*, 107 (Winter 1992–93): 585–606.

12. Richard Rose, *Governing without Consensus: An Irish Perspective* (Boston: Beacon Press, 1971); David E. Schmitt, 'Bicommunalism in Northern Ireland,' *Publius*, 18 (Spring 1988): 33–45; Robin Wilson, 'Polls Apart,' *New Society*, 83 (25 March 1988): 14–17; Christopher Hewitt, 'Catholic Grievances, Catholic Nationalism and Violence in Northern Ireland during the Civil Rights Period: A Reconsideration,' *British Journal of Sociology*, 32 (September 1981): 362–80; Bob Rowthorn and Naomi Wayne, *Northern Ireland: The Political Economy of Conflict* (Boulder, CO: Westview Press, 1988); J. L. P. Thompson, 'Deprivation and Political Violence in Northern Ireland, 1922–1985,' *Journal of Conflict Resolution*, 33 (December

1989): 676–99; John W. Soule, 'Issue Conflict in Northern Ireland: The Death of Legislature,' *Political Psychology*, 10 (December 1989): 725–44; Alan D. Falconer, 'The Role of Religion in Situations of Armed Conflicts: The Case of Northern Ireland,' *Bulletin of Peace Proposals*, 21 (September 1990): 273–80; Reed Coughlan, 'Employment Opportunity and Ethnicity in Northern Ireland: The Differential Impact of Deindustrialization in a Divided Society,' *Ethnic Studies Report*, 8 (January 1990): 34–45; Robert W. White, 'On Measuring Political Violence: Northern Ireland, 1969 to 1980,' *American Sociological Review*, 58 (August 1993): 575–85; Allen Feldman, *Formations of Violence: The Narrative of the Body and Political Terror in Northern Ireland* (Chicago: University of Chicago Press, 1991), esp. 261–69; Padraig O'Malley, 'Not Bloody Enough,' *New York Times*, 29 November 1993, p. A13; Marc Howard Ross, *The Culture of Conflict: Interpretations and Interests in Comparative Perspective* (New Haven, CT: Yale University Press, 1993), 152–82; Begoña Aretxaga, 'Striking with Hunger: Cultural Meanings of Political Violence in Northern Ireland,' in *The Violence Within: Cultural and Political Opposition in Divided Nations*, ed. Kay B. Warren (Boulder, CO: Westview Press, 1993), 219–53; Donald Harman Akenson, *God's Peoples: Covenant and Land in South Africa, Israel, and Ulster* (Ithaca, NY: Cornell University Press, 1992), 97–150, 183–202, 263–94.

13. Robert C. Oberst, 'Political Decay in Sri Lanka,' *Current History*, 88 (December 1989): 425–28, 448–49; S. J. Tambiah, *Sri Lanka: Ethnic Fratricide and the Dismantling of Democracy* (Chicago: University of Chicago Press, 1986); Sujit M. Canagaretna, 'Nation Building in a Multiethnic Setting: The Sri Lankan Case,' *Asian Affairs*, 14 (Spring 1987): 1–19; Lakshmanan Sabaratnam, 'The Boundaries of the State and the State of Ethnic Boundaries: Sinhala-Tamil Relations in Sri Lankan History,' *Ethnic and Racial Studies*, 10 (July 1987): 291–316; Robert C. Oberst, 'Federalism and Ethnic Conflict in Sri Lanka,' *Publius*, 18 (Summer 1988): 175–93; William McGowan, 'Third World Perspective: "Affirmative Action" Gone Awry,' *Los Angeles Times*, 13 May 1993, p. B7.

14. Arthur S. Banks, ed., *Political Handbook of the World: 1992* (Binghamton, NY: CSA Publications, State University of New York, 1992), 250–54; Anthony B. van Fossen, 'Two Military Coups in Fiji,' *Bulletin of Concerned Asian Scholars*, 19 (October–December 1987): 19–31; William E. H. Tagupa, 'The 1987 Westminister Constitutional Crisis in Fiji,' *Pacific Studies*, 12 (November 1988): 97–151; Brij V. Lal, 'Before the Storm: An Analysis of the Fiji General Election of 1987,' *Pacific Studies*, 12 (November 1988): 71–96; Stephanie Lawson, 'Fiji's Communal Electoral System: A Study of Some Aspects of the Failure of Democratic Politics in Fiji,' *Politics*, 23 (November 1988): 35–47; Stephanie Lawson, 'The Myth of Cultural Homogeneity and Its Implicaions for Chiefly Power and Politics in Fiji,' *Comparative Studies in Society and History*, 32 (October 1990): 795–821; Stephanie Hagan, 'The Party System, the Labour Party and the Plural Society Syndrome in Fiji,' *Journal of Commonealth and Comparative Politics*, 25 (July 1987): 126–40; Stephanie Hagan, 'Race, Politics, and the Coup in Fiji,' *Bulletin of Concerned Asian Scholars*, 19 (October–December 1987): 2–18; John Cameron, 'Fiji: The Political Economy of Recent Events,' *Capital and Class*, no. 33 (Winter 1987): 29–45; Timoci Bavadra, 'Fiji: The

Repression Continues,' *Arena*, no. 83 (Winter 1988): 10–16; John Sullivan, 'Repression Tightens in Fiji,' *Arena*, no. 84 (Spring 1988): 10–15; Roderic Alley, 'The Military Coup in Fiji,' *Round Table*, no. 304 (October 1987): 489–96; Ralph R. Premdas and Jeffrey S. Steeves, 'Fiji: Problems of Ethnic Discrimination and Inequality in the New Constitutional Order,' *Round Table*, no. 318 (April 1991): 155–72; Ralph Premdas, 'General Rabuka and the Fiji Elections of 1992,' *Asian Survey*, 33 (October 1993): 997–1009; 'Second Thoughts in Fiji,' *Economist*, 330 (5 March 1994): 37; Andrew Scobell, 'Politics, Professionalism, and Peacekeeping: An Analysis of the 1987 Military Coup in Fiji,' *Comparative Politics*, 26 (January 1994): 187–201; R. S. Milne, 'Bicommunal Systems: Guyana, Malaysia, Fiji,' *Publius*, 18 (Spring 1988): 101–13.

15. Carl Boggs, Jr., 'Revolutionary Process, Political Strategy, and the Dilemma of Power,' *Theory and Society*, 4 (Fall 1977): 359–93; Carl Boggs, *Social Movements and Political Power: Emerging Forms of Radicalism in the West* (Philadelphia, PA: Temple University Press, 1986); David Marquand, 'Preceptoral Politics, Yeoman Democracy and the Enabling State,' *Government and Opposition*, 23 (Summer 1988): 261–75; Michael W. McCann, 'Public Interest Liberalism and the Modern Regulatory State,' *Polity*, 21 (Winter 1988): 373–400; E.J. Hobsbawm, 'Inside Every Worker There Is a Syndicalist Trying to Get Out,' *New Society*, 48 (5 April 1979): 8–10; Sheldon S. Wolin, 'Contract and Birthright,' *Political Theory*, 14 (May 1986): 179–93; Sheldon S. Wolin, 'Democracy, Difference, and Re-Cognition,' *Political Theory*, 21 (August 1993): 464–83; Robert A. Dahl, *A Preface to Economic Democracy* (Berkeley: University of California Press, 1985); Richard W. Franke and Barbara H. Chasin, 'Kerala State, India: Radical Reform as Development,' *Monthly Review*, 42 (January 1991): 1–23; Maria Helena Moreira Alves, 'Four Comments on Kerala,' *Monthly Review*, 42 (January 1991): 24–28; Vanessa Baird, 'Paradox in Paradise,' *New Internationalist*, no. 241 (March 1993): 4–28; Jeffrey Stoub, 'From Redlining to Reaganism, NPA Puts Neighborhood Issues on National Agenda,' *Neighborhood Works*, 14 (June/July 1991): 1, 10–11; Richard Flacks, 'The Party's Over – So What Is To Be Done?', *Social Research*, 60 (Fall 1993): 445–70; Joel F. Handler, 'Postmodernism, Protest, and the New Social Movements,' *Law and Society Review*, 26, no. 4 (1992): 697–731.

## 7 Theories of the World System

1. Ron Pagnucco, 'Political Opportunities and Social Movements: Transnational Dimensions,' *States and Societies*, 10 (Winter 1993): 3–4; Bruce Russett and Harvey Starr, *World Politics: The Menu for Choice*, 4th ed. (New York: W. H. Freeman, 1992), 99–123; Jack S. Levy, 'The Causes of War: A Review of Theories and Evidence,' in *Behavior, Society, and Nuclear War*, vol. 1, ed. Philip E. Tetlock, Jo L. Husbands, Robert Jervis, Paul C. Stern, and Charles Tilly (New York: Oxford University Press, 1989), 222–58.

2. *The Complete Writings of Thucydides: The Peloponnesian War*, trans. Richard Crawley (New York: The Modern Library, 1951), 15.

3. Ibid., 331, 335. See too Daniel Garst, 'Thucydides and Neorealism,' *International Studies Quarterly*, 33 (March 1989): 3–27.

4. Niccolò Machiavelli, *The Prince* and *The Discourses* (New York: The Modern Library, 1950); Steven Forde, 'Varieties of Realism: Thucydides and Machiavelli,' *Journal of Politics*, 54 (May 1992): 372–93.
5. See Kenneth N. Waltz, 'Realist Thought and Neorealist Theory,' *Journal of International Affairs*, 44 (Spring/Summer 1990): 21–37; David A. Lake, 'Realism,' in *The Oxford Companion to Politics of the World*, ed. Joel Krieger (New York: Oxford University Press, 1993), 771–72; Patrick James, 'Neorealism as a Research Enterprise: Toward Elaborated Structural Realism,' *International Political Science Review*, 14 (April 1993): 123–48; Stephen D. Krasner, 'Realism, Imperialism, and Democracy: A Response to Gilbert,' *Political Theory*, 20 (February 1992): 38–52; Robert O. Keohane, 'Theory of World Politics: Structural Realism and Beyond,' in *Neorealism and Its Critics*, ed. Robert O. Keohane (New York: Columbia University Press, 1986), 158–203; Paul Huth, Christopher Gelpi, and D. Scott Bennett, 'The Escalation of Great Power Militarized Disputes: Testing Rational Deterrence Theory and Structural Realism,' *American Political Science Review*, 87 (September 1993): 609–23; Michael Loriaux, 'The Realists and Saint Augustine: Skepticism, Psychology, and Moral Action in International Relations Thought,' *International Studies Quarterly*, 36 (December 1992): 401–20; K. J. Holsti, *The Dividing Discipline: Hegemony and Diversity in International Theory* (Boston: Allen & Unwin, 1985), 7–81; Joseph S. Nye, Jr., 'Neorealism and Neoliberalism,' *World Politics*, 40 (January 1988): 235–51; Joseph M. Grieco, 'Anarchy and the Limits of Cooperation: A Realist Critique of the Newest Liberal Institutionalism,' *International Organization*, 42 (Summer 1988): 485–507; Emerson M. S. Niou and Peter C. Ordeshook, '"Less Filling, Tastes Great": The Realist-Neoliberal Debate,' *World Politics*, 46 (January 1994): 209–34.
6. Thomas Hobbes, *Leviathan* (New York: Liberal Arts Press, 1958), 86, 107.
7. Bruce Bueno de Mesquita and David Lalman, *War and Reason: Domestic and International Imperatives* (New Haven CT: Yale University Press, 1992), 181–217; John A. Vasquez, *The War Puzzle* (Cambridge, England: Cambridge University Press, 1993), 225–308; Charles W. Kegley, Jr., and Gregory A. Raymond, 'Must We Fear a Post-Cold War Multipolar System?', *Journal of Conflict Resolution*, 36 (September 1992): 573–85; Woosang Kim and James D. Morrow, 'When Do Power Shifts Lead to War?', *American Journal of Political Science*, 36 (November 1992): 896–922; Woosang Kim, 'Power Transitions and Great Power War from Westphalia to Waterloo,' *World Politics*, 45 (October 1992): 153–72. The likelihood of war depends less on the number of poles in the world system than on the distribution of combined resources among competing nation-states, the degree of overlapping memberships in opposed alliances, and the strategic beliefs of national government officials. See the discussion of Manus I. Midlarsky and Ted Hopf, 'Polarity and International Stability,' *American Political Science Review*, 87 (March 1993): 173–80; Michael Nicholson, *Rationality and the Analysis of International Conflict* (Cambridge, England: Cambridge University Press, 1992), 208–20; James D. Morrow, 'Arms versus Allies: Trade-offs in the Search for Security,' *International Organization*, 47 (Spring 1993): 209–33; William B. Moul, 'Polarization, Polynomials, and War,' *Journal of Conflict Resolution*, 37 (December 1993): 735–48.

8. Kenneth N. Waltz, *Theory of International Politics* (Reading, MA: Addison-Wesley, 1979), 60–210; Kenneth N. Waltz, 'The Origins of War in Neorealist Theory,' *Journal of Interdisciplinary History*, 18 (Spring 1988): 615–28; Glenn H. Snyder, 'Alliances, Balance, and Stability,' *International Organization*, 45 (Winter 1991): 121–42; Morton A. Kaplan, 'The Hard Facts of International Theory,' *Journal of International Affairs*, 44 (Spring/Summer 1990): 39–57; Alvin M. Saperstein, 'The "Long Peace" – Result of a Bipolar Competitive World?' *Journal of Conflict Resolution*, 35 (March 1991): 68–79; William R. Thompson, 'Polarity, the Long Cycle, and Global Power Warfare,' *Journal of Conflict Resolution*, 30 (December 1986): 587–615; John A. Vasquez, 'The Steps to War: Toward a Scientific Explanation of Correlates of War Findings,' *World Politics*, 40 (October 1987): 108–45; Miles Kahler, 'External Ambition and Economic Performance,' *World Politics*, 40 (July 1988): 419–51; Henk Houweling and Jan G. Siccama, 'Power Transitions as a Cause of War,' *Journal of Conflict Resolution*, 32 (March 1988): 87–102.

9. See Bruce Bueno de Mesquita, 'The Contribution of Expected Utility Theory to the Study of International Conflict,' *Journal of Interdisciplinary History*, 18 (Spring 1988): 629–52; Bruce Bueno de Mesquita and David Lalman, 'Empirical Support for Systemic and Dyadic Explanations of International Conflict,' *World Politics*, 41 (October 1988): 1–20; Roslyn Simowitz and Barry Price, 'The Expected Utility Theory of Conflict: Measuring Theoretical Progress,' *American Political Science Review*, 84 (June 1990): 439–60; Grace Isui Scarborough, 'Polarity, Power, and Risk in International Disputes,' *Journal of Conflict Resolution*, 32 (September 1988): 511–33; James D. Morrow, 'Social Choice and System Structure in World Politics,' *World Politics*, 41 (October 1988): 75–97; Christopher R. Mitchell, 'Ending Conflicts and Wars: Judgement, Rationality and Entrapment,' *International Social Science Journal*, 43 (February 1991): 35–55; Robert Jervis, 'Models and Cases in the Study of International Conflict,' *Journal of International Affairs*, 44 (Spring/Summer 1990): 81–101; Robert Jervis, 'War and Misperception,' *Journal of Interisciplinary History*, 18 (Spring 1988): 675–700; John Mueller, *Retreat from Dooomsday: The Obsolescence of Major War* (New York: Basic Books, 1989); John Mueller, 'Changing Attitudes towards War: The Impact of the First World War,' *British Journal of Political Science*, 21 (January 1991): 1–28; Kalevi J. Holsti, *Peace and War: Armed Conflicts and International Order 1648–1989* (New York: Cambridge University Press, 1991), 325–38; Jack S. Levy, 'Review Article: When Do Deterrent Threats Work?', *British Journal of Political Science*, 18 (October 1988): 485–512; Levy, 'The Causes of War,' 243–51; Christopher H. Achen and Duncan Snidal, 'Rational Deterrence Theory and Comparative Case Studies,' *World Politics*, 41 (January 1989): 143–69; Richard Ned Lebow and Janice Gross Stein, 'Rational Deterrence Theory: I Think, Therefore I Deter,' *World Politics*, 41 (January 1989): 208–24; Richard Ned Lebow and Janice Gross Stein, 'Deterrence: The Elusive Dependent Variable,' *World Politics*, 42 (April 1990): 336–69; Kenneth N. Waltz, 'Nuclear Myths and Political Realities,' *American Political Science Review*, 84 (September 1990): 731–45.

10. See Stephen D. Krasner, 'International Political Economy,' in *The Oxford Companion to Politics of the World*, ed. Krieger, 453–55; James A. Caporaso,

'Global Political Economy,' in *Political Science: The State of the Discipline II*, ed. Ada W. Finifter (Washington, DC: American Political Science Association, 1993), 451–81; Robert Gilpin, *The Political Economy of International Relations* (Princeton, NJ: Princeton University Press, 1987); David A. Baldwin, *Economic Statecraft* (Princeton, NJ: Princeton University Press, 1985): Richard Rosecrance, *The Rise of the Trading State: Commerce and Conquest in the Modern World* (New York: Basic Books, 1986), 55–59; Angus Maddison, *Phases of Capitalist Development* (New York: Oxford University Press, 1982), 44–45; Jacek Kugler and A. F. K. Organski, 'The End of Hegemony?', *International Interactions*, 15 (April 1989): 113–28.

11. Immanuel Kant, *Perpetual Peace*, ed. Lewis White Beck (New York: Liberal Arts Press, 1957); Nye, 'Neorealism and Neoliberalism,' 235–51; Grieco, 'Anarchy and the Limits of Cooperation,' 485–507; Robert Keohane, 'International Institutions: Two Approaches,' *International Studies Quarterly*, 32 (December 1988): 379–96; Stephen D. Krasner, *Structural Conflict: The Third World against Global Liberalism* (Berkeley: University of California Press, 1985); Jaap Nobel, 'Realism versus Interdependence: The Paradigm Debate in International Relations,' *Bulletin of Peace Proposals*, 19, no. 2 (1988): 167–73; Inis L. Claude, Jr., *Swords into Plowshares: The Problems and Progress of International Organization*, 4th ed. (New York: Random House, 1984), 378–408; Ernst B. Haas, *Why We Still Need the United Nations: The Collective Management of International Conflict, 1945–1984*, Policy Papers in International Affairs, no. 26 (Berkeley: Institute of International Studies, University of California at Berkeley, 1986); William K. Domke, *War and the Changing Global System* (New Haven, CT: Yale University Press, 1988); R.J. Rummel, 'On Vincent's View of Freedom and International Conflict,' *International Studies Quarterly*, 31 (March 1987): 113–17; R.J. Rummel, 'The Politics of Cold Blood,' *Society*, 27 (November/December 1989): 32–40; T. Clifton Morgan and Sally Howard Campbell, 'Domestic Structure, Decisional Constraints, and War,' *Journal of Conflict Resolution*, 35 (June 1991): 187–211; Randall L. Schweller, 'Domestic Structure and Preventive War: Are Democracies More Pacific?', *World Politics*, 44 (January 1992): 235–69; William J. Dixon, 'Democracy and the Management of International Conflict,' *Journal of Conflict Resolution*, 37 (March 1993): 42–68; William J. Dixon, 'Democracy and the Peaceful Settlement of International Conflict,' *American Political Science Review*, 88 (March 1994): 14–32; Bruce Russett, *Grasping the Democratic Peace:Principles for a Post-Cold War World* (Princeton, NJ: Princeton University Press, 1993), esp. 3–42, 172–138; Bueno de Mesquita and Lalman, *War and Reason*, 145–77; David Held and Anthony McGrew, 'Globalization and the Liberal Democratic State,' *Government and Opposition*, 28 (Spring 1993): 261–88; Friedrich Kratochwil, 'The Embarrassment of Changes: Neo-Realism as the Science of Realpolitik without Politics,' *Review of International Studies*, 19 (January 1993): 63–80; D. Marc Kilgour, 'Domestic Political Structure and War Behavior,' *Journal of Conflict Resolution*, 35 (June 1991): 266–84; Holsti, *Peace and War*, 335–53; Zeev Maoz and Nasrin Abdolali, 'Regime Types and International Conflict, 1816–1976,' *Journal of Conflict Resolution*, 33 (March 1989): 3–35; Jack S. Levy, 'Domestic Politics and War,' *Journal of Interdisciplinary History*, 18 (Spring 1988): 653–73; Robert Jervis, 'Realism,

Game Theory, and Cooperation,' *World Politics*, 40 (April 1988): 317–49; Denis MacShane, 'The New Age of the Internationals,' *New Statesman and Society*, 6 (30 April 1993): 23–26; Rosecrance, *The Rise of the Trading State*; Richard Rosecrance, 'Long Cycle Theory and International Relations,' *International Organization*, 41 (Spring 1987): 284–301; Arthur A. Stein, 'Governments, Economic Interdependence, and International Coopera- tion,' in *Behavior, Society, and International Conflict*, vol. 3, ed. Philip E. Tetlock, Jo L. Husbands, Robert Jervis, Paul C. Stern, and Charles Tilly (New York: Oxford University Press, 1993), 241–324; Dirk C. van Raemdonck and Paul F. Diehl, 'After the Shooting Stops: Insights on Postwar Economic Growth,' *Journal of Peace Research*, 26 (August 1989): 249–64; Pierre-Henri Laurent, 'The European Community: Twelve Becoming One,' *Current History*, 87 (November 1988): 357–60, 394.

12.  See the following works by Immanuel Wallerstein: *The Modern World- System: Capitalist Agriculture and the Origins of the European World-Economy in the Sixteenth Century* (New York Academic Press, 1974); *The Modern World- System II: Mercantilism and the Consolidation of the European World-Economy, 1660–1750* (New York: Academic Press, 1980); *The Modern World-System III: The Second Era of Great Expansion of the Capitalist World-Economy, 1730–1840s* (San Diego, CA: Academic Press, 1989); *The Politics of the World-Economy: The States, the Movements and the Civilizations* (Cambridge, England: Cambridge University Press, 1984), 1–57, 97–111, 147–58; 'Culture as the Ideological Battleground of the Modern World-System,' *Theory, Culture and Society*, 7 (June 1990): 31–55; 'World-Systems Analysis: The Second Phase,' *Review*, 13 (Spring 1990): 287–93; 'The Geoculture of Development or the Transformation of Our Geoculture?', *Asian Perspective*, 17 (Fall– Winter 1993): 211–25. See too Christopher Chase-Dunn, *Global Formation: Structures of the World-Economy* (Cambridge, MA: Basil Blackwell, 1989); Christopher Chase-Dunn and Thomas D. Hall, 'Comparing World- Systems: Concepts and Working Hypotheses,' *Social Forces*, 71 (June 1993): 851–86; Christopher Chase-Dunn, 'The National State as an Agent of Modernity,' *Problems of Communism*, 41 (January–April 1992): 29–37; C. P. Terlouw, 'The Elusive Semiperiphery: A Critical Examination of the Concept Semiperiphery,' *International Journal of Comparative Sociology*, 34 (January–April 1993): 87–103; Marian J. Borg, 'Conflict Management in the Modern World-System,' *Sociological Forum*, 7 (June 1992): 261–82; Robert W. Cox, 'Multilateralism and World Order,' *Review of International Studies*, 18 (April 1992): 161–80; Thomas Richard Shannon, *An Introduction to the World-System Perspective* (Boulder, CO: Westview Press, 1989); Daniel Chirot, *Social Change in the Modern Era* (San Diego, CA: Harcourt Brace Jovanovich, 1986); E. Spencer Wellhofer, 'Models of Core and Periphery Dynamics,' *Comparative Political Studies*, 21 (July 1988): 281–307.

13.  See Immanuel Wallerstein, *Unthinking Social Science: The Limits of Nineteenth- Century Paradigms* (Cambridge, England: Polity Press, 1991), 151–69, 187– 201, 257–72; Immanuel Wallerstein, *Geopolitics and Geoculture: Essays on the Changing World-System* (Cambridge, England: Cambridge University Press, 1991), 158–83; Wallerstein, *Politics of the World-Economy*, 41–43, 132–45; Immanuel Wallerstein, 'Typology of Crises in the World-System,' *Review*, 11 (Fall 1988): 581–98; Joshua S. Goldstein, *Long Cycles: Prosperity and War*

*in the Modern Age* (New Haven, CT: Yale University Press, 1988); Rosecrance, 'Long Cycle Theory and International Relations,' 284–301; Terry Boswell, 'Colonial Empires and the Capitalist World-Economy: A Time Series Analysis of Colonizaion, 1640–1960,' *American Sociological Review*, 54 (April 1989): 180–96; Terry Boswell and Mike Sweat, 'Hegemony, Long Waves, and Major Wars: A Time Series Analysis of Systemic Dynamics, 1496–1967,' *International Studies Quarterly*, 35 (June 1991): 123–49; Edward D. Mansfield, 'The Distribution of Wars over Time,' *World Politics*, 41 (October 1988): 21–51; Giovanni Arrighi, 'Marxist Century, American Century: The Making and Remaking of the World Labour Movement,' *New Left Review*, no. 179 (January–February 1990): 29–63.

14. Wallerstein, *Politics of the World-Economy*; David M. Gordon, 'The Global Economy: New Edifice or Crumbling Foundations?', *New Left Review*, no. 168 (March/April 1988): 24–64; Paul M. Sweezy and Harry Magdoff, 'A New Stage of Capitalism Ahead?', *Monthly Review*, 41 (May 1989): 1–15; Volker Bornschier and Christopher Chase-Dunn, *Transnational Corporations and Underdevelopment* (New York: Praeger, 1985), 80–116, 131–42; Birol Ali Yeshilada, 'World Market Recession and Economic Development: A Look at Alternative Rescue Policies for the Third World,' *International Journal of Contemporary Sociology*, 24 (January–April 1987): 57–69; Robert Z. Lawrence, 'Protection: Is There a Better Way?' *American Economic Review*, 79 (May 1989): 118–22; Stephen Gill and David Law, 'Global Hegemony and the Structural Power of Capital,' *International Studies Quarterly*, 33 (December 1989): 475–99; Russett and Starr, *World Politics*, 403–37.

15. Gordon, 'The Global Economy,' 24–64; Robert M. Marsh, 'Sociological Explanations of Economic Growth,' *Studies in Comparative International Development*, 23 (Winter 1988): 41–76; David Jaffee, 'Export Dependence and Economic Growth: A Reformulation and Respecification,' *Social Forces*, 64 (September 1985): 102–18; John R. Oneal, 'Foreign Investments in Less Developed Regions,' *Political Science Quarterly*, 103 (Spring 1988): 131–48; Robin Broad and John Cavanagh, 'No More NICs,' *Foreign Policy*, no. 72 (Fall 1988): 81–103.

16. James, 'Neorealism as a Research Enterprise,' 128–43; Jan Aart Scholte, 'From Power Politics to Social Change: An Alternative Focus for International Studies?', *Review of International Studies*, 19 (January 1993): 3–21; Morrow, 'Social Choice and System Structure in World Politics,' 75–97; Pierre de Senarclens, 'The "Realist" Paradigm and International Conflicts,' *Interational Social Science Journal*, 43 (February 1991): 5–19; Joseph S. Nye, Jr., 'The Changing Nature of World Power,' *Political Science Quarterly*, 105 (Summer 1990): 177–92; Alexander L. George, 'The Two Cultures of Academia and Policy-Making: Bridging the Gap,' *Political Psychology*, 15 (March 1994): 143–72.

## Part III

1. See Jane Loevinger, *Paradigms of Personality* (New York: W. H. Freeman, 1987), 11–48, 129–252; Albert Bandura, *Social Foundations of Thought and*

*Action: A Social Cognitive Theory* (Englewood Cliffs, NJ: Prentice-Hall, 1986), 1–46, 228–84, 335–91; David E. Apter and Charles F. Andrain, eds., *Contemporary Analytical Theory* (Englewood Cliffs, NJ: Prentice-Hall, 1972), 459–64.

2. George W. Bohrnstedt and David Knoke, *Statistics for Social Data Analysis*, 2d ed. (Itasca, IL: F. E. Peacock Publishers, 1988), 3–21; Edgar Kiser and Michael Hechter, 'The Role of General Theory in Comparative-historical Sociology,' *American Journal of Sociology*, 97 (July 1991): 1–30.

3. Roger Tourangeau, Kenneth A. Rasinski, and Roy D'Andrade, 'Attitude Structure and Belief Accessibility,' *Journal of Experimental Social Psychology*, 27 (January 1991): 48–75; Jason Young, Cynthia J. Thomsen, Eugene Borgida, John L. Sullivan, and John H. Aldrich, 'When Self-Interest Makes a Difference: The Role of Construct Accessibility in Political Reasoning,' *Journal of Experimental Social Psychology*, 27 (May 1991): 271–96; David Trafimow, Harry C. Triandis, and Sharon G. Goto, 'Some Tests of the Distinction between the Private Self and the Collective Self,' *Journal of Personality and Social Psychology*, 60 (May 1991): 649–55; Charles F. Andrain, *Foundations of Comparative Politics: A Policy Perspective* (Monterey, CA: Brooks/Cole, 1983), 17–19; Lee Sigelman, Carol K. Sigelman, and David Bullock, 'Reconsidering Pocketbook Voting: An Experimental Approach,' *Political Behavior*, 13 (June 1991): 129–49. For a discussion of the differences among laboratory experiments, quasi-experiments, and field experiments, see Christopher H. Achen, *The Statistical Analysis of Quasi-Experiments* (Berkeley: University of California Press, 1986), esp. 1–15; Morton Hunt, *Profiles of Social Research: The Scientific Study of Human Interactions* (New York: Russell Sage Foundation, 1985), 162–99, 256–62.

4. Arthur L. Stinchcombe, *Constructing Social Theories* (New York: Harcourt, Brace, and World, 1968), 15–38; Mats Ekström, 'Causal Explanation of Social Action: The Contribution of Max Weber and of Critical Realism to a Generative View of Causal Explanation in Social Science,' *Acta Sociologica*, 35, no. 2 (1992): 107–22; Randall Collins, 'Sociology: Proscience or Antiscience?', *American Sociological Review*, 54 (February 1989): 124–39; Fritz Machlup, 'Are the Social Sciences Really Inferior?', *Society*, 25 (May/June 1988): 57–65; Bruce J. Caldwell, 'Clarifying Popper,' *Journal of Economic Literature*, 29 (March 1991): 1–33; David M. Klein, 'Causation in Sociology Today: A Revised View,' *Sociological Theory*, 5 (Spring 1987): 19–26; Jerald Hage and Barbara Foley Meeker, *Social Causality* (Boston: Unwin Hyman, 1988), 1–74, 170–200; Douglas N. Walton, *Informal Logic: A Handbook for Critical Argumentation* (New York: Cambridge University Press, 1989), 198–238.

5. Gabriel A. Almond and Stephen J. Genco, 'Clouds, Clocks, and the Study of Politics,' *World Politics*, 29 (July 1977); 489–522; Carl G. Hempel, *Philosophy of Natural Science* (Englewood Cliffs, NJ: Prentice-Hall, 1966), 47–69; Morris Zelditch, Jr., 'Problems and Progress in Sociological Theory,' *Sociological Perspectives*, 35 (Fall 1992): 415–31; Stanley Lieberson, 'Small N's and Big Conclusions: An Examination of the Reasoning in Comparative Studies Based on a Small Number of Cases,' *Social Forces*, 70 (December 1991): 307–20; Norval D. Glenn, 'What We Know, What We Say We Know: Discrepancies between Warranted and Unwarranted

Conclusions,' in *Crossorads of Social Science: The ICPSR 25th Anniversary Volume*, ed. Heinz Eulau (New York: Agathon Press, 1989), 119–40.

6. Douglas V. Porpora, *The Concept of Social Structure* (Westport, CT: Greenwood Press, 1987), 43–103; Daniel Little, *Varieties of Social Explanation: An Introduction to the Philosophy of Social Science* (Boulder, CO: Westview Press, 1991), 105–12, 183–201.

7. Irving L. Janis, *Crucial Decisions: Leadership in Policymaking and Crisis Management* (New York: The Free Press, 1989).

## 8 The Learning of Political Attitudes

1. Jean-Jacques Rousseau, *Of the Social Contract or Principles of Political Right* and *Discourse on Political Economy*, trans. Charles M. Sherover (New York: Harper and Row, 1984), 4, 18.

2. Ibid., xiii–xl, 19; Sheldon S. Wolin, *Politics and Vision* (Boston: Little, Brown, 1960), 368–75; Patrick Riley, 'Rousseau's General Will: Freedom of a Particular Kind,' *Political Studies*, 39 (March 1991): 55–74; Pamela A. Mason, 'The Communion of Citizens: Calvinist Themes in Rousseau's Theory of the State,' *Polity*, 26 (Fall 1993): 25–49.

3. Walt Whitman, *Leaves of Grass*, ed. Jerome Loving (New York: Oxford University Press, 1990), 451–52.

4. Ibid., 128. See too 15.

5. Ibid., vii–xxx; Vernon Louis Parrington, *Main Currents in American Thought*, vol. 3: *The Beginnings of Critical Realism in America* (New York: Harcourt, Brace and Company, 1930), 69–86.

6. See the definition of 'principled tolerance' in Paul M. Sniderman, Philip E. Tetlock, James M. Glaser, Donald Philip Green, and Michael Hout, 'Principled Tolerance and the American Mass Public,' *British Journal of Political Science*, 19 (January 1989): 25–45.

7. James M. Olson and Mark P. Zanna, 'Attitudes and Attitude Change,' in *Annual Review of Psychology*, vol. 44, ed. Lyman W. Porter and Mark R. Rosenzweig (Palo Alto, CA: Annual Reviews, Inc., 1993): 117–54; John Mueller, 'Trends in Political Tolerance,' *Public Opinion Quarterly*, 52 (Spring 1988): 1–25; James L. Gibson, 'Political Intolerance and Political Repression during the McCarthy Red Scare,' *American Political Science Review*, 82 (June 1988): 511–29.

8. Robert D. Putnam, *The Beliefs of Politicians: Ideology, Conflict, and Democracy in Britain and Italy* (New Haven, CT: Yale University Press, 1973), 34–48; Philip E. Converse and Roy Pierce, *Political Representation in France* (Cambridge, MA: Harvard University Press, 1986), 111–40; Jon Pierre, 'Attitudes and Behaviour of Party Activists,' *European Journal of Political Research*, 14, no. 4 (1986): 465–79; Arthur Sanders, 'The Meaning of Liberalism and Conservatism,' *Polity*, 19 (Fall 1986): 123–35; W. Russell Neuman, *The Paradox of Mass Politics: Knowledge and Opinion in the American Electorate* (Cambridge, MA: Harvard University Press, 1986); Eric R. A. N. Smith, *The Unchanging American Voter* (Berkeley: University of California Press, 1989), 9–104, 223–27.

9. Herbert McClosky and Alida Brill, *Dimensions of Tolerance: What Americans Believe about Civil Liberties* (New York: Russell Sage Foundation, 1983), 320;

Herbert McClosky and John Zaller, *The American Ethos: Public Attitudes toward Capitalism and Democracy* (Cambridge, MA: Harvard University Press, 1984), 189–215; Paul M. Sniderman, Richard A. Brody, and Philip E. Tetlock, *Reasoning and Choice: Explorations in Political Psychology* (New York: Cambridge University Press, 1991), 70–92.

10. Mueller, 'Trends in Political Tolerance,' 15–16; Neuman, *Paradox of Mass Politics*, 132–68.

11. George C. Homans, 'The Present State of Sociological Theory,' *Sociological Quarterly*, 23 (Summer 1982): 285–99. For an analysis of the processing of political information, see Richard R. Lau and David O. Sears, 'Social Cognition and Political Cognition: The Past, the Present, and the Future,' in *Political Cognition*, ed. Richard R. Lau and David O. Sears (Hillsdale, NJ: Lawrence Erlbaum Associates, 1986), 347–66.

12. See John L. Sullivan, James Piereson, and George E. Marcus, *Political Tolerance and American Democracy* (Chicago: University of Chicago Press, 1982); John L. Sullivan, Michal Shamir, Patrick Walsh, and Nigel S. Roberts, *Political Tolerance in Context: Support for Unpopular Minorities in Israel, New Zealand, and the United States* (Boulder, CO: Westview Press, 1985).

13. M. Brewster Smith, Jerome S. Bruner, and Robert W. White, *Opinions and Personality* (New York: John Wiley, 1956); M. Brewster Smith, *Social Psychology and Human Values* (Chicago: Alkine, 1969), 14–32, 82–96; Gregory M. Herek, 'The Instrumentality of Attitudes: Toward a Neofunctional Theory,' *Journal of Social Issues*, 42, no. 2 (1986): 99–114.

14. Harold D. Lasswell, *Psychopathology and Politics* (New York: The Viking Press, 1960), 75–76.

15. T. W. Adorno, Else Frenkel-Brunswik, Daniel J. Levinson, and R. Nevitt Sanford, *The Authoritarian Personality* (New York: Harper and Row, 1950), esp. 222–79; Else Frenkel-Brunswik, 'Further Explorations by a Contributor to "The Authoritarian Personality",' in *Studies in the Scope and Method of 'The Authoritarian Personality,'* ed. Richard Christie and Marie Jahoda (Glencoe, IL: The Free Press, 1954), 226–75; Bob Altemeyer, *Right-Wing Authoritarianism* (Winnipeg: University of Manitoba Press, 1981); Bob Altemeyer, *Enemies of Freedom: Understanding Right-Wing Authoritarianism* (San Francisco: Jossey-Bass, 1988); Milton Rokeach, *The Open and Closed Mind* (New York: Basic Books, 1960).

16. Altemeyer, *Right-Wing Authoritarianism*, 14–80, 215–72; Sullivan, et al., *Political Tolerance in Context*, 175–242; Sullivan, et al., *Political Tolerance and American Democracy*, 163–241; McClosky and Brill, *Dimensions of Tolerance*, 338–70; Thomas T. Lewis, 'Authoritarian Attitudes and Personaliies: A Psychohistorical Perspective,' *Psychohistory Review*, 18 (Winter 1990): 141–67; Jay W. Jackson, 'Authoritarian Personality Theory of Intergroup Hostility: A Review and Evaluation of the Theoretical and Empirical Literaure,' *International Journal of Group Tensions*, 21 (Winter 1991): 383–405.

17. See John Stuart Mill, *On Liberty and Other Writings*, ed. Stefan Collini (New York: Cambridge University Press, 1989), x–xvii, 1–115; Peter Donovan, 'The Intolerance of Religious Pluralism,' *Religious Studies*, 29 (June 1993): 217–29; James L. Gibson, 'The Political Consequences of Intolerance: Cultural Conformity and Political Freedom,' *American Political Science*

*Review*, 86 (June 1992): 338–56; McClosky and Zaller, *The American Ethos*, 234–63.

18. See Paul Dekker and Peter Ester, 'Working-Class Authoritarianism: A Re-examination of the Lipset Thesis,' *European Journal of Political Research*, 15, no. 4 (1987): 395–415; Paul Dekker and Peter Ester, 'Social and Political Attitudes of Dutch Youth: Young Rebels, Trend Setters or Law-Abiding Citizens?', *Netherlands Journal of Sociology*, 24 (April 1988): 32–49; C. P. Middendorp and J. D. Meloen, 'The Authoritarianism of the Working Class Revisited,' *European Journal of Political Research*, 18 (March 1990): 257–67; C. P. Middendorp and J. D. Meloen, 'Social Class, Authoritarian-ism and Directiveness,' *European Journal of Political Research*, 20 (September 1991): 213–20; P. Scheepers, A. Felling, and J. Peters, 'Social Conditions, Authoriarianism and Ethnocentrism: A Theoretical Model of the Early Frankfurt School Updated and Tested,' *European Sociological Review*, 6 (May 1990): 15–29; Wim Meeus, 'Adolescent Rebellion and Politics,' *Youth and Society*, 19 (June 1988): 426–34; Bo Ekehammar, Ingrid Nilsson, and Jim Sidanius, 'Education and Ideology: Basic Aspects of Education Related to Adolescents' Sociopolitical Attitudes,' *Political Psychology*, 8 (September 1987): 395–410; Anthony Heath, Geoffrey Evans, and Jean Martin, 'The Measurement of Core Beliefs and Values: The Development of Balanced Socialist/Laissez Faire and Libertarian/Authoritarian Scales,' *British Journal of Political Science*, 24 (January 1994): 115–32; Frederick D. Weil, 'Structural Determinants of Political Tolerance: Regime Change and the Party System in West Germany since World War II,' in *Research in Political Sociology*, vol. 5, ed. Philo C. Wasburn (Greenwich, CT: JAI Press, 1991), 299–332; Raymond M. Duch and Michaell A. Taylor, 'Postmaterialism and the Economic Condition,' *American Journal of Political Science*, 37 (August 1993): 747–79; Michal Shamir, 'Political Intolerance among Masses and Elites in Israel: A Reevaluation of the Elitist Theory of Democracy,' *Journal of Politics*, 53 (November 1991): 1018–43; James L. Guth and John C. Green, 'An Ideology of Rights: Support for Civil Liberties among Political Activists,' *Political Behavior*, 13 (December 1991): 321–44; Paul M. Sniderman, Joseph F. Fletcher, Peter H. Russell, Philip E. Tetlock, and Brian J. Gaines, 'The Fallacy of Democratic Elitism: Elite Competition and Commitent to Civil Liberties,' *British Journal of Political Science*, 21 (July 1991): 349–70; Joseph F. Fletcher, 'Participation and Attitudes toward Civil Liberties: Is There an "Educative" Effect?', *International Political Science Review*, 11 (October 1990): 439–59; James L. Gibson, Raymond M. Duch, and Kent L. Tedin, 'Democratic Values and the Transformation of the Soviet Union,' *Journal of Politics*, 54 (May 1992): 329–71; Ian McAllister, 'Party Elites, Voters and Political Attitudes: Testing Three Explanations for Mass-Elite Differences,' *Canadian Journal of Political Science*, 24 (June 1991): 237–68; Susan Tiano, 'Authoritarianism and Political Culture in Argentina and Chile in the Mid-1960s,' *Latin American Research Review*, 21, no. 1 (1986): 73–98; John A. Booth and Mitchell A. Seligson, 'The Political Culture of Authoritarianism in Mexico: A Reexamination,' *Latin American Research Review*, 19, no. 1 (1984): 106–24; Barbara Geddes and John Zaller, 'Sources of Popular Support for Authoritarian Regimes,' *American Journal of Political Science*, 33 (May

1989): 319–47; Edward N. Muller, Mitchell A. Seligson, and Ilter Turan, 'Education, Participation, and Support for Democratic Norms,' *Comparative Politics*, 20 (October 1987): 19–33; Sniderman, et al., 'Principled Tolerance and the American Mass Public,' 37–42; Lawrence Bobo and Frederick C. Licari, 'Education and Political Tolerance: Testing the Effects of Cognitive Sophisication and Target Group Affect,' *Public Opinion Quarterly*, 53 (Fall 1989): 285–308; Mark Peffley and Lee Sigelman, 'Intolerance of Communists during the McCarthy Era: A General Model,' *Western Political Quarterly*, 43 (March 1990): 93–111; Clyde Wilcox and Ted Jelen, 'Evangelicals and Political Tolerance,' *American Politics Quarterly*, 18 (January 1990); 25–46; Daniel V. A. Olson and Jackson W. Carroll, 'Religiously Based Politics: Religious Elites and the Public,' *Social Forces*, 70 (March 1992): 765–86; Altemeyer, *Enemies of Freedom*, 51–99, 200–68; Kathleen Murphy Beatty and Oliver Walter, 'Religious Preference and Practice: Reevaluating Their Impact on Political Tolerance,' *Public Opinion Quarterly*, 48 (Spring 1984): 318–29; McClosky and Brill, *Dimensions of Tolerance*, 274–414; McClosky and Zaller, *American Ethos*, 189–287; Sullivan, et al., *Political Tolerance in Context*, 196–99, 207–32.

19. Sniderman, et al., *Reasoning and Choice*, 31–57, 120–39; James L. Gibson, 'Alternative Measures of Political Tolerance: Must Tolerance Be "Least-Liked"?', *American Journal of Political Science*, 36 (May 1992): 560–77; James L. Gibson and Raymond M. Duch, 'Political Intolerance in the USSR: The Distribution and Etiology of Mass Opinion,' *Comparative Political Studies*, 26 (October 1993): 307, 314–15; Dennis Chong, 'How People Think, Reason, and Feel about Rights and Liberties,' *American Journal of Political Science*, 37 (August 1993): 867–99; McClosky and Zaller, *American Ethos*, 234–302; 234–302; McClosky and Brill, *Dimensions of Tolerance*, 415–28; Rokeach, *Open and Closed Mind*, 71–80; Milton Rokeach, *Beliefs, Attitudes, and Values* (San Francisco: Jossey-Bass, 1968), 146.

20. Albert Bandura, *Social Foundations of Thought and Action: A Social Cognitive Theory* (Englewood Cliffs, NJ: Prentice-Hall, 1986).

21. See Lawrence Kohlberg, *Essays on Moral Development*, vol. 1, *The Philosophy of Moral Development: Moral Stages and the Idea of Justice* (San Francisco: Harper and Row, 1981); Lawrence Kohlberg, *Essays on Moral Developent*, vol. 2, *The Psychology of Moral Development: The Nature and Validity of Moral Stages* (San Francisco: Harper and Row, 1984); Anne Colby and Lawrence Kohlberg, *The Measurement of Moral Judgment*, vol. 1, *Theoretical Foundations and Research Validation* (New York: Cambridge University Press, 1987), esp. 1–61, 315–53; Shawn W. Rosenberg, *Reason, Ideology and Politics* (Princeton, NJ: Princeton University Press, 1988), 1–29; Shawn W. Rosenberg, Dana Ward, and Stephen Chilton, *Political Reasoning and Cognition: A Piagetian View* (Durham, NC: Duke University Press, 1988), 47–85, 127–85; Shawn W. Rosenberg, 'The Structure of Political Thinking,' *American Journal of Political Science*, 32 (August 1988): 539–66; Carol Gilligan, *In a Different Voice: Psychological Theory and Women's Development* (Cambridge, MA: Harvard University Press, 1982); Lawrence A. Blum, 'Gilligan and Kohlberg: Implications for Moral Theory,' *Ethics*, 98 (April 1988): 472–91; Charles F. Andrain, *Children and Civic Awareness: A Study in Political Education* (Columbus, OH: Charles E. Merrill, 1971), esp. 59–112; Robert

C. Luskin, 'Measuring Political Sophisication,' *American Journal of Political Science*, 31 (November 1987): 856–99; Philip E. Tetlock, 'A Value Pluralism Model of Ideological Reasoning,' *Journal of Personality and Social Psychology*, 50 (April 1986): 819–27; Altemeyer, *Enemies of Freedom*, 262, 321.

22.  Stanley W. Moore, James Lare, and Kenneth A. Wagner, *The Child's Political World: A Longitudinal Perspective* (New York: Praeger, 1985); Joseph Wagner, 'Political Tolerance and Stages of Moral Development: A Conceptual and Empirical Alternative,' *Political Behavior* 8, no. 1 (1986): 45–80; Joseph Wagner, 'Rational Constraint in Mass Belief Systems: The Role of Developental Moral Stages in the Structure of Political Beliefs,' *Political Psychology*, 11 (March 1990): 147–71.

23.  Bandura, *Social Foundations of Thought and Action*, 482–98.

24.  Kohlberg, *The Psychology of Moral Development*, 498–581; James Rest, Clark Power, and Mary Brabeck, 'Lawrence Kohlberg (1927–1987),' *American Psychologist*, 43 (May 1988): 399–400; Augusto Blasi, 'Moral Cognition and Moral Action: A Theoretical Perspective,' *Developmental Review*, 3 (June 1983): 178–210; Icek Ajzen, *Attitudes, Personality, and Behavior* (Stony Stratford, England: Open University Press, 1988), 112–45; Herek, 'The Instrumentality of Attitudes,' 99–114; Robert E. O'Connor, 'Political Activism and Moral Reasoning: Political and Apolitical Students in Great Britain and France,' *British Journal of Political Science*, 4 (January 1974): 53–78; Alberta J. Nassi, 'Survivors of the Sixties: Comparative Psychosocial and Political Development of Former Berkeley Student Activists,' *American Psychologist*, 36 (July 1981): 753–61.

25.  Samuel P. Oliner and Pearl M. Oliner, *The Altruistic Personality: Rescuers of Jews in Nazi Europe* (New York: The Free Press, 1988); Samuel P. Oliner, 'Altruism: Antidote to Human Conflict,' *Humboldt Journal of Social Relations*, 16, no. 2 (1991): 1–37. See too Kristen R. Monroe, Michael C. Barton, and Ute Klingemann, 'Altruism and the Theory of Rational Action: Rescuers of Jews in Nazi Europe,' *Ethics*, 101 (October 1990): 103–22; Kristen Renwick Monroe, 'John Donne's People: Explaining Differences between Rational Actors and Altruists through Cognitive Frameworks,' *Journal of Politics*, 53 (May 1991): 394–433; Neera Kapur Badhwar, 'Altruism versus Self-Interest: Sometimes a False Dichotomy,' *Social Philosophy and Policy*, 10 (Winter 1993): 90–117.

26.  See James L. Gibson, 'The Policy Consequences of Political Intolerance: Political Repression during the Vietnam War Era,' *Journal of Politics*, 51 (February 1989): 13–35; Gibson, 'Political Intolerance and Political Repression during the McCarthy Red Scare,' 511–29; McClosky and Brill, *Dimensions of Tolerance*, 232–73; Jennifer L. Hochschild, 'Dimensions of Liberal Self-Satisfaction: Civil Liberties, Liberal Theory, and Elite-Mass Differences,' *Ethics*, 96 (January 1986): 386–99; Sullivan, et al., *Political Tolerance and American Democracy*, 1–25, 254–63; John L. Sullivan, Michal Shamir, Nigel S. Roberts, and Patrick Walsh, 'Political Intolerance and the Structure of Mass Attitudes: A Study of the United States, Israel, and New Zealand,' *Comparative Political Studies*, 17 (October 1984): 319–44; David G. Barnum and John L. Sullivan, 'Attitudinal Tolerance and Political Freedom in Britain,' *British Journal of Political Science*, 19 (January 1989): 136–46; John L. Sullivan, Pat Walsh, Michal Shamir, David G.

Barnum, and James L. Gibson, 'Why Politicians Are More Tolerant: Selective Recruitment and Socialization among Political Elites in Britain, Israel, New Zealand and the United States,' *British Journal of Political Science*, 23 (January 1993): 51–76; David G. Barnum and John L. Sullivan, 'The Elusive Foundations of Political Freedom in Britain and the United States,' *Journal of Politics*, 52 (August 1990): 726–27; Peter Jones, 'Respecting Beliefs and Rebuking Rushdie,' *British Journal of Political Science*, 20 (October 1990): 415–37; Bhikhu Parekh, 'The Rushdie Affair: Research Agenda for Political Philosophy,' *Political Studies*, 38 (December 1990): 695–709; Paul M. Sniderman, 'The New Look in Public Opinion Research,' in *Political Science: The State of the Discipline II*, ed. Ada W. Finifter (Washington, DC: American Political Science Association, 1993), 228–31.

## 9 Electoral Participation

1. See Midge Mackenzie, *Shoulder to Shoulder: A Documentary* (New York: Knopf, 1975), 296.
2. Ibid., 33.
3. Jackie Duckworth, 'Sylvia Pankhurst as an Artist,' in *Sylvia Pankhurst: From Artist to Anti-Fascist*, ed. Ian Bullock and Richard Pankhurst (New York: St. Martin's Press, 1992), 36–51.
4. Mackenzie, *Shoulder to Shoulder*, 269–70, 283–84; Keith Curry Lance, 'Strategy Choices of the British Women's Social and Political Union, 1903–18,' *Social Science Quarterly*, 60 (June 1979): 51–61; Les Garner, 'Suffragism and Socialism: Sylvia Pankhurst 1903–1914,' in *Sylvia Pankhurst*, ed. Bullock and Pankhurst, 58–82; Joyce Gelb, 'Feminism and Political Action,' in *Challenging the Political Order: New Social and Political Movements in Western Democracies*, ed. Russell J. Dalton and Manfred Kuechler (New York: Oxford University Press, 1990), 137–55.
5. See Kay Mills, *This Little Light of Mine: Fannie Lou Hamer* (New York: Penguin Books, 1993).
6. Jon Elster, *Making Sense of Marx* (Cambridge, England: Cambridge University Press, 1985), 5–18; Douglas Moggach, 'Monadic Marxism: A Critique of Elster's Methodological Individualism,' *Philosophy of the Social Sciences*, 21 (March 1991): 38–63; David Lalman, Joe Oppenheimer, and Piotr Swistak, 'Formal Rational Choice Theory: A Cumulative Science of Politics,' in *Political Science: The State of the Discipline II*, ed. Ada W. Finifter (Washington, DC: American Political Science Association, 1993), 77–104; Dennis C. Mueller, *Public Choice II: A Revised Edition of Public Choice* (New York: Cambridge University Press, 1989), 364; Gordon Tullock, 'The Costs of Rent Seeking: A Metaphysical Problem,' *Public Choice*, 57 (April 1988): 15–24; William C. Mitchell, 'Public Choice Theory,' in *The Oxford Companion to Politics of the World*, ed. Joel Krieger (New York: Oxford University Press, 1993), 754–55.
7. Peter C. Ordeshook, *A Political Theory Primer* (New York: Routledge, 1992), esp. 7–60, 139–87; Elster, *Making Sense of Marx*, 358–67; Ralph H. Turner, 'The Use and Misuse of Rational Models in Collective Behavior and Social Psychology,' *European Journal of Sociology*, 32 (May 1991): 84–108; Michael

Hechter, 'The Insufficiency of Game Theory for the Resolution of Real-World Collective Action Problems,' *Rationality and Society*, 4 (January 1992): 33–40; Debra Friedman and Michael Hechter, 'The Contribution of Rational Choice Theory to Macrosociological Research,' *Sociological Theory*, 6 (Fall 1988): 201–218; Elinor Ostrom, 'Rational Choice Theory and Institutional Analysis: Toward Complementarity,' *American Political Science Review*, 85 (March 1991): 237–43; Aaron Wildavsky, 'Can Norms Rescue Self-Interest or Macro Explanation Be Joined to Micro Explanation?', *Critical Review*, 5 (Summer 1991): 301–23; William C. Mitchell, 'Virginia, Rochester, and Bloomington: Twenty-Five Years of Public Choice and Political Science,' *Public Choice*, 56 (February 1988): 101–19; George Tsebelis, *Nested Games: Rational Choice in Comparative Politics* (Berkeley: University of California Press, 1990), 1–47, 119–58; Ann E. Cudd, 'Game Theory and the History of Ideas about Rationality,' *Economics and Philosophy*, 9 (April 1993): 101–33.

8. Andries Hoogerwerf, 'The Market as a Metaphor of Politics: A Critique of the Foundations of Economic Choice Theory,' *International Review of Administrative Sciences*, 58 (March 1992): 23–42; Lawrence A. Scaff and Helen M. Ingram, 'Politics, Policy, and Public Choice: A Critique and a Proposal,' *Polity*, 19 (Summer 1987): 613–36; J. C. Glass and W. Johnson, 'Metaphysics, MSRP and Economics,' *British Journal for the Philosophy of Science* 39 (September 1988): 313–29; Jutta Weldes, 'Marxism and Methodological Individualism,' *Theory and Society*, 18 (May 1989): 353–86.

9. Peter Abell, '*Homo Sociologicus*: Do We Heed Him/Her?' *Sociological Theory*, 9 (Fall 1991): 195–98; Jon Elster, 'Rationality and Social Norms,' *European Journal of Sociology*, 32 (May 1991): 109–29; Steven Lukes, 'The Rationality of Norms,' *European Journal of Sociology*, 32 (May 1991): 142–49; Michael Hechter, 'Rational Choice Theory and Historical Sociology,' *Interational Social Science Journal*, 44 (August 1992): 367–73; Randall Collins, 'The Rationality of Avoiding Choice,' *Rationality and Society*, 5 (January 1993): 58–67; Daniel Little, 'Rational-Choice Models and Asian Studies,' *Journal of Asian Studies*, 50 (February 1991): 35–52; Daniel Little, *Varieties of Social Explanation: An Introduction to the Philosophy of Social Science* (Boulder, CO: Westview Press, 1991), 39–67; Turner, 'The Use and Misuse of Rational Models,' 91–106; Jack Dennis, 'The Study of Electoral Behavior,' in *Political Science: Looking to the Future*, vol. 3, *Political Behavior*, ed. William Crotty (Evanston, IL: Northwestern University Press, 1991), 66–74.

10. George C. Homans, 'Behaviourism and After,' in *Social Theory Today*, ed. Anthony Giddens and Jonathan Turner (Stanford, CA: Stanford University Press, 1987), 58–81.

11. James DeNardo, *Power in Numbers: The Political Strategy of Protest and Rebellion* (Princeton, NJ: Princeton University Press, 1985), 90–100; Dennis Chong, *Collective Action and the Civil Rights Movement* (Chicago: University of Chicago Press, 1991); Karl-Dieter Opp, *The Rationality of Political Protest: A Comparative Analysis of Rational Choice Theory* (Boulder, CO: Westview Press, 1989); Michael Thompson, Richard Ellis, and Aaron Wildavsky, *Cultural Theory* (Boulder, CO: Westview Press, 1990), esp. 1–100; James G. March and Johan P. Olsen, *Rediscovering Institutions: The Organizational Basis of Politics* (New York: The Free Press, 1989), 39–52, 117–72; Herbert A.

Simon, 'Altruism and Economics,' *American Economic Review*, 83 (May 1993): 156–61; Friedel Bolle, 'On Love and Altruism,' *Rationality and Society*, 3 (April 1991): 197–214; Robert Coles, *The Call of Service: A Witness to Idealism* (New York Houghton Mifflin Company, 1993); Samuel L. Popkin, *The Reasoning Voter: Communication and Persuasion in Presidential Campaigns* (Chicago: University of Chicago Press, 1991), 7–17.

12. James H. Kuklinski, Robert C. Luskin, and John Bolland, 'Where Is the Schema? Going Beyond the "S" Word in Political Psychology,' *American Political Science Review*, 85 (December 1991): 1341–56; Milton Lodge, Kathleen M. McGraw, Pamela Johnston Conover, Stanley Feldman, and Arthur H. Miller, 'Where Is the Schema? Critiques,' *American Political Science Review*, 85 (December 1991): 1357–80; Kay Lehman Schlozman and Sidney Verba, 'Sending Them a Message–Getting a Reply: Presidential Elections and Democratic Accountability,' in *Elections in America*, ed. Kay Lehman Schlozman (Boston: Allen and Unwin, 1987), 3–25; Donald R. Kinder and David O. Sears, 'Public Opinion and Politial Action,' in *Handbook of Social Psychology*, 3d ed., vol. 2, ed. Gardner Lindzey and Elliot Aronson (New York: Random House, 1985), 660–96; David Knoke, *Political Networks: The Structural Perspective* (New York: Cambridge University Press, 1990), 22–56; Manfred Kuechler, 'Issues and Voting in the European Elections 1989,' *European Journal of Political Research*, 19 (January 1991): 81–83; Paul M. Sniderman, James M. Glaser, and Robert Griffin, 'Information and Electoral Choice,' in *Information and Democratic Processes*, ed. John A. Ferejohn and James H. Kuklinski (Urbana: University of Illinois Press, 1990), 117–35.

13. Randall G. Holcombe and James D. Gwartney, 'Political Parties and the Legislative Principal-Agent Relationship,' *Journal of Institutional and Theoretical Economics*, 145 (December 1989): 669–75; Peter W. Wielhouwer and James L. Regens, 'Political Parties as Transaction Cost Minimizers,' paper presented at the annual meeting of the American Political Science Association, Washington, DC, 2–5 September 1993; Paul M. Sniderman, Richard A. Brody, and Philip E. Tetlock, *Reasoning and Choice: Explorations in Political Psychology* (New York: Cambridge University Press, 1991), 270.

14. Herbert Kitschelt, 'Class Structure and Social Democratic Party Strategy,' *British Journal of Political Science*, 23 (July 1993): 299–337; David Weakliem, 'Class Consciousness and Political Change: Voting and Political Attitudes in the British Working Class, 1964 to 1970,' *American Sociological Review*, 58 (June 1993): 382–97; Russell J. Dalton and Martin P. Wattenberg, 'The Not So Simple Act of Voting,' in *Political Science*, ed. Finifter, 198–202; G. Bingham Powell, Jr., 'Comparative Voting Behavior: Cleavages, Partisan-ship and Accountbility,' in *Research in Micropolitics*, vol. 2, ed. Samuel Long (Greenwich, CT: JAI Press, 1987), 233–64; Oddbjørn Knutsen, 'The Impact of Structural and Ideological Party Cleavages in West European Democracies: A Comparative Empirical Analysis,' *British Journal of Political Science*, 18 (July 1988): 323–52; Adam Przeworski, *Capitalism and Social Democracy* (New York: Cambridge University Press, 1986), 99–132.

15. Diane Sainsbury, 'Party Strategies and the Electoral Trade-Off of Class-Based Parties: A Critique and Application of the "Dilemma of Electoral Socialism",' *European Journal of Political Research*, 18 (January 1990): 29–50;

Jan-Erik Lane and Svante O. Ersson, *Politics and Society in Western Europe* (Beverly Hills, CA: Sage Publications, 1987), 39–153; Russell J. Dalton, *Citizen Politics in Western Democracies* (Chatham, NJ: Chatham House Publishers, 1988), 151–76; Charles F. Andrain, *Foundations of Comparative Politics: A Policy Perspective* (Monterey, CA: Brooks/Cole, 1983), 244–59; John R. Petrocik, 'Realignment: New Party Coalitions and the Nationalization of the South,' *Journal of Politics*, 49 (May 1987): 347–75; Edward G. Carmines and James A. Stimson, *Issue Evolution: Race and the Transformation of American Politics* (Princeton, NJ: Princeton University Press, 1989); Edward G. Carmines and Harold W. Stanley, 'The Transformation of the New Deal Party System: Social Groups, Political Ideology, and Changing Partisanship among Northern Whites, 1972–1988,' *Political Behavior*, 14 (September 1992): 213–37; Paul R. Abramson, John H. Aldrich, and David W. Rohde, *Change and Continuity in the 1988 Elections* (Washington, DC: Congressional Quarterly Press, 1990), 121–51; Warren E. Miller and Santa A. Traugott, *American National Election Studies Data Sourcebook, 1952–1986* (Cambridge, MA: Harvard University Press, 1989), 316; Kenneth D. Wald, Dennis E. Owen, and Samuel S. Hill, Jr., 'Churches as Political Communities,' *American Political Science Review*, 82 (June 1988): 531–48; Thomas D. Lancaster and Michael S. Lewis-Beck, 'Regional Vote Support: The Spanish Case,' *International Studies Quarterly*, 33 (March 1989): 29–43.

16. Bradley M. Richardson, 'European Party Loyalties Revisited,' *American Political Science Review*, 85 (September 1991): 751–75; Dalton and Wattenberg, 'The Not So Simple Act of Voting,' in *Political Science*, ed. Finifter, 202–06; Samuel H. Barnes, M. Kent Jennings, Ronald Inglehart, and Barbara Farah, 'Party Identification and Party Closeness in Comparative Perspective,' *Political Behavior*, 10 (Fall 1988): 215–31; Michael S. Lewis-Beck, *Economics and Elections: The Major Western Democracies* (Ann Arbor: The University of Michigan Press, 1988), 70–71, 156–59; Philip E. Converse and Roy Pierce, *Political Representation in France* (Cambridge, MA: Harvard University Press, 1986), 68–150, 764–86; Scott C. Flanagan, Shinsaku Kohei, Ichiro Miyake, Bradley M. Richardson, and Joji Watanuki, *The Japanese Voter* (New Haven, CT: Yale University Press, 1991), esp. 405–08; Jerrold G. Rusk, 'Issues and Voting,' in *Research in Micropolitics*, vol. 2, p. 116; Pippa Norris, 'Retrospective Voting in the 1984 Presidential Election: Peace, Prosperity, and Patriotism,' *Political Studies*, 35 (June 1987): 288–300; Pippa Norris, 'The 1992 US Elections,' *Government and Opposition*, 28 (Winter 1993): 51–68; Everett Carll Ladd, 'The 1992 Vote for President Clinton: Another Brittle Mandate?', *Political Science Quarterly* 108 (Spring 1993): 1–28; Arthur H. Miller, 'Economic, Character, and Social Issues in the 1992 Presidential Election,' *American Behavioral Scientist*, 37 (November 1993): 317–18; M. Kent Jennings, 'Idelogical Thinking among Mass Publics and Political Elites,' *Public Opinion Quarterly*, 56 (Winter 1992): 419–41; John P. Robinson and John A. Fleishman, 'Ideological Trends in American Public Opinion,' *Annals of the American Academy of Political and Social Science*, 472 (March 1984): 50–60; Miller and Traugott, *American National Election Studies Data Sourcebook*, 317; J. Merrill Shanks and Warren E. Miller, 'Partisanship, Policy and

Performance: The Reagan Legacy in the 1988 Election,' *British Journal of Political Science*, 21 (April 1991): 192–97; Warren E. Miller, 'Party Identification, Realignment, and Party Voting: Back to the Basics,' *American Political Science Review*, 85 (June 1991): 557–68, esp. 565; Bruce E. Keith, David B. Magleby, Candice J. Nelson, Elizabeth Orr, Mark C. Westlye, and Raymond E. Wolfinger, *The Myth of the Independent Voter* (Berkeley: University of California Press, 1992), 60–111.

17. Oddbjørn Knutsen, 'Cleavage Dimensions in Ten West European Countries: A Comparative Empirical Analysis,' *Comparative Political Studies*, 21 (January 1989): 495–534; Knutsen, 'The Impact of Structural and Ideological Party Cleavages in West European Democracies,' 323–52; Oddbjørn Knutsen, 'The Materialist/Post-Materialist Value Dimension as a Party Cleavage in the Nordic Countries,' *West European Politics*, 13 (April 1990): 259–73; Ronald Inglehart, *Culture Shift in Advanced Industrial Society* (Princeton, NJ: Princeton University Press, 1990), 248–334; Dalton, *Citizen Politics in Western Democracies*, 77–176; Torben Iversen, 'Political Leadership and Representation in West European Democracies: A Test of Three Models of Voting,' *American Journal of Political Science*, 38 (February 1994): 55–59; Anthony Heath, Geoffrey Evans, and Jean Martin, 'The Measurement of Core Beliefs and Values: The Development of Balanced Socialist/Laissez Faire and Libertarian/Authoritarian Scales,' *British Journal of Political Science*, 24 (January 1994): 115–32, esp. 129; David L. Weakliem, 'The Two Lefts? Occupation and Party Choice in France, Italy, and the Netherlands,' *American Journal of Sociology*, 96 (May 1991): 1327–61; Donald Granberg and Sören Holmberg, *The Political System Matters: Social Psychology and Voting Behavior in Sweden and the United States* (New York: Cambridge University Press, 1988); Richard G. Niemi and Anders Westholm, 'Issues, Parties and Attitudinal Stability: A Comparative Study of Sweden and the United States,' *Electoral Studies*, 3 (April 1984): 65–83; Lewis-Beck, *Economics and Elections*, 69–75, 159–60; Arthur Sanders, 'The Meaning of Liberalism and Conservatism,' *Polity*, 19 (Fall 1986): 123–35; Kathleen Knight, 'Ideology and Public Opinion,' in *Research in Micropolitics*, vol. 3, ed. Samuel Long (Greenwich, CT: JAI Press, 1990), 59–82; Robinson and Fleishman, 'Ideological Trends in American Public Opinion,' 56–59; William G. Jacoby, 'Variability in Issue Alternatives and American Public Opinion,' *Journal of Politics*, 52 (May 1990): 579–606; Miller and Traugott, *American National Election Studies Data Sourcebook*, 155–253.

18. G. Bingham Powell, Jr., and Guy D. Whitten, 'A Cross-National Analysis of Economic Voting: Taking Account of the Political Context,' *American Journal of Political Science*, 37 (May 1993): 391–414; Lewis-Beck, *Economics and Elections*, 33–162; Douglas A. Hibbs, Jr., 'Macroeconomic Performance, Policy and Electoral Politics in Industrial Democracies,' *International Social Science Journal*, 37, no. 1 (1985): 63–74; Douglas A. Hibbs, Jr., *The Political Economy of Industrial Democracies* (Cambridge, MA: Harvard University Press, 1987); Douglas A. Hibbs, Jr., *The American Political Economy: Macroeconomics and Electoral Politics* (Cambridge, MA: Harvard University Press, 1987); Heinz Eulau and Michael S. Lewis-Beck, eds., *Economic Conditions and Electoral Outcomes: The United States and Western Europe* (New

York: Agathon Press, 1985); Friedrich Schneider and Bruno S. Frey, 'Politico-Economic Models of Macroeconomic Policy: A Review of the Empirical Evidence,' in *Political Business Cycles: The Political Economy of Money, Inflation, and Unemployment*, ed. Thomas D. Willett (Durham, NC: Duke University Press, 1988), 239–75; Wessel Visser and Rien Wijnhoven, 'Politics Do Matter, but Does Unemployment? Party Strategies, Ideological Discourse and Enduring Mass Unemployment,' *European Journal of Political Research*, 18 (January 1990): 71–96; Arthur H. Miller and Stephen A. Borrelli, 'Policy and Performance Orientations in the United States,' *Electoral Studies*, 11 (June 1992): 106–21; Christopher H. Achen, 'Social Psychology, Demographic Variables, and Linear Regression: Breaking the Iron Triangle in Voting Research,' *Political Behavior*, 14 (September 1992): 195–211; Stephen Ansolabehere and Shanto Iyengar, 'Information and Electoral Attitudes: A Case of Judgment under Uncertainty,' in *Explorations in Political Psychology*, ed. Shanto Iyengar and William J. McGuire (Durham, NC: Duke University Press, 1993), 321–37; Donald R. Kinder, Gordon S. Adams, and Paul W. Gronke, 'Economics and Politics in the 1984 American Presidential Election,' *American Journal of Political Science*, 33 (May 1989): 491–515; Pippa Norris, 'The 1988 American Elections: Long, Medium and Short-Term Explanations,' *Political Quarterly*, 60 (April–June 1989): 204–21; J. Merrill Shanks and Warren E. Miller, 'Policy Direction and Performance Evaluation: Complementary Explanations of the Reagan Elections,' *British Journal of Political Science*, 20 (April 1990): 143–235; Shanks and Miller, 'Partisanship, Policy and Performance,' 129–97; Abramson, Aldrich, and Rohde, *Change and Continuity in the 1988 Elections*, 179–225; Morris P. Fiorina, *Retrospective Voting in American National Elections* (New Haven, CT: Yale University Press, 1981); D. Roderick Kiewiet, *Macroeconomics and Micropolitics: The Electoral Effects of Economic Issues* (Chicago: University of Chicago Press, 1983); Alan I. Abramowitz, David J. Lanoue, and Subha Ramesh, 'Economic Conditions, Causal Attributions, and Political Evaluations in the 1984 Presidential Election,' *Journal of Politics*, 50 (November 1988): 848–63; J. David Gopoian and Thom Yantek, 'Cross-Pressured Economic Voting in America: The 1984 Election,' *Political Behavior*, 10, no. 1 (1988): 37–54; Jason Young, Eugene Borgida, John Sullivan, and John Aldrich, 'Personal Agendas and the Relationship between Self-Interest and Voting Behavior,' *Social Psychology Quarterly*, 50 (March 1987): 64–71; Gregory B. Markus, 'The Impact of Personal and National Economic Conditions on the Presidential Vote: A Pooled Cross-Sectional Analysis,' *American Journal of Political Science*, 32 (February 1988): 137–54; Timothy Y. C. Cotton, 'War and American Democracy: Electoral Costs of the Last Five Wars,' *Journal of Conflict Resolution*, 30 (December 1986): 616–35; Keith Archer and Marquis Johnson, 'Inflation, Unemployment and Canadian Federal Voting Behaviour,' *Canadian Journal of Political Science*, 21 (September 1988): 569–84; Richard Nardeau and André Blais, 'Explaining Election Outcomes in Canada: Economy and Politics,' *Canadian Journal of Political Science*, 26 (December 1993): 775–90; Hans Rattinger, 'Collective and Individual Economic Judgments and Voting in West Germany, 1961–1984,' *European Journal of Political Research*, 14, no. 4 (1986): 393–416; Lee

Sigelman, 'Mass Political Support in Sweden: Retesting a Political-Economic Model,' *Scandinavian Political Studies*, 6, no. 4 (1983): 309–15; Paolo Bellucci, 'The Effects of Aggregate Economic Conditions on the Political Preferences of the Italian Electorate, 1953–1979,' *European Journal of Political Research*, 12 (December 1984): 387–401.

19. Donald R. Kinder, 'Presidential Character Revisited,' in *Political Cognition*, ed. Richard R. Lau and David O. Sears (Hillsdale, NJ: Lawrence Erlbaum Associates, 1986), 233–55; Miller, 'Economic, Character, and Social Issues in the 1992 Presidential Election,' 315–27; Scott Keeter, 'The Illusion of Intimacy: Television and the Role of Candidate Personal Qualities in Voter Choice,' *Public Opinion Quarterly*, 51 (Fall 1987): 344–58; Milton Lodge and Patrick Stroh, 'Inside the Mental Voting Booth: An Impression-Driven Process Model of Candidate Evaluation,' in *Explorations in Political Psychology*, ed. Iyengar and McGuire, 225–63; Martin P. Wattenberg, *The Decline of American Political Parties 1952–1988* (Cambridge, MA: Harvard University Press, 1990).

20. David E. Apter, *Choice and the Politics of Allocation: A Developmental Theory* (New Haven, CT: Yale University Press, 1971), esp. 6–104; Arthur H. Miller and Ola Listhaug, 'Ideology and Political Alienation,' *Scandinavian Political Studies*, 16, no. 2 (1993): 167–92; Christian Leithner, 'Economic Conditions and the Vote: A Contingent Rather than Categorical Influence,' *British Journal of Political Science*, 23 (July 1993): 339–72.

21. See Hans-George Betz, 'The New Politics of Resentment: Radical Right-Wing Populist Parties in Western Europe,' *Comparative Politics*, 25 (July 1993): 413–27; Hans-Georg Betz, 'The Two Faces of Radical Right-Wing Populism in Western Europe,' *Review of Politics*, 55 (Fall 1993): 663–85; Michael Minkenberg, *The New Right in Comparative Perspective: The USA and Germany* (Ithaca, NY: Institute for European Studies, Cornell University, 1993), 54–55; Piero Ignazi, 'The Silent Counter-Revolution: Hypotheses on the Emergence of Extreme Right-Wing Parties in Europe,' *European Journal of Political Research*, 22 (July 1992): 3–34; Piero Ignazi and Colette Ysmal, 'New and Old Extreme Right Parties: The French Front National and the Italian Movimento Sociale,' *European Journal of Political Research*, 22 (July 1992): 101–21; Michael S. Lewis-Beck and Glenn E. Mitchell II, 'French Electoral Theory: The National Front Test,' *Electoral Studies*, 12 (June 1993): 112–27; Nonna Mayer and Pascal Perrineau, 'Why Do They Vote for Le Pen?' *European Journal of Political Research*, 22 (July 1992): 123–41; Mark Gilbert, 'Warriors of the New Pontida: The Challenge of the Lega Nord to the Italian Party System,' *Political Quarterly*, 64 (January–March 1993): 99–106; Robert Rohrschneider, 'New Party versus Old Left Realignments: Environmental Attitudes, Party Policies, and Partisan Affiliations in Four West European Countries,' *Journal of Politics*, 55 (August 1993): 682–701; Robert Rohrschneider, 'Impact of Social Movements on European Party Systems,' *Annals of the American Academy of Political and Social Science*, 528 (July 1993): 157–70; and the following essays in *Challenging the Political Order*, ed. Dalton and Kuechler: Ronald Inglehart, 'Values, Ideology, and Cognitive Mobilization in New Social Movements,' 43–66; Dieter Rucht, 'The Strategies and Action Repertoires of New Movements,' 156–75; Herbert Kitschelt, 'New Social Movements

and the Decline of Party Organization,' 179–208; Ferdinand Müller-Rommel, 'New Political Movements and "New Politics" Parties in Western Europe,' 209–31; Manfred Kuechler and Russell J. Dalton, 'New Social Movements and the Political Order: Inducing Change for Long Term Stability?', 277–300.

22. See Schlozman and Verba, 'Sending Them a Message – Getting a Reply,' 3–25; John R. Petrocik, 'Voter Turnout and Electoral Preference: The Anomalous Reagan Elections,' in *Elections in America*, ed. Schlozman, 239–59; Richard W. Boyd, 'Electoral Change and the Floating Voter: The Reagan Elections,' *Political Behavior*, 8, no. 3 (1986): 230–44; Eric M. Uslaner, 'Looking Forward and Looking Backward: Prospective and Retrospective Voting in the 1980 Federal Elections in Canada,' *British Journal of Political Science*, 19 (October 1989): 495–513; Converse and Pierce, *Representation in France*; Heinz Eulau, 'The Congruence Model Revisited,' *Legislative Studies Quarterly*, 12 (May 1987): 171–214; Sören Holmberg, 'Political Representation in Sweden,' *Scandinavian Political Studies*, 12, no. 1 (1989): 1–36; Alan Ware, 'Parties, Electoral Competition and Democracy,' *Parliamentary Affairs*, 42 (January 1989): 1–22; Peter Taylor-Gooby and Hugh Bochel, 'Public Opinion, Party Policy and MPs' Attitudes to Welfare,' *Political Quarterly*, 59 (April–June 1988): 251–58; Ivor Crewe and Donald D. Searing, 'Ideological Change in the British Conservative Party,' *American Political Science Review*, 82 (June 1988): 361–84; Joel E. Brooks, 'Democratic Frustration in the Anglo-American Polities: A Quantification of Inconsistency between Mass Public Opinion and Public Policy,' *Western Political Quarterly*, 38 (June 1985): 250–61; Joel E. Brooks, 'The Opinion-Policy Nexus in France: Do Institutions and Ideology Make a Difference?' *Journal of Politics*, 49 (May 1987): 465–80; Joel E. Brooks, 'Mediterranean Neo-Democracies and the Opinion-Policy Nexus,' *West European Politics*, 11 (July 1988): 126–40; Joel E. Brooks, 'The Opinion-Policy Nexus in Germany,' *Public Opinion Quarterly*, 54 (Winter 1990): 508–29; Achen, 'Social Psychology, Demographic Variables, and Linear Regression,' 197.

23. Guy Fréchet and Barbara Wörndl, 'The Ecological Movements in the Light of Social Movements' Development: The Cases of Four Contemporary Industrialized Societies,' *International Journal of Comparative Sociology*, 34 (January–April 1993): 56–74; Herbert P. Kitschelt, 'Political Opportunity Structures and Political Protest: Anti-Nuclear Movements in Four Democracies,' *British Journal of Political Science*, 16 (January 1986): 57–85; Thomas R. Rochon and Daniel A. Mazmanian, 'Social Movements and the Policy Process,' *Annals of the American Academy of Political and Social Science*, 528 (July 1993): 75–87; Carol Hager, 'Citizen Movements and Technological Policymaking in Germany,' *Annals of the American Academy of Political and Social Science*, 528 (July 1993): 42–55; Étienne Balibar, '*Es Gibt Keinen Staat in Europa*: Racism and Politics in Europe Today,' *New Left Review*, no. 186 (March/April 1991): 5–19.

24. DeNardo, *Power in Numbers*, 58–86, 106–242; John Zaller, *The Nature and Origins of Mass Opinion* (New York: Cambridge University Press, 1992), 216–332.

25. Karl-Dieter Opp, 'Postmaterialism, Collective Action, and Political Protest,' *American Journal of Political Science*, 34 (February 1990): 212–35;

Przeworski, *Capitalism and Social Democracy*, 171–203; Adam Przeworski and John Sprague, *Paper Stones: A History of Electoral Socialism* (Chicago: University of Chicago Press, 1986).

## 10 Political Leadership

1. William Shakespeare, *Twelfth Night*, ed. David Bevington (New York: Bantam Books, 1988), 42.

2. Richard Lachmann, 'Elite Conflict and State Formation in 16th- and 17th-Century England and France,' *American Sociological Review*, 54 (April 1989): 141–62.

3. Plato, *The Republic of Plato*, trans. Francis MacDonald Cornford (New York: Oxford University Press, 1945), 195–96; Richard Rose, 'Steering the Ship of State: One Tiller but Two Pairs of Hands,' *British Journal of Political Science*, 17 (October 1987): 409–33.

4. George Bernard Shaw, *Man and Superman* (New York: Penguin Books, 1977), 169.

5. William Shakespeare, *As You Like It*, ed. David Bevington (New York: Bantam Books, 1988), 40.

6. See Robert D. Benford and Scott A. Hunt, 'Dramaturgy and Social Movements: The Social Construction and Communication of Power,' *Sociological Inquiry*, 62 (February 1992): 36–55; Robert D. Benford, 'Frame Disputes within the Nuclear Disarmament Movement,' *Social Forces*, 71 (March 1993): 677–701; David A. Snow and Robert D. Benford, 'Master Frames and Cycles of Protest,' in *Frontiers in Social Movement Theory*, ed. Aldon D. Morris and Carol McClurg Mueller (New Haven, CT: Yale University Press, 1992), 133–55; Jürgen Gerhards and Dieter Rucht, 'Mesomobilization: Organizing and Framing in Two Protest Campaigns in West Germany,' *American Journal of Sociology*, 98 (November 1992): 555–95.

7. See Reinhard Bendix, *Max Weber: An Intellectual Portrait* (Garden City, NY: Doubleday Anchor Books, 1962), 290–457.

8. See Steffen W. Schmidt, Laura Guasti, Carl H. Lande, and James C. Scott, eds., *Friends, Followers, and Factions: A Reader in Political Clientelism* (Berkeley: University of California Press, 1977).

9. Ann Ruth Willner, *The Spellbinders: Charismatic Political Leaderhip* (New Haven, CT: Yale University Press, 1984); Arthur Schweitzer, *The Age of Charisma* (Chicago: Nelson-Hall, 1984), 10, 51–53; David E. Apter, *The Politics of Modernization* (Chicago: University of Chicago Press, 1965), 266–312; David E. Apter, 'Mao's Republic,' *Social Research*, 54 (Winter 1987): 691–729; Craig Matheson, 'Weber and the Classification of Forms of Legitimacy,' *British Journal of Sociology*, 38 (June 1987): 199–215; Richard J. Ellis, 'Explaining the Occurrence of Charismatic Leadership in Organizations,' *Journal of Theoretical Politics*, 3 (July 1991): 305–19.

10. Bendix, *Max Weber*, 422–30; Fred Riggs, *Prismatic Society Revisited* (Morristown, NJ: General Learning Press, 1973), 24–30; Najmul Abedin, 'Administrative Reorganisation in Sudan: The Public Service and Central Administration, 1966–1983,' *Administration for Development*, no. 22 (January 1984): 31–48.

11.  David E. Apter, *Rethinking Development: Modernization, Dependency, and Postmodern Politics* (Newbury Park, CA: Sage Publications, 1987), 32–37; David E. Apter, *Choice and the Politics of Allocation* (New Haven, CT: Yale University Pres, 1971), 42–127; Li Cheng and Lynn White, 'The Thirteenth Central Committee of the Chinese Communist Party,' *Asian Survey*, 28 (April 1988): 371–99.

12.  David E. Apter, *Introduction to Political Analysis* (Cambridge, MA: Winthrop Publishers, 1977), 258–68; Sharon Kettering, 'The Historical Development of Political Clientelism,' *Journal of Interdisciplinary History*, 18 (Winter 1988): 419–47.

13.  Charles Lindholm, 'Lovers and Leaders: A Comparison of Social and Psychological Models of Romance and Charisma,' *Social Science Information*, 27 (March 1988): 3–45.

14.  Fred W. Riggs, 'Fragility of the Third World's Regimes,' *Interational Social Science Journal*, 45 (May 1993): 199–243.

15.  Apter, *The Politics of Modernization*, 410–11; Apter, *Introduction to Political Analysis*, 348–67; William H. Riker, *Liberalism against Populism: A Confrontation between the Theory of Democracy and the Theory of Social Choice* (Prospect Heights, IL: Waveland Press, 1988), esp. 115–212; Samuel L. Popkin, 'Political Entrepreneurs and Peasant Movements in Vietnam,' in *Rationality and Revolution*, ed. Michael Taylor (New York: Cambridge University Press, 1988), 9–62; Jean C. Oi, 'Communism and Clientelism: Rural Politics in China,' *World Politics*, 37 (January 1985): 238–66; and the following essays in *Leadership and Politics: New Perspectives in Political Science*, ed. Bryan D. Jones (Lawrence: University Press of Kansas, 1989): Bryan D. Jones, 'Causation, Constraint, and Political Leadership,' 3–14; Morris P. Fiorina and Kenneth A. Shepsle, 'Formal Theories of Leadership: Agents, Agenda Setters, and Entrepreneurs,' 17–40; Erwin C. Hargrove, 'Two Conceptions of Institutional Leadership,' 57–83.

16.  Apter, *The Politics of Modernization*, 94–99, 327–56; Erik H. Erikson, *Young Man Luther: A Study in Psychoanalysis and History* (New York: W. W. Norton, 1962), 42, 253–67; Erik H. Erikson, 'Identity and the Life Cycle: Selected Papers,' *Psychological Issues*, 1, no. 1 (1959): 18–166; James S. Coleman, 'Rational Organization,' *Rationality and Society*, 2 (January 1990): 94–105.

17.  Douglas Madsen and Peter G. Snow, *The Charismatic Bond: Political Behavior in Time of Crisis* (Cambridge, MA: Harvard University Press, 1991), 14–23; Lindholm, 'Lovers and Leaders,' 3–45.

18.  See Carlos de la Torre, 'The Ambiguous Meanings of Latin American Populisms,' *Social Research*, 59 (Summer 1992): 385–414; Madsen and Snow, *The Charismatic Bond*, 45–64, 126–47; David Rock, *Argentina 1516– 1987: From Spanish Colonization to Alfonsín*, rev. ed. (Berkeley: University of California Press, 1987), 249–321; Carlos H. Waisman, *Reversal of Development in Argentina: Postwar Counterrevolutionary Policies and Their Structural Consequences* (Princeton, NJ: Princeton University Press, 1987), 128–286; and the following three essays in Joel Krieger, ed., *The Oxford Companion to Politics of the World* (New York: Oxford University Press, 1993): William C. Smith and Aldo C. Vacs, 'Argentina,' 46–48; Frederick C. Turner, 'Perón, Juan Domingo,' 696–97; Marysa Navarro Aranguren, 'Perón, María Eva Duarte de,' 697.

19. Madsen and Snow, *The Charismatic Bond*, 150.
20. For a critical appraisal of the literature on revolutions and collective violence, see Harry Eckstein, *Regarding Politics: Essays on Political Theory, Stability, and Change* (Berkeley: University of California Press, 1992), 304–36.
21. Harold D. Lasswell, *Psychopathology and Politics* (New York: Viking Press, 1960), esp. 74–126; James C. Davies, 'Toward a Theory of Revolution,' in *Anger, Violence, and Politics: Theories and Research*, ed. Ivo K. Feierabend, Rosalind L. Feierabend, and Ted Robert Gurr (Englewood Cliffs, NJ: Prentice-Hall, 1972), 67–84; Ted Robert Gurr, 'On the Political Consequences of Scarcity and Economic Decline,' *International Studies Quarterly*, 29 (December 1985): 51–75; Ted Robert Gurr, *Why Men Rebel* (Princeton, NJ: Princeton University Press, 1970); James B. Rule, *Theories of Civil Violence* (Berkeley: University of California Press, 1988), 200–23; Jane Loevinger, *Paradigms of Personality* (New York: W. H. Freeman, 1987), 11–48, 160.
22. James S. Coleman, *Foundations of Social Theory* (Cambridge, MA: The Belknap Press of Harvard University Press, 1990), 479. See too J. Craig Jenkins and Kurt Schock, 'Global Structures and Political Processes in the Study of Domestic Political Conflict,' in *Annual Review of Sociology 1992*, vol. 18, ed. Judith Blake and John Jagan (Palo Alto, CA: Annual Reviews, 1992), 166–69; Faye Crosby, 'Relative Deprivation Revisited: A Response to Miller, Bolce, and Halligan,' *American Political Science Review*, 73 (March 1979): 103–12; Charles Tilly, *Big Structures, Large Processes, Huge Comparisons* (New York: Russell Sage Foundation, 1984), 102–05; Robert A. Hinde, 'Aggression and War: Individuals, Groups, and States,' in *Behavior, Society, and International Conflict*, ed. Philip E. Tetlock, Jo L. Husbands, Robert Jervis, Paul C. Stern, and Charles Tilly (New York: Oxford University Press, 1993), 22–25.
23. See Doug McAdam, John D. McCarthy, and Mayer N. Zald, 'Social Movements,' in *Handbook of Sociology*, ed. Neil J. Smelser (Newbury Park, CA: Sage Publications, 1988), 695–729; Sidney Tarrow, 'National Politics and Collective Action: Recent Theory and Research in Western Europe and the United States,' *Annual Review of Sociology 1988*, vol. 14, ed. W. Richard Scott and Judith Blake (Palo Alto, CA: Annual Reviews, Inc., 1988), 421–40; Charles Tilly, 'Models and Realities of Popular Collective Action,' *Social Research*, 52 (Winter 1985): 717–47; Charles Tilly, *From Mobilization to Revolution* (Reading, MA: Addison-Wesley, 1978); David Knoke, *Political Networks: The Structural Perspective* (New York: Cambridge University Press, 1990), 69–73; Nelson A. Pichardo, 'Resource Mobilization: An Analysis of Conflicting Theoretical Variations,' *Sociological Quarterly*, 29 (March 1988): 97–110; Jenkins and Schock, 'Global Structures and Political Processes in the Study of Domestic Political Conflict,' 170–72; and the following three essays in *Frontiers in Social Movement Theory*, ed. Morris and Mueller: Mayer N. Zald, 'Looking Backward to Look Forward: Reflections on the Past and Future of the Resource Mobilization Program,' 326–48; Clarence Y. H. Lo, 'Communities of Challengers in Social Movement Theory,' 224–47; Myra Marx Ferree, 'The Political Context of Rationality: Rational Choice Theory and Resource Mobilization,' 29–52.

24. S. N. Eisenstadt, 'Frameworks of the Great Revolutions: Culture, Social Structure, History and Human Agency,' *International Social Science Journal*, 44 (August 1992): 382–401; Paul Bagguley, 'Protest, Acquiescence and the Unemployed: A Comparative Analysis of the 1930s and 1980s,' *British Journal of Sociology*, 43 (September 1992): 443–61; Jae-Hung Ahn, 'The Politics of Collective Action by Labour in Hard Times: A Theoretical Discussion,' *Asian Perspective*, 14 (Spring–Summer 1990): 187–215.

25. See Charles D. Brockett, 'The Structure of Political Opportunities and Peasant Mobilization in Central America,' *Comparative Politics*, 23 (April 1991): 253–74; Timothy P. Wickham-Crowley, *Exploring Revolution: Essays on Latin American Insurgency and Revolutionary Theory* (Armonk, NY: M. E. Sharpe, 1991); Timothy P. Wickham-Crowley, *Guerrillas and Revolution in Central America: A Comparative Study of Insurgents and Regimes since 1956* (Princeton, NJ: Princeton University Press, 1992), esp. 302–26; Xueguang Zhou, 'Unorganized Interests and Collective Action in Communist China,' *American Sociological Review*, 58 (February 1993): 54–73; Evenly B. Davidheiser, 'Strong States, Weak States: The Role of the State in Revolution,' *Comparative Politics*, 23 (July 1992): 463–75; Roger Petersen, 'A Community-Based Theory of Rebellion,' *European Journal of Sociology*, 34, no. 1 (1993): 41–78; Daniel R. Sabia, Jr., 'Rationality, Collective Action, and Karl Marx,' *American Journal of Political Science*, 32 (February 1988): 50–71; Michael Hechter, *Principles of Group Solidarity* (Berkeley: University of California Press, 1987), 1–77, 168–86; Edgar Kiser and Michael Hechter, 'The Role of General Theory in Comparative-historical Sociology,' *American Journal of Sociology*, 97 (July 1991): 14–17; Tilly, *From Mobilization to Revolution*, 189–222; Craig Jackson Calhoun, 'The Radicalism of Tradition and the Question of Class Struggle,' in *Rationality and Revolution*, ed. Taylor, 129–75; Jack A. Goldstone, *Revolution and Rebellion in the Early Modern World* (Berkeley: University of California Press, 1991), esp. 1–62, 416–97; Jack A. Goldstone, 'Revolution,' in *The Oxford Companion to Politics of the World*, ed. Krieger, 786–90; Theda Skocpol, *States and Social Revolutions: A Comparative Analysis of France, Russia, and China* (New York: Cambridge University Press, 1979), 3–43; Theda Skocpol, 'Review Article: What Makes Peasants Revolutionary?' *Comparative Politics*, 14 (April 1982): 351–75; John Foran, 'A Theory of Third World Social Revolutions: Iran, Nicaragua, and El Salvador Compared,' *Critical Sociology*, 19, no. 2 (1992): 3–27; Gary Hawes, 'Theories of Peasant Revolution: A Critique and Contribution from the Philippines,' *World Politics*, 42 (January 1990): 261–98; Hudson Meadwell, 'Peasant Autonomy, Peasant Solidarity and Peasant Revolts,' *British Journal of Political Science*, 18 (January 1988): 133–40; Hudson Meadwell, 'Lords, States and Peasant Revolts,' *Social Science Information*, 29 (December 1990): 765–83; Bruce Cumings, 'Interest and Ideology in the Study of Agrarian Politics,' *Politics and Society*, 10, no. 4 (1981): 467–95.

26. David D. Laitin and Carolyn M. Warner, 'Structure and Irony in Social Revolutions,' *Political Theory*, 20 (February 1992): 147–51; James W. White, 'Rational Rioters: Leaders, Followers, and Popular Protest in Early Modern Japan,' *Politics and Society*, 16 (March 1988): 35–69; Robert W. White, 'From Peaceful Protest to Guerrilla War: Micromobilization of the

Provisional Irish Republican Army,' *American Journal of Sociology*, 94 (May 1989): 1277–1302; James DeNardo, *Power in Numbers: The Political Strategy of Protest and Rebellion* (Princeton, NJ: Princeton University Press, 1985), esp. 87–105; James S. Coleman, 'Free Riders and Zealots: The Role of Social Networks,' *Sociological Theory*, 6 (Spring 1988): 52–57; Coleman, *Foundations of Social Theory*, 486–502; Jeffrey Berejikian, 'Revolutionary Collective Action and the Agent-Structure Problem,' *American Political Science Review*, 86 (September 1992): 647–57; Dipak K. Gupta, Harinder Singh, and Tom Sprague, 'Government Coercion of Dissidents: Deterrence or Provocation?', *Journal of Conflict Resolution*, 37 (June 1993): 301–39; Edward N. Muller and Erich Weede, 'Theories of Rebellion: Relative Deprivation and Power Contention,' *Rationality and Society*, 6 (January 1994): 40–57; Edward N. Muller and Karl-Dieter Opp, 'Rational Choice and Rebellious Collective Action,' *American Political Science Review*, 80 (June 1986): 471–87; Edward N. Muller and Karl-Dieter Opp, 'Rebellious Collective Action Revisited,' *American Political Science Review*, 81 (June 1987): 561–64; Edward N. Muller, Henry A. Dietz, and Steven E. Finkel, 'Discontent and the Expected Utility of Rebellion: The Case of Peru,' *American Political Science Review*, 85 (December 1991): 1261–82; Edward N. Muller and Mitchell A. Seligson, 'Inequality and Insurgency,' *American Political Science Review*, 81 (June 1987): 425–51; Edward N. Muller and Erich Weede, 'Cross-National Variation in Political Violence: A Rational Action Approach,' *Journal of Conflict Resolution*, 34 (December 1990): 624–51; Karl-Dieter Opp, 'Grievances and Participation in Social Movements,' *American Sociological Review*, 53 (December 1988): 853–64; Karl-Dieter Opp, *The Rationality of Political Protest: A Comparative Analysis of Rational Choice Theory* (Boulder, CO: Westview Press, 1989); Karl-Dieter Opp and Wolfgang Roehl, 'Repression, Micromobilization, and Political Protest,' *Social Forces*, 69 (December 1990): 521–47; Karl-Dieter Opp, 'Repression and Revolutionary Action: East Germany in 1989,' *Rationality and Society*, 6 (January 1994): 101–38; Karl-Dieter Opp and Christiane Gern, 'Dissident Groups, Personal Networks, and Spontaneous Cooperation: The East German Revolution of 1989,' *American Sociological Review*, 58 (October 1993): 659–80; Sun-Ki Chai, 'An Organizational Economics Theory of Antigovernment Violence,' *Comparative Politics*, 26 (October 1993): 99–110; Jack A. Goldstone, 'Is Revolution Individually Rational? Groups and Individuals in Revolutionary Collective Action,' *Rationality and Society*, 6 (January 1994): 319–66; William Brustein and Margaret Levi, 'The Geography of Rebellion: Rulers, Rebels, and Regions, 1500 to 1700,' *Theory and Society*, 16 (July 1987): 467–95; Samuel L. Popkin, 'Political Entrepreneurs and Peasant Movements in Vietnam,' in *Rationality and Revolution*, 9–62.

27.  See David E. Apter, 'Yan'an and the Narrative Reconstruction of Reality,' *Daedalus*, 122 (Spring 1993): 207–32; Apter, 'Mao's Republic,' 691–729; Jean C. Robinson, 'Mao after Death: Charisma and Political Legitimacy,' *Asian Survey*, 28 (March 1988): 353–68; David Bachman, 'The Limits on Leadership in China,' *Asian Survey*, 32 (November 1992): 1046–62; John King Fairbank, *The United States and China*, 4th ed., enlarged (Cambridge, MA: Harvard University Press, 1983), 220–357; John King Fairbank, *China: A New History* (Cambridge, MA: The Belknap Press of Harvard

University Press, 1992), 269–341; Skocpol, *States and Social Revolutions*, 147–57, 236–81; Ralph Thaxton, 'On Peasant Revolution and National Resistance: Toward a Theory of Peasant Mobilization and Revolutionary War with Special Reference to Modern China,' *World Politics*, 30 (October 1977): 24–57; Ralph Thaxton, *China Turned Rightside Up: Revolutionary Legitimacy in the Peasant World* (New Haven, CT: Yale University Press, 1983); Cheng and White, 'The Thirteenth Central Committee of the Chinese Communist Party,' 371–99.

28. Barnett R. Rubin, 'Afghanistan,' in *The Oxford Companion to Politics of the World*, ed. Krieger, 3–5; David Gibbs, 'The Peasant as Counter-Revolutionary: The Rural Origins of the Afghan Insurgency,' *Studies in Comparative International Development*, 21 (Spring 1986): 36–59.

29. Daniel Little, 'Rational-Choice Models and Asian Studies,' *Journal of Asian Studies*, 50 (February 1991): 35–52; Daniel Little, *Varieties of Social Explanation: An Introduction to the Philosophy of Social Science* (Boulder, CO: Westview Press, 1991), 39–158; George C. Homans, 'Behaviourism and After,' in *Social Theory Today*, ed. Anthony Giddens and Jonathan Turner (Stanford, CA: Stanford University Press, 1987), 58–81; Harvey Waterman, 'Reasons and Reason: Collective Political Activity in Comparative and Historical Perspective,' *World Politics*, 33 (July 1981): 554–89; Sabia, 'Rationality, Collective Action, and Karl Marx,' 50–71; Muller and Weede, 'Theories of Rebellion,' 41–42.

30. Rule, *Theories of Civil Violence*, 238–68; James Tong, 'Rational Outlaws: Rebels and Bandits in the Ming Dynasty, 1368–1644,' in *Rationality and Society*, ed. Taylor, 98–128; DeNardo, *Power in Numbers*, 87–105; Dennis Chong, *Collective Action and the Civil Rights Movement* (Chicago: University of Chicago Press, 1991).

31. See Apter, *Choice and the Politics of Allocation*, 1–71, 105–54; Charles F. Andrain, *Comparative Political Systems: Policy Performance and Social Change* (Armonk, NY: M.E. Sharpe, 1994); DeNardo, *Power in Numbers*, 58–86, 106–242; Theda Skocpol, 'Social Revolutions and Mass Military Mobilizaion,' *World Politics*, 40 (January 1988): 147–68; Jeff Goodwin and Theda Skocpol, 'Explaining Revolutions in the Contemporary Third World,' *Politics and Society*, 17 (December 1989): 489–509; Erich Weede, 'The Impact of Interstate Conflict on Revolutionary Change and Individual Freedom,' *Kyklos*, 46, no. 4 (1993): 473–95; Ekkart Zimmerman, 'On the Outcomes of Revolutions: Some Preliminary Considerations,' *Sociological Theory*, 8 (Spring 1990): 33–47; Raj Desai and Harry Eckstein, 'Insurgency: The Transformation of Peasant Rebellion,' *World Politics*, 42 (July 1990): 441–65; Edward Friedman, Paul G. Pickowicz, and Mark Selden, *Chinese Village, Socialist State* (New Haven, CT: Yale University Press, 1991).

## Epilogue

1. See Thomas F. Mayer, 'Six Comments on Rationality,' *Science and Society*, 57 (Winter 1993–1994): 446–53; Keith Dowding, 'The Compatibility of Behaviouralism, Rational Choice and the "New Institutionalism",' *Journal of Theoretical Politics*, 6 (January 1994): 105–17; Charles Tilly, 'States and

Nationalism in Europe 1492–1992,' *Theory and Society*, 23 (February 1994): 131–46; Ted Robert Gurr, *Minorities at Risk: A Global View of Ethnopolitical Conflicts* (Washington, DC: United States Institute of Peace Press, 1993), esp. 15–138, 314–24; Karl-Werner Brand, 'Cyclical Aspects of New Social Movements: Waves of Cultural Criticism and Mobilization Cycles of New Middle-Class Radicalism,' in *Challenging the Political Order: New Social and Political Movements in Western Democracies*, ed. Russell J. Dalton and Manfred Kuechler (New York: Oxford University Press, 1990), 23–42; Lorna Weir, 'Limitations of New Social Movement Analysis,' *Studies in Political Economy*, no. 40 (Spring 1993): 73–102; Doug McAdam and Dieter Rucht, 'The Cross-National Diffusion of Movement Ideas,' *Annals of the American Academy of Political and Social Science*, 528 (July 1993): 56–74.

2. Émile Zola, *Germinal*, trans. Leonard Tancock (London: Penguin Books, 1954), 276.

3. Albert O. Hirschman, *The Rhetoric of Reaction: Perversity, Futility, Jeopardy* (Cambridge, MA: The Belknap Press of Harvard University Press, 1991); Albert O. Hirschman, '*The Rhetoric of Reaction* – Two Years Later,' *Government and Opposition*, 28 (Summer 1993): 292–314; Michael Thompson, Richard Ellis, and Aaron Wildavsky, *Cultural Theory* (Boulder, CO: Westview Press, 1990), 1–100; Aaron Wildavsky, 'Can Norms Rescue Self-Interest or Macro Explanations Be Joined to Micro Explanations?', *Critical Review*, 5 (Summer 1991): 301–23; Paul A. Sabatier, 'Policy Change over a Decade or More,' in *Policy Change and Learning: An Advocacy Coalition Approach*, ed. Paul A. Sabatier and Hank C. Jenkins-Smith (Boulder, CO: Westview Press, 1993), 13–39.

4. Anthony R. Oberschall, 'Rational Choice in Collective Protests,' *Rationality and Society*, 6 (January 1994): 79–100; Mark I. Lichbach, 'Rethinking Rationality and Rebellion: Theories of Collective Action and Problems of Collective Dissent,' *Rationality and Society*, 6 (January 1994): 8–39; Margaret Levi and Stephen DeTray, 'A Weapon against War: Conscientious Objection in the United States, Australia, and France,' *Politics and Society*, 21 (December 1993): 425–64; Paul F. Whiteley, Patrick Seyd, Jeremy Richardson, and Paul Bissell, 'Explaining Party Activism: The Case of the British Conservative Party,' *British Journal of Political Science*, 24 (January 1994): 79–94.

5. Zola, *Germinal*, 144, 146, 236.

6. Sun-Ki Chai, 'An Organizational Economics Theory of Antigovernment Violence,' *Comparative Politics*, 26 (October 1993): 99–110; Ruud Koopmans, 'The Dynamics of Protest Waves: West Germany, 1965 to 1989,' *American Sociological Review*, 58 (October 1993): 637–58; Manfred Kuechler and Russell J. Dalton, 'New Social Movements and the Political Order: Inducing Change for Long-term Stability?', in *Challenging the Political Order*, ed. Dalton and Kuechler, 277–300.

7. Jack A. Goldstone, 'Is Revolution Individually Rational? Groups and Individuals in Revolutionary Collective Action,' *Rationality and Society*, 6 (January 1994): 139–66; Lars Udéhn, 'Twenty-Five Years with *The Logic of Collective Action*,' *Acta Sociologica*, 36, no. 3 (1993): 239–61; Pamela E. Oliver, 'Formal Models of Collective Action,' in *Annual Review of Sociology 1993*, vol. 19, ed. Judith Blake and John Hagen (Palo Alto, CA: Annual Reviews,

Inc., 1993), 271–300; Thomas R. Rochon and Daniel A. Mazmanian, 'Social Movements and the Policy Process,' *Annals of the American Academy of Political and Social Science*, 528 (July 1993): 75–87; David S. Meyer, 'Peace Protest and Policy: Explaining the Rise and Decline of Antinuclear Movements in Postwar America,' *Policy Studies Journal*, 21 (Spring 1993): 35–51; Douglas R. Imig and David S. Meyer, 'Political Opportunity and Peace and Justice Advocacy in the 1980s: A Tale of Two Sectors,' *Social Science Quarterly*, 74 (December 1993): 750–70; Irving L. Janis, *Crucial Decisions: Leadership in Policymaking and Crisis Management* (New York: The Free Press, 1989).

# Index